Rear Cover: Wesley's Chapel, London where Peter and Valerie were married.
Chaplains Badge - ©Crown Copyright - MoD.

"PITS, PARACHUTES, AND PULPITS"

(Reminiscences from a Wheelchair)

By

Peter Bayley

Three Counties Publishing (Books) Limited

Published by

Three Counties Publishing (Books) Limited

P.O. Box 435 Leek, Staffordshire England, ST13 5TB
telephone 01538 380910 fax 01538 382204
email: tcpbooksltd@aol.com

ISBN 0 9544080 - 6 - 3

Typeset in Aster New Opti 11pt by Clermont Ferrand Int. Staffordshire, England.
and Printed by Biddles Limited, King's Lynn, Norfolk, England.

DEDICATION

When comforts are declining
He grants the soul again
A season of clear shining
To cheer it after rain

William Cowper (1731-1800)

To my wife, Valerie, without whose love, insistence, and continual encouragement, support and technical expertise, this book would never have been started, let alone completed.

CONTENTS

ACKNOWLEDGEMENTS

I can always remember being fascinated watching my mother create blankets made from tiny squares which she had crocheted from scraps of wool obtained from many sources. The finished product displayed a whole range of colour from the very brightest to the darkest. My life has followed the same pattern, in that it has been comprised of the people, events, and experiences which have both uplifted me and also which have caused me the greatest despair.

So many people have played a part in helping me to convey this that I cannot possible name them all, however, in the writing of this book I am particularly grateful to:

The late Lionel Murray (Lord Murray of Epping Forest); and Revd. David Wilkes OBE, QHC (Chaplain General HM Land Forces), for their introductions, proof reading, encouragement and reviewing.

Revd. Dr. Leslie Griffith (Lord Griffith of Burry Port) for his excellent review and Col. Peter Field MC. for proof reading matters relating to my time spent with Airborne forces.

Special thanks go to my sister, Joyce Rogers, for her constant, sensitive and practical support, and to Valerie, without whom I would have given up on myself long ago.

Revd. Peter Bayley's last official duty. July 24th 2004
Officiating at the Marriage of his step son, Dr. Dylan Bould to Dr Chilombo Kasanda

FOREWORD

To add another "P" to the challenging title of this book, this is the account of pilgrimage.

What his Ministry in my own church in Loughton showed, and years of friendship have confirmed, is that Peter Bayley has in full measure the qualities of the pilgrim, which John Bunyan lists in his stirring hymn: valour, constancy and the cheerful faith that keeps him going through good times and bad.

This is a tale well told. As a record of the life of a working class family in the 1940s and 1950s it has the great strength of being written by someone who lived it, as opposed to those who chronicle the life of others. Nor have I read a better account of life as it is lived in the barracks or the manse.

What comes through clearly is the sheer courage of the man, whether going down to dig coal in the bowels of the earth, jumping out of an aeroplane, or standing up as a Chaplain to commend his Saviour to men who, for the most part, were indifferent or downright hostile, and how much he enjoyed it.

Here is the "happy warrior" whom Wordsworth extolled. But even tougher, requiring a much higher level of endurance, is the way he has faced, and faced down, the awful spectre of multiple sclerosis.

This book is in itself a measure of Peter Bayley's refusal to cave in to adversity. Hand-in-hand with his courage goes his constancy and perseverance, to which the discipline of a working class upbringing and the later rigours of paratroop training both made their contribution. What rearing in the Methodist Church and Sunday school gave him, and army life did not weaken - quite the reverse- was the faith that has sustained him. Many readers, myself included, will take comfort in his admission of being assailed by doubts, and his response with bible in one hand and Leslie Weatherhead's "Christian Agnostic" in the other. He reminds us that an important part of faith-like love - is faith in one's fellow-men, whether waiting in a queue to leap from an aircraft or in a line to be ordained as a Methodist minister.

This is a marvellously readable book, informative, inspiring, cheerful. It is a pleasure to commend it.

LORD MURRAY OF EPPING FOREST
(former General Secretary of the TUC)

INTRODUCTION

In Pits, Parachutes and Pulpits the Reverend Peter Bayley tells the inside story of what shaped his life from his early days in a working class family in the Potteries to military service as a soldier and a chaplain. With humour and insight, humility and honesty, Peter Bayley shows how his Christian faith has informed, led and inspired his journey through life. Now afflicted by MS, he bravely invites his readers to accompany him on a voyage of discovery through the various phases of his past and present life.

As a Territorial Army chaplain I remember watching a television programme in which Peter was being interviewed about his work as a regular Army chaplain in West Germany; and like many I was most impressed by what he had to say. Imagine how apprehensive I was when a year later I joined as a full-time regular chaplain and found myself posted to Hohne in West Germany to succeed this remarkable man.

Clearly evoking his 1970s and 1980s experiences of chaplaincy, he accurately describes life in Germany long before the collapse of the Inner-German Border, illustrating it with sights and sounds so familiar to those who have lived through that era. Whether narrowly missing death in a coal mine deep underground, being ordered to parachute from an aeroplane at a low altitude, attempting not to miss flights back to the UK to visit his wife and new baby or facing down the ravages of MS, Peter Bayley captures the mood of the moment, and gently reminds us that under God all will be well.

This fascinating book deserves the attention of a wide audience. Many who know little of the pressures under which clergy live will find this very human story compelling and revealing. I warmly commend this very readable book.

17 December 2004.

Reverend David E Wilkes OBE OHC
Chaplain-General
United Kingdom Land Forces

PART I

OUT OF DARKNESS INTO LIGHT

On 25th September 1938 in Longton Cottage Hospital, Stoke-on-Trent, Staffordshire, my mother, Elizabeth (Betty) Bayley nee Thornhill, gave birth to a son and thus I entered the world. She and my father, a bricklayer, named me Peter. They had met in Trentham Gardens, a local beauty spot, and were so attracted to each other they lost all track of time. When they eventually decided to go home they discovered they had been locked in, and had to climb over the gates to get out!

On leaving school my mother had 'gone into service', and was working in the home of the local Medical Officer of Health when she was 'courting' my father. Family rumour had it that I was conceived in the back of the doctor's car because that is where a lot of their courting took place!

My father, William Harry, was the youngest of the four sons of Isaac and Olive Bayley, who lived in Newcastle-Under-Lyme, a bustling market town a couple of miles outside Stoke. There was also an elder sister, Nancy, who sadly died shortly after the end of the First World War. This tragic loss seriously affected my Grandma Bayley, who lapsed into a state of deep depression, from which she never recovered. My father was born in the 'Gasworks Tavern' in Newcastle and was weaned on beer! I understand he used to take his little tin mug and hold it under the pumps in order to sample the brew. He developed a taste for beer, which he never lost. Years later when I used to join him for the odd pint, he was fond of saying, "if mother's milk had tasted like this, I would never have left home!"

On leaving school he served a full apprenticeship to qualify as a bricklayer and kept half a dozen encyclopaedic volumes on his trade in the bookcase for the rest of his life. He was very contemptuous of many modern day workers who buy a few tools and call themselves bricklayers! He always made a point of examining every house I ever lived in and commenting on the workmanship. The house we are now living in was built in 1995 and we moved in a few weeks after it was completed. My father came to look at it, immediately found a few flaws in the brickwork and insisted the builders, who were still on site return and put things right; which they did!

Being in the Territorial Army (Royal Artillery) he was one of the first to be called up when, a year after I was born, War was declared. In order to prevent my grandmother Thornhill from being enlisted into the War effort, my mother went to work in a local munitions factory, so I spent the war years living with grandma and granddad Thornhill at 104 Knutton Lane, Newcastle-u-Lyme. I remember well being woken up in the middle of the night by the sound of air raid sirens, and being bundled down into the Anderson Shelter in the front garden until the 'All Clear' was heard. On the way I remember seeing search-light beams probing the sky looking for German bombers. My mother was sometimes very late coming home from work as the trains were stopped run-ning until the threat had passed. My grandma Thornhill was a formidable character with a fiery temper and a jealous nature. Like many of her genera-tion she had little schooling and went into domestic service at an early age. As a young woman she was involved in a fight and pulled a considerable amount of hair out of the other woman's head. She was taken to Court and the hair was displayed before the magistrates as evidence! Due to his poor state of health, my granddad was only able to undertake light work. He was employed in a little office and manned the public weighbridge working day and night shifts. My mother told how she was frequently dragged out of bed in the middle of the night and taken by my grandma to spy on granddad to make sure he didn't have a woman in his little office. He never did and would never have dared!

Although during the early years of the War my father managed to get home from time to time and was able to see his young family; the day came when he was sent overseas and my mother and I didn't see him again until the war was over. He had been gone for six months before my mother had any news of where he was or even if he was still alive. The news reports stated that some of our troop ships were being sunk off the west coast of Africa, exactly where she understood my father should be. Eventually she received a postcard from Cape Town, South Africa, which said quite simply: "We have entertained your husband".

This postcard, which my mother kept until the end of her life, was re-ceived with mixed feelings. It was evidence that my father was alive but it had been sent by a WOMAN, a point not missed nor appreciated by my mother, who also had a very jealous nature; something that she had inherited from my grandma! It turned out that my father had spent most of the war serving in the Middle East (mainly in Iraq). Years later he told us that he had in fact been part of a convoy which came under attack by German U Boats. When the attacks came, the drill was that all the soldiers on the troop ship had to remain below decks, (which usually meant being below the water line) seated with their arms folded and visible on top of the table, while armed officers manned the gangways!

My mother was the eldest of four children and I saw quite a lot of my two aunts, though very little of my uncle as he was also in the Army. There was only 17 years between my mother and grandma and they often went out together and were more like sisters. At least once a week they would go to one of the local cinemas, taking me with them. There were four cinemas in Newcastle then. On the way home the routine was always the same: we would call at a pub, "The Little Vine", and I would sit in the pub kitchen with a bag of crisps and a glass of lemonade, while they drank a glass of stout.

On Saturday afternoons I would go on my own to a cinema in Silverdale, not far away for what was called by the children, 'the three penny rush'! My grandma would give me six pence, which were spent as follows: 2 pennies for the bus fare, 3 pennies for the cinema, leaving me with one penny. I would buy a carrot for a half penny, and use the other half penny to scrape it with! The cinema was full of children so it was very noisy. After the main film there was a short serial, which always ended at a critical point, ensuring the audience returned the following week to find out what happened to the hero. As the serial ended the doors were flung open and there was a great rush to get out!

On Sundays my grand parents and my mother, if she wasn't working; would go to a nearby Public House, 'The Dunkirk'. I seemed to spend countless hours sitting on the step outside that 'pub' waiting for them to come out, so we could go home and have some dinner! On special occasions there might be a piece of cake and tinned fruit for tea: but only after I had eaten some bread and margarine. Butter was rationed and grandma would keep that hidden away for herself! So many things were either unavailable or strictly rationed, and my aunts would swap sweet coupons for clothing coupons, depending on who had the sweet tooth.

One day my grandma produced from her secret store, a tin of Grade I Salmon, which she had been saving. There was great anticipation around the table at this unexpected treat! The tin was opened and the salmon put into a basin. A vinegar bottle was fetched from the pantry, and a quantity poured over the salmon. Immediately there were cries of horror because of the smell. My grandfather had been keeping lighter fuel in what had been an empty vinegar bottle and that's what had been poured over the salmon! My mother said, "Well, that's ruined now", and promptly threw the contents of the basin onto the fire! There was a great WHOOSH of flames which went straight up the chimney; fortunately without setting it on fire! My grandfather came in for some real nagging.

One of life's great pleasures for me was travelling on a bus, preferably a double-decker when I could go upstairs and if I was really lucky occupy the front seat. However short the distance, I would never walk if I could possibly ride on a bus! If I could get hold of a few pennies I would get on a bus and go to Hanley, which was the main shopping centre in the district, just for the ride. Once I took my young cousin with me, who was only two years old. There was an indoor market in Hanley with an upstairs gallery, known as 'the Cock Loft'.

Here, amongst other things, rabbits, puppies, and baby chicks were sold. I was fascinated by the place and picked my cousin up so he could see these wondrous little creatures! When we got back to my grandparents, my cousin kept repeating over and over again; "cock loft, cock loft, cock loft"! It didn't take his mother, or my grandparents very long to work out where we had been; and I got a good 'telling off' for taking him to Hanley!

When the War ended there was great rejoicing and everyone streamed into Newcastle town centre to join in the celebrations. We rejoiced particularly because, unlike many of the other men who had gone to War, my father and all my uncles had survived and would soon be on their way home. The event was spoiled for me however, because I was forced to wear a ridiculous party hat, held on to my head throughout the proceedings with a piece of elastic. I had a thoroughly miserable evening!

When my father eventually arrived home he was hardly recognisable. His years in the desert had bleached his hair white and his skin was almost black! He arrived with two presents for me, both hand made out of wood. One was a tank and the other a Wellington Bomber. I thought they were wonderful and treasured them for many years. I was less impressed with another thing he brought back – DISCIPLINE. To use a phrase that seemed to be in common use at the time, I'd been 'granny reared and granny spoilt'. The fact that it was a phrase in common use made me feel better because it meant that it obviously didn't just apply to me!

My father picked up the tools of his trade and went to work for Parker's Brewery as a maintenance bricklayer. This enabled him to accumulate a considerable knowledge of the Public Houses in North Staffordshire and beyond! My granddad Bayley was working for the same brewery as a painter and decorator. I remember seeing him at the top of a ladder painting the outside of "The Bulls Head" in Newcastle.

Soon after this homecoming my parents managed to rent a small two up and two down terraced house a few doors away from the house where my other grandparents: granddad and grandma Bayley lived. This was in the Higherland area of Newcastle, only a few hundred yards away from the town. Our new home was next door to a Coal Merchants in Poole Street, and it was here that my sister Joyce was born on 3rd December 1946, thus making our families contribution to the post-war "Baby Boom". Even though we lived so close, I didn't see very much of my granddad and grandma Bayley. Granddad was very hard of hearing and just sat smoking his pipe, which was always filled with foul smelling 'thick twist'; while grandma sat very close to the fire, smoking cigarettes and saying very little.

Leaving grandma Thornhill to look after my baby sister, my mother found a number of cleaning jobs; this time in the Westlands, not very far from the

Higherland. If she was lucky, the families she worked for had little boys; and I was brought a succession of 'hand me downs' to wear. One of my aunts lived in nearby Basford and was working as a dressmaker. My mother used to do her washing and I was the one who collected it and returned it when it had been washed, dried, and ironed each week. My parents were still in the process of furnishing our little house and money was short.

There was no mains electricity in the house and all illumination came through gas mantles; neither was there any hot water. That was obtained by boiling kettles on the gas stove or from a small boiler in the kitchen. This was normally only lit at the weekend when we all had baths in a tin tub in front of the fire, and changed our underwear! The room for laundry was outside in the yard and contained an old mangle, dolly tub, dolly peg, and washboard. Living next door to a Coal Merchants was most frustrating for my mother, as freshly laundered garments would often get covered with coal dust as they were hanging out to dry, and would need to be washed all over again!

The coal we burned had to be brought in sacks through the kitchen, taken down some steps and emptied into the cellar underneath. There was no light in the cellar, other than that which filtered through the door of the kitchen. One morning my father went down the cellar steps to fill the coal bucket before going to work; and trod on a small kitten we had only recently acquired. As my father was wearing his big working boots, the poor kitten didn't stand a chance and was killed. We were all very upset about the tragic death of our new pet, none more so than my father.

The toilet was located next do to the washroom, which meant that each bedroom was equipped with a chamber pot for use during the night. The modern TV adverts make me smile as they extol the virtues of the various brands of toilet paper; we had to make do with a few sheets of old newspaper stuck on a nail behind the door! My parents would sometimes, usually at the weekend, leave me to baby-sit while they went to a pub called the 'Wagon & Horses', which was only about 100 yards away. I passed the time wither reading or listening to an old radio, which was powered by wet cell batteries. These had to be periodically taken to the garage across the road to be recharged.

One year I was allowed to have a few friends in for a small birthday party. Before blowing out the candles on my birthday cake, I was told I had to make a wish. Having only ever seen them on films, I wished for a banana! Something else I had never tasted was ice cream. One day the word was spread amongst the excited local kids that Millie's shop on the Higherland had some ice cream, but you had to take your own small basin. I dashed home to fetch a basin, persuaded my mother to give me a threepenny bit, and joined the queue. It was the first time I had ever tasted ice cream, and I have loved it ever since!

As well as suffering the usual childhood ailments such as measles, I was unfortunate enough to have scabies; a most unpleasant skin disease. The awful itching and scratching resulted in many scabs being formed and I attended a clinic several times a week. At the clinic I had to undress and was literally painted all over with some unpleasant medication and all the scabs that had formed were not too gently removed. The hardest thing to bear though was other children calling me " scabie Joe" !

Whilst living in Poole Street my father began the process of removing (often painfully) some of the bad habits I'd been allowed to acquire. Two examples will suffice. The first involved an examination of the thoroughness of my efforts when I claimed to have had a wash! He would always check in particular my neck and behind my ears, and if it appeared that the job hadn't been done to his satisfaction, I would receive a clout and be sent back to the kitchen sink to do it all again and again, until the required standard was achieved. The second example; one I will never forget was being taught to eat all of the food I was given! I recall a particular teatime when I was half way through eating a sandwich which I didn't really want and running out of the house with it, being all too anxious to play with my friends, I stuffed it behind the entry gate.

On returning home I found myself facing my father who had come home from work, and had found the abandoned, half eaten sandwich. He was in a towering rage. Whilst serving in Iraq he had witnessed children, badly undernourished, stealing food from the swill bins outside the cookhouse; and to come home and find his own son throwing food away really upset him, and he strapped my bottom in a way I have never forgotten!

Having said that, my mother never hesitated when it came to chastising me, but I seemed to incur her wrath over minor and inconsequential things. Mornings were particularly bad and she always seemed to be in a foul temper when she got up! My baby sister was always awake first and I was roused by her crying out, "Peter, Peter, take her down and put her in her chair", which I always did. Putting on the kettle and a saucepan of water ready for the porridge, getting dressed for school and laying the table, all had to be done before mother thundered downstairs. There would invariably be something that was not quite to her satisfaction and I would receive a clout, usually about my head. It was a rare day when I managed to get off to school without some punishment! Today I would probably be categorised as an abused child!

Another significant development at this time, which was to have far reaching consequences, was my involvement with the Higherland Methodist Church. Before marrying my father, my mother had been a member of the Salvation Army; she had proudly "worn the bonnet". My father however had been in the choir and the Boys' Brigade at the Methodist Church, and it was decided that

I should attend there. In 1946 I duly became a member of the Sunday school and of the Life Boys, the junior section of the Boys' Brigade.

So began my lifetime involvement with and later commitment to Methodism. How could anyone have possibly imagined that 49 years later I would become the Minister of that Church, or that the young ex RAF Spitfire pilot who led the Life Boys would still be very active in the life of the Church and the Brigade?

The annual Sunday School Anniversary was always a memorable event. All the children dressed in their best clothes would walk around the streets in the area led by the Boys' Brigade Band. As we walked around, money would be collected from the people who had come out of their houses to watch the parade. There were two Services and a tiered platform was erected in the Church on which all the children were seated; with the smallest sitting at the bottom and the bigger ones at the top. All the children had been rehearsing their songs for weeks and the Church Choir joined in with their contributions. It was on one of these occasions that I learned a song which is still a favourite of mine: "All In The April Evening".

THE MOVE TO BRADWELL

In 1948 the family moved to a Council house at Bradwell, a new post-war Estate about two miles north of Newcastle. In fact we were amongst the first people to take up residence. Our first house was commonly known as a 'steel house', and was supposed to last for a limited period. 55 years later they are still in use in many areas! The houses across the road were still being built in the traditional way using bricks. Most of them were still covered with scaffolding, and for the small group of adventurous lads living in the street they offered a great playground. We risked life and limb as we carelessly climbed and swung from the scaffolding and used the roofing laths as lances and swords. We were regularly cursed and chased by night watchmen who never succeeded in catching any of us!

As the Estate was still in the very early stages of development there were no shops, no bus service, and no Churches; but there was a public house called 'The Britannia', always referred to as 'The Brit'. My family were delighted with the house! After the very basic facilities of Poole Street we now had a bathroom, two indoor toilets, radiators heated by a back boiler from the kitchen fire; and to my father's great delight – a garden at the front and rear of the house. Washdays continued to upset my mother though, as our new home was only about half a mile away from a colliery and a factory, which made bricks and tiles. The prevailing wind was in the wrong direction, and laundry frequently had to be redone! We remained in the 'steel house' for only a couple of years before moving to a brick house five doors up the street. I know my father wasn't too happy about the move because of all the work he had done in the garden. The brick house had been built before the steel house we were vacating, so the garden was in fairly good shape!

The nearest shops of any size were about a mile away at Wolstanton, though there were a few small shops in Porthill, which was a little closer to home. One of my childhood tasks was to frequently trail back and forth to buy the family groceries, which were usually referred to as 'the rations' as the War- time ration books were still in use. My mother seemed to have a terrible memory and I frequently had to return to the shops for something she had gotten. One member of the family was once heard to say, "Bettty's head will never save Peter's legs"!

As there were no schools on the Estate I continued my education at Friarswood school in Newcastle. This meant walking to the main A34 road and hopefully catching one of the infrequent buses that ran between Newcastle and Talke. In 1950, to my parents delight and my astonishment I succeeded in passing the 11 Plus Examination. Actually I don't even remember taking it! I was allocated a place at the prestigious Wolstanton Grammar School: in those days an establishment of some reputation! One thing I failed to appreciate at the time, was the problem faced by my parents in finding the considerable amount of money to buy the vast number of items of uniform and sports wear demanded by the school. Of course there was only one shop in the area from which these items could be purchased, and they were incredibly expensive! I was consequently exhorted to take very good care of them, as they were so expensive to replace. Being a normal lad this was a most unrealistic expectation and I was often in trouble for dirtying or damaging items of school uniform!

My reward for passing my 'Scholarship' was a new bicycle. It was the cheapest in the shop and had to be returned within a few weeks because all the chrome came off! However, it was my bicycle and I couldn't wait to have it back once all the chrome had been renewed. I was still responsible for doing most of the shopping for the family and also for my grandparents, who had moved from Knutton Lane and were now living in their own little terraced house in Newcastle. Although today, we have the M6 Motorway and a dual carriageway on the A34, then there was only one road (the A34), and it was a single carriageway. All traffic on its way to and from Manchester, Liverpool, the north west of England; and Scotland used this road, and day and night it was always very busy. I made countless journeys to and from Newcastle with bulging shopping bags on both handlebars; while cars and heavy lorries passed me with only inches to spare. I think it's a wonder I survived!

Bricklayers, even very good ones like my father, were not very well paid in 1950, and it was common practice in the building trade to lay off workers during spells of bad weather. Also many of the building firms my father worked for seemed to go out of business, and he regularly changed employers. Consequently there was no such thing as a regular wage coming into the home. My mother, who handled all the family finances, turned out to be an absolute genius in juggling things to enable us to meet our commitments without getting into debt. So it was in September 1950, I presented my self, suitably equipped and attired at Wolstanton Grammar School. The next five years were largely wasted, for reasons, which will be revealed later, and I left school in 1955 without any formal qualifications.

In 1951 The Festival of Britain exhibition was held in London and Parker's Brewery organised a day trip for its employees and their families. We got up very early and caught a special train from Newcastle Station. It took nearly six hours to get to London; I thought we would never get there! I only remember two items from the Exhibition; the Skylon and an enormous stuffed Grizzly Bear! The journey back to Newcastle seemed to take for ever. Many crates of beer had been loaded onto the train and everyone was in high spirits. I went to sleep and was woken up just as the train was pulling into the Station.

Another 'Works Outing' was to Scarborough where my father had spent some time at the beginning of the War. As well a visiting the Castle and the town; we went to a beautiful Park where my father pointed out plants I had never seen before. One large plant he called African Rhubarb, and some tall red tipped flowers he described as 'red hot pokers'. This visit resulted in me gaining a little kudos a couple of years later when the Combined Cadet Force from school went to Scarborough for their annual Camp; and I was able to show some of the boys around! About the same time as I was settling into the routine of my new school, a new building was being opened on the Estate: a Methodist Church. It was a small dual-purpose building, which was to play a most significant part during my turbulent teenage years. Initially, taking my sister with me, I began to attend Sunday School. Later, and sneaking in before I was old enough; I joined the Youth Club, which met on three evenings a week. Mondays and Fridays were mixed and I discovered how attractive girls could be! I learned to dance to old 78 gramophone records and to play table tennis, billiards, and snooker. Wednesday evenings were for boys only; and on these evenings we were taught a little about gymnastics. Our tutor was a brick-layer, an acquaintance of my father, who had served in the Army Physical Training Corps. I really enjoyed this, particularly as I had joined a similar gymnastics club at School. The youth of the Church also met every Sunday morning, for discussion and argument in a meeting led by the Youth Club leader, who was also a Local Preacher. To round off our weekends, most teenagers would attend the Sunday evening Service, and then be invited to the homes of Church members for an informal get together and a cup of tea. There was a real sense of belonging and being valued. Many long-term friendships were forged, some of which in time led to marriages!

The support and advice I received from our full-time youth leaders, the first of these being Bill Cockell, and the second, Ron Kemp; who later became a Methodist Minister, was considerable and much appreciated. Their leadership and dedication played an incalculable part in the development of the new Methodist community in Bradwell. There was also a lady who was a member of the Youth Club helpers committee who befriended me and took an interest in me and in what I was doing. It is important for a young person that an adult from outside the family take an interest in them. The ladies name was Mrs. Rose Cumberbatch, always known as 'Cumby' by her friends, and she kept in touch with me over many years and wherever I travelled. She died recently at the age of 96 and it was a great privilege for me to give the address at her funeral.

Just a couple of hundred yards away from the Church, another new building had also opened on the Estate, one in which my parents were founder members. This was Bradwell Working Mens' Club, and my parents had been paying a small regular subscription towards its building. If you were to visit the Club today, you would find that the building, like the Church, has grown considerably in size over the years. You would also see my father's name engraved on the panelling in the entrance hall. He really made his mark in more ways than one! A small hut was built by this building, which served as the local Gardeners' Club. My father was a member and in addition to being a place where plants and gardening materials could be purchased at 'trade' prices; it was a convenient haven for my father whenever my mother was 'on the warpath'. Like a recent British Prime Minister, she was always determined to go on, and on, and on!

The opening of the Workingmen's Club and my parents regular attendance created a few problems for me; a minor one being the Methodist standpoint on alcohol, and the major one being my duty to baby-sit with my sister while they went to the Club! With monotonous regularity I had to leave friends and functions and rush off home to baby-sit, and I did this with increasing resentment as I got older. On one occasion I let my bicycle tyre down, pretending to have a puncture to justify my lateness home. I still received a clout from my father, who growled, "You can't fool me with tricks like that because I used to do the same when I was a lad". He may have been strict but he was always fair! Alcohol affects people in different ways. It made both my parents mellow, good tempered, and generous. I soon discovered the best time to ask them for anything was when they came home after a good evening at 'The Club'! To their credit they never changed their minds the following day.

As well as spending time looking after my sister; I was frequently expected to care for my two younger cousins. This was because two of my aunts were working, and my mother looked after their children. In practice, much of the 'looking after' was delegated to me! One cousin, a boy, was five years younger than me; and he would be with us mainly during school holidays. Wishing to spend time with my friends; engaging in the kind of games and activities twelve and thirteen years old boys enjoyed, I became increasingly resentful at having to take my young cousin with me!

My other cousin was only a baby and my aunt lived just over a mile away. She naturally wanted her baby daughter home every weekend, and one night during the week; the remainder of the week the baby stayed with us. It was my responsibility to collect her on Sunday evenings and push her large pram from Wolstanton to Bradwell. On Tuesday evenings she would be taken back to spend the night at home. I would also sleep at my aunt's house that night so I would be there to wheel her back to Bradwell early on the Wednesday morning before going to school.

There was an old cinema in Wolstanton known as 'The Bug Hut'; and my aunt gave me enough money to 'go to the pictures'. If the films being shown had a 'U' grading, I was allowed into the cinema. If however, a film was graded 'A', I was not allowed in without being accompanied by an adult. With others sharing the same predicament; I would wave my money under the noses of any adult entering the cinema and ask, "Will you take me in please?" Usually someone eventually would, and once we were past the ticket office I would go and sit on my own. There was a large wicker basket on the pram and lorries carrying coal frequently used the road I had to take to get home. Lumps of it frequently fell off and as I walked along I would pick up the coal and by the time I reached home the basket would be full! Friday evenings saw me pushing my cousin back home for the weekend.

The nearest Gas Works was at Chesterton in the neighbouring valley. Every week I would cycle there and collect two bags of coke, each one weighing half a hundredweight (56 pounds). One bag would be shoved inside the cycle frame; and the other placed on top between the handlebars and the saddle. It was then pushed home via a couple of steep streets. On the odd occasion when the cycle wasn't available, I would walk to the gas works and carry one bag home. It was hard work, but coke was cheaper than coal.

On 3rd January 1953, a Saturday; my granddad Thornhill had a heart attack and died. He was 59 years old. He had served in the Army during the First World War, achieved the rank of Sergeant; and spent three years as a prisoner of war. He had been a heavy smoker and enjoyed his beer. The early symptoms of his heart problems were not taken seriously by the family, who actually made light of his complaints about being short of breath and having chest pains; because he could always get to the local pub! I don't think he ever consulted a doctor. He was intelligent and knowledgeable, and I used to love to sit and listen to him talk about current affairs, the Earth, and the Universe.

It was a regular commitment for me every Saturday morning to cycle down to their home in Newcastle to do some shopping for them. When I arrived I was told the news and I was really shocked and very upset. At 14 I had never experienced the death of someone close to me before. Not many people had telephones in those days so, when I had composed myself, I cycled back to my home in Bradwell to break the news to my parents. Only my mother was at home and she was heartbroken by the news. I then set off to find my father who was working on a building site about two miles away. He was equally shocked and we walked back home together. There were of course many arrangements to be made but there were many people in the family to help. Grandma couldn't bear to be left alone so my mother decided that we would move in with her until after the funeral. It was only a small terraced house so it was a bit cramped to say the least. My sister and I had to sleep on a mattress in a small back bedroom with granddad 'laid out' in the next room. It was not the custom at that time to take the deceased to a Chapel of Rest. After a couple of days granddad was taken downstairs and put in his coffin in the parlour so that family, friends, and neighbours, could call in and pay their respects.

It had been decided that granddad should be cremated, and on the day of the funeral I was squeezed into the car immediately behind the hearse for the journey to the crematorium, which was about five miles away at Carmountside the other side of Hanley. I remember that as the cortege made it's way slowly through Newcastle, people stood still and men removed their hats as a mark of respect. After the service we returned home for refreshments and there were long discussions about the future of grandma, who had made it clear that she had no intention of staying on in the house alone. I distinctly remember my mother and my aunts arguing about who was going to take what from the house! Young as I was, it left me with a bad taste in my mouth; and I resolved there and then that when our parents eventually died, my sister and I would not behave in such an unseemly manner.

It was eventually decided that the house would be sold and that grandma would live with one of my aunts. The house was quickly sold for just over £900 and the money soon spent! Grandma treated herself to a fur coat and a television set, so we were able to watch the Coronation of Queen Elizabeth II. She bought me a new bicycle – a Philips Kingfisher with four gears and dropped handlebars, which served me well until it was stolen four years later!

One day a friend and I set off very early one morning on our bicycles for a day out. We had no particular destination in mind and after three hours we were on the outskirts of Chester. After a short break we decided to carry on and found ourselves cycling through Port Sunlight and on to New Brighton. We stayed there for two hours before setting off back home. We were determined to get home in time to go for a swim in Newcastle Baths. When we were about twenty miles from home our leg muscles began to complain! Pushing the pedals around became increasingly difficult; and in the last hour we made agonisingly slow progress. Far from going for a swim; by the time I reached home it was all I could do to stagger up the path to the front door! When we later studied a map, we discovered we had cycled 110 miles.

To earn extra pocket money I became a 'paper boy' for a Newsagent in Porthill. I had to be at the shop by 6.am Monday to Saturday, put my newspapers and magazines in order; deliver them and be back home for breakfast before going to school. At 5.pm I was back at the shop ready to deliver our local evening newspaper, 'The Sentinel'. On Wednesdays and Thursdays, owing to the weight of certain popular magazines such as 'Woman', 'Women's Own', and 'The Radio Times'; it was necessary to make two trips around the area I was responsible for. For this I was paid one shilling and one penny a round. On Sunday mornings I worked for four hours; because not only did I deliver the newspapers: I had to collect money from most of the customers as very few of them called in the shop to pay what they owed. Working on Sunday mornings earned me another four shillings; and if I completed a week without making any mistakes or omissions; I was given a bonus of one shilling. During the week before Christmas I would knock on the doors of my customers hoping for a 'Christmas Box! I composed a little verse, which I wrote on a postcard and gave to them when they opened the door.

"Through hail and rain and sleet and snow,

On my journey I must go.

I wear out gloves, and shoes, and socks;

So if you please, a Christmas Box!

It worked and I was usually given some money; even if, as one man said to me as he offered some coins, "here you are, if only just for your bloody cheek"! All the 'paper boys' at the shop compared their Christmas tips; and I was happy to be near the top of the list. On Saturdays, I would work for five hours on a stall in Newcastle indoor market; selling oatcakes, crumpets, scotch pancakes, and pikelets. For this I was paid ten shillings.

It was about this time that my mother went into hospital for an operation, which I later discovered to be an hysterectomy, which at that time was a major abdominal operation requiring a fairly lengthy period of convalescence. In common parlance she had had 'everything taken away'. After she had finally recovered, I couldn't help but notice a complete change in her character and attitude; she was a much nicer person! She had obviously been suffering for a long time before the operation had been deemed necessary, and this had undoubtedly contributed to her bad temper and to my mind, unreasonable behaviour! It also demonstrated what a patient and loving husband my father was.

A 'daughter' Church from Porthill Parish Church had now been built on the Estate, about 400 yards from the Methodist Church; but we had very little to do with them! The Bradwell community shared an ambivalent relationship with its Churches: they were always there, and were frequently the focus of the 'rites of passage' which were still a feature of life at that time. Baptisms, Weddings, and Funerals were 'Church occasions'. I had believed for some time, however, that God had a purpose for my life and in February 1954 I had a 'conversion' experience, which led to me becoming a committed Christian; and because of these nascent yearnings it wasn't really a difficult decision to make. I was invited by a group of young people to join in a Christian Endeavour meeting at a Church in Wolstanton. At the conclusion of the meeting I was invited to speak at the next meeting the following week. Before I realised what I was doing I had agreed!

My contribution to that and subsequent meetings of the Christian Endeavour led to the suggestion that I should consider training to become a Methodist Local Preacher. I considered this and allowed my name to be brought before the Local Preacher's Meeting of the Wolstanton and Audley Methodist Circuit. After due consideration it was agreed that my 'call to preach' be tested and I was placed 'on note'. This meant that I was put under the supervision of a fully accredited Local Preacher, who would also act as my mentor. In my case this was a fiery little man called Wilf Fox, affectionately known around the Circuit as "whosoever Wilf". A nickname acquired due to his habit of choosing a hymn which began "Whosoever will", and which had a rousing chorus at the end of each verse. At the conclusion of the hymn, when the congregation had closed their hymn books and had almost resumed their seats, Wilf would shout out "Halleluiah" and begin singing it again, causing the good people to reach for their hymn books, and struggle to find the right number!

I accompanied 'Wilf' for the next six months on his preaching appointments. First I was allowed to read the Lessons from the Bible, then I led the prayers and announced the hymns, finally it was my lot to preach the sermon. When all these things had been carried out to the satisfaction of Wilf and the Circuit Local Preachers, I was placed 'On Trial'. This meant that I was authorised to conduct services of public worship independently at Churches throughout the Circuit.

On one occasion I went to a Church in the village of Audley to conduct the evening Service. I arrived early and began my preparations. I put the hymn numbers on the board and opened the big pulpit bible at the lessons I had chosen, and then went into the vestry to talk to the Steward on duty. We were both a little surprised when another Local Preacher walked into the vestry. "Hello", I said, "What are you doing here"? He replied, "I'm planned to take the Service, what are **you** doing here"? The Circuit plan was consulted and I discovered I should have been at Audley Central Church about half a mile away. I didn't know that there were in fact three Churches in Audley! I ran down the hill to the Central Church just in time to prevent a relieved Steward from beginning the Service; for it was his responsibility to conduct the Service should a Preacher fail to turn up for any reason!

Being "On Trial also meant that I had to begin studying for my Local Preacher's examinations. The requirements being to pass three written examinations on the Bible and Christian Doctrine, conduct a Trial Service, and have an Oral Examination, which required some knowledge of the most important of John Wesley's sermons!

Being most enthusiastic to share my faith, I organised a Bible study/prayer group at school and half a dozen of us met most lunchtimes. I used to prepare and read my Bible during many boring lessons at the Grammar School; where we were more lectured to than taught! A sharp-eyed teacher would often confiscate the Bible. I therefore always made sure I had at least a couple of spares in my school satchel or desk! My evenings were spent either at the youth club or speaking at or attending meetings. Homework was rarely done and the subsequent periods of detention noted on my school reports together with many critical comments! This always resulted in arguments with my parents at the end of every term! I must admit to feeling a little guilty about letting my parents down, but obviously never guilty enough to change my priorities.

In my first term at the Grammar School I had been in the 'B' stream, but by the end of the term it was obvious that my academic qualities had been over estimated, and I was relegated to the 'C' stream where I remained for the rest of my time at school. One subject I did well in was German; at least for the first three years. In my fourth year I had a different German teacher and my performance deteriorated. He was a man who just seemed to drip sarcasm at every opportunity. It was obvious from the beginning that he didn't like me, and very soon the feeling was mutual! One day I made the great mistake of yawning during one of his lessons. "Boy", he yelled at me. "If you have to yawn in one of my lessons, you put your hand over your mouth: and if your hand isn't big enough, you lift the desk lid"!

Shopping was still my responsibility, and one evening each week I had to call at a grocers shop in Wolstanton on my way home from school, and collect what at that time were still called 'the rations'. On one occasion I had a school detention on the day I was due to do the shopping, which on that particular day included the family's evening meal. So I went to see the Headmaster (known to all the boys as 'The Beak'), explained the situation to him, and asked if the detention could be postponed to another evening. He refused! What a quandary I was now in! By the end of the school day, I had made my decision; I would do the shopping and face the wrath and cane of 'The Beak' the following morning. When I dressed the following morning I put on two pairs of underpants and my pyjama bottoms underneath my school trousers. After Assembly a prefect came and summoned me to the Head's office. I waited outside for about fifteen minutes; which I'm sure was a deliberate tactic designed to heighten the sense of impending doom!

When I eventually saw the Head he was absolutely furious. "You deliberately defied me", he thundered, swishing his cane. In a tremulous voice I reminded him of our conversation of the previous morning and concluded by saying, "Sir, I decided it would be better to face you this morning, than my mother last night had I arrived home without the shopping". He put the cane down, glared at me, and in a not unkindly way said, "Very well, but don't let it happen again"; and it didn't.

The Headmaster, Mr. Marples, was really quite an impressive man. I can still picture him as he strode down the aisle of the school hall every morning, his gown streaming behind him to take the morning Assembly. He was a man of dignity as was illustrated on the day he didn't appear at his usual time. The whole school sat, and waited, and wondered at the delay. The school organist, Mr. Spencer had decided that day to play the tune "Narcissus", which, at that time had become associated with the comic antics of the comedian, Norman Wisdom; and the Head had refused to enter the hall until something more appropriate was played!

In my third year I joined the school C.C.F. (Combined Cadet Force), and the things I learned about the military way of life were to give me a head start, and also enabled me to help other recruits when I joined the Regular Army a few years later. I also joined the school choir and drama society and took part in a number of concerts and productions. On the sporting side, after my first year I decided I would much rather spend one afternoon a week cross-country running rather than play rugby.

Again, this was to prove an advantage when I later joined the Army. In the summer I opted to do athletics instead of cricket, agreeing with Lord Mancroft, who reportedly said, "Cricket is a game which the English, not being a spiritual people, had to invent in order to have some concept of eternity!" One of our PE teachers had a small group of pupils who were interested in gymnastics. This appealed to me, as it was similar to the activities of our Wednesday club night at the Church; so I joined and soon became good enough to be part of the display team. In the summer months the team would often give displays at Church and village fetes and garden parties. Although I certainly hadn't made my mark at the school academically, I like to think I had made a small contribution to the life of the school in other ways!

The next time I visited the Head's office was to ask for permission to leave school when I had completed my GCE examinations (all of which I failed). I had been offered a place in September 1955 at Cliff College, near Sheffield, and I really needed to work for a few months to earn some money before I went. 'Cliff', as everyone in the Methodist Church knows, is an evangelical Laymen's Training College where young men (now young women too!) were sent by the Church for a years training in biblical studies, theology, and evangelism. Many did in fact go on from there to offer for the Methodist Ministry, as I myself did but not for several years. Anyway, there was much to do before I commenced my studies there – first I needed a job! I went to work less than a week after leaving school at the Chesterton Branch of the Silverdale Co-Operative Society.

At the Co-op my main job was to make sure all the shelves in the shop were kept well stacked and to keep the storerooms in good order. As the storerooms were located above the shop I was constantly going up and down the stairs, usually carrying heavy boxes. In addition, when the shop orders were delivered from the main Co-op warehouse, it was my job to take all the boxes and sacks upstairs to the storerooms. During busy periods I would help by serving customers and even learned how to take the bones out of a side of bacon without cutting a finger off! At the end of three months my muscles had been well built up and physically I was in very good shape for a youth who was just seventeen! This, along with lots of cycling was to stand me in good stead a few years later when I undertook the selection course to join 16th Parachute Brigade.

CLIFF COLLEGE

At last the day came when I was to leave home and travel to Cliff College. My Minister, Rev. J Arthur Hoyles, had kindly offered to take me to Hanley to catch the bus to Buxton where I was to change and catch the Sheffield bus. I had one enormous case containing all my worldly goods, and the princely sum of 30 shillings to last me until Christmas, when I hoped to get a holiday job. It took the coach about two hours to get to Buxton; then I had to wait ages for a connexion to Sheffield. The bus didn't go past the College so I was dropped off at a major crossroads about a mile away. My suitcase seemed to weigh a ton so I was very thankful when a lorry stopped (the driver had obviously seen me struggling), and I was offered a lift to the College. I had been allocated a room on the top floor and the views from my window must have been amongst the most beautiful in Derbyshire! It overlooked the River Derwent and a vista of hills covered with a great variety of colourful trees and bushes. The room itself was small, sparsely but adequately furnished and I was satisfied and very happy to be there; especially so as it wasn't costing me a penny! Students, and there were some, who could afford to make a financial contribution were expected to do so. Otherwise, all costs were met by donations (Cliff has many friends and supporters), and the Home Missions Department of the Methodist Church. No student was ever turned away on financial grounds

When all the students had arrived we gathered together in the lecture room to be introduced to each other and to the Staff; and of course to be informed about the rules governing the day to day life of the College. The rising bell was at 6.15am and we were expected to be washed and dressed and in the lecture room by 7:00am for roll call and to sing a verse of a hymn. Students then had to return to their rooms until 8.00am for a time of personal devotion, known as 'Quiet Time'. Then it was time for everyone to go to the lovely College Chapel for morning prayers, which was thankfully followed by breakfast in the dining room. Students took it in turns to do the washing up! After breakfast on the first morning, the students were expected to visit the College bookshop. Here all manner of things were on sale from Bibles to College badges and ties. The most important thing was to buy the Principal's notes on Theology; otherwise we would be unable to follow his lectures! By the time I had left the shop I had only fifteen shillings left!

Lectures were every morning for three hours and three evenings a week after tea. The other three evenings were taken up with a midweek Class Meeting, when lots of Cliff Choruses were sung and students were encouraged to talk about their own spiritual experiences (it was called 'giving a testimony') and people from outside the College community were allowed to attend these meetings. A small number of visitors were usually in attendance. On Friday evenings there was a Church service; and on Saturday evening there was a special prayer meeting for missionaries. On Sundays students were sent out to conduct services at Chapels over a wide area and I cycled (I'd sent my bicycle to the college by train) many miles in all weathers to fulfil this joyful task.

It was I suppose an almost monastic way of life (in fact everyone was referred to as 'Brother', which took a little getting used to.), and all students were expected to work in either the College (cleaning etc.) or the extensive gardens. This was down on the timetable as 'Manual' and was carried out between 2.00pm – 4.00pm every afternoon during the week. I, along with another student, Brother Ball, took on the responsibility of looking after the coal fired heating system. This meant going down to the boiler room several times a day to shovel fuel into the boiler and clean out all the clinker and ashes. It was a very dirty and dusty task and we needed to wear masks to prevent us breathing in the dust and fumes. The masks were only partially successful! If we failed to do the job properly all the radiators went cold and we had no hot water! This happened only once. The only exception to the above routine was when the hundreds of trees in the College grounds shed their leaves and everyone was mobilised to pick them all up; a mammoth task!

I hadn't been at Cliff many weeks when I committed my first misdemeanour. A friend and I hitch hiked to Chesterfield to see a newly released film "The Dam Busters". It took longer than we'd anticipated to hitch a lift back and we missed the missionary prayer meeting, thereby incurring the wrath of the Principal, Rev. 'Pop' Eagles! He could be a bit volatile at times and I later discovered that years before, whilst serving in the Army he had contracted malaria, which periodically still gave him a very bad time. In addition to this we discovered that a small group of students, appalled by the 'worldly' nature of our trip out, had held prayer meeting for us! A few years later it would take a period of agonising doubt and pain to disentangle myself from the narrow minded and theological conservatism of this environment. With hindsight, I was too young and much too immature to have gone to Cliff. I accepted without question all I was taught and would never have dreamt of expressing any doubts for fear of being called a 'backslider'. As far as the Bible and theology were concerned, my critical faculties were still at an embryonic stage, so I just soaked up everything like a big piece of blotting paper! In the meantime life went on.

For many years I had neglected to look after my teeth properly. Apart from cleaning them regularly I hadn't visited a Dentist for ages: now I was experiencing a lot of toothache! In fear and trepidation I made an appointment to see a Dentist in Bakewell, about four miles away. I cycled to Bakewell, sat in the waiting room thumbing through magazines without really seeing anything; until it was my turn to see the Dentist. His initial examination confirmed that I needed a lot of work doing on my teeth! That afternoon I had three teeth filled, and one extraction. I was then informed that I would need another appointment to have another three teeth filled on the other side of my mouth, and another extraction, which would entail cutting away part of my gum. I can honestly say that apart from the injections and a little discomfort, it was not a painful experience; my faith in the Dental Profession was restored and I have made regular visits to the Dentists ever since!

In the Autumn of 1955 I sat, and passed, all three of my Local Preachers written examinations with high enough grades to enable me later to offer myself as a candidate for the Methodist Ministry. What a contrast from my school results! I was now motivated in a way I never had been at school, and never again would I fail an examination; and there were many more to come.

In the spring of 1956 there was a shortage of men on the Evangelistic Staff of the College and I was selected to accompany one of the full time Evangelists, Lawrence Roddis (Lorrie) on a ten-day Mission to a Chapel in Long Lawford, near Rugby. I must have done quite well because I was invited to remain on the Staff – my student days at Cliff were over! Lorrie was a good leader of men and he taught me a lot. I remember well a talk he used to give entitled "From Plough to Pulpit", in which he related, to use his own words, how "a cursing swearing farm lad became a Christian and a preacher of the Gospel". A seed from those days must have been planted deep in my subconscious mind, which led me to choose the title for this book! I then spent several months partnered with another evangelist, Jim Beasley, who was an impressive preacher, especially in the open-air.

In the summer of 1956, Jim led a team of half a dozen students on a month long campaign to the beaches of Bridlington on the east Yorkshire coast. This was an annual event and we were accommodated in a local Methodist Church schoolroom. We had a special little portable platform which we erected a few yards from the beach and would hold special services for adults and children twice daily. The children's meetings, known as "Sunshine Corner", were especially well attended, by both children and adults! One of Jim's previous colleagues had been a soloist who had sung Gospel songs during the services, and Jim encouraged me to consider doing the same. I was very reluctant as I didn't consider my voice to be good enough, but Jim persisted and eventually I agreed. I sang my first solo in Bridlngton Methodist Church: it was from the Billy Graham Song Book and was well received by the congregation. Thus began a lifetime interest in singing, both as a soloist and as a choir member.

It was during this visit to Bridlington that I first met a 16-year-old girl who would later become my first wife. Maureen Vaughan was on holiday from Rotherham in south Yorkshire with a girl friend. It was just over a month later, after I had decided to return to Cliff for another few months; that I was part of another Mission team based at Attercliffe Methodist Mission, between Sheffield and Rotherham. She turned up at one of our meetings and following this we began to see each other at fairly regular intervals. During the Mission I stayed at the home of one of the Stewards. John and his wife Edna had four sons; the youngest being still in nappies, so it was quite crowded but they made me feel so welcome. When I finally finished at Cliff, John and Edna invited me to stay with them until I was 'called up' to do my National Service. John, who was a Director at one of the many Steel Works in Sheffield, offered to find me a job for a few months. It was a most generous offer, which I gratefully accepted.

John was as good as his word, and arranged for me to work at a factory about seven miles away; called Steads. This Company manufactured amber handled screwdrivers, springs, and 'Songster' gramophone needles. Work started at 7.15am, so I had to get up very early and cycle through the 'rush hour' traffic to the factory, which was on the outskirts of Sheffield. There was so much traffic, including trams; I considered myself fortunate to escape serious injury! Having no skills but a willingness and capacity for hard work; I was employed as a general labourer and given a variety of tasks: moving metal boxes filled with steel rods being one of them. One day I was given the job of cutting a great pile of steel rods into small pieces just over an inch long. These, I was informed, were components for the car manufacturing industry. An engineer set up a universal grinding wheel for this task and I got on with it. It took me about three hours to complete the job, and I sought out the Foreman to find out what he wanted me to do next. To my surprise he said, "a 'Time and Motion' study has been done on that job; and it should have taken you all day to complete it, so go and hide somewhere for the rest of the day"! Another task was to feed trolley loads of thin steel rods through a grinding wheel to sharpen the ends. These were then taken for the ends to be cut off by machines operated by women; before being returned so that what were now the ends of the slightly shortened rods could be sharpened. These were destined to become gramophone needles.

At the end of my time in Sheffield I returned home to Bradwell and waited to be called up to do my National Service. The first thing I did was to complete my training to be a Local Preacher. I conducted a Trial Service and had my oral examination; both of which were satisfactory, and in October 1956 at a Service of Public Recognition held in my home Church at Bradwell, I became a fully accredited Local Preacher of the Methodist Church. I was presented with a book called "The Bible as History" (I already had enough Bibles) and a letter from the President of the Methodist Conference. I was eighteen years old and one of the youngest Local Preachers in the country. I don't know whether 'The Beak' would have been impressed or not?

There was some delay at this time in calling up young men for National Service and I tried in vain to find temporary employment. Eventually my

Minister, who was a part-time Industrial Chaplain, suggested I went to work down the Pit (coal mine) and arranged for me to meet the Manager of Wolstanton Colliery who agreed to take me on. My parents were not at all happy about it! A relative of my mother had been killed in an accident underground, and one of my father's brothers had been buried for two days by a fall of rock. He hadn't been badly injured but the experience had scarred him for life. Anyway I decided to go for training.

LIFE DOWN THE PIT

WOLSTANTON COLLIERY

The training Pit was Kemble Colliery at Heron Cross near Stoke, and I spent a few weeks learning the basic skills needed to be a miner, and a great deal of emphasis was placed on the safety aspect. It was from here that my lovely bike was stolen. I walked to the Police Station in Stoke to report the theft but I never saw the bike again. Wolstanton Colliery was very, very different from the almost clinical conditions of the Training Colliery! I was first of all taken to the pithead baths and allocated two lockers, one either side of the showers. One was to deposit the clothes I had walked to work in, and the other to contain the clothing I would be working in underground. I was issued with a helmet, a sturdy pair of boots with steel toecaps, a pick, shovel, axe, and a pair of kneepads. Little did I realise how long I would have to spend on my knees! I bought a metal water bottle, sandwich tin, soap and towels. On my first working day I joined the men on the day shift. The shift working hours were from 6.00am to 1.30pm; and from 11.00pm to 6.30am.

Starting work at 6.00am meant being there at least an hour beforehand. After changing into working clothes, the miners would 'clock in' at the lamp house and pick up a battery, which fitted onto their belts, and a light, which clipped onto their helmets. Then they walked to the shaft, from where they would be lowered underground in cages to the pit bottom. Each cage had three sections, which would be packed with miners on the way down: and would bring three tubs full of coal to the surface. It took about half an hour to walk from the pit bottom to the coal face, and the further we walked, the hotter it became, so the practice was to gradually take off layers of clothing, hang them up on the odd nail, and get dressed again on the way out!

The first job I was given however, wasn't at the coalface, but at the Loader End. The miners shovelled the coal onto conveyor belts which eventually came to the Loader End where it was emptied into tubs, which were then hauled to the pit bottom, usually six at a time, to be taken to the surface in the same cages that brought the miners down. This was where some of the training I had been given at Kemble came to be used. The tubs were linked together and then the line of tubs was attached by means of chains to a continuously moving overhead steel cable. Each chain had a large hook at either end, and one chain was attached to the front tub and one to the rear.

The skill was to wrap one chain around the cable with the hook facing forwards to pull the tubs, and another chain fixed to the rear tub with the hook facing to the rear to stop the tubs running away whilst going down an incline. This had to be done without stopping the moving cable or losing ones fingers! In case of an emergency or shortage of tubs; the moving cable was stopped by pulling on a wire leading to the winch operator. One pull meant STOP, two pulls meant GO ON, and three pulls meant REVERSE. If the cable was stopped for more than a few moments, a colliery official would be on the phone or quickly on the scene to determine the reason! If the cable stopped, that meant the coal wasn't moving and that was bad news!

The major problem with working at the loader end was the amount of coal dust in the air. A small pipe was fitted to spray the coal with water as it came off the belt and into the tubs, but it was largely ineffectual. There was plenty of dust at the coalface as I was to discover later, but it wasn't as bad as at the loader end. One of my tasks was to hold a large wooden wedge under the front wheel of the front tub, and gradually allow it to move down the rails as it was filled with coal from the belt. Another task was to hold a metal sheet between the tubs to prevent the flow of coal from dropping between them as they moved forward. Any coal that did had to be shovelled up when there was a spare minute.

Owing to the distance from the coalface to the Loader End, two conveyor belts were used; one emptying on to the other. One man, usually an old collier would be stationed at the junction. His sole task was to watch the belts; and when one stopped he would press a large button to stop the other. If the belt between him and the loader end stopped it usually meant there was a shortage of empty tubs. It was a lonely and boring job and there were times when the old collier would 'nod off' and fail to stop the belt bringing coal from the face. Before long the man would be buried in coal; and occasionally when that didn't wake him, he would have to be dug out!

I was glad when my time on 'the haulage' came to an end and I was permitted to join the colliers at the coalface. My first day was memorable and a little frightening. Before the colliers went onto the coalface it was undercut to a depth of four feet six inches. A miner known as the borer would then drill holes at intervals all along the face. Another miner called a shot lighter equipped with a Davey Lamp to test for gas, would then ram an explosive charge into each hole to which was attached a detonator. After shouting a warning, he would 'blow the fronts' off the face bringing down tons of coal and creating clouds of coal dust. This was the first coal to be shovelled onto the conveyor belt by the colliers when they arrived. Three years after leaving the industry I was still coughing up coal dust!

The face I worked on was called 'Peacock 3'. As I crawled after the other miners over the recently blown 'fronts' I was informed that there was a fault on the face; which meant that for a distance of about 20 yards the seam of coal was reduced to about 30 inches and we had to crawl on our stomachs with our helmets touching the roof. Being my first day I was crawling along carrying and dragging a pick, shovel, axe, water bottle, and snappin tin containing my sandwiches! After finally arriving at my own 'yardage', the length of face I was expected to clear, I began shovelling the fronts onto the conveyor belt. That was the easy part. Then it was a matter of using the pick and shovel to bring down the rest of the coal. A priority was to check and where necessary renew the timbers holding the roof up. 'Peacock 3' was known to have an unstable roof, which was a rather disconcerting piece of information. Coal cutting machines had been tried on the face but the vibration had brought the roof down and buried them!

Working at the coalface was very hard but somehow satisfying. The conveyor belts stopped for twenty minutes during the shift; that was 'snappin' time when we ate our sandwiches and chatted. We were usually joined by a few older miners who, because of age or infirmity, were employed doing simple maintenance jobs. These were men who were definitely old before their time. They would look at me, young and innocent thing that I was, and say things like, "if tha's gor any sense lad, tha'll ger out"!

However, I carried on for several more months, one week on days followed by a week on nights. There was occasionally 'overtime' to be worked to ensure all was ready for the next shift. My mother always worried if I was late home! Then came the day when I had a very near brush with death. A large piece of coal had fallen out of the face and knocked down a wooden roof support I had put up. I remembered having seen a suitable length of timber on the other side of the conveyor belt. I had just got up off my knees and leaned over the belt to retrieve it, when a piece of rock about the size of a single bed crashed down onto the spot I had just vacated! A shower of much smaller pieces caught my back, and I still bear the scars, but my insides were churning. I visited the medical centre for a bit of minor patching up, went home, and terminated my employment there and then. My nerve had gone, and I never went down a mine again, until I did so as an Industrial Chaplain some nine years later.

REGULAR SOLDIER – 1957 - 1962

Having left the coal industry it was time to do my National Service. Maureen Vaughan and I had recently become engaged with a view to getting married the following year. Having no particular plans for a future career, and not relishing the prospect of earning a meagre twenty-eight shillings a week for the next two years, I decided to 'sign on' and become a Regular Soldier rather than a conscript. My three years in the School C.C.F. had given me enough confidence to believe I had at least the makings of a good soldier! So I went to the Army Recruiting Office in Stoke to begin the process of enlistment. This first of all required having a medical examination, which declared me fit enough to cope with the rigours of soldiering. The next day was spent doing written and intelligence tests, which classified me as an SSG2 recruit, (summed selection group) which indicated that I was above average. Not quite potential officer material, but one who could have a promising career. Having been 'sworn in', and made my oath of allegiance to serve the Queen and her heirs and successors, I was ushered out of the office by the Sergeant whose parting words to me were; "If I see you in three years time and you are not a Sergeant, I'll kick your arse for you!"

So on 14th November 1957 having duly made my oath of allegiance, I was enlisted to serve in the Royal Regiment of Artillery, and that was probably because the Recruiting Sergeant wore a Gunner cap badge! I was now 23532171 Gunner P. Bayley. My father was very pleased about this because he had served

November 1957/ 23 Intake Oswestry
Gunner Bayley is the 5th from the right on the second row

in the Royal Artillery during WWII. I had recently got engaged and planned to marry the following autumn, so my mother had mixed feelings about my military career! On the day of enlistment a soldier is given a days pay, a travel warrant, and a movement order giving instructions and directions to the Training Regiment. My orders were to report to 68 Training Regiment R.A., Parkhall Camp, Oswestry, Shropshire; as part of 57/23 Intake.

On arrival at the camp, I discovered that 57/23 intake was made up mainly of National Servicemen, who regarded the small group of Regular soldiers as being mentally retarded because they had been so stupid as to volunteer! First of all we were taken to our barrack rooms to leave our personal belongings, before being marched to the Quartermaster's stores and issued with our military uniforms and equipment. I was surprised at the vast amount involved and we certainly didn't march back to our barrack rooms, we staggered under the weight! The next job was to sort it all out and put it away. Where clothing like shirts were concerned we had been issued with three; the assumption being that one was worn, one was in the wash, and the other immaculately ironed laid out for inspection! My time in the CCF now paid off. I knew how all the various items of 1937 pattern webbing should be assembled, blancoed, and the way to clean all the brasses, especially those in almost inaccessible places. We cut pieces of cardboard to 'square off' haversacks, ammunition pouches, and bedding blocks.

One thing we all had to learn was how to transform two pairs of hard, pimply, ammunition boots (i.e. boots with metal studs in the soles and a piece of metal on the heels) into gleaming masterpieces of shining leather! The first thing to do was to flatten the pimples, and this was done by applying quantities of black boot polish on to the leather, heating up a spoon or fork handle with a candle, and sing pressure, gradually smooth them away. Then it was a case of applying water and more polish; and with a cloth, making little circles for hours and hours to produce a shine! Ironing battle dress uniforms and shirts to the required standard was also an arduous and time-consuming task. The best results were achieved using water, a shaving brush, and a sheet of brown paper to prevent singeing the cloth.

During the day much time was spent on drill, and learning to march properly. This was something I obviously hadn't managed to achieve with the CCF! I well remember the day when the drill instructor bawled at me across the parade ground, "Gunner Bayley: bend your knees, dig your heels in, swing your arms; and stop walking like a bloody duck!" We also made frequent visits to the gymnasium and went on long marches and runs. Our Platoon Sergeant was one of the old Army types who shouted a lot and had a very colourful vocabulary! One Saturday a group of us were enjoying a cup of coffee in a café in Oswestry, when we were joined by our Platoon Sergeant! He soon put us at our ease and turned out to be quite an amiable chap. Several weeks later we had a Pass Out Parade, which marked the end of the first part of our basic training. We were then allowed to go home for Christmas leave.

On our return, the soldiers who were to be trained as drivers and wireless operators were sent off to a Training Regiment near Rhyl in north Wales. The rest of us, who were to be trained in Gunnery, moved a few hundred yards to 17 Training Regiment in another part of Parkhall Camp, and were introduced to the 25 pounder Field Gun. Our new Platoon Sergeant was a Scot. His main aim, apart from training us in Gunnery, seemed to consist in making our lives as miserable as possible! This he did by increasing the number of drill parades and kit/barrack room inspections. We never seemed to stop cleaning the barrack room, the washrooms, and laying out our equipment and clothing; either on the bed or in our lockers: and everything had to be in the correct place and conform to the required measurements! However, we survived him, shone at another Passing Out Parade, and waited to be informed about our first posting. After a couple of weeks leave my orders were to report to The King's Troop, Royal Horse Artillery, stationed at St. John's Wood, London.

THE KING'S TROOP, ROYAL HORSE ARTILLERY

I had of course already heard about The King's Troop. They were the fearless horsemen who charged across the arena at Earl's Court towing ancient guns and firing Royal salutes on ceremonial occasions. What was to be my role in this famous unit? I found out soon enough! On my first morning I was roused by a bugle at 6.00am; taken to the stables and introduced to more than 100 horses. With other soldiers I "mucked out" the stables before breakfast. Then it was a case of combing the horses, brushing the horses, cleaning and polishing the harnesses of the horses, and eventually being taught how to ride the horses! This was the basic daily routine. In addition to making the horses shiny and beautiful, I had to give the same care and attention to the ceremonial uniform I was expected to wear. This entailed an awful lot of 'spit and polish'.

After a few months I decided that this wasn't really what I'd joined the Army for. It might have been fine for a National Serviceman to swan about with horses for a couple of years, especially being based in London, and many were very happy to do just that; but I was a career soldier and thought it was time to move on. The day after making this decision I went to see the Adjutant and requested a posting. He was quite dismayed, almost offended, that I should want to leave the unit, and my request was curtly denied.

Not long afterwards I was browsing through the papers pinned to one of the notice boards, and came across a little notice asking for volunteers to serve with the Artillery Regiment which was part of 16th Parachute Brigade. So I volunteered; but it was made clear that should I fail the selection course, I would be returned to The King's Troop. I was given a weeks leave before going on the course and I went home to break the news to my fiancee and my parents. The womenfolk were not all all happy at the prospect of me jumping out of aircraft! My mother said, "I used to worry myself to death when you were working down the pit; I don't know how I'm going to cope with you going up there"! My father simply took me on one side and said, "Just don't tell your mother when you are due to jump". Fair enough, but there was a lot to accomplish before I ever got near an aircraft!

33ᴿᴰ PARACHUTE LIGHT REGIMENT, ROYAL ARTILLERY

When my week's leave was over I travelled to Lille Barracks in Aldershot, and was informed that before going on the selection course for Airborne Forces, I would need to spend some time on a pre-para course! The physical training instructors at 33ʳᵈ wouldn't allow any soldiers to go to 'P' Company, as the selection course was called, at the Airborne Forces Depot until they were fairly sure they would pass. Soldiers serving with The Parachute Regiment, the infantry part of the Brigade, didn't have to go through 'P' Company as the testing procedures were incorporated into their basic training. 'P' Company was for all the other military units serving with the Brigade; and was composed of gunners, medics, engineers etc. The pass rate was only about 30%.

After a few weeks of toughening up, my instructors were satisfied that I would probably not disgrace the Regiment, and I was sent to Maida Barracks in Aldershot to join the next selection course. The hopeful, though apprehensive group, were first of all shown an old black and white film entitled "Theirs is the Glory". This was original film footage about the battle for Arnhem in September 1944, when as part of Operation 'Market Garden', the British 1ˢᵗ Airborne Division were dropped by parachute and glider to take and hold the bridge at Arnhem, for what was planned to be just a few days. For reasons now well known, the few days turned into many; with tremendous courage and tenacity being shown by the soldiers. Out of the 10,000 men who were dropped, approximately 8,000 were either killed or captured. The theme music chosen and played throughout the showing of the film was Wagner's "Ride of the Valkyries", which was adopted by The Parachute Regiment as it's Regimental March. The film had begun by showing soldiers in their barrack rooms chatting and laughing as they prepared for action. It ended by showing the same rooms, now occupied by many empty iron beds and the odd disconsolate soldier. The message was stark and simple. This was the history and heritage of the Airborne community we were now seeking to enter.

Now began the most difficult and testing fortnight of my life. On parade in the morning, the Sergeant instructor glared at his new squad of hopefuls and said, "Remember this, any fool can jump out of an aircraft, it's only the means of getting you where you are supposed to be. This selection course is to see if you've got what it takes to do the sort of jobs given to Airborne Forces once they are on the ground". Many television programs and films have been made about airborne and commando selection courses so I won't go into many details. I will just refer to two things. Firstly, to emphasise the fact, that every exercise and every test was preceded by the command 'GO'. Before the end of the course this word was embedded so deeply in our psyche that had we been standing on the edge of a cliff and someone had shouted 'GO'. I'm sure most of us would have jumped off!

Secondly there was a test designed to determine our aggressive tendencies: this was known as 'milling'. Quite simply this consisted of a one-minute boxing match, without any rules. Soldiers were paired off roughly by size and given one minute to knock hell out of each other! I was paired off with a stocky Craftsman from the REME (Royal Electrical and Mechanical Engineers). He obviously knew a bit more about this sort of thing than I, because within a couple of seconds I was flat on my back, dazed, and looking at the ceiling! With the roar of the spectators encouraging me, I managed to get to my feet and resume the battle, just managing to knock the Craftsman outside the ring of spectators before a bell brought the contest to an end. The instructors judged the bout to be a draw, but the blood that was spilt on the canvas was all mine! Sufficient to say that in the days that followed, none of us had ever been pushed so hard before. I well remember one day when I was having a real struggle to keep going, the Sergeant shouting in my ear, "You can lie down in the gutter and die, but you don't stop, you don't give up, you keep going" Those words have come into my mind on a number of occasions over the ensuing years, and have helped me to keep going when everything inside me seemed to be screaming, STOP! GIVE UP!

Every morning on parade there were a few more faces missing as those judged to be unsuitable were RTU'd (returned to unit). I'm sure that part of my motivation to pass the course was the sure knowledge that had I failed, I would have been returned to all those horses and all that went with them! Well, I passed the selection course, but still hadn't even seen a parachute or been anywhere near an aircraft. The following week we left Aldershot and were sent to the Royal Air Force Station at Abingdon, near Oxford, home of 1st Parachute Training School.

PARACHUTE TRAINING

The Motto of 1ˢᵗ Parachute Training School is "Knowledge Dispels Fear". I seem to remember that this was actually painted on a notice board by the entrance gate. For the next month we would be in the capable hands of RAF Physical Training Instructors. Their first and enduring task, they said, was to give us all confidence in our equipment, and in our instructors. The whole atmosphere was now totally different from that of 'P' Company, and even though the bravest was a bit apprehensive at the prospect of actually jumping out of an aircraft, we were a happier and more contented bunch!

A visit was arranged to the Parachute Packing Station and we were shown the procedure followed every time a parachute had been used. First of all any debris, like for example twigs, was removed, and the canopy carefully checked for any damage. The harness was also carefully checked. The parachute was then hung up to dry out completely before being taken to the packers, where it was repacked under strict supervision. Taking us to witness this procedure was to play an important part in giving us confidence in our equipment. After all, the question uppermost in the mind of any one considering jumping out of an aircraft is, 'can I have some guarantee that the parachute will open?'

The next two weeks were spent in intensive training, known hereafter as 'synthetic training'. We soon discovered that there was far more involved in parachuting than we had ever imagined. First of all several training films were shown, and a flight in a Hastings aircraft arranged, because most people in the squad had never flown before. The main parts of the training consisted of aircraft drill; exit, flight, and landing techniques. Steel helmets were worn most of the time. To be awarded our parachute wings and the coveted Red Beret, we would be required to complete eight jumps; two from a barrage balloon, and six from an aircraft, one of which had to be at night. In addition, two of the jumps from aircraft had to be with an equipment container secured to the parachute harness.

AIRCRAFT DRILL

A mock-up fuselage was used for this training. When dozens of paratroopers with all their equipment are on an aircraft, every man needs to know exactly what to do, and when and how to do it, or lives could be endangered. We wore dummy main and reserve parachutes for these exercises, and were divided into two 'sticks'; the Port (left), and the Starboard (right). There were stick commanders and RAF instructors to supervise. When the troops had boarded and were seated, the dispatchers would move down the fuselage giving each man a static line. One end of the static line was attached to an overhead cable and the other would normally be attached to the main parachute, but as we were wearing dummies we just held on to the other end. The command would then be given, "Prepare for action". Everyone would then stand up and each man was responsible for checking not only his own equipment, but also that of the man to his front and rear. When all checks had been completed, the air dispatcher would yell, "Tell off for equipment check": and the soldier at the rear end of the stick would yell back, "20 OK" (or whatever his number was, depending on the number of men in the stick), at the same time slapping the man in front on the shoulder. He in turn would yell "19 OK" – and so on down to the stick commander who would yell "1 OK, Port/Starboard stick OK" It was always necessary to yell because of the noise of the engines! Then the command was given, "Action stations", and the sticks moved down to the exit doors, which were located towards the front of the aircraft, in a controlled and disciplined manner, until the stick commander was just one step away from the door; with one hand holding his static line, and the other gripping the top of the exit.

There were two lights above the door, one coloured red, and the other green. When the red light came on the command was given, "Stand in the door", and every man took one pace forward. The stick commander now had one foot half over the edge of the door, and the palm of the opposite hand outside on the fuselage. After a few seconds the green light would come on and the dispatcher would slap Number 1 on the shoulder and yell, "GO". Number 1 would jump out onto the mat to be followed at roughly one-second intervals by the rest of the stick. Then it was a case of going back inside and doing it all again! Jumping with equipment i.e. a weapons container was a little more complicated, but more about that later.

EXIT TECHNIQUE.

Imagine travelling in a car and throwing a screwed up piece of paper out through the window. It wouldn't fall straight to the ground; but would be blown along the side of the car first. This is exactly what that happens when someone jumps out of an aircraft. The slipstream going past the door of an aircraft used for parachuting is blowing at about 100 miles per hour. The aim of the paratrooper is to launch himself into the slipstream hard, fast, and in as compact a position as possible. Any loose arm or leg would result in the trooper being buffeted about in the slipstream, and he would be spun like a top. The parachute is opened automatically by the falling weight of the trooper, and as it deployed, would have its rigging lines twisted, resulting in precious seconds being wasted while the trooper kicked himself out of the twists. Until this was done the trooper would have no control over his parachute, and could endanger not only himself but other troopers in the vicinity. Hence the necessity for making a good exit.

FLIGHT TECHNIQUE.

Once clear of the aircraft, the first thing to do was to look up and check that the canopy was properly deployed! Very rarely a rigging line was thrown over the canopy resulting in the trooper having two or more small canopies instead of one large one! If this happened the drill was to manually deploy the reserve parachute, which was secured across the chest. I have to say that in eight years of parachuting, it never happened to me, though I sometimes had to kick out of twists!

The next thing was to ensure that you had a little bit of air space to yourself, because there were likely to be many other parachutists around. If you found yourself about to collide with another, it was necessary to spread-eagle arms and legs so that you bounced off each others rigging lines instead of getting tangled up in them! Then, by pulling on the correct lift webs (there were four − two front and two rear on the troopers shoulders) to steer right away. Now it was time to look down at the ground below your feet and assess which way you were drifting; and using the lift webs again, try to correct the drift, so as to drop as vertically as possible. Should the trooper have been carrying a weapons container; it would have been released by now, and be dangling fifteen feet below on a nylon rope. Having successfully accomplished these essential tasks, preparation must now be made for landing and I'm not sure the reader will appreciate how little time has passed, and how much has been accomplished since leaving the aircraft. The dropping time from 1,000 feet is about 35 seconds!

LANDING DRILL.

Having corrected the drift, the trooper prepares to land. He has already spent many hours in the training hangar jumping from equipment set at various heights. In addition he will have jumped from a height of about 30 feet using a device known as 'the Fan' which controls the rate of descent, and also from a tower about 100 feet high operating on a similar principle. He will train and prepare for six different types of landing. Side left, side right, forward left, forward right, back left and back right. Having completed all the flight checks, he prepares for landing with knees slightly bent, elbows tucked in, feet at 90%, and chin on chest. The latter being very important if a backwards landing is anticipated, as it avoids head-whip. At a height of about 30 feet, the lower limbs are turned to take the fall in the anticipated direction. At the moment of impact the trooper turns and executes a roll, which minimises the risk of injury. Training is also given in case the trooper finds himself landing in trees or water.

JUMPING WITH AN EQUIPMENT/WEAPONS CONTAINER

On the parachute harness are two sets of D rings. The top two are for securing the reserve parachute; and the bottom two onto which the weapons container is clipped. Two quick release 'snap hooks' are used for this purpose. The container is also secured to the trooper's leg by a strap secured by a split pin. Fifteen feet of nylon rope is stowed in a pouch on the side of the container; this is kept in place by a piece of thin twine. A quick release jettison strap is also secured to the parachute harness waistband, so that the container can be released in case of emergency. It is most important for the trooper to check below before doing this because if another parachutist is underneath, a free falling container could cause his parachute to collapse with disastrous consequences! Having said all that, it is equally important that the trooper doesn't land with the container still strapped to his body; the result could be a broken back!

JUMPING FOR MY WINGS

Now it was time to put all the training and disciplines to the real test, and to discover how much patience was required! The motto of the RAF seemed to be, 'hurry up and wait'! And wait we did, sometimes for hours and hours. So many jumps were postponed or cancelled for a variety of reasons. Either the wind was too strong, or the aircraft was unserviceable, or hadn't turned up at all. We spent ages waiting around watching the wind speed indicator whizzing around hoping it would slow down sufficiently to enable us to jump; and this scenario was repeated throughout my years with Airborne Forces. Many hours were spent reading, talking, or playing cards. I learned a lot about playing cards hanging around on airfields! The RAF are very safety conscious and meticulous in all their pre-flight checks; of personnel and equipment. Transport Command was proud of the fact that they had never lost a passenger. A few may have died of frustration and boredom but that's another matter entirely! However, before we became acquainted with aircraft and their associated problems, we had to make two descents from a captive barrage balloon. I later discovered that most paratroopers hated balloon jumps because they didn't like the sensation of falling 150 feet before the parachute opened; which didn't happen when jumping from an aircraft, because being swept away in the slipstream meant the parachute opened at almost the same height, and more quickly.

1958, R.A.F. Abingdon. Parachute Selection Course.
Peter Bayley is on the third row 3rd from the right

Eventually the day came for us to make our first descent. The weather was good, the balloon was available and we were issued with our two parachutes: one main, and one reserve. Men come in different sizes, so we first of all had to ensure the parachutes fitted our own measurements!.. The waist belt and leg straps had to be adjusted accordingly and then checked by a PJI (Parachute Jumping Instructor). I seem to remember my measurements being two and a half hand spans. The lugs on the shoulder and leg straps were inserted into a quick-release box located on the midriff. Steel helmets were put on and we were ready to go! A final check by a PJI and we were marched out to the balloon. Even after all the training, the encouragement, and the confidence we now undoubtedly had in our equipment and instructors – there was still a sense of apprehension amongst our little group!

The balloon was secured by a steel cable, wound around a huge drum mounted on the back of a vehicle-operated winch. It would soon be ascending to a height of 800 feet carrying four men and a PJI. Having watched the operation several times already, it was now our turn. The cage we were about to enter, wasn't really a cage at all as it had no roof; it was more like half a metal box with a small section cut out to allow people to go in and out. A metal bar was placed across the opening to prevent anyone falling out unintentionally! There were four of us plus the PJI and we were each given a number. I was number 2! The PJI pulled out our static lines from the back of our parachutes, and attached them to a strong point in the cage, at the same time giving them a hefty tug to demonstrate to us that they were secure. He then leaned out over the bar and shouted to the winch operator, "Up 800 feet; four men jumping".

The operator repeated this instruction and began to release the brake. The cage lurched which made us all hang on, levelled itself, and began to rise. As we were all looking a bit glum, the PJI encouraged a bit of a singsong. This helped until we got to about 400 feet and somebody decided to look over the side and turned a funny colour. All were silent for the remainder of the ascent!

The first thing I noticed when we reached the required height was the wind! At ground level what had seemed a gentle breeze had now turned into a gale! The PJI looked down and received a signal from the ground indicating that we should proceed. He removed the bar from the exit and shouted, "Number 1, come forward". Number 1 in this instance was a Private soldier serving with the Royal Army Dental Corps, who had acquired a reputation for being a bit clumsy. Now he froze and said, "I can't do it Sergeant", which was very encouraging to the rest of us! The PJI managed to coax him to the middle of the cage, where he froze completely and wouldn't move another inch.

The PJI eventually shrugged his shoulders in a gesture of resignation and turned away. After a few moments he spun round and roared in a loud voice, "GO"! And the man jumped from where he stood. I don't know how he managed to clear the doorway, but he did, and dropped from sight. His parachute opened and he drifted gently down to earth. There were no more problems with the RADC soldier, or anyone else on the course for that matter.

It must be emphasised that it was vitally important for the man to have jumped on this occasion. During training, a soldier is entitled to refuse to jump and it is not considered a disgrace to make that choice. Indeed, in front of your peers, and considering all that a soldier has gone through to arrive at that point, it takes a lot of courage to refuse to jump. Had the soldier not jumped, he would have descended to the ground with the balloon and been RTU'd. He would not have been given another opportunity. Once a soldier has qualified and received his parachute Wings and Red Beret, he can be ordered to jump, and then the penalty for refusing to do so would result in a Court Martial. This may seem harsh, but later, with dozens of fully equipped paratroopers moving towards the exit doors of an aircraft, a soldier stopping and refusing to move forward at that critical time, would be endangering not only himself but also his comrades, and that is totally unacceptable. An airborne soldier must be 100% reliable.

Then it was my turn, and shuffling forward I stood at the exit point and adopted the required position. My mouth was dry and I had difficulty in stopping my knees wobbling. I hung onto the side! I knew I had to go, but didn't want to go before I was ready and had been finally checked over! The PJI tapped me on the shoulder and shouted, "GO", and I took one step forward and dropped.

My eyes were closed but then I felt a tug on my shoulders, looked up, and saw the wonderful sight of a beautifully deployed canopy. There were no other parachutes around. The next man wouldn't be dispatched until I was safely on the ground, but I went through all the drills, encouraged by a PJI shouting at me from the ground using a megaphone, and had an easy landing. Instinctively I pulled the now collapsed canopy towards me and whispered, "Oh you wonderful thing, thank you very much"! I experienced a feeling of elation. One of the Instructors had described parachuting as, "The second best thrill in a man's life"! A fairly accurate description!

The second descent from the balloon was much less stressful. This time, instead of going out from the side, we jumped through an aperture in the floor: a rehearsal for the day when we would do the same from the boom (upper deck) of the Beverley aircraft.

After days of hanging around due to bad weather or aircraft availability, we completed seven jumps. All that remained now was the night jump. When we paraded one evening for that, the PJI said, "Well lads, ready for your night jump? You'll find it's like jumping through nothing, into sweet f*** all!". The AZ (dropping zone) for all our aircraft jumps was at Weston on the Green, a few miles from Oxford, which meant flying low over the City with it's many lovely spires on our way there! Anyone sitting near the doors had a first class view of the city, but all prayed fervently that we would not be dispatched too soon! Oxford looks beautiful from the air, especially at night, but no one had any desire to land on top of it! However, all passed off successfully – we had done it! The only thing left now was to attend the Wings Parade when we were formally presented with our much coveted Parachute Wings and Red Beret. It was a truly memorable occasion: we had literally gone through blood, sweat, and tears to reach this day and my heart swelled with pride. It certainly never occurred to me that Pride was one of the deadly sins! I hitchhiked home the following weekend, wearing my uniform, and had no trouble whatsoever in being offered lifts. My family were also very proud of me, despite their original misgivings.

Having achieved the status of a Local Preacher, and now that of a trained Airborne Soldier, my confidence and sense of self worth knew no bounds. Those two events were to shape my character and personality. In the years ahead I would have the confidence and determination to attempt anything, and usually I would succeed! I will always be grateful to those who trained and encouraged me, and especially to those who had confidence in me.

BACK TO THE REGIMENT

When I returned to Aldershot, I discovered that my Regiment was away training at Otterburn in Northumberland. Instructions had been left with the Rear Party that I, along with a couple of other newly qualified recruits, should be immediately dispatched north to join them. On arrival at Newcastle-on-Tyne railway station we found that transport had been sent down to collect us. In just over an hour we arrived at the training camp and presented ourselves at Regimental Headquarters, which at that particular time was a hive of activity. The other two recruits were immediately sent out to join their Gun Batteries, but there didn't seem to be anyone around who knew quite what to do with me! Now I suffered a mild dose of deflated ego; I obviously wasn't so important after all, so I just sat down on a chair and waited. The Chief Clerk of the Regiment, a Staff Sergeant hereafter referred to as the 'Chief', was a pre-war regular soldier, and therefore by now, a man of considerable experience which commanded respect from all; came to me and said, "Come with me and I'll find you a job to do". He lead me to a corner of the main office, where there was a wooden structure fixed to the wall containing a number of pigeon holes, a filing cabinet, and a table covered with files, papers, envelopes, and other items of stationery. "You can be my Registration, Filing, and Dispatch Clerk", said the Chief. After giving me a few indications of what was required, he went away and left me to it!

I sat down at the table and began to bring a little order out of the chaos confronting me. The Regiment's training exercise in Otterburn was coming to an end, and we began to pack up ready for our journey back to Aldershot. Before we left, the Chief had a word with the Adjutant, the Officer responsible for all administrative matters in the Regiment, and said, "We're short staffed in the Regimental Office, so I'd like to keep Gunner Bayley as part of my staff". The Adjutant agreed, and I had a permanent job! It wasn't really what I'd expected when I joined the Regiment, but the prospect of working at the nerve centre was appealing, and I accepted the situation, little knowing what a good opportunity this would afford me for an interesting career. I was formerly posted to Headquarters Battery, the sub unit containing people like clerks, pay office staff, cooks, store men, etc. The Battery Sergeant Major (BSM) was a dynamic young Warrant Officer, who was obviously going places, and he certainly kept us on our toes!

On our return to Aldershot there was a period of sorting out and catching up to be done, and I began to understand the workings of Regimental Head-quarters. As the only Regular soldier in the main office, I saw it was impor-tant for me to understand something of the jobs and responsibilities of the other clerks. A major annual event was only a few weeks away, The Queen's Official Birthday Parade. All the units in Aldershot Garrison took part in this, and it involved many hours of preparation. There were drill parades and kit inspections galore! Full Battle Dress uniforms were worn, and as the weather was hot throughout, drill parades were very sticky and uncomfortable affairs.

The Birthday Parade itself was held on Thursday 10th June 1958, and went off successfully. The Queen, in her absence, was given three rousing cheers, and all units on parade marched past the Garrison Commander, who was taking the Salute. My Regiment marched past as the Bands played the Regi-mental March of the Royal Artillery, "The British Grenadiers". It was really quite a moving occasion.

QUICK MOVE

The Regiment was now granted 72 hours leave, a long weekend. As the new boy I was to remain as duty clerk, with the promise of 72 hours leave the following weekend. As the Brigade was on permanent stand by, it was routine for all leave addresses to be held by Battery Offices. That evening, having completed all my duties, I retired to bed with a book. I had just got comfort-able when a Regimental Policeman from the Guardroom came and summoned me back to RHQ. The Commanding Officer was having a meeting with his senior officers, and when it was over I discovered that the Brigade had been ordered to move to Cyprus ASP! There was as yet, no information as to the reason, or the time scale. I was particularly concerned about the latter, as I had fixed my Wedding date for 4th October! At 11.00pm I found myself in a Land Rover on the way to the main Post Office in Reading, clutching a sheaf of leave addresses and a telegram reading simply, "Return to your unit immedi-ately". Some soldiers had heard about the situation on the radio and were already making their way back. The others found the telegram waiting for them when they arrived at home.

This was just the kind of situation the Brigade practised for regularly, and the drills were immediately put into operation. By noon the following day, advance parties were on their way to Cyprus, and main parties followed during the next two days. At that time, the Brigade kept a stockpile of heavy equipment ready in Cyprus to cope with any eventuality in the Middle East. This meant we didn't have to take lots of equipment with us, and were there-fore able to move quickly. RHQ was packed and ready to go by midday on Saturday. I was informed that I would be moving out in the early hours of

Monday morning, so I approached the Chief to see if I could make a quick visit home. He agreed providing I was back by Sunday evening. At the time Maureen was staying with my parents in Bradwell so I set off there. She travelled back to Aldershot with me on the Sunday. The early hours of Monday morning were tinged with sadness, as army lorries filled with troops departed from Lille Barracks. There were a number of wives and children, some of them in tears, there to wave 'goodbye'. Maureen was also a little confused, as when she went to Aldershot railway station, she asked the time of the next plane to London!

CYPRUS

We arrived in Cyprus in the middle of the night and as we disembarked from the aircraft, it was like walking into an oven! England had been hot, but this was much hotter, and it was very humid. There were already tens of thousands of troops in Cyprus because of the ENOSIS, (union with Greece) movement, and the activities of EOKA, the terrorist organisation seeking to promote that end. Our purpose in being there was still a mystery to us; we were loaded onto lorries, each with an armed escort, and transported to a transit camp called Waynes Keep. Fortunately there was a large canteen, and we were able to obtain some refreshments while we waited for our next move. There was a juke box in the canteen, and one record which was played almost continuously was of the Everley Brothers, singing, 'Dream, Dream, Dream', which tugged at a few heart strings! In my mind's eye I can still visualise that canteen, with the fans in the ceiling attempting to circulate the air, and hear that record being played, over and over again. When morning came, we were again loaded on to lorries and taken to a barren piece of land called Kermia Camp, not far from Nicosia. On the way there we passed through many small villages, some flying the flag of Greece from almost every dwelling, and others the flag of Turkey. It really was an island of divided loyalties. At one point we paused to allow a Funeral Procession to pass. A Land Rover was carrying a coffin containing the body of a young Military Policeman who had been shot a few days earlier. It was a stark reminder of the security situation, and of the need to be constantly vigilant.

The word 'Camp' for our accommodation was a bit of a misnomer. Except for the tents, which had been erected for us by our advance party, who had obviously been working extremely hard in preparation for our arrival, there were no facilities whatsoever. A mini canteen was soon opened, which quickly sold gallons of Coca Cola and other drinks. Having not yet acclimatised, everyone had a raging thirst! Toilet facilities consisted of Deep Trench Latrines (DTLs), which could get a bit crowded; especially because it seemed that within a few days, most people were suffering from diarrhoea! The constant presence of swarms of flies was obviously a contributory factor! All meals had to be eaten with one hand, while the other hand wafted away the flies! There was a constant procession between the Medical Centre and the DTLs.

An armoury was not established, so we had to keep our personal weapons and ammunition with us at all times. My own weapon was a .303 Lee Enfield rifle. The advice of the Sergeant Major was to "treat it like a wife; keep it on your arm by day, and sleep with it at night". Woe betide any soldier found walking around the camp without his weapon! Because of the terrorist threat, security of weapons and ammunition was paramount. One unfortunate soldier lost one round of ammunition, and was awarded 21 days 'field punishment'. This meant he had to wear Full Service Marching Order (FSMO) at all times, was not allowed to walk anywhere, but had to run at all times, and was employed in digging DTLs. It was a lesson not lost on any man in the Regiment.

RHQ was established in one large tent, divided into offices by canvas screens. The conditions inside the 'offices' were most unpleasant, as the sides of the tent had to be kept mostly tied down to prevent the wind from blowing papers everywhere. Noise levels had to be kept low, and confidential matters whispered! The Quartermaster and his staff were very busy collecting vehicles, guns, and many other stores, and making sure they were all serviced and ready for action.

Soldiers were now allowed out of camp in groups of four, and were able to visit shops and cafes in the vicinity. The drill was for two soldiers to go inside, while the other two stood guard outside; then the couples swapped over. Occasionally a vehicle was made available to take groups for a swim in the sea near Kyrenia, on the northern coast. This was a most welcome break, and I managed to go several times. On one trip we made a slight detour and visited St. Hilarion castle, which had been built by King Richard the Lionheart for Queen Berengaria. The castle was situated on top of a mountain in the Kyrenia range, and the truck had a difficult job negotiating some of the hairpin bends. The views from the top were magnificent, making the effort of getting there well worthwhile!

Meanwhile, back at camp, the Regiment was still waiting, training, and preparing for, well we still didn't know! The Adjutant, who was a bit eccentric, had the bright idea that the Commanding Officer might appreciate having a little garden! The task of achieving this was passed to the Chief. He borrowed a 1-ton truck and trailer, and with all his staff on board, set out to find suitable soil. We drove around for hours without any success, finally ending up in an area known as 'The Pan Handle', in the north east of the island. A look at a map of the island will show how the area got its name. There we found not really what we were looking for, but something the Chief thought might suffice! A few plants were obtained and the 'garden' was laid out. We never discovered whether the CO liked his 'garden' or not.

Things were now happening in the Middle East to put us on a high state of alert, and double check our readiness to move. There was trouble in Lebanon, and we heard the Americans were sending troops. Thousands of Marines landed on the beaches of Lebanon, only to be met by bemused locals, who offered to sell them ice cream and cold drinks! We thought it was quite humorous, but were relieved there had been no trouble. Not long after this we were given the order to move, but not informed of our destination! The Americans didn't need any help, so we dismissed Lebanon from our minds. Having collected our equipment, we were taken to Nicosia Airport, where dozens of aircraft were lined up ready for us. No parachutes were issued so we assumed that wherever our destination might be, we would be landing in conventional fashion. There seemed to be some confusion about what was happening. Some aircraft had taken off, but some returned with troops still aboard. Then we were told to board a Hastings, and taxied out onto the runway ready for take off. It was only then that a member of the aircrew said to us, "Well lads, you're off to Jordan!" Most had never even heard of Jordan, let alone knew where it was located!

The earlier confusion had been caused due to the fact that after the first few aircraft arrived in Jordan; Israel closed the air corridor thereby isolating the first group. That was why the second group had been turned back and returned to Cyprus. I imagine there must have been frantic diplomatic efforts behind the scenes, as we were allowed through and after a short flight, landed at the airfield just outside Jordan's capital City, Amman, much to the relief of those already there!

JORDAN

We were told the reason we were in Jordan, was because King Hussein had requested our presence. The King's cousin, King Feisal of Iraq, had recently been assassinated, as had King Hussein's father a few years before. The King, who had been trained at the Royal Military Academy at Sandhurst, was fearful for his own safety, and had asked Great Britain for help. The British response was to send 16th Parachute Brigade, whose first task on landing, was to secure the airfield. Our information was, that while there were some doubts regarding the loyalty of elements of the Jordan Arab Army, the Arab Legion, founded by Glubb Pasha, with their distinctive red and white checked head gear, were fiercely loyal to the King. We kept a very watchful eye on the main road near the airfield, as the Jordan Arab Army moved it's 25-pounder field artillery up and down the road. Our most powerful weapons were the 4.2 inch Mortars of the Regiment, and a flight of RAF Hawker Hunter jets.

A few years earlier the RAF had used the airfield as one of their bases in the Middle East, and the accommodation used by them was still in fairly good condition. One two-storey building became our Regimental Headquarters, and for the first few weeks I slept on the tiled floor of the main office, using my groundsheet and a lightweight blanket. For food we depended on 24-hour ration packs, and after a few days these were collected in and the cooks with us managed to pool the contents and produce something a bit more palatable.

After all our aircraft had arrived, Israel again closed her air space to us, so it was not possible for us to receive supplies by air. All the equipment we had been unable to bring with us was on its way from Cyprus by sea, and it would take some weeks for it to arrive. Our 'sea-tail' would come through the Suez Canal, around the Sinai Peninsular, and into the Jordanian port at Aqaba. From there, it would travel overland by mountainous and hazardous roads to Amman. Meanwhile, essential supplies were brought in for us by the American Air Force. Every night, several huge Globemaster aircraft would land, be speedily unloaded by groups of Paras, and return to the base from which they came. When all our stores had been unloaded and sorted out, life became more comfortable.

An armoury was established, and as the immediate threat to our presence seemed to have passed, we were able to hand in our weapons and ammunition. Bivouac areas were designated and each man had his own little 'bivvy'. I had just pitched mine, when I noticed a sizeable hole just a few inches from one of the corners, out of which were crawling big black insects. I discovered that these were bull ants, capable of inflicting a nasty bite, and quickly moved my 'bivvy' to a safer location!

Jordan was hot but lacked the awful humidity of Cyprus, so we no longer felt the need to drink copious amounts. One concession had to be made to local culture. Because of the heat, most soldiers had taken to working without wearing a shirt, and local people found this offensive. An order was issued that this practise should cease immediately, and shirts were worn. As I worked indoors it didn't apply to me, but I had to have a shirt to hand in case I had to go outdoors for any reason. A few local tradesmen were now, after vetting, allowed onto the airfield. At Reveille every morning, they would tour the bivouac areas offering mugs of hot sweet tea. This was an excellent way to begin the day!

The Chief, who had previously served in the area, managed to convince these people that he was the person responsible for them being allowed to work in the Regiment! The fact that everyone called him 'The Chief' undoubtedly helped this misconception! Those working in the Headquarters soon had ample supplies of well-washed fresh fruit. Everyone had also now been issued with Khaki Drill Uniforms (KDs), and every day after morning tea, our uniforms would be collected, washed, starched, ironed, and returned to us by the evening. There was of course a charge for this service, but it was a mere pittance, and most people always paid a bit more than what was asked.

One Parachute battalion had been left behind in Cyprus, ready to reinforce us should that become necessary. The Regiment was one Gun Battery under strength, as it was away on duty in Aden. To bring the Brigade up to strength, a Battalion of the Cammeronians came from Kenya to join us. They soon made their presence felt. Every evening as they lowered their Colours, a piper played, and everyone on the airfield was expected to stop whatever they were doing and stand to attention. Taking sensible precautions, small groups were now permitted to visit the City of Amman. This was a fascinating experience, especially for those of us who had never visited the Middle East before, and many souvenirs were bought, much to the delight of the local tradesmen. They were really on to a good thing, as most of us had not yet learned to haggle over the asking prices! We visited the main Mosque, and the Guardians solemnly pointed out the place where the King's father had been assassinated.

There were several Chaplains with us, one of them happened to be a Methodist, Padre Brian Dougall. When he discovered I was a Local Preacher, he kindly invited me to share in a Service he was preparing for the Regiment. He also told me he was hoping to arrange for a small party to visit Jerusalem, and asked if I would be interested in joining them. Of course I jumped at the chance! The party left very early one morning in an Army lorry, while it was still bitterly cold. As we passed through the outskirts of the City, we saw refugee camps crowded with families living in appalling conditions. A few years later, they would be expelled from Jordan, and most would find themselves living in what we now call 'the West Bank' in Israel.

JERUSALEM

We crossed the River Jordan using the Allenby Bridge, and began the long climb out of the Jordan Valley up towards Jerusalem. By this time the temperature had risen and we were much more comfortable! On the way we passed the Inn of the Good Samaritan. Looking down from the modern road on which we were travelling, it was possible to see parts of the old road, which once joined Jerusalem to Jericho. It passed through barren and hostile terrain, and I couldn't look at it without thinking of the parable Jesus told. For a man to undertake such a journey alone would indeed have been a most hazardous undertaking! Soon the city of Jerusalem could be seen at the top of a distant hill, with the sun shining on the Dome of the Rock; it was a truly magnificent sight.

Arrangements had been made for our party to stay for three days at the hostel by St. John's Cathedral, and this was sheer luxury after the bareness of Amman airfield. The hostel was set in beautiful gardens, the atmosphere was cool, the food excellent; and we were very well looked after by the staff. At that time the City was divided between Israel and Jordan, with Jordan having responsibility for the old City. There seemed to be barbed wire and armed guards everywhere, and the places we were able to visit were restricted. It was a great experience to be able to wander around the old city, and to visit the Church of the Holy Sepulchre. To one brought up in the 'no frills' traditions of Methodism, I found this Holy site a bit of a 'culture shock'. The preponderance of Orthodox, Catholic, and Coptic furnishings and smells, were quite 'off putting'. I experienced the same feelings when we visited the Church of the Holy Nativity in Bethlehem.

By accident, a couple of us stumbled on the site of Pilate's Courtyard, which was by now several feet below street level. Carved on the flooring slabs were signs of the ancient games, reputedly played by the Roman soldiers. The place we all found most meaningful was the Garden of Gethsemane, with its ancient olive trees, some of which are reputed to be over 2,000 years old. Next to the Garden is the beautiful 'Church of all Nations', which had been only recently completed. It was built with money donated by many Roman Catholic countries, and contains the most incredible mosaics. It was the only place we visited which wasn't commercialised. In fact just the opposite: we were each given a special prayer card, with an olive leaf inside. I vowed that one day I would return and visit the other sites in the area, and probably look at the sites already seen with different eyes. It took about 30 years for me to return, by which time Jerusalem had been reunited. In fact I returned on five other occasions, and each time came away feeling I had been enriched by the experience.

On returning to Amman I found that the minds of most people were directed towards going home. We had achieved what we were sent to do, and the situation was now stable. Rumours abounded; one being that an aircraft carrier was making its way up the Gulf of Aqaba to take us home! This was just wishful thinking and the daily routine continued. However, some were returning to England, either because their tour of duty with Airborne Forces was coming to an end, or they were going to attend various training courses. My Wedding date was on the horizon, so I decided to make a determined effort to get home. I went to see the Regimental Second-in-Command, who was responsible for all training, and explained my predicament. He promised to do what he could to help, and about ten days later I received news that I was to go back to England on a Training Course. I sent a telegram home saying simply. 'Prepare for 4th October'. Little did I realise then how long it would take to get home!

RACE AGAINST THE CLOCK!

There was an irregular flight operating between Amman and Aqaba, using an old Valetta aircraft, and I had first of all to wait to be allocated a seat on that! When the day finally came for my departure, I boarded the aircraft carrying a suitcase, kitbag, plus my rifle and ten rounds of ammunition, which I was to hand in to the armoury when I got back to Aldershot. After a fairly short, but turbulent flight, the Valetta landed at Aqaba. The passengers were now transferred to a flat-bottomed ship known as an LCT (Landing Craft Tanks), and informed that the journey to Cyprus would take five days. We sailed down the Gulf of Aqaba, round the Sinai peninsular and into the Gulf of Suez; which led us into the Suez Canal, where we joined a convoy heading north. The weather was hot, so we lived and slept on deck. Half way through the Canal, we anchored in the Bitter Lakes, and waited for a south-bound convoy to pass. There was enough time for us to have a swim in the lakes, which was much appreciated.

We sailed through the night, and when we woke up in the morning we were anchored at Port Said; and there were local tradesmen all over the place attempting to sell their wares! Then the Captain appeared and roared, "Get those buggers off my ship," and the soldiers hurried to obey! Not to be deterred, they soon reappeared with ladders and tried to sell their wares to us through the rails. I didn't have any spare money, but did manage to exchange an old wrist- watch for a beautifully tooled leather handbag depicting typical Egyptian scenes; which was to be a present for my sister.

The journey to the port of Famagusta, on the east coast of Cyprus didn't take very long; then it was on to more trucks and back to the transit camp at Waynes Keep! The jukebox in the canteen was still playing, 'Dream, Dream, Dream', and I was very concerned when I heard how long some people had been waiting for a flight home! Every morning there was a 'flight parade', and the names of those lucky enough to have a seat on the flight that day were read out. The rest just went back to bed, sunbathed, read books, or sat in the canteen.

After three days of hanging about, I decided to go and see anyone I could find who might be in a position to help me get a seat on a flight. Time was running out, and it wasn't until Sunday 28th September that my name came up on the flight list. With a sense of relief I grabbed my belongings and boarded the truck for the airport. It was a Charter Flight, and after a short stop in Malta for refuelling, landed at Southend late in the afternoon. Coaches were available to take us to London, but I had a difficult choice to make. If I went to Aldershot to hand in my rifle, I wouldn't make it home that evening. If I went straight home, I would have to take the rifle with me, and make a special journey down to Aldershot later. I chose the latter and just managed to catch a train to Crewe. Fortunately, it wasn't unusual in those days to see a soldier carrying a rifle on the train! On arrival at Crewe, I jumped into a taxi and arrived home just as everyone was about to go to bed. They were surprised to see me, but relieved that I had got home in time. In these days when almost everyone has a mobile 'phone, it may seem strange, but my parents didn't have a telephone at all, so it hadn't been possible for me to inform them of my movements since sending the telegram from Jordan! The following day was spent talking and planning, and on the Tuesday I went down to Aldershot to deposit my rifle and ammunition in the armoury. I was really glad to get rid of them, they had kept me company for long enough!

We arrived back home late on Tuesday evening, to find a telegram from Maureen's father, reminding us that if the marriage license wasn't collected from the Registrar's office in Rotherham by 12.00 noon on Wednesday, we would not be able to marry on Saturday! I had been so preoccupied with the problem of getting home, I had completely forgotten about the legalities. We got up very early on Wednesday morning, caught a train from Stoke-on-Trent to Sheffield, via Derby, then a bus to Rotherham, and arrived at the Register Office to collect the license with just minutes to spare! Our next appointment was to visit the Minister who would be conducting the Marriage service at Rawnarsh Methodist Church. When we arrived at the Manse (as Ministers' houses are called), he glared at me and grumbled. "Oh, it's about time you turned up". I dug deeply into my reserves of grace and bit my tongue!

The Wedding took place as planned, and after a short honeymoon which was all we could afford, I returned to Aldershot to search for accommodation for us, leaving my new wife to stay with my parents. Married quarters were in very short supply, and allocated on a points basis. A soldier received so many points, for a) years of service, b) number of children, and c) months of separation in the previous three years. We were at the bottom of the list, so I set about scanning newspaper columns, and looking at cards placed in the windows of local shops. After a week or so, I found a small two roomed partially furnished flat, which was within our budget in Ash Vale, about a mile from Lille Barracks. The following weekend we moved in.

The training course I had come home for was cancelled, as the Regiment was now on its way home. There was much preparation to be done in advance of their arrival, and the Rear Party required my services. As each group arrived, they handed in their weapons and equipment, were issued with leave passes, travel warrants, pay, and sent away on leave. As the Chief passed through, he handed me a list of tasks to be completed before they all returned to duty. My wife managed to get a job working in a factory at Frimley Green, and we settled into a sort of routine. I put it that way, because once the Regiment returned to duty, there was no such thing as predictability!

The Chief was pleased with what I'd done so far, and promised to send me to Woolwich in the New Year, to attend a training course at the Royal Artillery Clerks' School. There were about 20 prospective Clerks on my course, and not a single NCO (non commissioned officer) among us. I don't know whether it was just a case of being in the right place at the right time, or my Red Beret; but the Lieutenant Colonel commanding the School, promoted me to the rank of Lance Bombardier (L/Bdr) for the duration of the course. It was my responsibility to march the course at the correct times, between our living accommodation and the School, and to ensure that our Barrack Rooms were kept clean and tidy. On the course we were taught basic typing skills, and the various duties performed by clerks in the Royal Artillery. At the end of the course, which lasted three weeks, we all had to take a typing test, and pass written examinations. Those who were successful were now classified as, Clerk GD (General Duties), Group B, Class 3. We were given a badge to wear, and a pay rise of seven shillings a week. (Today's equivalent is 35p). Course Reports were sent to our Regiments, and on my return to 33rd, I was informed that my temporary promotion had been made permanent. That was the first step on the promotions ladder, and a pay rise of another seven shillings a week! The School didn't offer residential courses for upgrading to B2, but did offer a correspondence course, and I immediately enrolled.

My wife was now pregnant, intentionally so, the baby being due to arrive towards the end of October. We didn't have what you might call 'good neighbours', and hadn't yet made any friends. The Regimental training program for the coming months meant I was going to be kept very busy, including a number of periods away from home, culminating in a NATO Exercise in Norway in September. After a family conference, it was decided that my wife would return to Bradwell, and be cared for by my parents until the baby was born. The move was organised, and I moved back into Barracks.

I worked on my correspondence course, and within a few months passed the examination. I was now a B2 Clerk, with a different badge, and another seven shillings a week! My next goal was to study for my Army Certificate of Education in Maths and English. To do this I attended classes at the local Royal Army Education Corps Centre in Aldershot and passed the examinations. Having passed these examinations, and knowing there was a vacancy for a Bombardier, Assistant Chief Clerk, I was cheeky enough to ask for it, and was promoted. I had been in the army for less than two years.

During the Regiments time in Cyprus and Jordan, it hadn't been possible to do any parachuting, so arrangements were made to remedy that. Our nearest DZ was Frensham Common, an area south of the road between Guildford and Farnham. A Balloon was made available and many soldiers were able to make at least a couple of descents. One day I was due to go on leave for a week, and was scheduled for an aircraft descent. The aircraft was a Beverley and I was listed to jump from the upper deck, called the Boom. Jumping from the Boom was a pleasant experience, as you drop into the slipstream. On this occasion, the pilot slightly overshot the DZ, and the last four troops landed in trees! Realising there was no avoiding the trees; I carried out the appropriate drill. I wriggled back into my seat strap, brought up my knees to protect my essentials, and crossed my arms in front of my face. I hit the tree about 30 feet from the ground, landed on a sturdy branch, and wrapped my arms around the trunk. My parachute collapsed right over the top of the tree. I released myself from the parachute harness without too much trouble and climbed down to the ground. It didn't happen very often, but on this occasion there was a AZ clearance party, so I was able to get away on leave as planned. When I returned from leave, I was told that I hadn't been too popular with the DZ clearance party, as it had taken them more than two hours to disentangle my parachute from the tree. I didn't feel bad about it; after all I wasn't the pilot who overshot the DZ!

NORWAY – EXERCISE 'BAR FROST'

My next descent proved to be even more memorable, for a number of reasons. The Brigade was flown out to an airfield just north of Trondheim, in southern Norway, where we prepared for the NATO Exercise; which was to take place about 180 miles inside the Arctic Circle. The object was to test the defences of the Norwegian Army units in that area. The RAF informed us that the weather in that area had been atrocious, and the odds against us being able to parachute in were high. Another problem was the DZ, which was waterlogged, and of a size which limited the number of troops that could be dropped at any one time. (We were assured that Norwegian troops with ropes would be on hand, to help anyone unfortunate enough to land in a deep pool!) It would take three passes to dispatch a Beverley load, and after each pass it would take the aircraft exactly six minutes to complete the circuit, as it turned and banked between the mountains. I was one of the troops listed to make the journey north, travelling on the upper deck, but who would then have to climb down and exit the 'plane from the freight bay. It was necessary to practise this in the aircraft on the ground, and it took ten minutes! We had to continue practising until the drill could be completed in six minutes!

Another worry for me was the weight of the equipment to be carried. In addition to personal weapon and equipment, some troops had to carry items for others, like signallers, who needed more then they themselves could possibly carry. I was given a wet cell battery, secured to a metal frame and weighing 20 kilograms to pack with my own kit, total weight 48 kilograms. In addition I would be wearing two parachutes, and because we would be travelling over water, if not landing in it, a life jacket!

When all preparations had been completed, there was just enough time to catch a bus and pay a quick visit to Trondheim. The Norwegians were very friendly and helpful, which may have been due in part, to the fact that British Airborne Forces had played a significant role in the liberation of the country towards the end of the 2nd World War. Many Norwegians today speak English, but that didn't seem to be the case in 1959. Of course, none of our little group spoke Norwegian, but we got by until the time came when we asked for directions to a toilet. We tried German, French; and of course, English. All without any success. Almost at the point of extremity we stumbled on a toilet by accident, and roared with laughter when we saw the sign above the door, it was called a Menns! On returning to the airfield, final checks were carried out and we boarded the aircraft. The weather had improved over the DZ, and the RAF confident that we would be able to parachute in. Those of us travelling on the upper deck stacked our containers in the freight bay before climbing up.

We took off and flew for several hours up the West coast of Norway. Looking out of the Port windows we could look down into the sea. From the Starboard windows, we looked straight into the side of a mountain. This made for a turbulent and uncomfortable flight, and for the first and only time in my life, I was airsick! As we neared the DZ, the order was given to the troops below to, 'Prepare for Action'. After equipment checks came the order, 'Action Stations', and the troops shuffled towards the exits, watched by a soldier looking through the floor of the upper deck. 'Red On', 'Stand in the Door', and after a few seconds, 'Green On – GO', and in ten seconds the first stick were away. The static lines, and the bags which had contained the parachutes, were pulled into the aircraft, and the next stick began to get ready. The Beverley was turning and banking, and it was difficult for the troops to keep their balance. They completed their drills and were out of the doors. The soldier looking down into the freight bay gave us a signal, and we began to climb down the fuselage, hanging on grimly as the aircraft began its circuit. Because time was short, the air dispatchers gave us a hand to fit our containers; when mine had been fitted I could hardly stand up! The lights above the exits came on and while it wouldn't be true to say we were pushed out, I was certainly given a lift towards the door, for which I was grateful. I it was such a relief to get out! There were no problems on the way down, and I had a good landing well away from any pools of water. Rolling up the parachute, I clipped it to the reserve 'chute, hoisted the container on to my back, picked up the parachutes, and struggled off the DZ to the RV (rendezvous point).

RHQ was located near an old barn, and after handing our parachutes back to the RAF, we unpacked our containers and I was happy to deliver the battery I had brought with me to a grateful wireless operator. Thoughts now turned to food. We had been issued with 24 hour ration packs, so I got out the little 'tommy cooker', as it was called, lit a couple of hexamine blocks, opened a couple of cans and proceeded to cook a meal'. A colleague was heating some water so we could have a mug of hot tea. The date was 25th September 1959, my 21st Birthday. It wasn't much of a party, but I thoroughly enjoyed it! It was now growing dark, and it was time to try and get some sleep as we had an early start the following morning. It was bitterly cold and all I had was a ground sheet and a lightweight blanket. Sleeping bags and thick winter jackets were for the next generation of soldiers! I realised the only addition to what we had in the Middle East, was a woollen pullover. Not many managed to get any sleep that night. In the morning, after a wash and shave in ice cold water (there hadn't been time to heat any), we set off to find the Norwegian Army. Breakfast, consisting of hard tack biscuits, an oatmeal block, and a drink of water, were consumed on the way.

We heard that some of the Norwegian units had bicycle patrols in the area, and it was considered great sport to lay a rope cross the road, and cause the leaders to dismount in an undignified manner! As this was a NATO Exercise, a team of Umpires were in the area to monitor and also to judge which side 'won' in the contacts that occurred. A strong force of Norwegians had dug themselves into a strong defensive position, half way up a mountain from where they could see, and dominate all approaches. 1st Battalion, The Parachute Regiment (1 PARA), quickly made their way around to the other side of the mountain. They climbed the mountain and went over the top during the night, coming down behind the unsuspecting defenders in a devastating dawn attack. The Umpires were left in no doubt about who won that particular encounter! The following evening, with a Gun Battery positioned on each side, RHQ found another barn, this time filled with hay. Those of us not detailed for Guard duty, burrowed into the hay to keep warm, and managed to get a few hours sleep. As we were getting ready to move in the morning, a Platoon of the 'enemy' was spotted in the valley below our position. They began to climb the hill towards us, completely unaware of our presence. There were no Umpires in the area, so the Second-in-Command (2IC) called a hurried conference and said, "there's nothing else for it; we'll have to charge the buggers". Word was passed to the Gun Batteries and at the time appointed, the 2IC yelled, "Charge"! Grinning broadly and waving his shooting stick in the air, he led a couple of hundred screaming Paras down the hill towards the 'enemy'. When they saw the approaching horde bearing down upon them, the Norwegians promptly dropped their weapons and surrendered. Both sides had a good laugh about it afterwards!

Those who had planned the Exercise had obviously overestimated the time it would take for the Brigade to achieve it's objectives, as the Exercise ended two days earlier than anticipated. We were flown home from an airfield in northern Norway, and after tidying things up in Aldershot; I went home for the weekend. On Sunday, our 1st Wedding Anniversary, I caught an overnight train from Stoke-on-Trent, and arrived back in barracks in time for first parade on Monday morning.

On Tuesday morning 6th October, I was having my breakfast in the dining room, when a Regimental Policeman from the Guard Room came in and put his hand on my shoulder. "Congratulations Bombardier Bayley", he said, "you've just become a Dad! Your wife's just had a baby daughter, and they are both well". Apparently, my wife had started in labour just an hour after I left on the Sunday evening. She was three weeks early, and had asked my father to phone the Regiment, as I had already arranged to have leave of absence, as I wanted to be home for the birth. My mother however, said, "Leave him where he is, he's better off out of the way", and as usual my father did as he was told! I saw the Chief as soon as he came into the office, informed of the news, and he sent me back home for another week. On returning home, it was apparent that my wife had had a most difficult time, so much so that my father couldn't stand to remain in the house while she was in labour, and spent hours walking up and down the street, leaving my mother and the midwife to cope.

Had I been there, I could at least have walked up and down the road with him! However, all was well, and we had a beautiful seven and a half pound daughter, whom we named, Vivien Janet,

After a week at home I returned to Aldershot to try and find us a home. I knew there was no chance of getting a married quarter, but there was a possibility of a Hiring, which was civilian accommodation meeting laid down specifications, which the Army would pay for, charging me rent I would have paid had a quarter been available. It took me three weeks to find something suitable. It was an attic flat with two bedrooms in Farnborough, just a few hundred yards from the main runway of the Royal Aircraft Establishment, and a mile or so away from Lille Barracks. There was one other military occupant in the house, a Corporal serving with the Band of 2 PARA, and his wife and children. They occupied the ground floor and the basement. They told me we'd soon get used to the noise of the aircraft, which passed very low over the house, and very frequently too! Together with representatives from the Regiment, and local Barracks Office, I inspected and signed for the flat, which was furnished; hired a van, and went to collect my family. We did get used to the noise of the aircraft, which did indeed pass very low over the house. When standing at the kitchen sink at the back of the flat, I felt I could almost shake hands with the pilots as they came in to land! My parents came down to visit us, and I had neglected to warn them about the aircraft. My poor mother was just unpacking, when a huge Jet passed over the house and almost scared the life out of her!

Once we had settled in, I arranged to go to the Clerks' School to take my B1 examination. In addition to all that had gone before, I needed instruction on Military Law, especially the documentation required to set up and see through, a Court Martial.

I passed the course, and was awarded a different badge, and another small pay rise! I was now in possession of qualifications, which could, given time and recommendations, take me up to the rank of Staff Sergeant. It was then I did something really stupid.

One evening a week, the Regimental Gymnasium was used for Bingo! This was very popular, particularly with the families. Tables were brought from the main dining room for this purpose. At the end of the evening, it was the duty of the Regimental Fire Piquet to return the tables to the dining room and sweep and clean the Gym. One evening I was the NCO in charge of the Fire Piquet. Having completed the tasks, I prepared to go home, having already arranged with an NCO who was a single man, to cover for me during the night. This was normal practice. We had been using the Duty Driver and his Land Rover to transport the tables, and the driver kindly offered to give me a lift home. At the time I was learning to drive, and to use a phrase in use at the time, I was 'cab happy'! So I said to the driver: "Move over, I'll drive", and he did. I drove out of the barracks and hadn't travelled more than a few hundred yards, when I looked in the mirror, and saw behind me a Military Police vehicle.

I drove very carefully home and when I stopped outside the house the MP vehicle stopped behind me and two MPs got out and came to my window. "Can I see your license please", said one of the MPs. "I'm afraid I don't have one", I replied. He took out his notebook, and I was ordered to get out of the vehicle. I produced my Identity Card and Provisional license; but then he asked for the Vehicle Work ticket, which was the authority for the vehicle to be on a particular journey, I asked the driver to produce it; but he said, "I don't know where it is, this isn't my vehicle"! I was ordered into the passenger seat and we were escorted back to barracks, and handed over to the Guard Commander. He entered the details in his log which would be on the Adjutant's desk first thing in the morning, and told me to go home.

I was in the Office very early the following morning, and told the Chief exactly what had happened before the Adjutant saw the Guard Report. The Military Police report arrived later that day, and I was formerly charged with the offences of driving without a license, on an unauthorised journey, and without the Vehicle Documents. The duty Driver was absolved of any offence, as I said I had ordered him to allow me to drive. A few days later I appeared before my Battery Commander, and the charges against me were read out. Because of my rank and the seriousness of the charges, I was remanded to appear before the Commanding Officer. I paraded outside the Regimental Sergeant Major's office on judgment day, and was marched in to see the CO.

The charges were again read out, and I pleaded 'guilty as charged'. The CO said, "You are a bloody fool Bombardier, and you are severely reprimanded". After the RSM had marched me outside, he said, not unkindly, "It could have been worse, you could have lost your stripes"!

As it was a 'severe reprimand', not just a reprimand, the details were entered on to my Regimental Conduct Sheet, and the Royal Artillery Records Office informed. To this day that Conduct Sheet will be in the archives there. When I left the Army two years later, my Certificate Of Discharge indicated my record of Conduct as being 'Very Good'. Without the above offence, it would have been 'Exemplary'! Years later, when serving as an Army Chaplain, I couldn't help but wonder if I was the only Chaplain with such a document stored away!

It was about this time that the Regiment was informed at it had been granted RHA (Royal Horse Artillery) status. The RHA had always been considered the crème de la crème of the Royal Artillery, and the Regiment considered it an honour to have the title bestowed on it. The officers in the Regiment were particularly delighted with this elevated status, but it meant little to the rank and file, who were not at all thrilled with the Regiments new title. From henceforth we were to be known as 7th Parachute Regiment. Royal Horse Artillery, (which was soon to shortened in everyday usage to simply 7th RHA) which many soldiers considered a trifle ridiculous, and which for a time, elicited a few disparaging comments from around the Brigade, which didn't help! There was of course a Parade, and all were issued with a different cap badge, indicating that we were no longer just Gunners, but members of an elite unit.

CRISIS OF FAITH

Many years before, when the Army had been much larger, a significant number of soldiers declared themselves to be 'Methodists'. The Methodist Church, determined to minister to these men, made funds available and the Aldershot Methodist Military Trust was founded. Among other facilities, two Garrison Methodist Churches were built. One was in the centre of Aldershot, and the other at North Camp, near Farnborough. I, and my family attended the latter. The congregation, now mostly civilians were very friendly and supportive, and a crèche provided. Owing to my uncertain military commitments, I was unable to commit myself to conduct Services in the Circuit on any future dates; but did offer to conduct Services should any Local Preachers be unable to fulfil their appointments for any reason. This was an offer frequently taken up by the Superintendent Minister of the Circuit.

An increasing problem for me was the content of my sermons. I had been thinking very seriously about all I had been taught at Bradwell, and particularly at Cliff College. My mind was full of doubts and questions. I had been driven to abandon theological 'certainties', and felt I was not only adrift and severed from my roots, but also disloyal. In particular I was questioning the literal interpretation of the Bible, and consequently the whole doctrine of salvation. There seemed to be a terrible inconsistency in believing in a God of Love who, according to conservative evangelical theology, laid down criteria which consigned most of humanity to the eternal dustbin, as they couldn't possibly fulfil them. Furthermore, if every person is of intrinsic value to God, the Cross of Christ, far from being a Victory, must be a crushing defeat for the intentions of the Almighty!

The festival of Easter posed equally difficult questions. If God did in fact send Jesus to die on the Cross for the salvation of the world; it would make Him the author and perpetrator of a barbaric murder: and characters like Judas and Pontius Pilate, mere puppets with God pulling the strings!

Padre Brian Dugall had moved on, and been replaced by another Methodist Chaplain, Padre Douggie Dennis. I arranged to see him, and we spent a long time talking through the issues bothering me. Eventually he helped me to see that the conclusions I had reached in my thinking were shared by many in the Church, and that previously I had been out on a limb but hadn't realised it! This was a great help and comfort to me, and I was now prepared to move on. John Robinson, Bishop of Woolwich, had written of a 'New Reformation'. The Reformation initiated my Martin Luther many years ago, had encouraged the quest for a 'gracious' God. Now, claimed the Bishop, the quest was for a God who was 'worthy'. I found this concept most helpful, as there was no way I could believe in, let alone worship, a God whose actions I deemed to be beneath what I, as a mere human being would find acceptable.

GOODBYE TO LILLE BARRACK

The Regiment was now informed that Lille Barracks was programmed for demolition and rebuilding, starting with the Sergeant's Mess. While all this work was being carried out, the Regiment was to move into Oudenarde Barracks, on the way to Aldershot. The previous occupants, the Army Catering Corps, had left the barracks in fairly good order, so it wasn't long before we were able to move in. The Regiment also had a new Regimental Sergeant Major, who had a reputation for being a bit of a martinet! This turned out to be the case, and soldiers would take significant detours around the barracks to avoid going anywhere near his office, which was only a few yards away from the Regimental Office where I worked! One night someone actually broke into his office and trashed it. Strangely enough, he seemed quite pleased that he had been singled out for such attention! Fortunately for the office staff, the RSM was an old comrade of the Chief, so we were treated with a little more leniency than most!

When the new Sergeant's Mess had been completed in Lille Barracks, the RSM decided to allow the Bombardiers to move into the old one at Oudenarde Barracks. He believed that it would be good for them to be responsible for their own Mess, instead of just having a separate room in the NAAFI Canteen. He argued it would be good training for the time when most would eventually become members of the Sergeant's Mess. He nominated me to be the first PMC (President of the Mess Committee); and with a couple of other enthusiasts, we set about arranging things. A bar had to be organised, stocked, and manned by one of the members doing a monthly duty. There was a full size Snooker table, darts corner, music centre, and we managed to obtain enough tables and comfortable chairs to establish a lounge area. This enabled us to hold social evenings, and for members to bring their wives into the Mess. It was a great success, and all credit to the RSM for his foresight and support in enabling it to be successfully completed. In due course, Bombardiers/Corporals Messes became widely established in the Army, but I like to think we were amongst the pioneers.

1960 Bombardiers Outing to Southsea. Peter is on the first row 3rd from the left

CALL TO THE METHODIST MINISTRY

Things were now going well for me. I was happy in my work and had my family with me, and yet there was something missing. My wife was one of those who said to me, "you are meant for more than this". I knew she wasn't very happy with the Army way of life, so I didn't credit too much weight to that argument. I was also presented with another opportunity,which was tempting! One day my downstairs neighbour said, "I've heard you singing upstairs, and I know the Band are looking for a vocalist for some forthcoming engagements. I've mentioned this to the Bandmaster, and he would like you to come for an audition; how about it?" As I did enjoy singing, I agreed to meet with the Bandmaster, sang a few songs, and was invited to accompany the Band on a couple of engagements. My singing was well received by the audiences, and the Bandmaster said, "Why don't you transfer to the Band, and I'll make sure your voice is properly trained"?

This would have meant leaving the Royal Artillery, transferring to the Parachute Regiment, and reverting to the rank of Private soldier. As I was probably within months of being promoted Sergeant, I declined the Bandmaster's offer. I sometimes wonder where life might have lead me had I chosen that particular path! However, the feeling that I should explore the possibility of offering for the Methodist Ministry was growing stronger, and I decided to have another talk with Padre Dennis. The difficulties seemed enormous. I was a Regular soldier on a nine years engagement, of which I had completed only 3; and I was married with a young daughter. I also knew that Methodism at that time had strong reservations about accepting married men as Candidates for the Ministry.

To leave the Army before completing my engagement would mean purchasing my discharge, which would cost £200, an awful lot of money in 1960. Padre Dennis advised me to visit London, and discuss things with the Connexional (National) Candidates Secretary. I arranged to meet him at his office in Westminster Central Hall, and we discussed the situation. He agreed the problems were considerable, but not insurmountable. Methodism was now prepared to accept married candidates, providing assurances were given that the candidate promised to maintain his family during training, which entailed spending four years in Theological College, followed by two years on probation before Ordination. The Church would not at that time, accept any responsibility. It had only recently been decided to accept married men for training. Previously Ministers had not been allowed to marry until they were Ordained; a fact which many older Ministers frequently reminded those of us who entered training colleges already married, or who got married during training!

The next step was for my wife and I to talk things through, and see if arrangements could be made to make it possible for me to offer and train for the Methodist Ministry. After much thought, prayer, discussion, and consultation: we decided to ask my mother-in-law if she would be prepared to look after Vivien, freeing my wife to go back to work, thus enabling us to save enough money for me to purchase my discharge from the Army and train for the Ministry. She readily agreed to help, and once again we packed up our home, and I took my family back to Rotherham, where my wife soon found a job as a Copy Typist. Once again I moved back to live in Barracks, but at least this time, I was able to have a room of my own!

Except for Exercises and duties, I was able to get home most weekends to see my family. This was proving expensive, so I decided to invest in a motorbike. My brother-in-law was 'into' motorbikes, so, one Saturday morning he accompanied me to a dealers in Sheffield, where I bought a motorbike! It was an AJS 500cc Twin, which was a big powerful machine, especially for one who had never ridden a motorbike before! I had chosen such a machine, because it was my intention once I had passed my Driving Test, to add a sidecar to it, thereby enabling me to transport the family, and not just myself! I spent the Saturday afternoon learning how to ride the bike, and set off, a little apprehensively early on the Sunday morning to ride back to Aldershot. Having hitch-hiked between Aldershot and Rotherham many times, I didn't need to consult a road map. On the way I had one slight mishap, when I came off the bike whilst negotiating a small roundabout near Warwick! I wasn't hurt, and the bike was undamaged. I made the trip several times before applying to take my driving test. Having recently passed a driving test in a Land Rover, I didn't find it too difficult to pass the motorbike one. The next step was to buy a sidecar, and have it fitted; this I did a few weeks later.

Fitting the sidecar made the machine more stable, but it was like learning to drive all over again! Driving a three-wheeler, when the steering wheel isn't central, poses particular problems, especially when driving around left hand bends. When negotiating left hand bends, the bike is happy to turn left, but the sidecar wants to go straight on! I decided it was much easier to drive a Land Rover, and it took me a little time to master the motorbike combination.

The procedure for offering for the Ministry took a whole Connexional year, and it would be September 1961 before I would be able to begin the process. In the meantime Army life went on. There were more Exercises, many of them on Salisbury Plain where there were several Dropping Zones. Practise Camps when the Regiment went away for 2-3 weeks; sometimes to a Training Camp on Salisbury plain, or to Sennybridge, near Brecon in South Wales. This became a little bit boring, as we needed to practise the same things over and over again. The end of National Service was in sight, but we still had a considerable number of conscripts serving with the Regiment, who were still learning the basics. Every time we went 'into the field', it was a case of teaching them things like; how to camouflage a vehicle, how to erect an Airborne Shelter; and how to live and move tactically, etc.

Many people today say that National Service should be brought back, as it would be good for young men. I'm sure it would; but it wouldn't be good for the Army, as it would seriously affect the ability of soldiers to be truly professional.

Someone once said, "That which isn't regularly inspected, deteriorates", but there was no chance of that happening in the Army! In addition to routine inspections, there was an Annual Administrative Inspection. This required lots of preparation and rehearsals, and was usually carried out by the Brigade Commander and his Staff. The day began with an inspection of the Regiment on Parade. The Brigadier would then select one Battery to perform a specific task, which could be anything from Gun Drill to an inspection of their living accommodation and equipment. While this was going on, his Staff would be inspecting the Regimental and Battery Offices; checking that correct procedures were being followed, and that classified documents and soldier's personal documents were being kept secure and up to date. The results of the inspection were anxiously awaited, as the verdict could well affect career prospects!

Another important inspection for the Regimental Office; was when an Inspection Team from the Royal Artillery Record Office came to check all the documents of every soldier. It was this inspection, which made even the Chief a bit nervous! We would be given notice of this inspection, which gave us a little time to carry out our own checks, but he visiting team would invariably find errors and omissions. Once again, the verdict would be anxiously awaited, and anything less than 'Good', would be regarded as unacceptable, and another inspection could be expected before too long!

Peter with friends
Tom Bartram and
Ernie Heyes in 1960

CANDIDATING FOR THE METHODIST MINISTRY

In September 1961, I could have offered to Candidate from the Aldershot Circuit, but because I was known much better back home, I decided to offer from there. I informed the Superintendent Minister of the Wolstanton and Audley Methodist Circuit of my intention, and he duly gave notice to the September Quarterly Meeting: the governing body of the Circuit. It was now a requirement that before the December Meeting; I conduct Services in as many of the Circuit Churches as possible, so that people had an opportunity to hear me. The Chief regretted my decision, as he believed I had excellent career prospects in the Army, but promised me his full support. As a result I managed to get home the majority of weekends and preached in most of the Circuit Churches.

It was during one of these visits home I almost came to grief! I was planned to take a Service one Sunday at a Church in Audley (I found the correct one this time), and took my sister with me in the sidecar. One the way home afterwards, I was driving down a long hill and took a left hand bend too quickly. The combination couldn't take the bend, and went straight across the road and into a hedge on the other side. Fortunately for us, there was no traffic coming the other way, or the outcome could have been disastrous! Both of us were a bit shaken by the experience, but neither was hurt. I dragged the machine out of the hedge and back on to the road; kick started the machine and set off home; but not before I had exacted a solemn promise from my sister to say nothing of the incident to my parents! She didn't, and I never made the same mistake again!

In October I was promoted to the rank of Acting Sergeant, and informed that I was shortly to be posted to the RA Clerks' School as an instructor. The Chief was away for a while and I acted as Chief Clerk for a few weeks. I moved out of Oudenarde Barracks into the new Sergeant's Mess in Lille Barracks, which was very comfortable. Before I left the Regiment, the Bombardier's Mess organised a farewell party for me. Speeches were made thanking me for my role in making the Mess a successful venture, and I was presented with a silver plated tea service engraved with the words, "Presented to Bombardier W Bayley"? An understandable mistake, because everyone with the name Bayley, (however spelt) was always called 'Bill'; in the same way that everyone by the name of Clarke was called 'Nobby'. Whites were always 'Chalky', Millers always 'Dusty', and Murphys always 'Spud'! In reply I thanked them for their kind words, support, and generosity. I also confessed that my achievements in the Mess had been made possible because I had behind me an irresistible driving force! These comments caused a wave of laughter, as the RSM was standing behind me grinning broadly! So I left the Regiment and for the time being, Airborne Forces; and moved to Woolwich.

On arriving at Woolwich, an historic Military Garrison and The Royal Regiment of Artillery Depot, I booked into the Sergeant's Mess, and then went to the Clerks School. I already knew most members of the Staff there, and arranged to see the Officer Commanding the following morning. He was a Lieutenant Colonel who had 'come through the ranks', and was affectionately known as 'Mother'! We had met several times before and he gave me a warm welcome to the School. He was surprised when I told him that I was in the process of offering for the Methodist Ministry, and in the days ahead did his best to encourage me to reconsider. He assured me I had a good career in front of me if I stayed in the Army, and pointed to his own achievements as an example. Of course I had no idea then, but I would also eventually end up with equivalent rank, but by taking a very different route! When he saw I was determined to carry on with my candidature, he promised to support me in any way possible, and was as good as his word.

I attended the December Quarterly Meeting in uniform, and as the rules required, gave an account of my Conversion, Call to Preach, and Call to the Ministry. I then answered questions from members of the Meeting. There were a few, predictably from people with pacifist convictions. There were over 60 members attending the meeting, and when the vote was taken as to my suitability for the Ministry; 2 voted against me, and four were neutral. This was more than sufficient for me to proceed with my candidature.

The next step was to sit three, three hour written examinations, which I succeeded in passing with a comfortable margin. Then I had to take 2 Trial Services in Churches outside my home area. Arrangements were made, with the London South East District of the Methodist Church, for me to conduct Services at Bromley and Bexleyheath. The congregation in both Services contained three Ministers and three Lay People, whose responsibility it was to write a report on each service, and award a mark for a) the Service, and b) the Sermon. I was awarded above average marks in each case. A sermon in manuscript also had to be submitted to the Connexional Candidates Secretary at Westminster, together with a list of books I had read, denoting particularly those read during the past year. I would be questioned on this at a later Committee, and awarded a mark.

At the Clerks' School I was paired with a Staff Sergeant Instructor, and between us, ran courses lasting three weeks for potential clerks. At the end of the course the students took a trade test, and if successful, became B3 Clerks. Writing later in my Certificate of Discharge Book, 'Mother' wrote that as an Instructor; I had been an 'unqualified success'.

The School Staff were all enthusiastic players of Bridge, and so I had to learn to play! The game was played during every lunch break, and occasionally whole evenings were devoted to playing in the Sergeant's Mess. Sometimes a group of Staff and students would visit one of the Public Houses in Woolwich, of which there were many. One in particular had a very good duo, a pianist and a drummer; and customers were invited to participate in the entertainment.

After listening to a few of the contributions, I passed the comment that I thought I could do better! Before I knew what was happening I was on the platform, and expected to perform before a noisy and inattentive crowd. In a way I was restricted to what the pianist could play, so we settled on 'Granada'. As I sang, the whole pub went very quiet, and at the end I received tumultuous applause and cries of 'More'! I offered 'Love is a many splendoured thing', 'Moon River', and called it a night! Subsequent visits to the pub, and there weren't many, found me on the platform! It was good experience and I enjoyed it.

The next hurdle in my candidature, which was an important one, was to appear before the Chester & Stoke-on-Trent Methodist District Candidates Committee. I was on leave in Rotherham at the time, and the Committee was due to meet at a Church in Chester. It was a fine day and I decided to travel in uniform, leaving early to ensure I found the Church, and arrived in good time. I've always been paranoid about arriving late for anything! When I was about 15 miles from Chester, I had a puncture in the front tyre of my motorbike, and I didn't have a jack! Unlike cars, motorbikes with sidecars don't carry a spare wheel; neither was I a member at that time of any motoring organisation, which might have helped me. There was nothing for it, but to walk along the road until I came to a garage, which I did and after about a mile or so I found one. They very kindly lent me a jack, and I walked back to the bike, jacked it up, and proceeded to take the wheel off. This proved to be a difficult and dirty business, as I don't think the wheel had ever been off the bike since it left the factory!

Fortunately I had taken my uniform jacket off and placed it with my hat in the sidecar, because by now I was very hot and sticky and my hands were covered in oil. Eventually I succeeded in getting the wheel off, and rolled it to the garage. It turned out to be more then a puncture; I needed a new inner tube! I held my breath as the mechanic looked through his stock; and heaved a sigh of relief when he found an inner tube, which was the correct size. He quickly fitted it, inflated the tyre, and I rolled it back to the bike. With an anxious eye on the time, I quickly put the wheel back on, wiped the worst of the oil off myself with some rags, and set off again, stopping only to return the jack and express my thanks to the mechanic for his help.

The District Candidates Secretary was waiting anxiously for me when I arrived at the Church and, as there were several men to be interviewed, moved my name down the list to give me the opportunity to get cleaned up! All the men's toilet had to offer, was cold water, a small piece of soap, and toilet paper. I did my best and was glad that I wasn't going on parade, only to an interview! The Secretary had explained the situation, and I think the Committee made allowances for my less than immaculate appearance. There were about a dozen Ministers on the Committee, including my own Superintendent from Wolstanton. They had before them all the results of the tests and examinations I had already completed, including information about my school record!

One member of the Committee immediately drew my attention to that! Looking at me with a rather puzzled look on his face, he said, "Mr. Bayley, I see that you took your School Certificate in seven subjects, and you failed them all; how on earth did you manage it?" Rather sheepishly I replied that it wasn't really very difficult; hastening to emphasis the fact that since leaving school, I hadn't failed a single examination, and had achieved the rank of Sergeant in the Parachute Brigade in just four years. Another member of the Committee obviously took exception to me being a Regular Soldier, and adopted a hostile attitude towards me. I answered his questions about what it meant to be a Christian and a professional soldier calmly and with conviction. Other members then moved on to different subjects, including my family commitments. Afterwards, my Superintendent informed me that I had been awarded an above average mark for the interview, and that my antagonist was a pacifist and a member of CND. He also told me that his blatant antagonism had in fact won me the support of other members of the Committee!

Having satisfied the District Committee, I was now expected to attend the Ministerial Session of the District Synod. There were over 100 Ministers in the District, and having to appear before them was a daunting prospect. They had all been informed of my achievements to date, and each candidate was sent into the Church separately. Again, I chose to wear uniform, indicating I was still a serving soldier, and realising it would draw a few questions about the Army, giving me an opportunity to express myself. It was a good interview, and I was recommended to go on to the penultimate stage of the selection process by an overwhelming majority. This meant being interviewed by the National Candidates Committee, which made its recommendations to the Church's governing body, The Methodist Conference. In 1962 there were more than 100 candidates, and the Committee convened in two of our Colleges. I was required to spend two days at Hartley Victoria College, in Manchester.

The Committee was made up of about 30, mostly Ministers; and as there were a large number of candidates, formed three sub-committees. Each candidate was interviewed for about half an hour, and graded between A & D. Those graded A by the sub-committee were recommended for acceptance by the Conference, en bloc, while those graded D were recommended for rejection en bloc. Those graded B & C, had to appear later before the full Committee, and were later considered individually by the Conference; those graded B usually being accepted, and those graded C usually rejected.

It was during this interview, I was questioned about my book list, for which I had been awarded an average mark. The questions were all about one particular book, 'Impatient Giant', which was about China! It was quite an ordeal and I was glad when it was over! I then waited anxiously for several hours, and was greatly relieved when told I had been awarded an A grade, and was free to leave. A few weeks later I received a letter from the Conference Office, confirming my acceptance, which I handed to my Officer Commanding at the School, whom I believe had been doing a little research behind the scenes on my behalf regarding my discharge from the Army.

It was now time for me to make a formal application for my discharge from the Army, and I had the money ready! Imagine my surprise and pleasure, when I was awarded a Discharge, 'Free on Compassionate Grounds:' and I have those very words before me now, in my Army Certificate of Discharge book. The Church had five Theological Colleges, each linked to a local University, and I was to be trained at Hartley Victoria College, Manchester. This suited me very well, as it wasn't very far from either Bradwell or Rotherham. I was to begin training in September, but first I had to formerly disentangle myself from the Army! All my uniforms, equipment, and bedding had to be handed into the Quartermaster's Store; and I had to tour the Garrison collecting signatures on the Clearance Certificate, proving that I had no debts or equipment outstanding in any department. All that remained was to say 'farewell' to 'Mother' and my colleagues at the School, load up my personal belongs in the sidecar, and depart. This I did with mixed feelings. I had enjoyed my years in the Army, and was only becoming a Minister because I felt it was something I had to do in order to live with myself. I was mindful of the advice I'd received from a Minister at Bradwell some years previously. He had said, "We only want men in the Ministry who can't keep out". At the time I hadn't really understood what he was saying, but now I did and it certainly applied to me!

HARTLEY VICTORIA COLLEGE – MANCHESTER

1962 – 65

Knowing each student had two rooms in College; a small bedroom and a sparsely furnished study in another part of the building, I began collecting a few things together to make life comfortable! I hired a small van and transported these to Hartley a few days before term commenced. Having left the Army only two weeks before, I found going to Theological College a bit of a culture shock. I was 24 years of age, married with a daughter, and had spent the past five years in the Army. Most of the other new students were much younger, single, and hadn't yet done very much with their lives. On the first evening there was a meeting, when introductions were made and we met the College Staff.

We were given a couple of days to form ourselves into 'tea clubs', of three or four students who would meet together in the late afternoon for tea, sandwiches, fellowship, and mutual support. This was an old tradition, and many friendships were formed which lasted far beyond College days. After 'sounding out' a number of students, I became one of a group of four, who stayed together for the next three years. Timetables were issued, and a few basic College rules were emphasised. Having subjected the students to a most thorough and exhaustive selection procedure, The Methodist Church offered training programs to suit each one. If a student already held a University Degree, he would be offered a post-graduate course at Manchester University. A student possessing the required number of 'A' levels, or wishing to obtain them; would be encouraged during the first year to study for them. If successful he would then study for an external London University Degree in order to become a Batchelor of Divinity; attending lectures at the College and at Manchester University. Thers like me, having no formal qualifications, would do the basic College Course, which in many ways was probably the best practical preparation for Ministry in the Methodist Church.

The Principal, The Rev. Dr. Percy Scott, whom, we soon discovered to be a fanatical supporter of Manchester United Football Club, interviewed and advised all the new students about their proposed studies; and also asked what financial contribution they were able to make to the College! Staffordshire County Council, believing that the Church itself should fund such courses, had given me a grant of £75 for the year; so I told the Principal that I wouldn't be able to make any contribution. Given my family commitments, he reluctantly accepted this!

After a couple of weeks, all except the first year students, put on a mini-concert in the Common Room, which was very enjoyable, and only spoiled by the fact that they expected the new boys to do the same the following week! After a hurried meeting, we cobbled together a program and had a quick rehearsal. My contribution was to sing a couple of songs, which ensured me a place in the College Concerts, which were held every term, and attended by 'friends of the College', as well and students and their families.

We were fortunate in that one of the older students was an accomplished organist and pianist. There were also a number of non-theological students studying at the University who used Hartley as a hall of residence, and played a full part in the social activities of the College. It was the 'Non-Theologs' who provided the sound and electronic resources for the concerts. It was refreshing and encouraging to discover how talented many of our Ministers are. A resource I was to use on a number of occasions during my Ministry!

I soon got used to the daily routine; morning prayers in the College Chapel, usually conducted by one of the Staff; breakfast, lectures all morning, afternoons free for either study or leisure activities, tea club, evening meal, lectures, and evening prayers in the Chapel; usually conducted by a student. Every Friday evening there was a Service in the College Chapel, after which there was a mad dash for the exit by those of us who were married; at that time only half a dozen or so! Most Sundays, students were expected to conduct Services in Churches within a radius of about 30 miles of the College, and that commitment determined how long a student could remain at home, or indeed, whether he could go home at all! I managed to get to Rotherham to see my family most weekends, even if it meant getting up very early on the Sunday morning to travel to my appointment. I used to ride over the Pennines using the Woodhead Pass, via Penistone, and down to Rotherham. My motorbike and sidecar proved most reliable, even in appalling weather conditions, and never let me down once!

One Sunday morning when I was unable to go home for the weekend, I had to catch a train from the old Manchester Exchange station to go to my preaching appointment. When I arrived at the station, my train was already standing at the platform. The carriages were old and there was no corridor. Each compartment could take eight – ten passengers. As the train began to move I was the only passenger in the compartment, when I heard the sound of someone running along the platform. A man, still running, reached my compartment and opened the door to get in. He then caught sight of my clerical collar and changed his mind. He slammed the door shut and carried on running along the platform. He obviously preferred to risk missing his train rather then share a compartment with a parson!

I found most of the lectures interesting and challenging. In fact, I found the first year to be quite destructive in a way, as I was forced to question almost everything I had always believed in! This was healthy, and I certainly didn't object to it. Some of the students however, hadn't been through what I earlier described as a 'crisis of faith', and found things very difficult. Given the many subjects we were studying, I came to resent the inordinate amount of time spent learning New Testament Greek, especially as there were excellent modern translations available! I knew it was a good discipline and did well, but remain unconvinced as to its value, unless one was of an academic nature, and intended to continue using it in the future.

Finance was a problem, and would continue to be so. Books were expensive and I needed to purchase a great number as the courses progressed. When I went home during vacations, I looked for work and managed to find a job working in the Butchery Department of the Rotherham and District Cooperative Society. This work entailed driving a mobile Butchers Shop around the area. There was a butcher on board who prepared the meat and served the customers. All I had to do was drive! Sometimes I would drive other vans, delivering meat to the many shops in the area belonging to the Society. The Society had its own slaughter men; but it was a while before I could bring myself to watch the sheep and cattle being slaughtered and butchered. I was also surprised at the speed and efficiency of the process.

At the end of my first year, two things happened. The Principal had been satisfied with the progress I had made, and offered to enrol me on a three years course at the University. The first year would lead to me obtaining a Certificate in Biblical Knowledge, and the next two years to a Certificate in Theology. This would mean me attending some lectures at the University, and would enable me to obtain a full grant of about £300 a year! How could I refuse? I accepted gratefully.

Secondly, he asked me if I would be prepared to spend the summer, looking after two churches in the Long Eaton Circuit, between Nottingham and Derby. He already knew I was planning to bring my family to live in Manchester after the summer vacation. "You can take your family with you and live in the Manse", he said, " and the Circuit will pay you a quarters stipend". I discussed this with my wife, and we agreed to go. Apparently, the Minister there had got himself into all kinds of trouble, I never found out exactly what, and neither did the Circuit, but he left giving no indication of his intentions. A week before I was due to go, I drove down to meet the Superintendent Minister, and together we broke into the Manse, which had obviously been vacated in a hurry judging by all the things that had been left lying around! The Superintendent told me I would be responsible for two churches; Trinity, in the middle of the town, so called because it had only recently been created by uniting with two other churches in the town; and a smaller church at Chilwell, a few miles up the road towards Nottingham.

A week later we packed our belongings and moved to Long Eaton. The people gave us a very warm welcome, and helped us to settle into the Manse, which was a large house in need of some maintenance. Neither the Manse, nor its over grown garden were really our responsibility, but in the three months we were there, we did our best to improve both. Trinity was a thriving Church with many activities. It possessed a well-equipped office, manned by volunteers, which enabled the Church to operate smoothly and efficiently. All they really required from me; was to conduct Services on Sundays, visit the sick and housebound, and speak at a few meetings. Chilwell had similar expectations. It was not in my nature however, just to let things 'tick over'! One thing in particular troubled me, and that was the appearance of the front of the Church, situated as it was in the middle of the town.

The woodwork and the iron railings were badly in need of painting, the small 'garden' in front of the Church was overgrown and looked a real mess, and a new Notice Board was urgently required. I discussed this with the Church Stewards, and they agreed with me that something should be done. They agreed that there was no way they would ever allow their own homes and gardens to get in such a state, and that the condition of the exterior of the Church did present a poor witness to the community. With the help of a small group of volunteers, I set about organising a 'face lift' for the Church.

The painting didn't take long, and a new Notice Board was designed and ordered. We then turned our attention to the 'garden'. One big old bush had to be removed, but the roots proved too much for us. Knowing that there was an Army Ordnance Depot at Chilwell, I telephoned the Adjutant, explained the problem to him, and asked if he could loan us a Land Rover and tow chain for an hour. This, I said, could be a good Community Relations exercise! He agreed, and the following afternoon a Land Rover and tow chain arrived at the Church. Watched by a curious little crowd, the driver wrapped the chain around the roots, and dragged them out of the ground. He was also kind enough to take them away and dispose of them! After that, tidying up the garden was easy, the new Notice Board was erected, and the church no longer looked neglected and uncared for. The Church published a monthly magazine, and the next issue contained two cartoon sketches, one showing the statue on top of the Old Bailey Courthouse, holding a sword in one hand, and the scales in the other, with the caption 'Justice Administered'. The other cartoon showed a sketch of me in clerical collar, holding a pot of paint in one hand, and a brush in the other. The caption now read, 'The New Bayley, Just As He Ministered'.

It was during my short time in Long Eaton, I had my first experience of conducting Funerals. Most were of elderly people, but my first funeral was of a young married woman in her late twenties who died of cancer. I had visited her in hospital several times, and had long conversations with her husband. I was feeling my way very carefully through this tragic situation, especially as there had been nothing to prepare me for it during my time at College, nor would there be during the remainder of the course! It was very much, 'on the job' training, and learning as you went along! The young woman had been very popular and the church was full for her funeral. I used the order of service from the Methodist Service Book, but altered and added pieces to make it more personal. I found it to be a very moving experience, and also a little upsetting. It was impossible not to become emotionally involved, which was something I had to learn, to a certain degree in later years, otherwise I would have been crushed by the burden.

As well as conducting Sunday Services at Long Eaton and Chilwell, I was expected to visit other Churches in the Circuit. I remember taking an evening Service at one Church, where I was taken to task for using the New English Bible! The little group that accosted me after the service claimed that the King James Edition, the Authorised Version of 1611, was 'The Word of God', and no other! The discussion then moved on to the question of life after death, and they were most disturbed when I confessed that I didn't believe in Hell. "Don't you believe in the flames?" I was asked. "Good heavens, no", I replied. They walked away, convinced that I was beyond redemption, and I went away saddened that we had such people active in the Church!

It was about this time that a Report was published on the 'Conversations' taking place between the Methodist Church and the Church of England. This was a challenging document, and important enough to warrant a meeting between the congregation of Trinity, and the Parish Church to discuss some of the main proposals. The Parish Church was of the Anglo Catholic branch of the Church of England, and the Notice Board outside advertised the main Sunday Morning service, not as Matins, but as Mass. After a short discussion, the Vicar declared that, "As the Methodist Church was the first to leave the Church of England, it should be the first to return!" It was obvious that because of his deeply entrenched position, it was going to be a 'dialogue of the deaf', and no further meetings were planned as the Methodist Church was seeking unity, not absorption!

On a lighter note, living in the Manse meant that for the first time, we had a telephone! It was situated at the end of a long hall near the front door. My three years old daughter Vivien, found this instrument particularly fascinating; and whenever it rang, it would be a race down the corridor to see who could get there first. On the occasions she succeeded, which were many, she would pick up the telephone, say 'Hello', and put it down again! These were the days before one could dial 1471, and we had to trust to the caller trying again later. Of course the regular callers, who knew all about my daughter's antics, always did.

One of the Church members was an upholsterer by trade, and he had noticed that the seat of my motorbike, and the canopy of the sidecar were getting rather worn and in need of repair. He very kindly offered to replace the covers for me, and did so, making a first class job of it, and refused to accept any payment. This was just one of the many acts as kindness we received. Another was when we needed to go to Manchester for a day, and were loaned a car. Our time in Long Eaton was coming to an end and it would soon be time to return to College. The big problem was that as yet, we had nowhere to live, and needed to visit the City to try and find suitable accommodation. Setting off early one morning, we arrived in Manchester in time to buy the early edition of the local newspaper. After searching for several hours without any success, we found a small ground floor flat in Chorlton-cum-Hardy, a couple of miles from the College. It had a kitchen, living room, and a small bedroom with twin beds. Bathroom and toilet facilities had to be shared with a young couple living upstairs.

The rent was £5 per week. It was far from ideal, especially the bedroom as Vivien would need one bed, and my wife and I would have to manage in the other single bed, but we were running out of time so we accepted it, hoping it wouldn't be too long before we found something more suitable.

On returning to Long Eaton, we attended 'Farewell' meetings in both Churches, and with a tinge of sadness, went back to Manchester, where a number of things needed to be organised before the beginning of term. I did return to Long Eaton several times during the next two years to conduct special services, and it was good to do so. Vivien was not yet old enough to start school, so we found a nursery that would take her, but only from 9.00am – 12,00 noon. My wife had found a job in the centre of Manchester, working in the office of an Insurance Company, so I had to alter my College timetable a little. Taking Vivien to, and collecting her from the nursery meant I had to miss morning prayers, and also the last morning lecture. Little wonder the Colleges weren't too keen to accept married men with families! I looked after Vivien every afternoon, did the shopping, the washing; and got the tea ready for when my wife came home from work. Then it was back to College until 9.30pm.

Sometimes I spent afternoons in College, and managed to do a little work while Vivien played with toys or colouring books; and she joined my 'tea club'! One day, during tea, she suddenly turned to one of the students and said, "Do you have hairs on your bottom?" For a moment there was a stunned silence, a moment of embarrassment, and then gales of laughter!

Money was becoming less tight as my wife now had a better job, working at the offices of the Central Electricity Generating Board in Didsbury; and we decided it was time to look for more suitable accommodation. We found another, much larger ground floor flat not very far away, and still in Chorlton-cum-Hardy. The rent was a little more, but we felt we really had to move.

Now that I was doing a course at the University, I was awarded a larger grant, as previously indicated. The problem was, that this grant was sent to the Principal, and I had to see him at the beginning of each term to persuade him to part with it, as he still sought contributions for the College! I pointed out to him that all my wife's earnings went on paying the rent and nursery fees, and that we still had to buy food and pay bills. This was to be the routine at the beginning of every term, before he handed the cheque to me. I remember saying to him on one occasion, "OK, you keep the money, I'll just send you the bills!"

When we were living in Farnborough, I had bought a bicycle (that was before the motorbike), and I now decided to bring it back into service, putting a child's seat on the back, so that I could transport Vivien around. As part of my new course of study, I was expected to attend a number of lectures each week at the University, and a bicycle was more practical than a motorbike and sidecar.

Our financial situation meant it was necessary for me to work during every vacation, and fortunately I never had any problem in finding employment, though that often meant working nights. Through the nursery, we managed to find someone to look after Vivien when I was at work, and we were fortunate enough to retain her services when Vivien started School. Most vacations I found work at Walls, which had it's Meat and Ice Cream factories located at Hyde, just outside Manchester. Sometimes this entailed working on a production line, putting pastry lids on meat pies, or simply loading the pies onto large metal trays, ready for the oven. When the pies were cooked, the racks of trays had to be taken to the cooling room, before they were bagged up ready for dispatch. There was one occasion when there were several students from the College working there, and as two of them were pushing a rack full of trays filled with hot pies to the cooling room, they went around a bend in the overhead rail a bit too quickly, and every tray, full of hot pies slid off the racks and onto the floor! The Foreman, understandably, wasn't pleased. He stood in front of us, and swore at us for about five minutes without repeating himself once. He had a vocabulary a Sergeant Major would envy!

I also worked for a short time in the section where sliced bacon, attached to metal grills was passed through baths of brine. I was unable to cope with that for long as my arms had an unfavourable reaction to being covered in brine for long periods. So, I was moved to the loading bay, where articulated vehicles were stacked with almost 1,000 large metal containers loaded with bacon, sausages, and various types of pies. It was a case of taking the containers off a conveyor belt, and loading them about six high onto the lorry. It was hard, back-breaking work, but I was still fit enough to quite enjoy it! The lorries were then dispatched around the country to local Depots, where their cargo was off loaded on to smaller vehicles for distribution to local shops.

When working in the Ice Cream section, which was in a different location; I wasn't employed on the production section, but was again working to dispatch the products all over the country. This involved taking order forms into the Deep Freezer, bringing out the required items, packing them in dry ice into special containers, and putting them out for dispatch.

One summer vacation was spent working at the Head Office of Renold Chains, near Manchester Airport. The Company were giving a free issue of three million shares to about 7,000 shareholders, and had taken on half a dozen temporary staff to help with all the paperwork involved. The process involved going through a number of stages, and we spent hours pouring over ledgers, and using what would now be considered old fashioned adding machines; preparing share certificates, and balancing the totals at each stage. This sometimes proved to be difficult, because if we didn't come up with the correct total, it meant going through the whole process again, using alphabetical lists giving 26 sub-totals to be compared with others. It was an interesting, if sometimes frustrating job, but I enjoyed the experience.

Revd. Peter Bayley – Bus Driver

One of the members of our 'tea club', who had at one time worked as a lorry driver, told me of a garage he had discovered, just up the road in Moss Side. This garage was the Depot for a small number of buses, and the owner taught people to drive them, for a price of course. I believe he did in fact, train many drivers for Manchester Corporation. The Corporation usually insisted that people worked for two years as a conductor, before they would teach them to drive. Some conductors decided to short-circuit the system by obtaining their Public Service Vehicle License, after taking lessons with the man from Moss Side! I discussed with him the possibility of obtaining a PSV License. He not only agreed to teach me, he also offered me part time employment if I passed the test! I thought this was too good an opportunity to miss, so I began lessons. I was taught to drive a 1944 Leyland Double Decker with a crash box. In the Army I had learned to double-de-clutch when changing gear. Now it was a case of moving out of gear into neutral, waiting about four seconds until the revs had almost died, before putting it into the next gear! I also had to get used to the size of the vehicle. As it was a half-cab, that wasn't too difficult. I say that because a few months later, I had to drive a coach for the first time, and when I sat in the drivers seat, it felt as though I was driving the side of a house! After five hours tuition, I put in for my test, and failed. I was positioned at the top of a hill, turning left on to a main road. As I turned, I caught my back wheel on the edge of the pavement, and that was enough to fail me. I had another hours tuition, took the test again, and this time I passed. The tuition and tests had cost just £19!

I began my part time job the following week. This meant getting to the garage before 6.am, driving around parts of Manchester picking up workmen, and delivering them to a factory at Trafford Park. I returned in time to take Vivien to School before going to College. I did the return trip at teatime, collecting the bus at 4.30pm. The Principal knew what I was doing; the only thing he objected to were the odd occasions I parked the bus outside the College! Sometimes I would take workers to a factory near Stockport, which made cardboard boxes.

One day I was asked to take a crowd of children and a few adults from a local Church to Blackpool. It was a bit of a drag with the old Double Decker, but it made it! But when it was time to come home, I discovered one of the tyres was flat! There was no way I could change the wheel, so I had to telephone the garage, and they said they would send another coach. It took about five hours to arrive, as they had to find a driver who was free. People were making frantic telephone calls explaining the situation, and asking people to tell others the reason for the delay. When the coach did arrive, the driver, who was most disgruntled at having his Saturday evening ruined, slumped down on the back seat and said, "You can drive back to Manchester"! I was a trifle apprehensive about this, not having driven a coach before, but I had no option but to take the wheel. As mentioned earlier, it was like driving the side of a house, and I drove very cautiously and slowly until I gained a bit more confidence!

Eventually, and without further incident we arrived home, to be met by a crowd of anxious parents. It was a very relieved driver who drove the coach back to the garage!

On another excursion I had to collect a ladies lacrosse team from the other side of Stockport, and take them to Liverpool. When the team had boarded the Double Decker, I asked the lady in charge of the team if there was a more direct way to join the road to Liverpool, without going back through Stockport. "Oh yes", she said, "I'll show you the way". She guided me through the suburbs and back roads, and down a long country lane, where we came to a bridge, which was obviously too low for the Double Decker to pass under. I stopped the bus and said to the lady, "You didn't tell me about this bridge, did you?" "Oh, " she said, "I usually come down here in my mini." "Well, you're not in a mini now", I growled! By this time there was a long line of vehicles behind the bus, unable to pass due to the narrowness of the lane. There was nothing else for it, but to reverse the whole column back up the lane until we came to a place when I could turn the bus around. This wasted valuable time, as well as adding miles onto the journey I had hoped to save by taking the 'short cut'! We arrived in Liverpool just in time for the match, and I remained in the bus reading a book until it was time to take the team back to Stockport, using the conventional route!

As part of the continuing 'Conversations' between Methodism and the Church of England, it was suggested it might be a good idea if Methodist Theological Students spent a weekend with an Anglican Vicar, and Anglican Theological Students spent a weekend with a Methodist Minister. This seemed a good idea to me, so I put my name down to take part in this 'getting to know you better' exercise. Hartley was 'twinned' with an Anglican College in the Liverpool Diocese, so it was logical for Hartley students to visit parishes in that area, and I was invited to spend a weekend in a Parish in one of Liverpool's more affluent suburbs. It was a very wet day as I made my way there, so I was dressed in all my waterproof motorbike leathers. Having found the Vicarage, I made my way up the drive and parked my combination, now leaking a little oil, behind the Vicar's smart saloon car.

I went to the side door, as it seemed somehow inappropriate to present myself at the front door in my dripping condition! The Vicar's wife, a most charming lady, showed me into the cloakroom where I proceeded to change out of my travelling clothes into something more suitable. About half way through this process, the Vicar's wife popped her head around the door and said, "Would you like a bath or a shower before tea?" Not wishing to be any trouble I replied, "No thanks, I'm fine, I had a bath last night"! Buried deep in my subconscious was the old family routine of more than 20 years ago, when we had a bath once a week in a tin tub in front of the fire! When I returned home and told my wife what had happened, she was horrified that I should say such a thing; and so was I! The weekend progressed satisfactorily; socially, and in the Services I shared with the Vicar. It did much to repair the negative impressions of working with Anglicans I had come away from Long Eaton with.

At the end of my second year, I passed the required examination and was awarded the Certificate in Biblical Knowledge. Not wishing to spend another two years at College, I suggested to the Principal that I double up on my lectures and take the Certificate in Theology examinations the following year, thus completing my course. I could then leave to go into Circuit as a Proba-

1962 -1963 Hartley Victoria College. Peter is 4th row up, 4th from the right

tioner. I didn't expect him to agree with my suggestion, but to my surprise he did. Perhaps he thought it might be a good idea to get rid of me a year early!

During my final year I worked extremely hard, attending extra lectures and spending more time reading, studying, discussing, and arguing. I mentioned earlier that I found the first year to be quite destructive, as I was encouraged to seriously question so many aspects of my faith, particularly the authority and use of Scripture, and Theology. My second year was spent in what I can only describe as, a 'fluid' state. So many things were moving around in my mind, but not many were inclined to settle! I compared the experience to pouring water into a U Tube. As the water is poured into one half of the tube, the weight and pressure forces it up the other side, and for a while, it moves up and down each half, until finally settling half way up each side. As I prepared myself to leave the 'ivory towers' of Hartley Victoria, two things happened to help this final process.

The first was an informal talk we had from the Superintendent Minister of the Manchester Mission, which he entitled, 'Half time Ministry'. He was a man of considerable experience and insight, and I was intrigued and challenged by what he had to say. The main point he was making, was that it was not the function of a Minister to spend all his time and energy, on Church people and Church structures; but considering most people didn't belong to the Church anyway, it was vital that a Minister spend time and energy involved with people and structures in the community outside the Church. Whether Church members would accept Ministers putting this theory into practice, was another matter entirely. It certainly wasn't uncommon to find Church members who really believed that they paid their Ministers to look after them!

The second event that was to shape my future Ministry, was when students in their final year spent a few days at Luton Industrial College, which trained, encouraged, and supported full and part-time Industrial Chaplains. The College Principal, Rev Bill Gowland, was a charismatic Minister, who had pioneered the work of the Church in Industry, in the Methodist Church. He had been responsible for founding the Industrial College, which operated under the auspices of the Home Mission Department of the Methodist Church. He emphasised that it was the mission of the Church to work, not just for the redemption of the individual, but also the redemption of society; and, he was fond of saying, "You can't redeem what you don't understand"! I was delighted when he introduced the man who was to speak to us about 'Trade Unionism'.

His name was Moses Parker, who had been a member of the Church in Long Eaton! Moses had been a full time Trade Union Official in the East Midlands for more than 20 years, and was a Local Preacher who would only agree to conduct evening Services, because his Union Branch meetings were held on Sunday mornings; and he considered his attendance at that meeting to be a priority! I well remember him leaning over the lectern and saying, in an almost pained and rasping voice, "If only I could get half a dozen Christian men to take an interest in the Trade Union Movement, there's nothing we couldn't do – but they are all too busy at Church!" He also joked about his name, saying, "I come from a large family, and I just missed the New Testament; all my elder brothers and sisters were given names from the New Testament; by the time I was born, they'd run out of names, so I was named Moses"! All I took away from Luton, dove-tailed in with the concept of 'half-time Ministry' mentioned above.

In my continual quest for a 'worthy God', I had been greatly helped by reading many books written by the late, Rev. Dr. Leslie Weatherhead, who was for many years, Minister of the City Temple Church in London. He was once referred to by a Minister as, "The man whose books are on all our shelves, and whose illustrations, in all our sermons!" I heard him preach only once, and that was at the Manchester Mission Anniversary. He asked a capacity congregation, "Why is it, whenever people go wrong in life, the very last place they want to come to, is the Church?" The reasons were, and in some cases still are, that we are not known to be people who are kind, loving, forgiving, and understanding. We do have a reputation though, for being judgmental and having wagging fingers and sharp tongues! That may seem unfair comment, and in many cases it undoubtedly is; but what is in no doubt, is that the Church, throughout it's many branches and denominations, has, in so many ways from its public pronouncements to its liturgy: succeeded in making people feel guilty!

Some years ago, after his retirement, Dr. Weatherhead published a book entitled, "The Christian Agnostic". His views, especially on the Bible, resulted in pages of letters to the 'Methodist Recorder' and other Church journals, as well as media comment. At this point in my life, it's not difficult for me to describe myself as, "a Christian Agnostic", and to agree with Weatherhead when he wrote, "The older I get, the smaller becomes the area of fundamentals"; those things which are really important: and like him, I am happy to say that there are in my mind, drawers containing many items, filed under the heading, 'Awaiting further light'

In the last term of my final year at Hartley, there were two things uppermost in my mind; firstly, where was I to be stationed to serve my three years as a Minister on Probation, and secondly, the final examinations towards my Certificate in Theology. The first was settled first! One day the Principal sent for me, sat me down, looked at me gravely, and said, "Mr. Bayley, would you have any objections to going back to Stoke-on-Trent?" I had to smile as I said that it wouldn't be a problem! He explained the appointment would be to the Longton & Fenton Circuit, and that I would have responsibility for a new Church, opened the previous year on a large Council Estate. Having spent nine years living on such an Estate at Bradwell, it seemed to me, and obviously to the Stationing Committee, to be an appropriate 'launching pad' for my Ministry.

The following week I arranged to visit the Longton & Fenton Circuit to meet the Minister I would be taking over from, and to look at the Manse. The Council Estate consisted of about 2,000 houses, and was divided by a busy main road. The larger part of the Estate was in Blurton, and the area across the main road was known as Newstead. The Manse was a small two bedroom council house in the middle of Blurton, with the Circuit paying the rent. The membership of the new Church was small, but lots of work was carried out with children and young people. There was a large Sunday School, Companies of the Boys' Brigade, and the Girls' Brigade; and a large Youth Club with more than 100 members. The Church was a Home Missions project, and therefore received funding to provide for a concentrated Ministry for five years. All this initial information indicated a most challenging beginning to my ministry.

The University examinations were now almost upon me, so I concentrated on some last minute 'cramming'. Coming out of one of my final lectures, I discovered that my bicycle was missing, child seat and all. I searched the surrounding area, to no avail. It had obviously been stolen, and was never seen again! The Certificate in Theology examinations consisted of six three hours papers taken over a period of just over a week. When the results came out later, one of the College Tutors kindly sent me a postcard informing me that I had passed all six papers. The Principal also informed me that I had been awarded a £5 prize, which was given to the student deemed to have made the most progress during his time at College; and that really was a surprise!

My final day at College was marred by a domestic crisis. For a couple of days my wife had been suffering severe headaches, which became so bad I sent for the doctor. He examined her and asked questions about her medical history. When he discovered that she had suffered from tuberculosis in her teens, he immediately sent for an ambulance, which arrived very quickly. I arranged for a neighbour to look after our daughter, and we sped off in the ambulance, with sirens sounding and headlights flashing, to an Isolation Ward in a North Manchester Hospital.

The Doctors suspected TB Meningitis, and my wife was barrier nursed while tests were carried out. The tests proved negative, and after a week the headaches stopped as mysteriously as they had started, and she was discharged. The Doctors said that she had probably just had a viral infection, but it was all very scary!

Having completed my course at Hartley, there were still several weeks until I was due in Blurton, so I looked for another temporary job. I found one with a well-known firm of Dry Cleaners. As part of a promotions venture, they were offering a prize of a new Mini Car, and it was my job to drive this Mini

Car, with a large board on top advertising the competition, all around Manchester and the neighbouring towns. I was expected to visit the many braches of the firm, and park the car outside each one for a period of time, giving local people an opportunity to examine it, and hopefully enter the competition. When this venture was completed, I still had a little time left, and the firm found a job for me working in one of the local branches, where I was taught to load and operate a large dry cleaning machine!

My parents now surprised me by offering to buy a car for me before I went into Circuit. They hadn't much money to spend, so we toured the local second-hand car dealers looking for something suitable. Having looked at many cars, we decided upon an old 1948 Lanchester, with pre-select gears, and a fluid flywheel; neither of which I understood anyway. It was an impressive looking car, and after a trial run, we bought it for £35. I now needed to sell my faithful old motorbike and sidecar, which I did without much trouble for £30!

So my years at Hartley Victoria College came to an end. I wasn't sorry, as I was anxious to get to work in Blurton, and to begin to live something like a real family life after all the turbulence and pressures of the previous five years. I was grateful to the College and its traditions, rooted as it was in Primitive Methodism; and to the tutors who challenged me, taught me, and opened my mind. Unfortunately they didn't teach me how to be a Minister! My time working in Long Eaton had given me a foretaste of what was to come; that meant continual 'on the job' training, and learning how things should be done by doing them, and seeking help and guidance from Circuit colleagues.

Top Left: Peter aged 10

Top Right; Peter aged 20

Right: Peter and his sister, Joyce, pictured at her wedding

Above: Mini Golf with other Officers 1977
Below: Men at prayer 1977

LONGTON & FENTON METHODIST

CIRCUIT – 1965 -70

There were four other Ministers in the Circuit, the Superintendent being Rev. Percy Sanders, who had spent the first part of his Ministry working as a Missionary in West Africa: a Ministry which had taken its toll on his health. As I was to be a Minister on Probation for the next three years, the support and guidance I would need from the Superintendent was most important. My family and I were given a warm welcome at a special Circuit Meeting. At the end of the evening I was given an envelope by the Senior Circuit Steward, containing a cheque for one quarter's Stipend & Allowances. It is still the practice of the Methodist Church to pay Ministers quarterly in advance, though this is now done centrally from Westminster. When I left the Army three years previously, my pay was about £1,000 per year. Now I was to receive only £600, plus £15 per quarter, for Postage, Travel, and Stationery! No one joins the Ministry of the Church for the money, but you do need enough to pay the bills!

I could walk around the Estate, but visiting people in local Hospitals, and visiting other Churches in the Circuit for meetings and Services was impossible without a car, and that was to prove the biggest drain on family finances. It has taken a number of years, but Ministers are now paid a more realistic Stipend, plus sufficient allowances to run a car! The Manse was very small, and the dining room had also to serve as my study. Vivien was now six years old and my wife and I decided it was time to increase the size of our small family! It had been out of the question while I was training, as we were dependant on my wife working.

The new Methodist Church was located right on the edge of the Estate, backing on to one of the biggest Coal Mines in the country. Hem Heath Colliery employed about 2,000 men and was one of the few in the country drawing more then one million tons of coal a year. There were two other Churches on the Estate; a daughter Church of the old Church of England Parish Church in Blurton, and the responsibility of the Curate, which was about 400 yards from my Church; and a Roman Catholic Church, across the main road on the Newstead side of the Estate. When the Estate was planned, it was obvious that the prime sites had been given to the Public Houses, of which there were 5!

The Methodist Church was a dual-purpose building, with the Sanctuary area at the front, and a large hall with a stage at the rear, which could be divided into two smaller halls using large foldaway partitions. The outside area belonging to the Church was as the builders had left it, and next to the

Church was a children's playground! Vandalism was, and still is, a major problem! Another major problem I was soon to discover, was that due to the autocratic style of my predecessor's Ministry, the Church had been denuded of most of the lay leadership. The Minister cannot possibly fulfil the Ministry of the Church by himself! For the Church to function efficiently, it needs dedicated people, to take responsibility for the property, finances, children, music, and tasks relating to the wider work of the Church, at home and overseas. I needed to find people to fill many vacancies, and it wouldn't be easy!

I did eventually manage to find, and enthuse people for these tasks, but it was a constant battle to keep things going. They were good, lovely people; but most, in their daily lives and work, were not used to accepting responsibility, or acting on their own initiative. There was much to be done, but any time I stopped, so did they. My style of leadership soon evolved into leading from the front, pushing from the back, and working alongside!

The first Saturday saw my wife and I sweeping out the hall, and putting out the chairs in preparation for the Sunday Service. This was the routine for the first few weeks until I decided, that one way or another, we had to employ someone to clean the premises! The Church itself couldn't afford to do this, so I decided to use funds from the Youth Club; after all, I reasoned, they were the group who made most of the mess! After a week or so, I managed to find two ladies, who agreed to do the job; and they did a good job for us over the next few years.

The next few months were spent getting to know my Church members and many others in the wider Church community. As already mentioned, there were lots of children and young people, many of whom came to Church on the Sunday evenings. The Girls' and Boys' Brigade Companies were thriving, and I held regular Parade Services for them. After a few months, I felt things were progressing fairly well in the life of the Church. Repairing the damage caused by vandalism was an expensive and time-consuming business, stretching patience and tolerance to the limit. I managed to obtain some second-hand iron railings to install around the Church, which did cut down the amount of damage caused, but the Church was still well within throwing range; and replacing broken windows was a regular and expensive task.

As the weather grew colder, we began to experience problems with the oil fired heating system. When we first ran out of oil, I found I was the one expected to check on the tank and order re-supplies! As there was no way of checking the amount of oil in the tank, I had a gauge installed, as well as a frost stat, which increased the amount of oil used, but avoided the chance of having burst pipes. Nothing in the Hartley syllabus about such things! The winter of 1965/6 was very cold and I began to have serious problems with my car. I was unable to move it for a while, and the engine block froze, as there was insufficient anti-freeze in the system. Sadly it had to be towed away to a scrap yard, where it was cannibalised by Lanchester enthusiasts. Being without a car made life difficult, and, some in the Circuit noticed this. I was amazed to arrive home one day to find an old Hillman Californian parked outside the Manse. It was an old but reliable car, and it took me a while to discover where it came from. When I did eventually discover the identity of my benefactor, he would accept no more than a sincere 'thank you'

One evening while looking through the local newspaper, The Evening Sentinel, I saw that the North Staffs Operatic and Dramatic Society were holding auditions for their next production, which was to be "Guys & Dolls". I went for an audition and was given a small part in the production, as the gangster, Benny Southstreet, which involved singing a couple of songs as part of a trio.

It was no hardship while there was only one rehearsal a week, but as the dates for the show grew nearer, more rehearsals were needed. During the week of the show, there was little time for anything else! The show was a great success, and my appearance was featured in the Evening Sentinel under the headline, 'METHODIST MINISTER TURNS GANGSTER – ON STAGE'! It was also described as a 'sexy' show, because in some scenes the chorus girls were scantily dressed! The Societies next production was, 'West Side Story', and I would have loved to be part of it, but it was now obvious to me that I really wouldn't be able to devote the necessary time.

We were struggling financially, so I decided to seek part time employment to help make ends meet! Two miles down the road at Trentham, was a coach firm called Thompson Tours, owned by a lady called Mrs Thompson! One day I called to see her, produced my PSV license, and asked if she employed any part-time drivers. It turned out that most of her drivers were part-timers, and she offered to add me to the list. She asked me to present myself at the garage at 5.30am the following morning, so that her traffic manager could give me a test drive! I arrived in good time and boarded a coach with him. Now these coaches were luxurious compared to those I had driven in Manchester, and were a real pleasure to drive. The traffic manager told me to drive to Tunstall, one of the five towns making up the Potteries conurbation, and arrive there by 6.00am. to pick up my first passenger. There were more people to pick up in Burslem, Hanley, and Newcastle-u-Lyme, before driving to the Motorway Services at Keele on the M6. I had just delivered the Day Shift to work! We then went into the café for a free breakfast while the shifts changed over.

After breakfast we went back to the coach and found the people who had been working through the night, on board waiting to be taken home. Many of them lived in the rural areas around Newcastle, which meant driving along many narrow country roads. When the last passenger had been dropped off, I was told to drive to Kidsgrove, not far from Tunstall, and began driving through the Potteries again, picking up schoolgirls, and taking them to a Grammar School just outside Newcastle. Then it was back to the garage at Trentham.

The traffic manager was satisfied with my driving, and I was offered the job of doing the same trip every morning, Monday to Friday. For this I would receive £5 a week! I was back home by 9.00am, so it couldn't be said that I was neglecting my Church work!

Driving for Mrs Thompson soon had a favourable spin off for the Church. A matter of concern had been the small number of children attending Sunday School from the Newstead side of the Estate. The reason for this was, understandably enough, the reluctance of parents to allow their children to cross the busy main road dividing the Estate.

Those were the days when children we sent on their own to school and Sunday school, not taken everywhere by their parents, as is today's practice! I had already been told that the Local Authority had no plans to provide a Pedestrian Crossing, or Foot Bridge to enable people to cross the road safely; so the only way to help the children would be to provide transport. I explained the situation to Mrs Thompson, and asked if we could hire a coach for a couple of hours on Sunday afternoons. To my delight, she agreed, and pleased me even more when she said there would be no charge, providing I drove the coach! Of course I agreed, had some leaflets printed and distributed around Newstead, offering the service and giving timings and pick-up points. One of the teachers accompanied me, as it was important to have an adult on board to help the smaller children, and to maintain order! It was a great success with a considerable number using the coach. After depositing the children at the Church, I would go home for an hour before collecting and delivering the children back home.

We were now expecting our second child and it was necessary to encourage the Circuit to find us a larger house. I made enquiries around the Estate and heard about a three bed roomed house that would soon be coming available, only a few hundred yards away from the Manse. The Circuit had words with a local Councillor, the matter was resolved, and a few weeks later we moved! The new Manse was near to one of the Public Houses, and backed on to the Primary School attended by Vivien. The extra space was most welcome, and preparations were made in readiness for our new arrival. My wife saw the local Midwife regularly, and as no problems were anticipated, a home delivery was planned. When the first signs of labour manifested themselves, my mother, who was working at the time, came over immediately to help. She stayed for two weeks waiting for the birth, but nothing happened; it was a false alarm, so she went back home and returned to work! According to the Midwife, such things were not uncommon, and assured us there was nothing to worry about. Sure enough, in the early hours of 5th July 1966, my wife really went into labour and I phoned the Midwife, who quickly arrived and took charge of the situation. Having missed the arrival of my daughter into this world, it was a very moving experience to be present, and helping, at the birth of our son. He arrived a week later than anticipated, weighed in at nine and a half pounds, and we decided to call him Simon Peter. My mother came over again and stayed for another two weeks. Her help was very much appreciated, as was my father's who was especially delighted to have a Grandson!

Whilst working at the Central Electricity Generating Board in Manchester, my wife sat by, and helped a lady who was blind. She had a Golden Labrador guide dog. My wife thought the dog was absolutely wonderful, and was most interested to learn that it was possible to acquire a dog from the Society, which had to be rejected if for any reason, it was considered unsuitable. Consequently, as soon as we arrived in Blurton, we put our name down on the waiting list for a guide dog reject.

Just a few weeks after Simon's birth, we were notified that a dog was available for collection from a training unit in Lancashire, and was ours for a small donation. It was a bitch, and we were informed the reason it had been rejected was because it had proved to be 'traffic shy'. We collected the dog the following Saturday. It was a beautiful affectionate dog, whose name was 'Trailer of Ashbrook'! 'Trailer' certainly wasn't a name we would have chosen, but she was a mature dog and we couldn't really expect her to adjust to a new name, so we were stuck with it. We had all kinds of problems with her. She had to be confined to the house, or be taken out on a lead. If she managed to escape through an open door, she would just run away, sometimes for miles. Fortunately we had our telephone number engraved on her collar, and would receive calls from people who had taken her in, asking us to collect her!

Meanwhile, the Methodist Church at Bradwell, having previously built a large hall for its youth work, had eventually built a Church. My sister Joyce had arranged to get married there, and with the permission of the Minister, I was invited to officiate at the marriage ceremony. It was the first Wedding to take place in the new Church, and I married my sister to Eric Rogers, a young man she had met at work, on 22nd November 1966. The Reception was held at a venue in Newcastle, attended by family and friends, and was a joyous affair. We didn't stay late because of Simon, and the dog! When we arrived home, we saw immediately that we had left the dog for too long! The house was covered in a thick layer of dust! We had left the dog in the kitchen with food and water, but she had obviously got bored and tried to scratch her way out. She had scratched most of the plaster off the walls right down to the brickwork. There was an awful lot of work to be done before we got to bed that night, which was the last thing we needed with a new baby in the house!

The final straw was when the dog began to be very threatening whenever food was around. One day while she was eating, Vivien happened to get too close to her, and was bitten. Sadly it was time to find another home for Trailer. After making some enquiries, we found her a home just out in the countryside, with a retired policeman who already had one Labrador. She quickly settled, and when we visited to check on her a couple of weeks later, she was obviously very happy there.

Having a new baby, who wasn't sleeping well at night, and getting up at 5.15am to collect my coach was proving too much. We couldn't send the baby back, so I had to give up the early morning job! Still needing to supplement my income, I started work as a part time Religious Instruction Teacher at a local secondary modern School. I hadn't received any training as a teacher, but I worked through the agreed syllabus, using a few schemes of work left by other teachers, plus a few of my own. I found it to be very hard work, and I don't think I was particularly successful as a teacher, but I stuck at it for two years before returning to the coaches, but more of that later.

Owing to a reduction in the number of Ministers in the Circuit, I was asked to take responsibility for the Methodist Church at Trentham, just two miles down the road. The contrast with Blurton couldn't have been greater. The Church building was an old village chapel with 18 dedicated members. It had originally been part of the Trentham Estate, owned by the Duke of Devonshire. Trentham was now an affluent suburb of the Potteries, and hundreds of new homes were planned for the area. Small as it was, I saw that it was a church with tremendous potential. It had a small, but growing Sunday School, but the Church hall was badly in need of maintenance and redecoration. The mothers of the children 'volunteered' the help of their husbands to carry out a major refurbishment of the hall! A portable tower scaffold was borrowed and the work began. The work was completed in record time, and the men folk began to take more of an interest in the Church. I met with the local Vicar, and we organised a team of volunteers to visit each new house in the area, to welcome the people, and inform them of the local Church facilities. It worked well, and both Churches experienced a growth in Church attendance as more and more homes were built. The Methodist Church soon needed to expand it's premises, but in this it was severely limited, located as it is on the corner of a main road, and sandwiched between a Bank and a large suburban house.

Over the next few years, interior walls were demolished and exterior walls pushed out to the absolute limit! A Youth Club was opened for the teenagers in the community, which only met once a week on Friday nights because most had lots of homework to do during the week. I assumed responsibility as Youth Club Leader. Cooperation with the Parish Church was excellent and arrangements were made for joint Services to be held during the main Christian Festivals. The ladies of both Churches met together, and a joint Men's Supper Club was founded, meeting monthly during the winter months in a variety of locations, with an after Dinner Speaker to round off the evening. It was a great success.

At Blurton, things were also progressing well. I had formed a good working relationship with the Curate living on the Estate, and our congregations began to work well together. . We faced similar problems and challenges and were able to support each other. We were both concerned that, even though we had a good Medical Centre on the Estate, there was no Chemist's shop. People needing medicines on prescription had to catch a bus to either Longton or Heron Cross to find a Chemist. I heard that one of the shops on the Estate was soon to be vacated, and that a local Bookmaker was hoping to acquire the premises. Even as a Methodist Minister, I had nothing against Bookmakers, but I sincerely believed the community badly needed a Chemist's Shop! I took the matter up with the local Council, and was informed that they had been unable to find a Chemist who wanted to work on the Estate. Within three days I had found one, and informed the Council. I had simply visited several Chemists and asked if they, or anyone of their colleagues was seeking to expand.

A Chemist operating in Dresden, halfway between Blurton and Longton, told me he had been trying to get onto the Estate for some time, but without success. Six weeks later, he opened a shop on the Estate!

The outside area surrounding the Blurton church had been bothering me for some time, and I decided it was time to call a few people together to discuss the matter. It was decided to clear the ground, and prepare it for covering with turf. Having taken all the measurements, I visited a supplier about ten miles away and negotiated a price and delivery date. Having prepared the ground, which involved the removal of lots of rubbish; a large working party, including my father and some senior boys from the Youth Club assembled early one Saturday morning, and spent the whole day laying the rolls of turf. It made a tremendous difference to the appearance of the Church. All that was necessary now to complete the job, was a new Notice Board, a petrol driven lawn mower, and a list of people prepared to cut the grass! To encourage others, I put my own name on the list.

HEM HEATH COLLIERY

I saw the colliery every day, and remembering how much I had been inspired by my visit to Luton Industrial College, made an appointment to see the Manager. He was a little puzzled when I asked if I might visit the colliery as their Chaplain. He suggested I visit the Canteen, but I requested access to every part, including going underground. I explained that many of his workers lived on the Estate where I was the Minister, and that I believed it to be important that I understood, and indeed needed, to share in a part of their lives outside the domestic. After chatting about things for a while, he agreed that I could do as I had requested, though I would need to be accompanied when going underground for safety reasons. I then explained I would also need permission from the Trade Unions, or I risked being perceived as a Management spy! He agreed to arrange for me to meet the leaders of the many unions representing the men working at the colliery.

The meeting was arranged for the following week, and when I entered the room I was surprised how many Union representatives were present; and they were as suspicious as a wagonload of monkeys! I spent the first ten minutes telling them about the things I didn't want to do, like conducting Church services, distracting men while they were working, or attempting to raise money in any way! I explained that I wanted to understand more about their working environment, visit miners who were sick or in hospital, join in social activities, and generally be available for anyone who might need to talk about anything. Some of them had seen me around the Estate, and in the local pubs; and some had children who attended our Sunday School and Youth Club. After some discussion among themselves, it was agreed that I should be allowed to visit the colliery as I had requested; the consensus being, 'that it couldn't do any harm'!

I reported back to the Manager, and we arranged a date for my first visit underground. When I arrived, suitably dressed and wearing a clerical collar, I was issued with a helmet, battery, and light. I wore the clerical collar because it would save a lot of explanations, and I wasn't going to be working anyway! The Safety Officer was to accompany me on this occasion, and as we made our way to the shaft he received a telephone call regarding an accident underground. A large piece of coal had fallen out of the coalface, and a miner's foot had been badly crushed. Four miners were in the process of carrying the injured man on a stretcher to the pit bottom. The Safety Officer needed to see the man, and visit the scene of the accident in order to make his report, so we set off along the appropriate roadway to meet them. When we saw the lights of the group in the distance, the Safety Officer said to me, "When we meet up with them, try and keep out of sight, because if the injured man sees you, he'll think it's all up with him!"

This was an indication of the way clergymen are to be seen as being associated with bad news and tragedy. It reminded me of a story related to us at Luton by Bill Gowland. One night he decided to visit the men on the night shift in a local factory. Looking up from the factory floor, he noticed a large overhead crane, operated my a man who spent the whole shift sitting in a little cabin, moving the crane back and forth along the factory. Bill had climbed up a ladder into the roof space, walked along the catwalk, and opened the door of the little cabin. When the operator saw him, he went white and said, "Is the wife dead?" The poor man couldn't conceive of any other reason why a parson should visit him in that situation! So, when we met up with the outgoing party, I did as recommended and kept out of the way, visiting the miner later in hospital. When the Safety Officer had spoken to the group, we proceeded to the site of the accident.

As we went further into the mine, I noticed significant differences in the equipment and conditions compared to those in Wolstanton Colliery where I had worked ten years earlier. Instead of tubs filled with coal, there were now much larger mine cars. Instead of dozens of miners shovelling coal, there were only three or four at one end of the coal-face, cutting out a small area, called a stable, just large enough to fit in place a coal cutting machine, which would travel the length of the face, cutting the coal and automatically loading it on to the conveyor belt. When a length of coal had been cut and loaded, a miner operating a couple of levers, hydraulically lowered the roof supports, moved them forward, and elevated them back into position again. Having done all that by hand, I was most impressed!

While the Safety Officer was drawing sketches and taking statements from some of the miners, I took the opportunity to chat with some of the others. One or two I knew and they and others seemed quite pleased to see me, and we met up later in the canteen for a mug of tea and a sandwich! On subsequent visits, I saw other areas underground, and not always with the Safety Officer! When visiting the areas 'on top', I was free to wander as I wished, visiting the medical centre where I was informed of any workers in Hospital, the workshops where routine maintenance was carried out, the screens, where the coal was sorted by size and other materials like stone removed, before being loaded into railway wagons for transportation to a nearby power station: and never forgetting to visit the lone workman who operated the winding gear, moving the huge cages up and down the main shaft. These cages were used for lifting coal and miners,(not together) up and down the shaft, which I was reliably informed, was the biggest in Europe!

My wife and I were once invited to present the prizes at the Annual Sports & Social Evening, which turned out to be a most enjoyable occasion, and enabled us to meet socially, many of those only ever seen at work; and also meet their wives.

After whirling around the dance floor doing the 'Gay Gordon's', one old miner said to me, "I'm surprised to see a man in your position gallivanting around the floor like that!" I said to him, "Do you know what happens if I cut my wrist?" He looked a bit puzzled and said, "No, what happens?" I said, "Blood comes out; the fact that I wear this white plastic thing around my neck, doesn't mean I was hatched from an egg"! It was perhaps, a not too subtle attempt at emphasising the humanity of the Ministry. It was an evening when I felt useful contacts had been made, and that I was now more of an accepted member of the community, not only at the Colliery, but also around the Estate.

I hope the reader will note that part of the title of this book is 'Reminiscences'. I have never kept a diary and some of the events I am writing about are not all necessarily in strict chronological order! This is particularly true of my time in the Longton & Fenton Circuit. So many things happened and I recall most of them, but they may not all be in the correct order!

The interior of the Blurton Church, and especially the hall, was by now in need of redecoration. Lots of time, expense and effort had been spent on the outside; and I lost count of the broken windows we had replaced, including some small stained glass ones at the front, which had air rifle pellets shot through them. Finance was a problem, so there was no way we could afford to have professional decorators. It would have to be a DIY project, but we lacked the equipment to tackle the high walls and ceilings. Then I heard of a builder, Mr. Cornes, who was a Methodist in a nearby Circuit, but with his office and yard a few miles away in Hanley. I went to see him, explained the situation, and asked if we could borrow some A ladders and planks for a couple of weeks. He first wanted to see the situation for himself, and so, settling myself in the front seat of his Rolls Royce, I took him to see the Blurton church! When Mr. Cornes had seen the building, and some of the problems we were having, he readily agreed to help. A few days later, a lorry arrived and off loaded all I had requested. A working party was assembled, including some senior members of the Youth Club, and men who weren't even members of the Church. Working evenings and weekends, the work was done in about a fortnight.

Every Christmas, a group from the Church would visit all the five Public Houses on the Estate to sing Carols and collect money for the Church. On one occasion a disagreeable man came up to me and said, in an aggressive manner, "You're always here after bloody money you are". I recognised the man, and asked, "Didn't I Baptise your grand-daughter last year?" He agreed that I had. "And didn't I conduct your Mother-in-Laws funeral the year before?" Again he agreed, so I went on, "And didn't you expect the Church to be there when you needed it, and didn't you expect it to be clean and warm?" He nodded, so I said, "Right, so put some money in the tin", and rather shamefacedly he did. That man wasn't at all typical; the majority did appreciate what we were trying to do for the community, and were pleased to see us in the pubs, not only at Christmas, and not always after money!

As a Minister on Probation, I was expected to continue with my studies, and a Minister from a neighbouring Circuit was appointed to supervise me. I was doing so many other things, I didn't have time for very much studying. My supervisor described me as a pragmatist! As he was also a part time Industrial Chaplain, we were 'on the same wavelength' and travelled together to Luton for Conferences, further training, and inspiration. Every year I had to attend the District Probationers Committee with my Superintendent Minister, so that my progress could be assessed. The Chairman of the District knew the Circuit well and was very supportive in all I was trying to achieve.

The Methodist Ministers' Housing Society, which provides homes for retired Ministers, launched an appeal for funds as the demand was outstripping supply, and more property was required. We discussed this at our Staff Meeting, and I suggested that the Ministers put on a Concert to raise funds as our contribution to the appeal. My argument was that the crowds would be drawn, not so much by the programme, but by who was performing! I offered to organise the event and arranged for it to be held at Blurton, as they had the biggest hall and a good stage. A date was agreed, and the event was well publicised around the Circuit. With minimum rehearsals, the show went ahead and was an outstanding success! I acted as Master Of Ceremonies, and the extended Church hall was packed to capacity. It was a truly hilarious evening; people saw another side of their Ministers, and lots of money was raised for the Society.

A new Superintendent Minister was now appointed to the Circuit. Rev. Howard Trevis was a very experienced Minister, now in his final appointment before retirement. I owe a lot to him for his support and wise advice. He and his wife moved into a different house from his predecessor, recently acquired by the Circuit, and very close to the Estate. Certain grants became available, and it was agreed a proper Manse should be purchased for me! A lovely house with four bedrooms became available almost opposite the Superintendents, and the Circuit bought it, with carpets and fittings, for £4,500! The previous occupant had been an elderly lady, who had been related to Harry Wheatcroft, and the garden was absolutely full of roses; front, rear, and down the side! It was a beautiful house, and I was now able to have a study. The worst time of the year was when the roses needed pruning; there were an awful lot of thorny branches to be disposed of!

Since being given the old Hillman Californian car, which served me well for a while, I had several 'old bangers', which meant frequent visits to a nearby scrap yard to search for spare parts. We decided the time had come to get a vehicle we could rely on, but would be inexpensive to run and maintain. I went to see my Bank Manager and borrowed £360 to buy a new three wheel Reliant Van; later adding two rear seats, but no rear windows to keep it in the lower tax bracket! I was amazed how versatile it was. I remember packing my family and my parents into it, and touring North Wales! It coped well with all the hills even when fully laden. To help pay for this, I went back to work for Mrs. Thompson, but not to work the early morning shift! Now I took the night shift to the Motorway Services, and took the afternoon shift home. This meant working from 10.pm to midnight, six evenings a week.

Sometimes I was asked to drive in the late afternoon to take workers from the Colliery Workshops to their homes around the Potteries, terminating at Biddulph. There was one passenger who was the most foul-mouthed man I had ever encountered; and he always sat behind me. Many of the other workers were clearly uncomfortable by his continual flow of bad language. One day one of them said to him, " Just watch your language, you've got the Vicar driving today!" The man immediately responded, "I don't give a f*** about the

Vicar". I turned straight around and said to the man, "And I don't give a f*** about you either"! He was so shocked by my response that he shut up like a clam and didn't say another word: either on that or subsequent journeys.

My wife decided she would like to help out as well, and went back to work part time as a Nursing Auxiliary at the City General Hospital in Newcastle. She worked on the Children's Ward, and found it very satisfying, except for those occasions when a child died, which she found very upsetting. While she was at work Simon was looked after by a lady who lived near the Church. She thought the world of him, and he enjoyed going to her home. Having two older boys of her own, and a dog, Simon was quite 'spoiled'! My wife was working flexible hours, and I was usually able to drive her to and from the Hospital. One day I was going to collect her, taking Vivien in the van with me. She was sitting in the back, when I was forced to make an emergency stop to avoid a lady who stepped into the road in front of me. Poor Vivien was thrown between the front seats, and hit her head on the dashboard. It was a nasty cut, and there was blood everywhere! Giving her a handkerchief to hold to her forehead, I decided the best thing to do, was to continue to the Hospital where she could be examined and treated. I took her straight to the Children's Ward, where the Ward Sister cleaned the wound and put in a couple of stitches. Vivien was very brave, and quickly recovered from the shock, but I decided to exchange the Reliant Van for a Ford Anglia car, which would offer greater protection for little passengers!

The Superintendent Minister asked me to become the Circuit Youth Secretary, probably because most of the Youth in the Circuit were at Blurton, and also because I was the youngest member of the Circuit Staff. When details of this appointment were known and circulated, I began to receive literature from many quarters! One leaflet offered Holidays for Youth Groups at a resort in Belgium, not very far from Ostend. I consulted with several people around the Circuit, and it was agreed that even though it hadn't been done before, it was worth trying. In no time at all I had enough names to fill a coach, including eight adults, the minimum needed to help in supervising a crowd of energetic teenagers! I hired a coach from Mrs. Thompson, which I drove to Dover. Another driver was with me to take the coach back to Trentham. When we arrived in Ostend, I was dismayed that there was no coach waiting to take us to our Hotel. After waiting for half an hour, I telephoned the tour operator, who promised to look into the matter. On hour later a coach arrived, and the driver informed me that the Hotel would not be able to accommodate us until the afternoon of the following day!

Apparently there had been a mix up in the bookings, and we were to be taken to another resort on the other side of Ostend for the night. The accommodation was most unsuitable, and my party were understandably very dissatisfied.

Telecommunications weren't very good then compared to today, but I eventually managed to contact the tour operator again and conveyed our intense displeasure! He was most apologetic and promised that all would be well on the morrow, and fortunately for us, and the reputation of the tour operator, it was!

The Hotel was good, and close to the sea for those who wanted to swim. There were lots of shops and cafes in the area, and some of us quickly became addicted to Belgian waffles and cream! Ostend was quite close and public transport good. Coach trips were organised to Brussels, and to a little market town just over the border in Holland. Some wished to visit the First World War Memorial at Ypres, and this was arranged. Those who made the trip, some for family reasons, were profoundly moved by the experience. In the evenings we organised our own entertainment, and during the night the adults took turns in patrolling the Hotel to keep the boys and girls apart! The homeward journey was uneventful, and all agreed that except for the initial problems, we had all enjoyed ourselves. It was agreed that we should return the following year, and with a few changes in the composition of the party, we did!

As a result of my campaign to get a Chemists Shop on the Estate, and my dealings with the local Authority, I decided to take more of an interest in local political matters. It was disturbing to discover that the turnout for the last local Council elections had only been 30%. My parents had been active in the Newcastle-u-Lyme Constituency, as members of the Labour Party for many years, so I decided to join the Labour Party, and began to attend the monthly meetings of the local Ward. There were eight Wards in the Stoke-on-Trent (South) Constituency, and Jack Ashley was our Member of Parliament. The Labour Party had controlled the City Council for many years, and a degree of complacency was evident. It was said that even if a monkey offered as a Candidate; providing it was wearing a yellow ribbon, it would be elected! The next Local Elections were some months away, and I suggested we began to prepare for them immediately. This raised a few eyebrows, and muttered comments about the obviously inexperienced 'new boy'!

When I joined the Labour Party, I subscribed to receive regular up-dates and information on Party Policy and 'tools for the job'. One 'tool' in particular fired me with enthusiasm and I sent off for more details. It was an efficient canvassing aid known as 'The Reading System', because it had first been used to good effect in Reading! It entailed a lot of extra work for Party activists, but my Ward agreed to give it a try. The system consisted basically of pads of carbonated lists, on which volunteers wrote the names and addresses of everyone on the Electoral Register.

There were about six sheets on each pad, and when completed, were fixed to a large board, and kept in the Ward 'Office', which was usually a Party Member's living room. Party literature had to be delivered to every house in the Ward, and as many people as possible spoken to. As well as seeking commitments to work or vote for the Party, it was important to compile lists of those needing help in getting to the Polling Stations on the day. On the day of the Election, a member of the Party had to be outside each Polling Station; not to conduct an 'exit poll', but simply to determine who had voted. This information was then passed to the Ward Office, and the names of those who had voted, crossed off the prepared lists.

Many more people voted than the previous year and most helpers were available during the evening hours. By continuing to supply the helpers with up to date lists, precious time was saved by not knocking on the doors of people who had already voted. As helpers reported in to the Ward Office, the next sheet was simply torn off the carbonated pad, and given to them. They then knew exactly where to concentrate their efforts to encourage as many people as possible, to go to the Polling Stations before they closed. Some of us then went to Longton Town Hall to watch and wait as the votes were counted. Our candidate was elected, which was no surprise. What was most satisfying was that the turnout was 50%, a most significant increase. As a result of this successful experiment, other Wards decided to adopt the 'Reading System'. This was to be critically important when the time came to fight the next General Election!

Our MP, Jack Ashley had been in Hospital for an operation on his ears. He had suffered from poor hearing for years, and it was hoped the operation would help. Most unfortunately, the opposite happened, and Jack was left completely deaf. When the results were known, Jack offered his resignation to the Constituency General Management Committee, but they refused to accept it. Jack agreed to remain as our MP, and very quickly mastered the art of lip reading. He was given his own seat in the House of Commons, from where he could continue to participate in the business of the House. As many people know, he became a Champion for the deaf and others who were in any way disabled. He was also able to continue due to the tremendous help and support he received from his wife, Pauline. An additional earpiece was fitted to their telephone, so that as a caller was speaking to Jack, he was lip reading from Pauline what was being said, and answering the caller. It was a strange experience, having a conversation with a man you knew to be deaf!

My active involvement with the Labour Party, not unexpectedly, caused a little disquiet among some of my Church members, particularly at Trenthem, which was strongly Conservative. I insisted on exercising my right, as a citizen, to be involved politically; and as there is no other kind of politics in this Country, other then Party politics, I had to 'nail my colours to the mast' somewhere, and I had chosen the Labour Party. At no time, did I ever talk about Party Political matters from the pulpit, although I did sometimes write letters to the Evening Sentinel on current topics.

More changes were now taking place within the Circuit, and I was asked to be responsible for another Church just outside Longton, at Lightwood. This was an old Chapel with its roots in the old United Methodist tradition. This usually meant that, while they acknowledged the need of a Minister for specific functions, they really liked to do things their own way without Ministerial interference! In this respect, it was a very different set up from my other two Churches. The membership of the Church was quite small, about 30, but there was a large Sunday School, and so yet again, my ability to relate to children was most important. Trentham was now doing very well, and apart from pastoral needs, was more than capable of looking after itself. It was financially sound and had good lay leadership. Blurton still required a strong hand on the tiller, but was now much better at getting on with things without me. I'm sure that one of the aims of leading is to enable people to do without you!

It didn't take very long before I got to know the people at Lightwood, and to feel at home amongst them. There was strong lay leadership, and the Church was efficiently managed. Their one fault was that they refused to 'go by the book' in some matters the Methodist Church considered necessary. Someone, I never did find out whom, left some money to the Church. This should have been declared and sent to the Property Division of the Church in Manchester, whose responsibility it is to ensure the money is spent wisely. The folk at Lightwood committed the money to projects, without even telling me about it, never mind getting permission from the Property Division! I made my displeasure known, and some relationships became a little strained! One thing they were determined to do, was to obtain new pews. Someone saw an advert in a Church newspaper, offering pews for sale from a Church in Lymm, not far away in Cheshire. I went with a small group to inspect them, and when we saw what a lovely condition they were in, made an offer, which was accepted. The Church was also offering a pulpit for sale. It was really much too large for the small chapel at Lightwood, but it was such a magnificently carved pulpit, we couldn't resist the temptation to buy it!

Relations were strained even more when I discovered a date had been agreed with the Mayor of Stoke-on-Trent to perform the Opening Ceremony following the refurbishment, again without consulting me, though they expected me to be present! I was furious at what was at least gross discourtesy, and my initial reaction was to refuse to attend. My Superintendent calmed me down, and we both attended the ceremony! His advice to me, which has proved accurate throughout the years, was, "Peter lad, in this job, you'll find members of the Lord's awkward squad where ever you go!"

ORDINATION

My Probationary Period was coming to an end, and I attended my final District Committee, which was satisfied and referred me to the Synod for their judgment. They agreed to send me to the Methodist Conference, which that year was meeting in London, for final acceptance. Before Conference met, there were two final things to be done. A few days after Synod, those from the District being sent for Ordination, attended a Service of Public Testimony at a church in the Longton Mission Circuit. During this Service, the Ordinands spoke of their personal experiences, and affirmed their commitment to serve the Church as Ministers. Attending a National Ordinand's Retreat was the final preparation before making our final vows.

I don't think the Retreat, which was held at 'Hereward the Wake' House in Northampton, was as quiet and contemplative as the organisers would have wished. Most were meeting friends they hadn't seen since leaving Theological College, and there was a lot of gossip to catch up on! Coming to the end of what had been a very long and exhaustive number of years, most were on 'a bit of a high'. It had been eight years since I decided to offer for the Ministry; seven years since I began the process of 'Candidating'. A couple of evenings saw quite a few of us in Northampton town, where, for the first time, I discovered the pleasures and difficulties of Ten Pin Bowling!

The Methodist Conference in 1968 met in Westminster Central Hall. I was given accommodation with a Methodist family living near Barnet in north London, and travelled daily on the 'tube' to Westminster. One day all Ordinands were lined up on the stage of the Central Hall, and presented to the Conference for acceptance. My wife and parents had come down to London and were present at this ceremony. In that year, there were almost 100 Ordinands, and several special Ordination Services were held that same evening in Churches around London. I was ordained on 18th June 1968 at Bowes Park Methodist Church. It was a very moving, satisfying, and never to be forgotten experience. I remember spending the following day with my family, visiting among other places, The Tower of London.

During my daily visits to Westminster Central Hall, while the Conference was getting on with its business, I had several meetings with the Secretary of the Royal Navy, Army, and Royal Air Force Board, whose responsibility it is to recruit and recommend Ministers to serve as Chaplains with Her Majesty's Forces. Having enjoyed my time in the Army, I was more then happy to consider serving as a Chaplain should a suitable vacancy arise. The Methodist Church had comparatively few Chaplains compared to the Church of England, because Chaplains were allocated on a strictly denominational basis, approximately one Chaplain for every 850 servicemen and women. Those joining the Forces, had to declare their Denomination or Faith. Many weren't really sure and, understandably enough, were registered as belonging to The Church of England, that being the Established Church of the Nation. Sadly, as I was later to discover, the Church of England had more vacancies than it was able to fill.

There were no anticipated vacancies for Methodist Chaplains for some time, so I put the idea to the back of my mind and returned home to get on with the job of being a Circuit Minister. Blurton was beginning to have problems with the Boys' Brigade. The Company had been founded and Captained by one man since 1964. He and his wife had done a tremendous job, and it was a very successful Company. Then a family with strong Brigade connections transferred to Blurton from another Church in the area. Three members of the family were trained B.B. Officers, and their help with the Company and in the Church was very much welcomed and appreciated. All went well for some time until, in small and subtle ways, they began to challenge and undermine, the position of the Company Captain, who had as the Constitution demanded, been appointed by the Leaders Meeting of the Church.

Matters came to a head, just prior to what was the most important event in the B.B. year, the Annual Enrolment Service, when Officers and Boys make their vows and receive their new Membership cards. There had been major disagreements about how the Company should be organised. I met with the Officers a number of times, and it became obvious to me that attempts were being made to dislodge and replace the Company Captain; and I was having none of it. I had a final meeting with them on the Sunday afternoon, just a few hours before the Enrolment Service, and the matter remained unresolved. I told them that under the circumstances, I was not prepared to conduct the Service, and that it would have to be postponed. Many had been invited, especially the boy's parents. It was one of the most difficult decisions I ever had to make, and probably one of the most difficult Services I had to conduct. The Captain had met with the boys prior to the Service. I don't know what he said to them before sending them home. One half of the Church was full of parents and the normal congregation; the other half was empty, except for the Captain, who sat alone. I don't remember much of what I said, apart from expressing my sadness and affirming my support for the Captain. The other Officers left the Church, and I conducted the Enrolment Service a few weeks later.

The Circuit, meanwhile, was looking for ideas to raise funds. One of the smallest Churches in the Circuit was at Cross Gate, out in the countryside near Hilderstone. It was a very small, but lovely chapel with considerable grounds, and they offered to host a Circuit Garden Party; and I was asked to organise it! I called a meeting of representatives from all the Circuit Churches; I think there were 16 of them, in order to decide what produce or game they planned for their Church stall. This was important to prevent duplication. A major concern was to enable people to attend who had no access to private transport, public transport being practically none existent. I had already anticipated this, and had already arranged for a coach to be available at minimum cost, as I would be driving it. All I needed to do was to work out a route around the Circuit, do a trial run to determine timings, and circulate the details of pick up points and timings to the Churches. The weather was fine, lots of people attended, an encouraging amount of money was raised, and the event was deemed a great success; to be repeated the following year!

The Secretary of the Forces Board contacted me about an unexpected vacancy occurring for a Chaplain to serve in the RAF the following year, and invited me to attend a meeting of the Board for interview. I discussed this with my family and the Circuit Stewards, and went to London for the interview. There were three others being interviewed, and the position wasn't offered to me! Several months later, the same thing happened when a vacancy unexpectedly came up in the Royal Navy. The Secretary informed me that it was considered I was best suited to the Army, and that the next vacancy occurring in the Army would be offered to me without further interview; but that could be several years away.

My work for the Labour Party continued, and was set to become more significant. An Agent was being sought to work in the Constituency for our MP, Jack Ashley. This meant coordinating the work of the eight wards, and the task appealed to me. I was interviewed by the General Management Committee and offered the job, which carried a small remuneration, plus expenses.

I met with Jack and the Constituency Chairman, Sir Albert Bennett, and we discussed the state of the Party. They were a little concerned about one or two 'extremist' elements seeking to obtain positions in the management of the Party, which was something of which I was only vaguely aware. Jack held a regular 'surgery' for his constituents on Friday evenings in a room in Longton Town Hall, and I usually met with him and Pauline afterwards and, if time permitted, went for a drink and a chat. Jack invited me to visit the Houses Of Parliament, preferably on either a Tuesday or Thursday, so that I could be present for Prime Minister's Questions. I accepted this kind invitation, met Jack for lunch in the Member's Dining Room, and then took my seat in the Gallery of the House ready for what was then, one of the twice weekly 'confrontations' between The Prime Minister, Harold Wilson, and the Leader of the Opposition, Ted Heath. It was a very interesting experience, and there was no doubt in my mind that the Prime Minister certainly dominated the House, at least on that occasion!

One of the problems in the Constituency was the small number of members attending the Annual General Meeting, and I made it a priority to try to remedy this; as small attendance enabled official positions to be filled by people who were not necessarily representative of the Party, even though they and their supporters dominated the Meeting. Before the next AGM I made a point of visiting every Ward Meeting and urging them to attend what was a very important meeting. I was most gratified by the turn out, and very pleased when Officials were elected who more accurately reflected the convictions of the usually 'silent' majority!

A colleague, who was a Minister in a neighbouring Circuit, and an active member of the Labour Party, had decided to stand as a candidate in the forthcoming local elections. I was too busy to give him much help, but did manage a couple of evenings knocking on doors canvassing for him. The response was positive and encouraging. One man in particular gave me a lot to think about when he said, "I'll certainly vote for the Minister, it's great to have somebody standing for the Council, who isn't a railway man or a bloody bus driver"! He had nothing against either profession, but was making an important point, that Local Councillors couldn't possibly be truly representative, because in order to get time off to attend the many committees and fulfil their responsibilities, they would have to be wither self employed, trade union sponsored, or retired! My colleague won the seat with a large majority, and served the City well for a number of years. I was encouraged to consider standing as a candidate in my own Ward at a later date. To do this I had first to become an officially recognised Party Candidate, and this entailed being recognised and recommended by the Labour Group on the City Council. I was interviewed and my name added to the list of potential candidates.

A brutal civil war was being fought about this time in Nigeria, and our newspapers and television screens were constantly filled with heart breaking pictures of starving Biafran children. Most people in England had never seen anything like it before and the nation responded magnificently to the regular appeals for aid and finance. I was therefore very pleased when I was asked to host a Missionary Deputation to the Circuit by a Minister serving in Nigeria. Arrangements were made for the Missionary to visit Churches and senior Schools, and to stay with a number of Church members. I had the opportunity to have long conversations with him, and was most disturbed by the information he shared with us.

He claimed that the British public had been grossly misinformed about what was really happening in Nigeria. He was based on the island of Fernando Po, just off the coast of Nigeria, which was the operational base for relief supplies on their way to the mainland. Did we know, for example, that the civil war had been started when the Biafrans bombed the Nigerian Capital, Lagos? Did we know that the Biafrans had hired a well known Public Relations Company based in Switzerland, to 'sell' their case to the world: and that they had obviously made a very good job of doing so? And that it was some time before the Nigerian authorities realised what was happening, and began to publish their side of the story? Of course most people had no idea, and while they continued to supply aid to both sides, treated future reports with caution and suspicion. For the first time, and certainly on many occasions in the future, I understood the jibe directed at the media, and journalists in particular: 'Why spoil a good story for the sake of the truth'?

Early in 1970 I received a 'phone call from the Secretary of the Forces Board, informing me that a vacancy had come up for a Chaplain to serve with the Army, and would I be available to join the Royal Army Chaplains' Department at the beginning of July? I had a meeting with the Superintendent Minister and the Circuit Stewards, and they agreed to release me early from my engagement. It so happened that my replacement in the Circuit was serving as a School Chaplain, and would be free to join the Circuit in July. I informed Jack Ashley and the Constituency Labour Party, and they began to look for a replacement: at a special meeting of the General Management Committee, a replacement was found. As the Forces Board can only make recommendations, it was necessary for me to visit the Chaplains' Branch at the Ministry of Defence in London, and be interviewed by the Chaplain General, and Deputy Chaplain General. During the interview, I expressed my desire, especially as I was already trained, to serve with the Parachute Brigade. This request was noted, but as there were at the present time, no vacancies, I would be posted to Germany to serve with 2nd Battalion, The Royal Green Jackets, who were stationed in Munster.

In the meantime there was much to be done and many preparations to be made. Having served in the Army, I had a fair idea of what action I needed to take. Knowing that there was an Army unit near Litchfield, I telephoned the Quartermaster, told him I was about to join the Army as a Chaplain, and asked if he would be kind enough to send me some packing cases. Within a few days, an Army lorry arrived at the Manse, unloaded a pile of flat packed packing cases and a message to 'phone the Quartermaster when they were ready for collection. The cases were assembled using strong screws to secure the bottom, and a lesser number to secure the top once the cases had been filled. A large yellow square had to be painted on the top, and on one of the sides. My name, and the address of the Battalion in Germany, was then painted on the yellow squares in black paint. One evening when I was out at a Church meeting, my wife was hosting a sewing circle in the lounge of the Manse. When she came out to go into the kitchen to make some tea for the group, she was horrified to find that our dear little son, Simon, who was almost four years old, had been prowling around when he should have been asleep; found the paint and brushes, and decided to paint the staircase! When I arrived home I found a group of ladies doing their best to clean it off! It also occurred to me that I wasn't as physically fit as I had been when I left the Army in 1962, so I decided to go for a little jog for half an hour. After less than 15 minutes, I accepted that I really was out of condition, and would have to do some serious training before I put on a uniform again!

Having examined my wardrobe, it was apparent that the suits I possessed were a little past their best, and I would need new ones before putting in an appearance at the Officer's Mess of a distinguished Regiment! My Bank Manager was very understanding, and gave me an overdraft to cover the many new items I would require. As I was moving to Germany, I was entitled to buy a tax-free car, so I ordered a new Ford Cortina, and very unwisely as it turned out, asked for a left hand drive model. It seemed a good idea at the time, but my tour of duty turned out to be much shorter than anticipated!

Then a real bombshell disrupted my preparations. The Prime Minister, Harold Wilson, called a snap General Election! Within twenty four hours the person who had succeeded me as Jack's Agent, decided it was too much for him to handle; and I had Jack and Pauline on the doorstep, asking me to organise the Election Campaign! I tried to explain how much I had to do before leaving to join the Army, but they prevailed and I gave in. Organising a General Election campaign involved much more than a local Council election, as I was soon to discover. Jack and Pauline were very worried, as were all the other MPs in North Staffordshire, because the date of the Election was right in the middle of what was known locally as the 'Potters Holiday Fortnight'. This was the time when all the Pottery factories, and other major industries in the area closed down, and most people went away on their annual holidays. This meant that not only would many voters be away, but also many of the party activists, who would usually spend a lot of time and effort preparing for Election Day. Fortunately, the Party Chairman was going to be around, and he had been involved in many campaigns, and offered me sound advice.

There was so much to do, and very little time to do it! The first thing I had to do was to book space on major hoardings around the Constituency to put up Election notices. We adopted as our Election slogan, "LABOUR FOR JACK ASHLEY", which would appear on major hoardings, window posters, and 'day-glow' circles, which could be displayed anywhere. Jack was busy preparing his Election manifesto and address, which would be delivered to every house in the Constituency. A major problem was finding enough envelopes to put them in! The Election had been called so unexpectedly, all the usual suppliers of envelopes had been caught out and had no stock.

Every Constituency in the country was desperate to acquire envelopes. I eventually managed to track down a firm in Blackburn, Lancashire, which promised to supply me with the 40,000 envelopes I required, but they were unable to deliver them so I had to make arrangements to collect them. The people in the Wards had done a great job in gathering enough volunteers together, ready to address and deliver the literature. All they needed were the envelopes. I decided to go to Blackburn myself to collect them. To do this I hired a van, which, I was told, had a diesel engine. There was very little fuel in the tank, so I stopped at the first garage I came to and filled up.

2 miles down the road, the engine spluttered and died. I found a telephone (no mobile 'phones then) and called the hire firm, and they admitted I had been given the wrong information: the vehicle I had been given had a petrol engine! It took them about an hour to bring me a replacement van with a full tank of petrol. Fortunately in 1970, the roads weren't nearly as congested as they are now, and I managed to get to the factory in Blackburn before they closed! As soon as I got back, I toured the Constituency and delivered boxes of envelopes to all the Wards. In addition to addressing the envelopes, the helpers also had to fill in the carbonated pads we had used so successfully in the local elections.

The next thing to concentrate on was finance, and a special Bank Account had to be opened, as in a General Election, every penny has to be accounted for. I was amazed how many forms I, as the election agent, had to fill in during the next few weeks! Donations were received from many quarters, but as Jack was an MP sponsored by the General & Municipal Workers Union, they provided most of the funds needed to fight the Election. All donations, however large or small had to be declared, and receipts obtained for all money spent. Much had already been spent on advertising, van hire and petrol, envelopes and Election literature. Fees also had to be paid for the use of the premises used as the eight Ward Offices. Jack and Pauline toured the Constituency, speaking at meetings and knocking on doors. I did my share of that but had to take time out to pack some cases ready for shipment! My work as a coach driver had also been terminated.

I had been ordered to report to the Royal Army Chaplains' Department Depot, Bagshot Park, Bagshot, Surrey, on 6th July. I would be expected to spend about three weeks there, obtaining uniforms, attending courses in the area, and receiving general instructions on Army life, and how to function effectively as a Chaplain in a Military environment. I had filled in and dispatched the forms requesting a married quarter, and was informed that it would probably be a couple of months before a house became available for us. The Manse would have to be vacated so that my successor and his family could move in, and it was agreed that my wife and children should stay with my parents in Bradwell until they could join me in Germany. My new car had arrived and I was very pleased with it. Because of the amount of luggage I would need to take with me, I put a luggage rack on top. The new suits I had ordered, still 'made to measure' in 1970, were also ready and the final packing case had been filled.

I telephoned the Quartermaster in Litchfield, and he made arrangements to collect them, informing me that it would take about six weeks for them to arrive in Germany. As the holiday season was now well under way, I thought I had better book tickets on a Ferry to get to Germany. Having studied a map of Europe, I saw that there were many possible routes to Munster. Having been given a date when I would be finished at Bagshot, I booked tickets on an overnight car ferry from Harwich to Bremerhaven, which should allow me to arrive in Munster in time for lunch. I wrote and informed the Commanding Officer of 2 RGJ of my intentions.

Having made all possible preparations for the General Election, all that remained was to hope for fine weather on the day, and by all means possible, encourage people to come out and vote! The weather was fine and we worked none stop throughout the day until the very last minute when the Polling Stations closed. A loud speaker had been installed on the roof rack of my car, and as I toured the Constituency, calling regularly at all the Ward Offices to assess progress, I was able to call on people to come out and vote for Jack! We then went to scrutinise the votes being counted and to wait anxiously for the result.

In spite of so many people being away on holiday, Jack was returned to Westminster as our MP with a comfortable majority. There was a Celebration Party, and we were able to express our appreciation to those who had worked so hard to make the victory possible. There were still a number of forms to be completed, but I would have to take them to Bagshot with me and complete them there!

My Churches had arranged meetings to bid farewell to me and my family, and it was sad to have to leave so many people who had become good friends over the previous five years. We were given a number of beautiful gifts, one in particular is still being used today: a Royal Doulton Dinner Service, which was a gift from the people of Trentham.

When I finally departed, my car was packed to capacity, and had two large cases on the roof rack! On arrival at Bagshot, I was delighted to find the Deputy Warden, who would be responsible for the three Chaplains joining at that time, was Rev. Brian Dougall, whom I hadn't seen since leaving Jordan twelve years earlier. I was Commissioned into the Royal Army Chaplains' Department, on 7th July 1970 as a Chaplain to the Forces Fourth Class (Captain): and given a new Army Number; I was now 489267! The following day we were taken by Brian Dougall to a Military Tailors in Camberley to be measured up for uniforms. A generous Uniform Allowance had been paid into our bank accounts, and Brian ensured we spent every penny of it! There was a long list of items we were expected to buy: two uniforms, Mess Kit, shirts, overcoat, hats, rank badges, etc. Having left the Circuit, I had moved from being paid a quarter in advance, to being paid monthly in arrears! This was quite a gap and I was experiencing serious cash flow problems! The Military Tailors were quite used to this situation, and I had no problem in arranging to pay for my uniforms over a period of time. We were then taken to the Quartermaster's Department at the Royal Military Academy, Sandhurst, and issued with various items of Military clothing from boots to berets.

I had finally completed all the forms relating to the recent General Election; and so one evening I drove over to Jack's house in Epsom to obtain his signature on some of the forms, before posting them to the Electoral Registration Officer. Jack and Pauline thanked me for all my work on their and the Party's behalf, and wished me 'all the best' for my future career as a Chaplain in the Army. Thus ended another chapter in my life, and I drove back to Bagshot.

Bagshot Park belongs to the Crown, and had been used as the RAChD Depot since 1946, by kind permission of King George VI, who had been concerned that Army Chaplains had no Base or Depot to call their own! The grounds and gardens were extensive and beautifully maintained. The house itself was impressive, and the interior, which contained a Memorial Chapel and Museum, was much loved by generations of Chaplains. The panels in the corridors had been exquisitely carved by craftsmen from India; who had camped in the grounds whilst carrying out the work.

Brian Dougall had written an excellent handbook for the guidance of Chaplains, and many hours were spent going through it with him. It contained information about everything from writing official letters, to modes of dress for different occasions. It was a document I kept close at hand for many years. We were not required at weekends, so I went home, rising at 4.00am on Mondays to arrive back at Bagshot in time for breakfast. As part of our 'basic training', we attended an Army Methods of Instruction Course, at an Army Education centre at Beaconsfield; where we were introduced to a variety of audio/visual teaching aids, and required to give two presentations during the week. The tailor visited the House for the final fittings of our uniforms, and informed us they would all be ready for collection the following week. Having collected them, I repacked the car, now having three cases on the roof rack; thanked the Staff at Bagshot, and set off to catch the ferry to Germany, really looking forward to taking up my first appointment as a Battalion Chaplain.

PART II

HIGH FLYING

2ND BATTALION, THE ROYAL GREEN JACKETS, (2RGJ) AUGUST 1970 – MAY 1971

STATIONED IN MUNSTER, GERMANY.

The ferry from Harwich glided smoothly into its berth in the North German port of Bremmerhaven just as I finished a substantial Continental breakfast. Drivers were requested to return to their vehicles on the car deck and prepare to disembark. Returning to my car, I checked it over, paying particular attention to the heavily laden roof rack.

As I sat in my car, waiting for the bow doors to open, my mind flickered over the events of previous years, which had brought me to this time and place. I was about to begin not only a new chapter in my life, but a very different way of life as an Army Chaplain. I remembered my time working as a coal miner, and the narrow escape I had from serious injury or even death which had caused me to leave the industry; subsequently spending five years in the Army as a Regular soldier. I recalled my service with the Royal Artillery Regiment in the 16th Parachute Brigade; and I hoped that these experiences would help me as I strived to become an effective Chaplain. I thought of the hardships endured by my family, not only during the years of training for the Methodist Ministry, but also in my five years as a Circuit Minister. This had been on a large Council Housing Estate, where I had become embroiled in local politics; and had to supplement my income by driving a coach, and by teaching RE (Religious Education) in a local Secondary Modern School: not at the same time I hasten to add! In spite of the obvious difficulties of Service life, I was hoping that our quality of life would be enhanced, and that I would be able to make a significant contribution to the military community. Vehicles began to move and my reverie was over. As I drove off the ferry, I entered a different country and began a new life.

After passing through various checkpoints, I wound my way out of the docks and on to the road going south towards Bremen, where I would leave the single carriageway and join the Autobahn. Initially I drove slowly and very carefully, never having driven on the right hand side of the road before! It took longer than anticipated to reach the Autobahn, and when I did, I discovered that substantial sections of the Bremen ring road were in the process of being resurfaced, which slowed me down even more. Having passed the road works, I increased my speed and tried to make up for lost time. This was a mistake as there were still some very uneven parts of the carriageway waiting to be re-paired, as I discovered when I hit a very bumpy patch and felt something break on the luggage rack! I slowed down and pulled off the road at the next exit to check the damage. One of the metal rails had broken, which meant I had to re-pack the car in order to lighten the load on top. Having informed the Commanding Officer of my ETA (estimated time of arrival), I now resigned myself to the fact that I was going to be late and carried on, driving as fast as I dared, watching carefully for the road signs to Munster. I had been given accurate directions from the Autobahn to Oxford Barracks, home of 2RGJ, and on arrival I called at the Guardroom to ask for directions to the Officer's Mess.

Having parked the car, I went into the Mess and was warmly greeted by the Commanding Officer who, when I apologised for my late arrival, grinned broadly and said, "I thought you were being a bit optimistic"! He then lead me into the Mess, where almost every officer in the Battalion had assembled to welcome me, which was a bit overwhelming, and certainly something I never experienced again in any of my subsequent postings.

After an excellent lunch, which was a foretaste of the very high standard of catering in 2RGJ, members of the Mess staff helped me to unload the car and carry the contents up a couple of flights of stairs, to the room which would be my home for the next few months until a house became available, and my family able to join me. I unpacked only what was necessary before going downstairs for Dinner.

The following morning I had a meeting with the Commanding Officer, a devout Roman Catholic, who assured me that his door would always be open to me. I then toured the building and introduced myself to the staff of Battal-ion Headquarters. The Quartermaster (QM) showed me a small room which was to be my office, and arranged for me to meet with a member of his staff and the out going Chaplain, to inspect and sign for the Church and its con-tents! Oxford Barracks had originally been built to accommodate units of the German Army, as had all the other barracks in the Garrison. The Church was located right at the top of one of the large accommodation blocks: in fact it looked just like a converted attic! As most Chaplains belonged to the Church of England, the Church was furnished and equipped to meet their needs and expectations. Having checked and counted so many unfamiliar items, I signed the inventory and decided that most items would have to be stored away dur-ing my tenure, as I certainly wouldn't be using or displaying them!

The one thing I was really going to miss was the Methodist Hymn Book. Hymns Ancient & Modern was a very poor substitute, and choosing appropriate hymns every Sunday turned out to be quite a chore, especially as I had to lead the singing! My organist was a young Lieutenant, and the Treasurer a Royal Signals officer attached to 2RGJ. As there were no maintenance costs, all Church collections were donated to various charities. Instructions issued by the Chaplain General, specified charities he expected to be supported, but there was a degree of flexibility. When I examined the contents of the office I found a considerable number of files, and a cursory look was enough to convince me that I certainly hadn't escaped from paperwork by joining the Army!

2RGJ was part of 4th Guards Armoured Brigade, whose headquarters were a few miles away on the other side of the City. The Senior Chaplain came to welcome me and to give me useful information about the Garrison. There were five Chaplains including a Roman Catholic Priest, three Protestant Churches, and a Chapel in the British Military Hospital (BMH). The Senior Chaplain (SCF) was the Hospital Chaplain, but all Chaplains were expected to take turns in conducting Services in the Chapel, which were always held early on Sunday mornings to enable Chaplains to get back to their own Churches in time for the Morning Service.

I was issued with two vehicles, a Mini for use around the Garrison on official business, and a Land Rover for use on Military Exercises. Both vehicles would be held and maintained by 2RGJ. However, before using either vehicle, or obtaining concessionary Petrol Coupons for my own car, I had to obtain a BFG (British Forces in Germany) driving licence. This meant studying the German Highway Code and passing the 'tick test', having been given a number of alternatives for action in specific situations. I discovered the most important thing about driving in Germany is 'the Rule of the Right'. Roads where a driver has the right of way are clearly marked at regular intervals. In all other situations a driver must give way to traffic coming from the right. Unlike British Traffic laws, in Germany there are no 'grey' areas: a driver is either in the right, or in the wrong! I once heard a Services Liaison Officer briefing a crowd of new arrivals say, "Make no mistake about it, a German driver will die happy if his gravestone can be engraved with the words, "He Had The Right Of Way". I passed the 'tick test' and was issued with a BFG Licence, and a card on which Petrol Coupons issued would be recorded. These coupons could only be used at BP petrol stations, and at ESSO stations on the Autobahn. A map was available showing the location of all stations in Germany. All that remained was to obtain new BFG number plates for my car, and ensure I had a GB sticker, a First Aid Kit and Warning Triangle in the vehicle.

I was informed that an important aspect of serving with the Army in Germany was to be always ready for quick deployment should there be an imminent threat from the East. These drills were regularly practised under the code name 'Quick Train,' and could be initiated by the CO, who would expect to see his Battalion formed up, and ready to move to their deployment areas within two hours. Should the 'call out' be during the night, Buglers would tour the married quarter 'patches', and certain soldiers living there were tasked to make sure everyone heard, and made their way into the Barracks as soon as possible. On occasions it could be the Brigade, the Division, the Corps, or even a NATO Exercise. Every soldier had to have his equipment ready at all times, and all tracked and 'soft skinned' vehicles always maintained and fuelled. As the Padre, I would deploy with the Doctor and the RAP (Regimental Aid Post).

The next few days were spent finding my way around and getting ready for another move. The Battalion were preparing to travel to a place called Larzac in the south of France for a Battle Group Exercise. In addition to the Battalion, there would be a Squadron of tanks from the Blues and Royals, and other supporting units. I should point out that by this time, all units in Germany were mechanised, and 2RGJ was a mechanised Infantry Battalion equipped with dozens of APCc (Armoured Personnel Carriers), which were tracked vehicles weighing about sixteen tons. My Land Rover was to be taken down to Larzac with the road party, and I would be travelling with the majority of the Battalion, overnight by train. Before departing for France I conducted my first Sunday Service. There was a good congregation, but how many of them were regular worshippers, and how many had come to see what the new Padre was like remained to be seen! Talking to many of them afterwards, I detected that they had enjoyed the Service, but were surprised how bare the Church appeared without all the Anglican seasonal colours. I hoped they would soon get used to it. Some obviously missed the Anglican liturgy, but others with a Free Church background were glad of the change. I accepted the fact that I was responsible for ministering to all denominations except Roman Catholics, and planned a variety of Services so as to please all the people some of the time. I knew that Anglican Chaplains were bound by Canon Law to conduct specific Services: as a Methodist I had the freedom to 'ring the changes' and intended to use it.

When the train departed for France, I found myself sharing a compartment with two other Officers. One was a young Second Lieutenant, and the other a Captain. The Captain had been a Regimental Sergeant Major with another RGJ Battalion, achieved a Commission, and was now serving as second-in-command of a Rifle Company. He was an unforgettable character, and we were to get to know each other very well during the next two years. His soldiers referred to him either as 'the cockney Captain', or as 'Captain Hurricane'. We ate the 'haversack rations' provided for our evening meal and chatted away happily until it was time to try and get some sleep. The Captain said to the young 2/Lt, "I am a Captain, and I am sleeping here". He pointed to one of the long seats in the compartment. "The Padre is a Captain, and he is sleeping there". He pointed to the other long seat. "You are a Wart, and you will sleep out there in the corridor". Before I had time to say a word, the young man had disappeared! Apparently, in this particular part of the Army, young Officers were often referred to in this manner! It was a very noisy, stop/start sort of journey, and I doubt whether anyone managed to get much sleep. When we arrived at the terminus, lorries were waiting to take us to the French Army camp, which was to be our base while we trained in the area. There was a little village a few hundred yards down the road, but the nearest town was miles away.

I thought this situation would be an ideal opportunity for me to get to know the Battalion, and when I saw the Training Schedule, worked out a programme that would enable me to spend some time with each of the Rifle Companies. Having sought approval from Battalion HQ, I sent a Memo around the Battalion entitled, "The Padre's Progress'. My Land Rover had arrived and I had a map of the training area, so I was free to move around without inconveniencing anyone. There was however, one exception. An Adventure Training camp had been established by a lakeside many miles away, and it was agreed that I could visit that location by helicopter! I had never flown in a helicopter before, so I decided to leave that particular treat until I had seen the soldiers at work before watching them play. Having been a Gunner in my previous service, it was interesting to see how the Infantry operated 'in the field'.

Early one morning I joined a Company on a march across country. When we came to a river I looked for a bridge, and as there was no bridge in sight, asked a Corporal how we were going to get across the river. He looked at me and grinned. "Just follow me Padre", he said, as he waded into the river, which came up to his waist!

Of course I followed, trying hard not to loose my balance and my dignity as my feet negotiated their way around the many small, submerged rocks. It took another two hours marching before my boots stopped squelching and I dried out! We arrived back at the Company location and enjoyed a good evening meal. Food always seems to taste exceptionally good after a hard day in the open air! It was a warm, pleasant evening, and a group of us sat around talking and swapping jokes. The CSM (Company Sergeant Major) was quite a comedian and seemed to have an inexhaustible supply of funny stories and anecdotes. In addition to other sources, my father had always kept me well supplied with jokes from the building sites. (He had never really accepted the fact that he had fathered a Clergyman!) Some of these were repeatable, and I was able to make my contribution to the evenings entertainment. There was much enjoyment and laughter until after midnight, when a soldier came with a message from the Company Commander: "Tell the Sergeant Major and the Padre to go to bed, so we can all get some sleep!"

Having visited the Rifle Companies, I accepted an invitation from the Bandmaster to join them on a 'Community Relations' engagement to play in the town square at Rochefort, famous for its cheese. I hadn't heard the Band play before, and I was most impressed by their professionalism. As well as playing the kind of music expected from a Military Band, they included a number of stirring pieces associated only with the Light Division, which is made up of The Royal Green Jackets, and the Light Infantry. I thoroughly enjoyed the performance, as did the townspeople, who wined and dined us royally afterwards! It was a very happy bunch that returned to Larzac in time for bed! So began what turned out to be a very good relationship with the Band, and especially the Bandmaster, who was a Yorkshireman, and had begun his Army career as a member of the Kings Own Yorkshire Light Infantry.

The helicopter, which took me up to the lakeside camp, was a Sioux. It was very small and looked like a big bubble with two seats inside! The pilot was a young Sergeant in the Army Air Corps. He carried out his pre-flight checks, made sure I was comfortable and properly strapped in, gave me a head set so we could talk to each other, and lifted off. The weather was lovely with good visibility, and from 5,000 feet the views were spectacular. I was almost sorry when we arrived at the lakeside camp, where we spent two hours talking to the men there and having some refreshments. On the way back I said to the pilot, "What happens if you have an engine failure in one of these things?" He smiled and said, "I'll show you", leaned forward and turned it off! The machine began to slowly descend, spinning gently: it reminded me of a sycamore leaf. I tried not to appear concerned, but to reassure me the pilot said, "This is a routine drill, when we get near to the ground, I look for a suitable place for a gentle bump down". However, before we got anywhere near the ground, he restarted the engine and we arrived back in camp in a conventional manner!

The CO had suggested that we should have a Church Service in the open air for the whole Battle Group on the Sunday before we returned to Munster. I met with the Bandmaster to see what music the Band had brought with them, and together we chose a few popular hymns. I drafted out an Order of Service, which included the words of the hymns we had chosen, and asked the Chief Clerk to produce six hundred copies: in the event, some had to share as I had neglected to include the Blues and Royals! As this would be my first Service with the whole Battalion, it was vital that it went well. I felt very keenly that I was 'on trial', and spent a considerable amount of time preparing what was for me, a short, but memorable sermon. As any public speaker will know, it's much more difficult to produce a short talk than a long one! It was a fine Sunday morning, and over eight hundred soldiers paraded for the Service. Encouraged by the Bandmaster they sang the hymns well, and my sermon, in which the serious message was interspersed with humorous anecdotes, was well received. Judging by the comments I received after the Service and in the Mess over lunch, I had got off to a good start, and the Battalion were happy with their new Chaplain! Relieved and encouraged, I returned to Munster in good heart.

EXERCISE 'PARSONS' PLEASURE'

Every year in Germany, all the Chaplains took part in an Exercise organised and run by a military unit, in consultation with the Assistant Chaplain General (ACG). This was designed to train and practice Chaplains in basic military skills. These included First Aid, Nuclear, Biological, & Chemical (NBC) drills, Tactical movement using maps and compass, driving across country using four wheel drive, basic fault-finding and maintenance of the Land Rover, and camouflage. Chaplains were expected to assemble at the designated base camp, with their Land Rovers fully equipped with tools, jerrycans for petrol and water, camouflage nets and poles. In addition they were required to take all their personal equipment, which by now, thankfully included a sleeping bag, which was a great improvement on the thin, green lightweight blanket and groundsheet I remembered from my previous service! Field Communion sets, which had been issued to us at Bagshot in rather large, heavy boxes, which had been designed to serve as portable Altars when necessary, also had to be taken and inspected.

Apart from the use of weapons, Chaplains are expected to be as physically fit and professional in basic military skills, as the soldiers they were serving with. 'Parsons' Pleasure' was organised to ensure these standards were met. Coming back from France, I had less than a week to prepare myself, and my equipment for this. I felt I was really being thrown in at the deep end! The Exercise was challenging and useful, and I particularly enjoyed the opportunity to meet all the other Chaplains. One morning I was chosen to lead Morning Prayers in a forest glade. This I did in typical Methodist extemporary fashion, much to the delight of other Free Church Chaplains, and the bewilderment of those whose devotional lives were tied to the Book of Common Prayer or Missal!

After handing in my equipment and dealing with all the post, which had accumulated during my absence, I decided it was time to find my way around the Garrison. Using my Mini, I visited all the other Barracks, the Military Hospital, and discovered where the Churches were located. Then I needed to find out where all the married soldiers lived: the Army called them 'quarter patches'. The Battalion had more than three hundred married soldiers, and they were scattered in 'patches' all over the Garrison.

Munster is a beautiful city, which has been rebuilt and accurately restored after the War using the original plans. It is a strongly Roman Catholic area, and I was told that many people opposed Hitler during his rise to power. When he achieved absolute power, he surrounded the City with military barracks, and is reputed to have said: "When I have conquered Europe, I will come back and conquer Munster". Towards the end of the War, the German Garrison was composed of elite troops. The City was 'carpet bombed' by the Allies and almost totally destroyed. Displayed in the entrance to the Cathedral are a number of photographs showing the devastation caused by the bombing. The City is 'twinned' with Coventry.

While I was living in the Mess I used to play table tennis with the young officer who was also my Church organist. One day he asked me if I played squash, and when I said no, he offered to teach me. I thought I was reasonably fit, but after fifteen minutes on the squash court I was completely exhausted! However I continued to play at regular intervals, and gradually built up my stamina. I soon realised that it was important to find a partner who was about the same standard, or just a little better. I began to play regularly with one of the Sergeant Majors; he hadn't been playing the game long, and we often played together during my time with 2RGJ. As my game improved I was able to add to my list of partners, and found it to be an enjoyable and valuable form of exercise.

There was still no sign of a married quarter for me, so I decided to fly home for a long weekend. I booked a flight from Dusseldorf to Manchester and sought advice on the best way to get to the airport. I was advised to, "just drive down the Autobahn and look for the signs". I drove a considerable distance and saw no signs! I left the road and studied the map, which was something I should have done before setting out! The 'helpful' chap had neglected to tell me the point at which I had to change Autobahns! By this time I was well south of Dusseldorf and the most direct way to the airport was to drive to and through the City. This I did, keeping an anxious eye on the clock and following the airport signs. When I finally arrived it was well past the check in time. I parked the car and sprinted into the departure area. The last call for the flight has been made, but someone kindly shouted out, "He's got a ticket, open the gate", and they did!

I gave the family a 'first impressions' account of our new home, and promised that it wouldn't be long before I returned to collect them. I knew there were people working behind the scenes on my behalf. Only a couple of weeks later I was offered temporary accommodation in a flat just two miles from the Barracks in a German village. It was a lovely flat in a small block and the other occupants were all from the Battalion. I was assured it would only be for about a month until a house became available, so I accepted the offer and made arrangements to go home to collect my family. The Army would have flown them out, but that would have taken a little time to organise. Our packing cases had arrived safely, and were in the Quartermaster's Store. All German houses and flats have cellars, so I arranged for them to be delivered and deposited in the cellar, where I unscrewed the lids ready to take out just the things we would need until the next move. Over the next sixteen years, during which we lived in thirteen houses, I was to become quite an expert on packing and unpacking!

I booked a passage from Zeebrugger to Dover, and travelled overnight to catch the early morning ferry. This time I studied the map in great detail before setting off! I was about half way between Dover and London on the M2, when a stone thrown up by a passing vehicle shattered my windscreen! There were small pieces of glass everywhere, and it was quite an unnerving experience. I drover slowly and carefully to the next service station and contacted the AA.

Within a few minutes they had contacted a garage in a nearby village, and they said they would be able to fit a new windscreen straight away. I drove to the garage, had a meal in a local café, and was on my way again within two hours. It was not an experience I would care to repeat! The rest of the trip was thankfully uneventful and we all arrived safely back in Munster the following day.

There was a Primary School and Play Group in Oxford Barracks, and as I had already made sure there were places available for the children, they were able to start straight away. My wife had not yet learned to drive, so while we lived in the flat I had to arrange to transport the children to school, and take my wife shopping. When we moved into a house a few weeks later, both school and NAAFI (Navy, Army, & Air Force Institute) shop were within walking distance. I was surprised and pleased, when I found that one of my new neighbours was someone I had known in Aldershot years before. Then he had been a Corporal in 23rd Parachute Field Ambulance: now he was a Captain working in the Military Hospital. Our wives became good friends, which was an added bonus.

It was now autumn, and there were so many large trees in the Barracks, it reminded me of my time at Cliff College! For several weeks it seemed that every available soldier was busy sweeping up piles of leaves. The Battalion had been in Oxford Barracks for almost four years, and they were quite used to the routine, which, from comments passed, didn't make the task any the less disagreeable.

One night I was called to the Maternity Ward in the Military Hospital. Apparently I was the only Chaplain they had been able to contact. A young wife, whose husband was serving with the Army Air Corps, had prematurely given birth to twins. They had been born six weeks early and weighed just over two pounds each. I was asked to baptise them, just in case they didn't survive. I discovered this to be common practice in the Army, and was known

127

as 'emergency' baptism. Theologically, I was opposed to the whole idea, but it wasn't possible to discuss theology with distraught parents at 3.am, so I baptised the twins, who both happily survived, and completed the necessary documentation. Had the staff been unable to contact a Chaplain, then one of the nurses would have baptised the babies. Providing water was used and the babies baptised in the Name of the Father, the Son, and the Holy Spirit; the baptism would have been considered valid by all Christian denominations and could not be repeated.

Parents would often request a Church Service afterwards so they could celebrate the event with family and friends. They were usually puzzled when I agreed to conduct a Service where they could give thanks, offer prayers, and make their vows; but not baptise the baby or babies again. Away from the anxiety and stress in the Maternity Ward, it was usually possible to reason with the parents. Baptism is in no way to be regarded as a kind of insurance policy against a premature or sick baby dying. If we believe in a God of Love, how could He possibly discriminate against a newborn child?

I had never come across this kind of situation before, but it was to occur several times in the years ahead. It was usually, but not always, initiated by nursing staff who were Roman Catholics.

Formal Dinner Nights were a regular feature of life in the Mess. The CO and other Officers often used these occasions to entertain guests or return hospitality to those who had entertained them. They were grand evenings with the Mess Silver on display and always a first class menu. The Band would play before and during the meal, and after playing the Regimental/ Corps Marches of the guests, they concluded by playing the Regimental March of the Royal Green Jackets. After a short break the Band would usually offer a little light entertainment. As the Padre, I would always be asked by the CO to say 'Grace' before the meal commenced. One evening, being very much aware of the sumptuous meal before us, I prayed particularly for the starving and those in great need. Afterwards, one of the Senior Officers said, "That was a very sombre Grace, Padre". I think the point he was making, was that people were being constantly bombarded by the media, and from the pulpit on these matters, and that something a little lighter would be more appropriate and appreciated. I took the point, and on the next Dinner Night offered the following Grace:-

We thank Thee, Lord, before we dine,

For food, and comradeship, and laughter.

So may we feast and drink good wine,

And still rejoice the morning after.

That was well received, and entered into a large book kept in the Mess, known as 'The Lie Book' (why is was so called I never discovered). It was a volume containing snippets about people and events over many years, and Members and guests could frequently be seen browsing through it. The problem for me now, was that I was expected to produce an appropriate Grace on every occasion! This was a practice carried on, not just with 2RGJ, but with every unit I served with for the next sixteen years: it was a treadmill, which was impossible to either stop or get off!

At a subsequent Dinner Night I learned a very important lesson. The Warrant Officers had all been invited to the Mess, and I found myself sitting next to the Bandmaster, who was on my left. It was a most enjoyable evening and we found lots to talk about. As the evening progressed, I was completely unaware of the hand that kept reaching over my right shoulder and topping up my glass of red wine. Being engrossed in conversation, I was continually reaching out and drinking from my wine glass. At the conclusion of the Meal, it was time to 'pass the port' as the conversation continued. Then it was brandy and coffee. When the evening was over, I hadn't a clue how much I had drunk, but as we left the Mess, I knew I was in no fit state to drive! The Bandmaster lived in a house in the Barracks, and my home was a few hundred yards outside the rear of the Barracks.

I parted company with the Bandmaster about fifty yards from his door and made my way home, arriving at about 1.30a.m. When I awoke I had the most awful hangover, I thought I was going to die. After a couple of hours, I hoped I was going to die! Then my wife, who showed me no sympathy whatsoever, insisted that we go to Munster, as she wanted to visit the Market. As we made our way through the crowds, my head still felt as though a Corps of Drums was practising for a Military Tattoo, when we met the Bandmaster and his wife. She berated me saying, "Padre, what were you doing keeping my husband out until 4.a.m. this morning?" I replied, "I left your husband about 1.a.m. and I honestly have no idea what happened to him after that"! Thereafter, I always kept a watchful eye on who was putting what into my glass!

My wife found the social life very difficult. In fact it was a real culture shock and she didn't enjoy it at all. On the first Ladies Guest Night she was seated between two Officers. One asked, "Do you ride?". "No I don't", she replied. "Then do you sail", he asked. Again she replied in the negative, and he didn't speak to her again! I have to say that wasn't typical, but thereafter I had to break with convention, and prevail upon certain Officers to ensure that in future, my wife was seated next to people she felt comfortable with. This was something that continued throughout my career and I usually had to apply a 'three line whip' to get her into the Officers' Mess. She was prepared to go to the Mess for the occasional Curry Lunch, and more than happy to attend functions in the Sergeants Mess!

One day the CO sent for me, asked me to sit down, and said, "Peter, the Battalion has been ordered to move to Northern Ireland next year, and we would very much like you to come with us. It will be for two years and of course our families will be coming with us". I replied that I would be delighted to go with the Battalion, but in the first instance the decision wasn't mine to make: the Chaplains' Department at The Ministry of Defence would have to authorise such a move. I would also have to discuss the matter with my wife, who was only just beginning to settle down.

The following morning I went to see my Senior Chaplain, who said he would pass the request up the chain of command. It got as far as the ACG at Corps HQ who said, "No, Padre Bayley has to stay in Munster and be the Chaplain to the incoming Battalion". I reported back to the CO, who snorted, "I haven't even started yet. Next week I'm going to a meeting in London and I'll see what can be arranged". I don't know what meeting he attended, or to whom he spoke, but within a week I was informed that I would be going to Northern Ireland with 2RGJ! In spite of the constant flow of bad news coming out of Northern Ireland, my wife confessed that she wasn't enjoying life in Munster, and would be more than happy to go with the Battalion. We also discussed the possibility of having another baby! She said, "You know I've always wanted three children, but we couldn't possibly afford it before. Now we are better off financially, and you won't be around as much as I would like, so?" What could I do but agree: I was more than happy at the prospect. A couple of months later, she happily informed me that she was pregnant. The new baby would be born in Northern Ireland.

The move to Northern Ireland was to take place in May 1971, but there was much to do before then. After four years in Munster there were lots of 'farewells' to be organised, and soldiers had to undergo special training to prepare them for their new role. I attended a meeting when many of these matters were discussed. Someone suggested the possibility of a Battalion Concert/Review/Show, to be held in the large Gymnasium, which would accommodate the Battalion and it's families. Most people thought this was an excellent idea, and I volunteered to organise it! The CO looked at me, and said with just a note of concern in his voice, "Are you sure you can do this Padre?" I assured him I had organised such events before, and he told me to go ahead. When I had consulted the Adjutant about dates for the Concert and planning meeting I sent a letter to all the Rifle Companies, he Officers and Sergeants Messes, the Wives Cub: and the Bandmaster and the Bugle Major. Each agreed to produce a contribution for the Concert, and a couple of rehearsals were planned so that a programme could be agreed. The Sergeant Major with the reputation for being a bit of a comedian agreed to be the Master of Ceremonies! There was plenty of time for everyone to prepare their contributions so I was happy to leave them to it, confident they would all produce something acceptable by the time we met again. I met with the Band to practice a few solos and prepared a couple of monologues.

All the Garrison Chaplains were invited to attend a special service in the Cathedral, when the Lutheran Bishop of Westphalia would be speaking about his recent visit to Ethiopia. More than sixty other Clergymen from many different Christian denominations attended the Service, and although my very basic command of the German language meant I was unable to follow most of his sermon, a colleague gave me the a short summary. After the Service, we were invited to join the other Clergy for refreshments in an adjacent building. We found ourselves sitting at a table with a dozen or so Germans, whose command of the English Language put most of us to shame! There were ample quantities of food and wine, and it wasn't long before conversation was flowing freely. Our hosts were very interested when they discovered that one of my colleagues was an Australian, and came from the place where Captain Cook had first landed. They though it a fascinating coincidence that another colleague came from the place in Yorkshire where Captain Cook had been born. After a lull in the conversation, someone asked me where I came from, and I said, "I come from Stoke-on-Trent". There was a pause, and then someone asked if there was anyone famous they should know who came from Stoke-on-Trent. Well, I could have said "Josiah Wedgewood", but a little gremlin whispered in my ear, 'say Reginald Mitchell'; so I did. They looked puzzled. "What was he famous for?" They asked. "He was the man who designed the 'Spitfire' I replied. They smiled politely and changed the subject! Afterwards I realised that perhaps I'd been a bit insensitive, and regretted what I'd said.

On the evening of the Concert, the Gymnasium was packed to capacity. Every group and individual taking part had made an effort and performed well. As always on these occasions, the success was due, not just to the performance, but who were performing! Many people, including some senior figures, were seen in a new light after the event. The Band made a significant contribution, not least in the way they presented themselves. The CO's nickname amongst the soldiers was 'Egg on Legs'. When the curtains were opened, the Band had on their music stands, not the usual Regimental Colours and Badge, but a piece on material on which had been painted a large Yellow Egg on little Red Legs! The CO was sitting in the front row with his wife, and laughed uproariously. I will never forget The Bugle Major, a magnificent figure of a man who led the Band on Parade, now dressed as a woman, with ribbons tied to his enormous moustache, singing 'The Marrow Song'!

One evening I was sitting in the lounge at home reading. My wife was upstairs in the bathroom when I heard her cry out. I rushed upstairs to see what was wrong, and was horrified when she cried that she thought she was losing the baby. My neighbour was a doctor at the Hospital, and fortunately he was at home. He came straight away and confirmed my wife's fears. She was immediately rushed to Hospital, where she remained for the next two weeks. The baby was saved, and my wife was instructed to 'take things easy' for a while. The problem now, was that the house had to be thoroughly cleaned and packed up for our move to Northern Ireland; and there was no way she could possibly be involved in that process. Arrangements were made for her and the children to stay with my parents until the move was completed, when I would collect them and take them to our new home. I paid two Sergeant's wives we were friendly with to clean the house, while I filled all the packing cases again! As the whole Battalion was moving, all freight, including that belonging to families was loaded into huge containers, and as everyone was having three weeks leave, would be in our new location before we were.

There was just one thing left to do. I had a left hand drive car, which was just a year old, and I didn't want to take it to Northern Ireland. I managed to come to an arrangement with a young Captain, who was a member of the 'advance party' for the Battalion relieving 2RGJ. He had a 1.6 Triumph Vitesse which was five years old, but with low mileage and in beautiful condition. We agreed to do a swap, with him giving me some money to make up the difference! It wasn't an ideal family car, but with a luggage rack on top, served us well for the next two years. It was though, an ideal car for the many country roads I travelled in Northern Ireland. We paid our farewells to Munster with a Battalion Parade. Local dignitaries, both military and civilian were invited, together with several Senior Officers from The Royal Green Jackets. When it was all over, I packed up my little car and headed for home.

NORTHERN IRELAND – MAY 1971 – OCTOBER 1972

I decided to report to our new base early, so that I could sort out our new married quarter, and hopefully the packing cases, before returning to collect the family. I travelled to Northern Ireland for the first and only time, from Liverpool to Belfast. On all subsequent occasions I used the ferry from Stranraer in Scotland to Larne, just north of Belfast. It was a much longer drive, but the sea crossing was only two hours!

The Battalion's new home was in Shackleton Barracks, which had until very recently been an RAF Station: in fact there were still a few RAF personnel there in the process of handing over the Station to the Army. Because of the mounting problems in the Province, the Army Garrisons were being strengthened. Now, instead of the usual type of Barracks, the Battalion had a large airfield with loads of space and an excessive amount of accommodation. It was located on the coast of Loch Foyle by a little village called Ballykelly, about half way between Londonderry and Coleraine: both being about fifteen miles away. The nearest little town was Limavady, which was four miles away. The railway line between Londonderry and Coleraine ran across the bottom of the airfield which, when we arrived was populated by dozens of large arctic hares the size of small dogs!

There was more than enough accommodation for the Battalion's families. In fact, over a hundred houses were occupied by families belonging to another Battalion stationed in Londonderry. There were also extra Officers quarters, some of which had been unoccupied for months, as was apparent from the state of the gardens! I had been allocated one such property, and it was to take months before the jungle was tamed! The inside of the house wasn't too bad and could soon be tidied up. From the kitchen window there was a lovely view across Loch Foyle to the mountains of Donegall, which are in the Irish Republic. There were some fabulous sunsets, that is, when it wasn't raining: and when it did rain, it rained horizontally! I arranged for our packing cases to be delivered, put them in the garage, and went home to collect the family.

They were pleased with the house and it's location, even though it would take some time to bring it up to standard. The children were particularly anxious to see their new school in the village. A few months earlier, the Headmaster had visited Munster and given us lots of information. We had heard that the standard of education in the Province was high, and we were not disappointed. I was delighted when Captain 'Hurricane' and his family moved in as our next-door neighbours. They were a 'down to earth' family and we got on well with them.

The Battalion was now part of 8th Infantry Brigade, with its Headquarters in Ebrington Barracks, Londonderry, which had originally been built as a base for the Royal Navy.

The Senior Chaplain was based there, and as his name was Bailey, it caused a little confusion when I arrived! The Battalion was now made up of four Rifle Companies, having added a Company from the temporarily disbanded 3 RGJ. One Company was based in Londonderry, one Company deployed to a number of towns and villages in Londonderry County, one Company on 30 minutes standby to reinforce any Company needing help should unforeseen trouble arise: for example, spontaneous rioting; and the fourth Company remained behind in Ballykelly engaged on local duties in camp and patrolling the areas where the families were living. They spent three to four week in each location before exchanging duties with another Company. Periodically the Battalion exchanged roles with the Londonderry Battalion, and assumed responsibility for the City. These heavy and continuous responsibilities meant that married soldiers rarely spent any time with their families. We now had a first class Families Officer, who had been a Superintendent Clerk and knew how to cope with most domestic situations. In the main married quarters 'patch' there was a small NAAFI Shop, and an excellent Families Club. This was open every day, and also used to stage special events. For example, one evening a week was 'BINGO' night, and on occasions I became a proficient 'caller', having picked up the 'jargon' when accompanying my parents to the Working Mans Club in Bradwell!

There were two Churches in Shackleton Barracks. One was an old stone, musty building, at the bottom end on the camp, i.e. towards the Loch, which served as the Roman Catholic Church. The Brigade Roman Catholic Chaplain would say Mass there every week, usually on Saturday evenings. The other Church was and old wooden building at the top end of the camp, which had been emptied of its contents when the RAF moved out! I arranged with the RC Chaplain to use his Church for a few weeks until I could make my own Church fit to be used. A few miles along the coast at Magilligan Point was a Training Camp, used by the Territorial Army and the Army Cadet Force. I heard that this Camp was in the process of being closed down: in fact in a couple of months it was to be turned into an Internment Camp.

I learned that the Camp contained a fully furnished Church, although it was not in good condition. I went to the Camp, inspected the Church, and found many items that could be very useful to me in Ballykelly. I telephoned the Senior Chaplain at HQ Northern Ireland in Lisburn, and asked if I could remove anything useful before the Camp closed down. He agreed, so I obtained the use of a four-ton truck, and with the help of a couple of soldiers, moved most of the contents to my Church in Ballykelly. Within a week or so, the Church and its new furnishings had been given a good cleaning and I began to hold Services there. There was a useful hall attached to the Church, which was soon serving as a venue for a Playgroup, the Sunday School, and also used as a vestry.

Because of the recent significant increase in the size of the Military forces in the Province, there were not enough civilian vehicles available for all Chaplains to be issued with cars. Due to the security situation, Chaplains would always wear civilian clothes and a clerical collar, and never drive around in Military vehicles! It was to be almost a year before I was eventually issued with an official vehicle, which was a light blue Ford Escort Estate. In the meantime I used my own car to travel on duty around the Province, for which I was paid a generous mileage allowance! My soldiers were stationed in several strategic locations around Country Londonderry, sometimes being accommodated either in or alongside Royal Ulster Constabulary Stations. It became my practice to visit each location at least weekly, and more often as events dictated. One of the little jobs I found myself increasingly doing, was shopping for the soldiers, who were unable to get to the shops. Wearing my clerical collar and civilian clothes, I was able to visit the shops in the City centre with my shopping list and buy Birthday Cards, Anniversary Cards, and any other items a soldier might need.

The nearest Hospital was the Altnagelvin in the Waterside (mainly Protestant) district of Londonderry. In addition to serving the people of the City, the Hospital also treated soldiers and their families. The nearest Military Hospital was at Musgrave Park near Belfast, with the more serious casualties being treated at the Royal Victoria Hospital in Belfast. After emergency treatment and stabilisation, soldiers were often sent back to Hospitals in England until they were hopefully fit enough to return to the Battalion.

My first visit to Londonderry was quite an 'eye opener'. Since learning of our posting, I attended a number of briefings and information meetings about the current activities of the Civil Rights Movement and the methods and aims of the IRA; and something of the historical background. I paid particular attention to television and newspaper coverage of events there.

I remember well standing on the walls of the old City, overlooking the infamous Bogside and Creggan Estates; and being most surprised to see how normal and comparatively modern everything seemed! The Estates reminded me of Bradwell, where I had been brought up, and of Blurton, where I had been a Minister for five years. The houses looked to be in good repair, a large modern Roman Catholic Church dominated the scene, as did the Church of Ireland Cathedral situated within the old City walls; and there was a School, which obviously wasn't very old. Directly beneath the City walls to my left was the Brandywell area, consisting of old terraced houses, and to my right, a tall block, the Rossville Flats, which we were to discover, provided a good vantage position for snipers! The Bagside Inn was about 150 yards from the walls, and to its left, painted on the side of a house, and much photographed, were the words, "YOU ARE NOW ENTERING FREE DERRY". Before the Creggan Estate, which covered the hill above the Bogside had been built, it had inspired Frances Alexander to write the famous Easter Hymn, "There is a green hill far away, without a city wall".

Rioting by mobs throwing stones and petrol bombs was a regular evening activity, which usually went on until long after midnight. This kept the security forces busy as they strove to keep the mobs from getting into and wrecking the City centre, and destroying its commercial heart. 'The Marching Season', when men belonging to the Orange Order or the Apprentice Boys, would march wearing their distinctive regalia with their pipes and drums along traditional routes, were usual 'flashpoints'. Extra troops were brought in to help cover these occasions, and 3rd Regiment Royal Horse Artillery (3RHA) had recently arrived in the Province, and was stationed with 2RGJ in Ballykelly. While they were with us they became my pastoral responsibility. When I first visited them, I was delighted to discover that their Chief Clerk, now a Warrant Officer, was one of the clerks trained by me at Woolwich back in 1962! He was to be a valuable link in my dealings with the Regiment.

While there was much activity, attempts were made to have a social life!

On our first Dinner Night in the Mess, I included these words in the 'Grace'.

> May this first feast on Emerald soil,
>
> Strengthen us for future toil,
>
> And grant us Lord, in this location;
>
> Patience with the Irish Nation!

Subsequent Dinner Nights were often cut short, disrupted, or cancelled altogether. I was therefore moved on another evening to add the words,

> May those who work for Civil Rights,
>
> Not disrupt our Dinner Nights!

The Methodist Church in Ireland is a quite small but significant Christian denomination, with Churches in both Northern Ireland and the Irish Republic, all coming under the authority of the Methodist Conference in Ireland. In Londonderry there were two Churches, and there was a Church in Limavady. I soon got to know the Ministers quite well, particularly the one who lived in Limavady. When military duties permitted, I would sometimes conduct an evening Service for him. A system evolved which he described as 'a supper for a sermon'! I was also able to conduct Services in Portstewart and Portrush, on the north coast; and at Coleraine. I found these contacts to be an important link between the Military and civilian communities.

Limavady was a mixed community, with 60% being Protestants, and 40% Roman Catholics. I was assured that the two communities got on very well together, and that there was never any trouble. My daughter Vivien, after a short time at the school in Ballykelly, was offered a place at Limavady Grammar School. The following year there was trouble in the town, when bombs were detonated by the Police Station and in the town centre. Local people were certainly not responsible for these atrocities, but, like many other peaceful communities in the Province, were victims of 'imported terrorism'.

The divisions that do exist between the communities go back hundreds of years and are very deep. It has been said that 'the people of Northern Ireland have no history, only current affairs.' The Battle of the Boyne didn't happen over three hundred years ago, it was yesterday! Had there been an easy solution to the 'problem', it would have been found generations ago. It is an immensely complex situation, and there are no easy answers. After being in the province for three months, I thought I knew all the answers. When I left after living there for eighteen months, I was just becoming aware of some of the questions! Having said all that, I found the vast majority of the people charming and friendly, and deeply ashamed of the images portrayed of them around the world. I was later to return to the Province on three subsequent tours of duty, and was always happy to do so. However, to return to 1971!

The beginning of August saw the introduction of Internment without Trial, and the match was set to the powder keg! In early morning raids, the Army and Police arrested hundreds of people, mainly in Belfast and Londonderry. There was widespread rioting throughout the Province, and over a hundred barricades were erected in the Bogside and Creggan areas of Londonderry. This was considered unacceptable by the authorities, and after a couple of weeks, a military operation was launched to dismantle them. For the first time I put on my 'combat' uniform and accompanied my Battalion. I had attended the CO's briefing, and apparently someone at Brigade HQ had questioned the wisdom of having Chaplains around during the operation. My reply was to say that if I couldn't be with my soldiers in such situations, I might as well leave the Army and go back to being a civilian Minister! My point was well taken, and the CO told me to get my kit.

I did so and waited at the bottom of the road, getting a lift in the back of Captain Hurricane's Land Rover. On arrival in the City, I positioned myself with Battalion HQ, so that I could monitor what was going on, and keep out of the way of those actually doing the job. There were three military units involved in the operation, and within a few hours, all rioting and resistance had been quelled: and all barricades dismantled except one. The remaining one was very large and located outside the Bogside Inn. Half a dozen women and girls had positioned themselves on top of the barricade. There were Television crews from several countries filming all that was happening, which put the young Platoon Commander on the ground in a dilemma. Should he order his soldiers to physically remove these protesters from the barricade in front of all the TV cameras? He decided to consult his superior officer, who in turn decided to do the same, and the dilemma was passed right up the chain of command. While all this was going on, the initiative was lost and the mobs regained their courage and came back onto the streets. The answer finally came back that the women were to be left where they were. I discovered later that this had been a political, and not a Military decision. That same night the barricades were put up again, and the year began when the Bogside and Creggan became 'NO GO' areas for troops and police!

The situation now became much more serious as firearms began to be used regularly against the security forces. Batons and shields had been carried by troops when faced with mobs throwing stones and petrol bombs: CS gas, rubber bullets, and 'snatch' squads had been used to disperse them. Now, gunmen used the cover provided by the crowds, to use rifles, sub-machine guns, and pistols to fire on soldiers and police. Nail bombs were also used against them. 'Home made' bombs, which became much more sophisticated as time went on, were increasingly used against prime targets in the City, and Bomb Disposal teams were regularly called out. Security forces wearing 'flack jackets' and carrying weapons now became the norm. Small armoured vehicles, known as 'pigs' had been taken out of 'mothballs' and were used to carry small numbers of troops. Land Rovers had been fitted with covers, which offered protection against petrol bombs and low velocity bullets, and windscreens had been covered with metal grills. Soldiers had been injured tackling rioters: now they were to suffer more serious, and sometimes fatal injuries.

The strain on soldier's families was considerable. Waving 'goodbye' to a husband or father as he leaves on a troopship or an aircraft for a war zone is difficult enough: when he's only fifteen miles down the road in the United Kingdom, it is more difficult to live with, or even begin to come to terms with he possibility that he could be severely injured or killed. Local radio and TV covered all that was happening. People in England heard and saw only a fraction. Families with the Battalion stationed in Londonderry, whose homes were nearby, heard every bomb. I knew wives who never missed a news bulletin. In 1971, the BBC had a studio in Londonderry. On one occasion, the newsreader said, "A soldier has been shot in Londonderry, there is no news yet about his condition". Can you imagine the effect of that news item on all the wives who were listening? Fortunately that particular soldier wasn't seriously injured, or even married, but the proximity of the media sometimes made our task in caring for families more difficult. If one of our soldiers was killed or injured, it was the highest priority the family was visited by members of the Battalion, before they heard via the media or the 'bush telegraph'. Our Families Officer and a wife would make the initial visit, and I, as the Padre, would visit within the hour. My first task would be to visit the hospital, see the soldier if possible, and talk to the Doctors, again if possible. This was an issue we had discussed at some length when we first arrived, and I had made it clear that as I needed to visit families regularly for a variety of reasons, it was unwise for my frequent presence on 'the patch' to be associated with bad news or tragedy.

Our first casualty was a Corporal who was shot in the leg just above the ankle. He told me he didn't feel a thing at the time: just found himself on the floor and wondered why he was there! It was only when he tried to get up and looked at his leg that he realised he had been shot. Then the pain hit him and he was rushed to Hospital, where he remained for some time before being flown back to England to the Joint Services Rehabilitation Unit (JSRU) at Chessington. Several months later he was able to return to the Battalion and resume his duties.

One day I was visiting him in the Altnegelvin Hospital, and chatting to an elderly man in the next bed who lived in the Bogside. He asked me what people in England were saying about the Northern Ireland situation. I told him that many people thought the ordinary people in the Province should stand up against the thugs. He gave me a weak smile and said sadly, "Listen, Reverend, when a man comes to your front door with a gun, you call him 'Sir'!"

The first fatality was a young married Bombardier from 3RHA who was shot dead by a sniper at an Army post between the Bogside and Creggan. His body was flown home where he was given a Military Funeral. I conducted a Memorial Service for him at Ballykelly, which was attended by his family, who had flown over for the Service, and members of his Regiment who had been unable to attend his funeral. As an ex young married Bombardier in the RHA myself, it was a particularly poignant occasion for me. During the next few weeks the Battalion suffered two more casualties. The first was a Major, a Company Commander, who was shot in the stomach. He was married, with children, and was kept in Hospital in Londonderry for a long time, fighting a succession of infections. Eventually he was he was sent back to England and for a time seemed to be making progress. He then suffered further infections, and by this time having little strength left to fight them, died at the end of January 1972, almost five months after being shot. He was buried with full Military Honours in Winchester, following a Service, which I conducted in the Church at the Royal Green Jackets Depot. So many attended the Service, that the journey to the Cemetery brought Winchester to a stand still.

The second was a mature, experienced Rifleman, much respected by his peers, who was shot through the neck while he was on the walls of the City. He was paralysed from the neck down and after a time in Hospital in Londonderry and Belfast, was sent to Stoke Mandeville Hospital, near Aylesbury. I visited him there on two occasions, and was amazed at his progress. He was propelling himself in a wheelchair and had a cheerful and positive attitude. Coming from a coal mining area, where his family still lived, he was eventually found a place in a Nursing Home not far from his family, which specialised in caring for men who had been seriously injured in the mines.

At the beginning of September I was attending a meeting with other Chaplains in Lisburn, when I received a telephone call from my wife informing me that she thought the arrival of our baby was imminent! I left the meeting and rushed home, telephoned the Cottage Hospital in Limavady, and took her straight there. I remained with her until our lovely second daughter was born on 7th September 1971. She was without a name for a few days, until we finally settled on the names of Karena Diane. She was a very good and contented baby, who was soon sleeping through the night: which reminds me of others who were suffering from sleep deprivation!

Because there were things happening 'around the clock', the Officers in Battalion HQ manning the Operations Room, were getting little sleep, although things were generally quieter during the night. I joined a small group of 'volunteers', like the Paymaster, the QM, and even the Doctor, to man the Ops Room during the night, so that the staff could get some sleep! As an ex Regular soldier, I knew how to use a radio and was happy about handling routine 'traffic' on the Battalion and Brigade Networks (Nets), and answering the telephones. Before assuming a duty, I would be briefed on the current situation by a member of the Staff, before he went to a room not many yards away to get some sleep. There was a signaller on duty in the room below, and if anything important happened, he would be sent to rouse the Staff, and they would be back in the Ops Room within minutes to assume control.

One morning, at about 7.30a.m., the Ops Staff were still in bed, having been up until 3.0a.m., when I was informed that no less then three bombs had been planted in buildings in the City centre, and only a hundred yards or so away from our HQ, which was located in the main Police Station! I immediately called for the Bomb Disposal unit and sent the signaller to wake the Staff. Before they could arrive and take control, the door opened and in walked the Brigade Commander, who looked very surprised when he found the Padre controlling the Ops Room! All the bombs went off before the Bomb Disposal unit arrived, doing considerable damage to the buildings around us, but causing no casualties. The Brigadier couldn't have been too unhappy about my role, as my name continued to appear on the duty forecast lists!

The 'No Go' areas continued to cause great frustration and anger amongst the Army and the RUC. Gunmen and bombers could leave the Bogside and Creggan, inflict death, injury, and damage, and return knowing they would not be pursued! The Northern Ireland Secretary at the time was William Whitelaw, who soon became known as 'Willie Wet'! One tactic of the gunmen was to use children to set fire to old buildings and dilapidated property. Of course the Fire Service had to be called out to prevent the flames spreading to homes nearby. The firemen, understandably, refused to enter the area without a military escort, who then became targets for snipers. One day I was in an Observation Post (OP), with a Company Commander (a Major) overlooking the area when such a sequence of events was under way. On that occasion nothing happened, but the Major said to me, "Padre, before this week is over, I'm going to loose one of my soldiers". He was right: a few days later a young soldier was shot dead as he protected firemen.

While most terrorist activities were quite blatant, there was a sinister element also at work. My mother-in-law had a friend whose son and his family lived in Limavady. He was working for an Insurance Company, which had an office in Londonderry. She encouraged us to make contact with them and eventually we did, visiting each other for meals and a chat. My wife was very glad to meet people from 'home'. One day he telephoned me and asked to see me as a matter of urgency. He sounded quite upset so I went to his home the same evening. When I arrived we sat down and he said, "We are leaving tomorrow to go back to England and I want you to know why, just in case you have been compromised in any way.

A few days ago I left the office and went to where my car was parked. Before I could get in, I was grabbed by some men and bundled into the car. They drove into the Bogside, put a bag over my head and drove around for a while. Then they began asking me lots of questions about my job and why I was in Londonderry. They put a gun to my head and asked me about military matters. I told them my only knowledge was when I spent two years in the RAF as a National Serviceman." They drove him around a little longer, and then said, "But what about your friend, the Army Padre in Ballykelly?" He told them how we came to meet, and eventually they were satisfied, drove him out of the Bogside, took the bag off his head and pushed him out of the car. They kept the car, which ended up on one of the barricades.

As you can imagine, he was quite devastated by this experience, and his Company moved him out of Northern Ireland as soon as possible. The following day I saw the Battalion Intelligence Officer, and told him what had happened. He said he would make some enquiries, but I didn't really believe he would come up with anything. To my surprise he did! A couple of weeks later he told me what he had discovered. My friend had gone into his office one Monday morning, and as people do, was asked if he'd had a good weekend. Amongst other things, he mentioned that he and his family had been to my home for a meal. Apparently, on of the girls who worked in the office had links with one of the gangs in the Bogside, and thought it worthwhile to pass this little tit bit of information on to them. They obviously thought it worth checking out, picked up my friend and interrogated him.

One security problem we had was the number of soldiers who became involved with local girls. A regular Dance was held at Ballykelly for troops not on duty. Girls came from miles around and queued at the Camp gates, as each one had to be 'signed in' by a soldier. There had been an incident at an Army barracks near Belfast, when a girl had left a bomb in the ladies toilet. The bomb had exploded, causing damage to the property, but fortunately injuring no one. These Dances and other encounters resulted in me conducting forty three marriages during my eighteen months in Ballykelly, many of the girls coming from homes in Londonderry. On more than one occasion, I had to stand at the front of the Church and say to the congregation, "Will you please put your cigarettes out, we are about to begin the Service!" Some of the couples were obviously ill matched, and the marriages didn't last long. Others were well matched and the marriages were long and happy. A very concerned Company Commander came to see me one day and said, "Padre, can't you refuse to marry these people?" I said, "Of course I can, but we are in the United Kingdom, and if I refuse to marry them, they will simply go to the Register

Office in Limavady, and get married there: whereas, If I marry them and they have problems, they will be more likely to come to me for help". Of course this policy resulted in me baptising many babies, which led to me having problems with some in the Chaplains Department!

Having enjoyed excellent working relationships with Anglican Clergymen when I was a Circuit Minister, I was amazed and saddened to discover that relationships between the Christian denominations in the Army were years behind what was happening in the civilian Churches. The vast majority of soldiers were only nominally Church of England/Methodist/Baptist etc. To them, the Padre was the Padre, and they weren't the slightest bit interested in which Denomination he was. During my years as a Chaplain, I always explained to those who came to me, that I was a Methodist, but would be happy to arrange for them to see a Church of England Chaplain. This offer was never once taken up. The response was invariably, "But you are our Padre, aren't you?"

I mentioned earlier that living in Ballykelly, were about a hundred families from the Battalion based in Londonderry. Some of them asked about having their children baptised, and I duly passed on these requests to their Chaplain. After a few months he said to me, "It doesn't make any sense for me to travel to Ballykelly, or to bring families from there to Londonderry, when

Christening of Dale Henny
26th September 1972 Ballykelly 2RGJ

Christening of John Michael
26th September 1972 Ballykelly 2RGJ

you are on the spot. Why don't you do the Baptisms in your Church?" Of course I agreed and did several Baptisms for him. When the documentation reached the Senior Chaplain in Lisburn, who was a very traditional Welsh Anglican, he telephoned me and told me I was not to Baptise children from Church of England families, and that also applied to the families of 2RGJ! This led to a number of heated phone calls. I said that I had been baptising children from my own Battalion for the past eighteen months, and wasn't going to stop now! He said he would take the matter up with the Chaplain General and the Bishop to the Forces. I said, "With respect, I am a Methodist Minister, and the Bishop to the Forces has no authority over me"! A week later I had a phone message left for me saying, "In future, all Baptisms must be by Denominations, if requested". I phoned back straight away and said simply, "I have no argument with that"

As well as conducting a Sunday morning Service in my Church in Shackleton Barracks, I would also conduct Services in the Company Locations and at Battalion HQ. When possible I arranged with the Brigade Roman Catholic Chaplain to share in these Services. We would conduct a short, informal Service together, and then divide into two groups and offer Mass and Holy Communion to those who wished to receive the Sacrament. On Easter Sunday I visited as many locations as possible to offer the Sacrament. In one place, as I was preparing for the Service, two soldiers came to me and said, "Padre, we are Roman Catholics and because our Priest has so many places to visit today, he is not able to come here: may we come to your Service and take Communion?" I made sure they understood the difference between the two services, which they did, and happily gave them Communion with the others who came to the Service. I must emphasise that no pressure was ever put on soldiers to attend Church Services, except on Remembrance Sunday. On that day a Service was held for all soldiers not on essential duties, and their families, in a huge hangar at the bottom of the airfield. The hangar had been built to accommodate the Nimrod aircraft, which replaced the old Shackletons, but they were never deployed to Ballykelly.

In an attempt to stop bombs and weapons from being brought into the City, and to check the identity of vehicle occupants, Vehicle Check Points (VCPs) were set up on roads in the immediate area. Some were permanent; others were temporary and set up quickly, sometimes as a result of intelligence reports. One day, a young soldier manning a VCP with three others, was shot twice. He was rushed to Hospital, but sadly, he died. A little later I was talking to the Doctors who treated him, and was most surprised when they told me that the soldier shouldn't have died from his wounds, which weren't serious enough to have been fatal. They thought that he had really died of shock: he knew he'd been shot, convinced himself he was dying, and did.

His comrades manning the VCP had also obviously been shocked, taken cover, and tried to identify where the shots had come from. A perfectly normal reaction under the circumstances, bearing in mind these were still comparatively early days in the Army's role in combating urban terrorist activities. We, and that includes the Chaplains, were still very much on a learning curve. If the wounded soldier had been, comforted, reassured, joked with, and buoyed up, he would probably have survived. Such actions were very soon to become the norm, and formed part of a soldier's pre-Northern Ireland training.

On a lighter note: one day the Bandmaster came to see me and showed me a letter he had received about an Army Group/Singer Competition. He urged me to enter, and after thinking about it for a few days, I allowed my name to go forward. I had to be prepared to sing two songs, and after some discussion, decided on 'My Way', and 'If I Ruled The World'. In Germany and England there were 'heats', but as I turned out to be the only entry from Northern Ireland, I found myself in the Final without having sung a note!

The Finals were held in a Theatre in north London. I don't remember the name of the Theatre, but it was the one used for the regular BBC broadcast of 'Friday Night is Music Night'. The competition was held one evening in the Theatre, which was empty except for the judges, which included Tony Blackburn and Geoff Love. I was surprised how seriously the event was taken by other competitors, some of them had obviously entered the competition in previous years, and 'knew the form'. They were 'dressed up to the nines' whereas I turned up in casual dress! We were permitted one brief rehearsal in the afternoon, and I felt a bit intimidated by the professional pianist who was to accompany me. His hands flew up and down the keys and I found it difficult to come in at the right time! The same thing happened at the actual competition, and I made a poor start. However, once I got started, I sang 'My Way' without any problem. Afterwards the judges made their comments and announced their decision. I came third, which meant that I would be performing before a full house the following evening. Three singers and three groups had been selected for the public performance. For this I had relinquished my casual attire, and wore a Dinner Jacket!

Leslie Crowther was the Master of Ceremonies. As he chatted to, and then dismissed the people who had been performing before me, he said, "Bless you", as they left the stage. When I was introduced, I said to him, "Do you know you could get into trouble?" He looked puzzled and a bit confused. "What do you mean?" he said. I replied, "You can't just go around blessing people like that you know". He looked even more puzzled and asked, "Why not?" I said, "Where's your Union Card?" Then he remembered that I was a Chaplain, and we had a good laugh about it! I was feeling more relaxed and confident than I had for the actual competition, began singing at exactly the right time, and received a great ovation at the end of my performance!

During the reception afterwards I chatted with many people. Geoff Love informed me that he had once served with the Royal Green Jackets, and I met a BBC Producer, who said he would find a job for me if I left the Army! Having only recently joined the Chaplains Department, and thoroughly enjoying my work, I wasn't even remotely interested in exploring his offer!

It was during one of our visits to my parents that my mother had an accident, which affected her for the rest of her life. She was carrying her new grand daughter to 'show her off' to a neighbour, when she tripped and fell onto a concrete path. In order to protect the baby, she fell onto her knees and twisted her ankle as her foot slipped off the path. It didn't seem serious, but as time passed her foot became quite twisted so that she could hardly walk at all, and ended up having to use a wheelchair.

I was a little concerned about what was happening to our soldiers who had been sent back to Hospitals in England for specialist care and rehabilitation. Checking with our own Battalion Medical Centre, I discovered that we had eleven soldiers in six Military Hospitals in England. When a soldier has been in Hospital for sixty days, he is 'Y' listed. This means that he is 'struck off strength' of his unit, and administered by the Infantry/Regimental/Corps Record office. The Royal Green Jackets had a Territorial Army Battalion in the London area, and they were very conscientious about visiting our soldiers in Hospital, providing they knew were they were! Hospitals would often move soldiers to different Hospitals, and were notoriously bad about informing anyone that they had done so! I discussed this with the CO, and he agreed to send me to England for a week to 'track down', and visit our soldiers. The Adjutant contacted the Royal Green Jackets Depot in Winchester, and they agreed to supply me with a car and pick me up from Heathrow Airport.

I took with me a pile of stamped addressed envelopes to give to the soldiers in Hospital, with instructions that they were to inform the Battalion should they be moved to other Hospitals. I spent three days visiting soldiers in Hospitals at Millbank, London; Woolwich, Aldershot, Mount Vernon in North London, Stoke-Manderville, and Chessington. They all seemed pleased to see me and gave me a variety of messages to take back to the Battalion, and to friends they knew I would be seeing in other Hospitals.

Not all the soldiers were in Hospital as a result of injuries inflicted by the IRA or riotous mobs. The soldier I visited in the Specialist Burns Unit at Mount Vernon was there as a result of an unfortunate accident. He had been part of a small unit inspecting a derelict house, and flipped a cigarette end into what he thought was an empty tin. Unfortunately for him, the tin was half full of paint thinner and exploded, inflicting terrible burns. The assessment was that he was suffering 66% burns to his face and body. When I saw him, the Doctors had done a considerable amount of work on his face, but most of his body looked as if it was covered with black leather.

My last visit was to the Joint Services Rehabilitation Unit at Chessington. Some of the soldiers there would soon be returning to the Battalion. I was saddened and disappointed, when some soldiers, including a number wearing Red Berets complained that no one ever came to see them! This was something I was to rectify a few months later when I returned to the Parachute Brigade.

After almost exactly a year, the political decision was made to dismantle all the barricades in the Bogside and Craggan, and bring to an end the 'No Go' areas. The Army would have been quite capable of doing the job many months earlier, but were not permitted to do so. By this time, some of the barricades were of a considerable size, and many were suspected to contain 'booby traps'. Now, the biggest military operation since Suez was mounted, and it was code-named 'Operation Motorman'. Many extra troops were brought in, many to wait in Ballykelly until the start of the operation. A young Warrant Officer, a bomb disposal expert, was attached to 2RGJ. He had been going on leave with his family when he was stopped at the German border, and ordered to Northern Ireland.

My Church and Hall were taken over by 2nd Field Hospital. Beds were put up in the Church, and the Hall was used to accommodate the Staff and store equipment. Fortunately it was never used, but its very deployment was indicative of the seriousness with which the authorities were treating the situation.

It was a massive operation, and there was no way it could be kept secret. Any 'most wanted' members of the IRA would have ample time to slip over the border into the Republic. Was this perhaps intentional, to avoid the possibility of large scale 'fire fights'? Several of the larger barricades had concrete set in them and would be difficult to remove. However, plans had been made to cope with them. During the hours of darkness preceding the deployment of troops, a number of Armoured Engineer vehicles brought from Germany by sea, were off loaded from a ship, which had slipped unobtrusively alongside the quay in Londonderry. They were in fact, old Centurion tanks, without gun turrets, but with massive bulldozer blades mounted at the front. They quickly demolished the larger barricades and returned to the ship, which sailed before dawn. I think the 'powers that be' were being very wary. The last thing they needed were photographs in the Press, or TV coverage of 'Tanks In The Bogside'! I think it was a good decision, and very efficiently executed.

The main operation began at 4.00 a.m., and I moved with my Battalion through the Brandywell area of the City. There were troops entering the area from all directions, and with the aid of Royal Engineers and Bomb Disposal units, were systematically demolishing and taking away all the barricades: and there were over a hundred of them. There was very little resistance: I think there were two people, not soldiers, killed during the operation. As we moved carefully along the terraced houses of the Brandywell, people came out and said, "Thank God you've come", and offered us cups of tea. I remember seeing headlines and photographs in the past saying, "A Thousand People Marched From the Creggan and Bogside". What they didn't point out was that there were more then twenty five thousand who didn't march! The fact is, that for a year, a community of almost thirty thousand people were effectively 'controlled' by terrorists, with the full knowledge and acquiescence of the British Government.

Later in the day, I was having a cup of tea with our Bomb Disposal Warrant Officer, who had successfully 'made safe' a number of devices during the morning. A few days after Operation Motorman had been completed, I was immensely saddened to learn that he had been killed in another part of the Province while attempting to disarm a bomb.

With the opening up of the 'No Go' areas, the return of regular patrols considerably reduced the number of serious incidents, and the Battalion resumed its routine commitments. Sadly, another young solder was killed, bringing the number of fatalities suffered by the Battalion to four. I was at home when I heard the news and I think the stress of the past year was beginning to tell. I just broke down and cried.

I was informed that the Parachute Brigade would shortly be looking for at least one Chaplain to replace those leaving, and I informed the Chaplain General that I was still willing to serve with them. Having done 'P' Company back in 1958, I was informed I would not have to do it again, but would be required to do a Parachute Refresher Course. No date for my posting had been fixed, but I decided I had better increase my physical fitness levels. I had continued to play squash regularly, but really needed to concentrate on running more to build up my stamina again. Since arriving in Northern Ireland I had spent countless hours in my car and driven thousands of miles around the Province.

The airfield provided an ideal running area and I began running four miles every day. After a week, I got out of bed one morning, and could hardly walk! My achilles tendons were so painful. I saw the Doctor, who told me that my tendons were very bruised and that I should cease running for at least two weeks. The problem was, that I'd been running on concrete in ordinary running shoes. In future I would always run in DMS Army boots with thick rubber soles, and I had no further problems!

My posting order eventually arrived. I was to report to First Battalion, The Parachute Regiment in Aldershot at the end of October. I PARA was just coming to the end of a two year tour in Belfast, and only their Rear Party would be in Aldershot when I arrived. Before they returned to Aldershot, they would have some well deserved leave, which would give me time to settle my family in and do my Parachute Refresher Course. So it was back to filling the packing cases, organising my move, and saying 'farewell' to 2RGJ. As much as I wanted to return to Airborne Forces, I was very sad to leave 2RGJ. We had been through much in the past two years, and had laughed and cried together on many occasions. As a Battalion, they had shown me, and my family much kindness, and from them I had learned a lot about being a Chaplain. They will always have a very special place in my heart.

1ST BATTALION, THE PARACHUTE REGIMENT ALDERSHOT – OCTOBER 1972 AUGUST 1974

There was a Methodist Chaplain serving in Aldershot, and he took it upon himself to ensure we had a Married Quarter to move into as soon as we arrived. A new 'patch' of Officers Quarters was in the process of being built, only a few hundred yards from Mons Barracks, home of I PARA, and we were among the first occupants. As the first occupants of the house, there was a lot of cleaning and tidying up to be done once the builders had gone. The hard, bare piece of ground meant to be the garden would need a lot of time and effort! A few weeks later we were delighted when our friends from Munster moved into a house in the next cul-de-sac. My friend from the 50s had now been posted to 23rd Parachute Field Ambulance, as the Adjutant.

Across the road in Mons Barracks, I introduced myself to the Rear Party, and took over the Chaplain's Office and car, which was a Morris Minor Estate. I went and paid my respects to the Garrison Senior Chaplain, a very affable Irishman, and to the Methodist Superintendent Minister. I told him I was unable to offer him any firm dates when I would be able to conduct services in the Circuit, but would be happy to help out whenever possible. I visited the Garrison Methodist Church in North Camp with my family, and it was a pleasure to meet again people we had known when we last attended that Church back in 1960/61. Aldershot was the only place I served as a Chaplain, where I didn't have my own Church. For the next two years I used the two Garrison Methodist Churches for Baptisms and Weddings, and conducted Services in them whenever I could, but they were both part of the Aldershot Methodist Circuit and had civilian Ministers. I felt it was a strange arrangement, but it worked well.

The most important thing now, was to visit the RAF Detachment in Aldershot and talk to them about doing a Parachute Refresher Course. Personal courses obviously weren't on offer and I would join others doing routine training. I think I explained earlier, the necessity for all Airborne soldiers to do two hours 'synthetic' training before each parachute jump, so there was always something going on in the Training Hangar. The Instructor I spoke to asked, "How long is it since you last jumped Padre?" I replied, "Oh, it must be about eleven years". He grinned at me and said, "Well, we now use different aircraft, different parachutes, and different equipment: apart from that, nothings changed!" During my time away, the Hastings and Beverley aircraft had been phased out. The Argosy had come and gone, and the Brigade now used the C 130 Hercules. The main parachute now had a 'skirt' fitted around the periphery, designed to stop a rigging line being thrown over the canopy as it deployed; and the personal equipment container had been slightly altered. After spending two or three days brushing up on my aircraft, exit, flight, and landing drills, it was time to join a group due to make a jump. When I arrived at the hangar a few days later, the Instructor said, "You're in luck Padre, we've got an Andover aircraft today coming in at RAF Odiham; and that's a real Gentleman's aircraft!"

During the next few weeks I did several jumps with different groups from the Hercules and the Balloon, until the RAF Instructors were satisfied that I was suitably 'refreshed'! I noticed one main difference from my previous experience: Everything 'seemed' to happen more slowly, and I was much more aware of what was going on around me: in fact I quite enjoyed the experience. I think as a young soldier, I had probably gone through the process automatically, and in a bit of a daze. Now I felt more confident, and in control.

1 PARA were now beginning to drift back in groups from their post Northern Ireland leave, and would soon be busy brushing up on their Parachuting skills and conventional military training. During the previous three years, the Battalion had spent twenty seven months in Northern Ireland. There was a lot to be done in a short time, as we had been informed that we would be going to Cyprus the following May for six months, as part of the United Nations peacekeeping force there.

There was one thing I was determined to do before becoming embroiled in Battalion activities, and that was to visit the JSRU at Chessington. I telephoned the Admin Officer, who remembered me from my previous visit and agreed a suitable time and date for me to visit. He also agreed to gather together all members of the Parachute Brigade so that I could meet them all. I had discovered that it was unwise to visit such establishments unannounced, as many of the people I wanted to see could well be involved doing other things! When I walked into the room to meet them, I was amazed how many there were! Some were there as a result of injuries received in Northern Ireland: others as a result of injuries due to parachuting, playing sport, or following more routine medical problems. Many were disgruntled, feeling they had been forgotten! I made a list of their names, military units, and any particular problems they had. When I got back to Aldershot, I typed it out, and took a copy to the Brigade Major at Brigade HQ. He immediately sent a sharp letter to all units on the list, and the soldiers at Chessington began to receive regular visits.

Time was now spent getting to know the Battalion, and building up relationships with those I would be dealing with regularly. People like The CO and the Staff of Battalion HQ, Company Commanders, the RSM and Company Sergeant Majors, the Quartermaster an his Staff; and of course the Families Officer, the Doctor, the Paymaster, and the Bandmaster. When dealing with soldiers or families experiencing difficulties, it's amazing how many of the aforementioned become involved! The Padre is definitely one of a team, and no matter how well I got on with 2RGJ, they were now history and I had to begin again from 'square one'! The fact that I had previously served as a Regular Soldier with the Brigade was undoubtedly an asset.

Time passed quickly, and before I knew it, it was Christmas! For the first and only time in my Ministry, not having responsibility for a Church, I had Christmas off! We decided to spend Christmas with my parents in Newcastle-u-Lyme, and the New Year with my in-laws in Rotherham. Early in the New Year, 1973, I began to have stomach trouble. I went to see the Doctor and he decided to send me to the Military Hospital for tests. Routine tests revealed nothing, so it was decided to have a look internally. The process began with an enema, followed by a bowel wash. What little dignity I had was disappearing fast, and 'the little' was to follow shortly! I had to kneel on a bed, naked, with my bottom at about 45 degrees. The Doctor said, "We don't do many of these, would you mind awfully if some of the nursing staff came in to watch?" What could I do but agree to his request? Half a dozen nurses trooped into the room, trying not to giggle at the sight of a Padre with his bottom stuck up in the air! A small trolley was wheeled in with the instruments covered with a white cloth. The cloth was removed and the Doctor picked up what looked like a long metal tube, which appeared to me to be inordinately wide! I said, "You're not going to shove . . . . . ." and he said, "Oh yes I am", and after putting some jelly like substance on it, he did! Having inserted it, he began to move it around, muttering to himself. It wasn't painful, but it was most uncomfortable. There was obviously a light on the end of the tube, and the Doctor said to the nursing staff, "Come and have a look". Whatever they might have been looking for wasn't there, so the instrument was removed and I returned to the ward.

The way I was feeling afterwards is difficult to put into words. I felt quite disturbed by the experience, even violated. A few days later I was given a barium 'meal' to drink, and I watched its progress through my system on a monitor by the bedside. The cause of my problem soon became evident: I had a small ulcer, which had probably been caused by my hectic lifestyle and stress during the past eighteen months in Northern Ireland. The treatment was fairly simple. It consisted of tablets, a careful diet, and a less stressful existence. I could only guarantee the first two!

Now it was time to prepare for our departure for Cyprus. Apart from packing, I felt I needed to sell my lovely Triumph Vitesse, which had served us so well for the past two years. My wife was not yet able to drive and I didn't want to leave it standing unused for six months. It was sold within a week to a young man who came with his father to inspect it. After a trial run, they met my asking price without any problem.

A week before we were due to leave, I was sent for by the Brigade Commander. He instructed me to go to Cyprus, take it easy, and get rid of my ulcer! He then gave me a copy of a Signal, which informed me that I had been awarded a 'Mentioned in Despatches' for distinguished service in Northern Ireland. I was quite speechless and most surprised. A few days later I received a formal Certificate, signed by the Defence Minister, Peter Carrington, and an oak leaf to wear with my General Service Medal.

What was equally unexpected were the large number of letters I received congratulating me on receiving the Award. They came from all over, including the Chaplain General, and the General Officer Commanding forces in Northern Ireland. A few weeks later someone informed me that etiquette dictated I reply to the letters! This task was completed with some difficulty from Cyprus. I found it hard to choose appropriate words to express my sentiments on receiving the Award.

UNITED NATIONS FORCE IN CYPRUS (UNFICYP) – MAY – NOV 1973

On the day of our departure, tears were shed as we boarded coaches to take us to the airport. Six months is a long time, even though there was to be two weeks leave for everyone about half way through the tour. At least, unlike Northern Ireland, there was no element of danger involved. We flew in aircraft of RAF Transport Command to Cyprus, and after a short break in Malta for refuelling: landed at RAF Akrotiri, which at that time was the largest RAF Station in the world. On the way to our base just north of Limasol, we drove through groves of oranges, lemons, and grapefruit, and the smell was absolutely gorgeous! I was to make the journey through the groves many times, as any sick or injured soldiers were admitted to the RAF Hospital on the base.

Battalion HQ and one Rifle Company were based in an old camp, consisting of dilapidated wooden buildings which had been built many years before by Kitchener. Other Companies were based, one in the south of the Island, and the other about half way to Nicosia, at the junction where the road went on to Larnaca and Famagusta. There were several other nationalities making up the UN Force, each with its own area of responsibility. There were Swedes,

Irish, Fins, and Canadians. They all had their own Chaplains, and we would get together once a month for both business and social reasons: each contingent taking their turn to act as host. My recollections of our visit to the Irish Battalion in Larnaca are a bit vague. This was due in no small part to the fact that we were all given several mugs of Irish coffee when we first arrived! This was because we didn't all arrive together, and as each Chaplain arrived, our host brought out another round of drinks!

In addition to the soldiers, there were UN Police contingents from Australia, Denmark, and Sweden. The Australian Police contingent were based just down the road from I PARA, and I naturally assumed pastoral responsibility for them. They were a most hospitable bunch, and were very popular, not least because they had the only air - conditioned bar on the island: appropriately called 'The Hop Inn', with its kangaroo motif on the door! The only other British Troops were a Squadron of light tanks, based in Nicosia, very close to the French Speaking Canadians. There were also British units based in the two Sovereign Base areas of Dhekelia and Episkopi, but they were not part of the UN Force. This occasionally led to some friction as they weren't bound by the strict orders applying to UN Soldiers, who had to wear uniform at all times, and be back in barracks no later then 11.00p.m!

The first thing we had to do was to change uniforms! Our Red Berets were swapped for the Blue Berets of the UN, and daily working dress changed to Khaki Drill shirts and trousers. I had been given a Tropical Uniform allowance and was measured for a Dress uniform, which I only needed to wear on about four occasions. My 'home' for the tour was a small, stone, one room building, onto which some previous occupant had fixed the sign 'The Vicarage'! Fine mesh had been fitted to the door and window to keep mosquitoes and other insects out, but no attempt had been made to repair a number of holes in the ceiling!

This didn't bother me until the day I saw a large rat snake in the tree outside my door. I watched it for a while, and then to my horror it made its way along an electricity cable, and disappeared into my roof! I didn't get much sleep that night, as I could hardly take my eyes off the holes in the ceiling! I was informed on the following day, after sharing my experience with some 'old' soldiers, that most people in Cyprus were more than happy to share their homes with a rat snake, for obvious reasons.

I soon found it was possible to follow the Brigade Commander's instruction that I should 'take it easy'. Because of the heat, we started work very early and finished at lunchtime. It was impossible for me to go visiting people in the afternoons, because no one was around! For the past twelve years I had been what could only be described as a 'workaholic'. Now I drove around visiting my soldiers in the morning, and either got back to base for lunch, or ended up on a beech for a swim or to relax in the shade. In Cyprus I learned how to relax, took my tablets, and made a feeble attempt to watch my diet! At the end of the tour, I went for a medical examination, and there was no trace of the ulcer.

A new Doctor joined the Battalion just as we arrived in Cyprus. He was a charming Irishman from Dublin. He had not quite completed his parachute course, having slightly injured himself just two jumps short of obtaining his Wings! We had brought our own Parachute Jumping Instructor with us, an RAF Officer, as it was hoped we would be able to do some parachuting in Cyprus. It was a priority to get the Doctor to complete his course! The Dropping Zone (DZ) was to be the beach not far from Akroteri, and we fervently hoped the pilots would be 100% accurate when they gave us the green light to jump, as we didn't want to end up in the sea! The jumps were planned to take place very early in the morning, before the wind got up. I was surprised how windy Cyprus was during the day! We had been informed that a couple of years earlier, a parachutist had landed on the beach by the waters edge; and before he had time to collapse his parachute, been dragged into the sea by the wind, and being unable to disentangle himself, unfortunately drowned. Our jumps were thankfully uneventful, and the Doctor was presented with his Wings!

The old building that was supposed to serve as a Church in the UN camp was in a bit of a state, and had obviously not seen much use. I managed to come up with an acceptable alternative. About a mile down the road towards Limasol, was an RAF married quarter 'patch' called Berengaria, with Churches to serve all three main denominations. Unlike the Army, which had Chaplains who were either Roman Catholic or Protestant, the RAF had three branches. RC, C of E, and CSFC (Church of Scotland and Free Church). The CSFC Chaplain, who happened to be a Methodist, worked at Akroteri and Episcopi (the RAF HQ), lived in Berengaria, and was responsible for the Church there! When we first met, it was immediately obvious that we were 'on the same wave length' and became good friends. He very kindly offered to share his Church with me during my tour, and I publicised details of all Church Services at Berengaria in the UN Camp.

The few who were regular worshippers were happy to make the short journey down the road, and benefited from being part of a 'normal' congregation; and were also able to share in the social life of the Churches. Every three weeks I would conduct a Service at Ziggi, in the south of the island, where we had about a Company and a half stationed.

The main duty of the soldiers was to man Observation Posts (Ops) in strategic positions. Their task was to observe, and make reports on any suspicious activities between the Greek Cypriot and Turkish Cypriot communities. Under no circumstances were they to intervene; just observe and report. You can imagine how utterly boring this quickly became for Airborne soldiers! They also had to watch out for any UN Vehicles passing along the road below them: then they were expected to step out of their shelters and give a smart salute. Any soldier failing to do this was liable to be reported for lack of vigilance!

I mentioned earlier how, having to obey UN Orders, could sometimes lead to problems with the other British soldiers stationed on the island. One evening, a group from I PARA were in a bar in Limasol having a good time. At about 10.30pm they began to make a move to get back to camp before 11.00pm. Some other soldiers in the bar began to make fun of them with comments like, "Bye, bye boys, off you go to bed like good boys". This inevitably led to a 'punch up', damage was caused to the bar, and the UN Police were called. The soldiers were arrested, charged, and taken back to their respective camps. The following morning I saw about half a dozen of them outside the CO's Office. Some were a bit bruised but seemed quite cheerful. Two UN Policemen insisted on making their report personally to the CO, who listened politely then said, "I have only one question for you; did we win?" The soldiers were marched in, pleaded guilty as charged, and accepted their punishment, part of which was to pay for damage caused. The CO did take the matter seriously and dealt with it accordingly, but soldiers have been having fights and smashing up bars for many, many years; so it was no big deal!

The tank squadron in Nicosia had gone back to England and been replaced by another. They were 16/5th Lancers and I went to visit them and introduce myself. I talked with the Squadron Leader for a while and asked questions about his Regiment. He was appalled to discover that as a Staffordshire man, I was unaware that 16/5th Lancers were my County Armoured Regiment! He informed me that the majority of his men came from North Staffordshire, and asked if I would like to meet the Squadron end speak to them on my next visit. I said that I would be delighted and arranged a visit for the following Wednesday. When I arrived, the Squadron had been gathered together in a small cinema. They were all huddled down in their seats, and didn't look at all pleased at being there! I jumped up on to the stage, looked them over for a minute, and then said in North Staffordshire dialect, "Ay up lads, 'ow at, or rate"? And they perked up and grinned from ear to ear. I spoke to them for about half an hour, then we all moved over to the Squadron Club and in no time at all, we'd swapped enough stories to make me think I was distantly related to many of them!

Subsequent visits to the Squadron were a pleasure. Little did I know that seven years later, I would be Chaplain to the whole Regiment, when I was posted to the Royal Armoured Corps Centre, at Bovington in Dorset!

I PARA kept the medical staff busy, and I made frequent visits to the Hospitals in Akroteri and Dhekelia. Most soldiers were admitted as a result of injuries sustained while playing sport, usually Volley Ball on concrete pitches! Thinking back over my eight years with Airborne Forces, there is no doubt at all in my mind that playing sports is far more dangerous that parachuting! A bandsman spent a short time in Hospital after putting his hand into a small shrub containing a viper while in the process of sitting down on a stone. Another soldier in an OP was pumping up a primus cooker, when it blew up, burning him rather badly. Fortunately, much time in the sun had given him an impressive tan; otherwise he would have suffered much more.

Following the victory of the Battalion team in the Island Tug-of-War competition, the team went out in the evening to celebrate. In the morning, a nineteen years old member of the team was found dead in bed. He had drunk far too much, gone to sleep on his back, and choked to death. Once again, soldiers were reminded about the 'buddy' system, and ensure that if one of their friends had too much to drink, it was their responsibility to put him to bed on his side in the semi prone position. Better still, to put him in the Guardroom for the night where he could be constantly observed. The young man's body was sent back to England for burial, and I conducted a Memorial Service for him in his Company location.

One of the social highlights for the British Community on the Island during the summer, were the Band Concerts which were held in the Curium, an open-air amphitheatre set in the cliffs between Limasol and Paphos. That summer there were two military bands performing together, and the event was traditionally organised by the RAF. The amphitheatre was packed to capacity. People brought their cold boxes containing their supper, and bottles of wine. The Bandmaster suggested I sing a couple of solos as part of the programme. I practised and performed songs from "South Pacific", and "Fiddler of the Roof". The atmosphere was incredible, and the audience very light hearted and most appreciative. It was for me, an unforgettable experience.

The months of July and August were unbearably hot and humid. I would frequently have to get up a couple of times during the night and take a cold shower! It was a good time to take a break and I decided to return to England for two weeks leave. Indulgence (free) flights with the RAF were available but

August 1973 Peter sings at a band concert at Curium, Cyprus

couldn't be guaranteed, so I flew home using a civilian airline. I took the family to Bournemouth, where we had a most enjoyable holiday. The weather was good for the whole time, and I just couldn't believe it when I got sun-burned! That was something I had managed to avoid during the past three months in Cyprus, even though I had spent many hours in the sun. I had come home with a good tan, and got burned on top of it! I managed to get an indulgence flight back to the island for the second part of the tour.

Not wishing to take things too easy, I used to go for a run most days, usually about 4.30p.m., when the temperature had dropped a bit!. Shortly after our arrival, a young Officer had introduced me to a circuit, which went up into the hills behind the camp, close to where a new Dam was being built. The route then went down into a valley, and around to another hill, which led back to the camp. It took about forty minutes over very uneven ground to complete the circuit and it was necessary to run in a strong pair of boots! After cooling off for half an hour, I would have a shower, get dressed for the evening, stroll across to the Mess and order a pint of Carlsberg. Losing so much bodily fluid during the run, left me with an incredible thirst, and the Carlsberg was the finest thing I'd ever tasted!

These regular runs were to pay quite a dividend near the end of the tour. The first Company based at the Nicosia/Larnaca junction had trained by running up a considerable hill to a Monastery at the top, called Stavravouni. It was a hard slog and took about 55 minutes of hard running and climbing. Indeed the last hundred feet or so were more of a scramble than a climb! Subsequent Companies carried on the tradition, and it was decided to hold an inter-platoon race to the top. The Sergeants challenged the Officers to do the same, and of course the challenge was accepted. On the day of the race I joined the Officers team, and my personal stock rose a few points when I surprised a few people, particularly from the Sergeants Mess, when I beat many of them to the top! There was one particular Officer, an ex-Regimental Sergeant Major, who had always given me the impression that he had little time for Chaplains, or what they represented. After I had beaten him on the climb to the top, his attitude towards me changed completely!

One day the Australian Police Superintendent asked me to call on him. When I had sat down in his office, he said, "Peter, you are our Chaplain aren't you"? I replied in the affirmative. "Well then," he said, "We've been invited to a Church Service with the Swedish Police Contingent in Famagusta, would you like to come with us"? Of course I agreed, and on the day I was collected, and squeezed into a large red Mercedes saloon for the journey to Famagusta. On our arrival we were directed to a large corrugated iron building with a bell on top, which served as the Lutheran Church in the camp. It was only then I heard that I was expected to preach! It was a most unusual service, and began with a large, bearded Swedish policeman singing the Louis Armstrong hit song, "What a Wonderful World". After a few words of welcome, the bearded police-man gave us another solo, this time it was, "Somewhere over the Rainbow"! There were a couple of hymns, known and sung only by the Swedes: then I read a Lesson and preached. Fortunately the congregation's knowledge of the English language was good!

After the Service we were invited to their Mess where we enjoyed a very good meal. The bearded policeman then treated us to another song and a few jokes. The Australian sitting next to me had been at the Band Concert at Curium. He gave me a nudge and whispered, "Come on Padre, it's got to be your turn now". Feeling National honour was at stake, I sang a song and told a joke! The Swede responded with another rendition, and I received another nudge.

This went on for about an hour until the Superintendent thought it was time for us to leave! Thanks were expressed on both sides for a most entertaining evening. We squeezed back into the Mercedes and I went to sleep! I was awakened just as the car stopped by my 'Vicarage'.

The tour ended on a very sad note. One of our Platoon Commanders, a Scotsman, had served in the Territorial Army for a few years before taking a Regular Commission, and was therefore older than his contemporaries. He was very popular with his soldiers, and with his fellow Officers. He made jokes about being 'the oldest Lieutenant in the Army'. One day he decided his Platoon should race to the Monastery at Stavrovouni. He didn't run with them, but took a long wheel based Land Rover to the top to give them a lift down. There were soldiers hanging on all over the vehicle when it left the road and turned over. Most were thrown clear, three ended up in Hospital with minor injuries, but the Lieutenant received fatal injuries. He was married but had no children. I had met his wife when she had visited him in Cyprus only a few weeks earlier. She decided he should be taken home, and given a Military Funeral in Scotland.

After consultations with the CO, it was decided that I, and a small party from the Battalion, should return to England with him. I travelled to Scotland and conducted his Funeral. As the Battalion were within a few weeks of completing their tour of duty in Cyprus, it was decided I should remain in Aldershot. It was quite ironic that after more than two years serving in Northern Ireland, without suffering any casualties, the Battalion should lose two soldiers in sunny Cyprus! Most of the soldiers were very pleased when they returned to Aldershot. In Cyprus they had become very bored and frustrated with the routine and inactivity of being UN Soldiers. Now they could put their Red Berets back on, and get on with what they considered to be the 'real job'!

After some well deserved leave, the Battalion came back just in time to bid 'farewell' to the CO, and to meet his successor. They were also informed the Battalion was to be posted to Berlin the following summer. Except for the tour in Northern Ireland, the Battalion's families had never been out of England before and the news was received with mixed feelings. Most were absolutely delighted, but others felt a little concerned at the prospect of being 'enclosed' in West Berlin. They were reassured when they found out that West Berlin was much larger than they had imagined; in fact it was twenty miles across and had many lakes and forests. Another incentive was the superb shops, not only in the City itself, but also as Allied Forces, we would be entitled to use the American and French Army shopping facilities! Another piece of good news (for the soldiers at least) was that we were to go to Kenya in January for a months training. This would be an excellent opportunity for training in various types of terrain, and at an unaccustomed altitude. It would also enable our new CO to test and assess his troops, and for the Battalion to discover their new CO's priorities, expectations, and modus operandi. I think I must have been one of the first to experience the latter!

For the last few months in Cyprus, I had been entrusted with looking after the 'extra Messing' account for the HQ Officer's Mess. In addition to the rations supplied to the Mess by the Quartermaster, extra items, such as various kinds of cheese; would be purchased from local shops by the Mess Sergeant. Each Officer paid an amount according to his rank, for 'extra Messing' on his monthly Mess bill. Battalion Officers serving in other locations regularly visited the HQ Mess, and dined well, as did guests from other units on the island. Having no previous experience in such matters, I sought the advice of the outgoing Mess Sergeant. His advice was simple, but as it turned out, inaccurate. "Oh", he said. "You just find out what they want, buy it, and they pay for it"! The result of this policy was that the Extra Messing account went deeply 'into the red', and this was a major item of business at the first Mess Meeting back in England under the new CO. Every Officer had to pay an additional amount to balance the books. As the person responsible (ignorance being no excuse!) I apologised profusely, but the CO ordered me to pay double the amount levied on the other Officers!

KENYA – JANUARY 1974

The Brigade Roman Catholic Chaplain had arranged to accompany the Battalion to Kenya. He was a most amiable chap and I knew we would work well together. It was quite a long flight to Kenya. We flew by Britannia turbo prop aircraft to Nairobi, stopping to refuel in Cyprus. From Nairobi, which I learned was 6,000 feet above sea level, we journeyed north for about 100 miles to our base camp at Nanyuki, just a few miles north of the Equator. It was a tented camp, located by what I can only describe as an old colonial Country Club, which had seen better days. Officers were invited to use the facilities, including a squash court. I had been playing squash regularly with the Battalion Second-in-Command (2IC), and we soon discovered the increased speed of a squash ball in Equatorial temperatures! A couple of days after our arrival, I went for a run with a group around the sports field. Feeling good, I decided to do an extra lap and experienced the worst headache I'd ever had. The reason was, that I hadn't given myself enough time to acclimatise to the altitude!

The temperature during the night was another thing that caught me completely unawares. After the blistering heat of the day, it was bitterly cold during the night: it's the only place I've ever been where I needed to put on so many clothes before going to bed! The following day, it was a case of stripping off a layer at a time as the temperature rose.

Kenya offered a variety of training areas, from the foothills of Mount Kenya to the desert parts in the north of the country. The Rifle Companies rotated, spending time training in each area, and I was able to spend time with each of them. I had no vehicle of my own, so it was a case of hitching rides as and when others were making the trip. The favourite location was Archer's Post in the north of the country, located very near to the Samburu wild life

Reserve. The Battalion Second in Command invited me to join him on a trip to Archer's Post. After spending time with the Company, we visited the game Reserve. Before driving around the Reserve we had some refreshments at a café by a shallow river, and sat at an outside table by a wall about three feet high separating the café from the river. There were signs at intervals on top of the wall warning diners to 'Beware of Crocodiles'. The other side of the signs, facing outwards to the river, read, 'Beware of People'! To emphasise the seriousness of these signs, the Manager informed us a young woman from the village had been taken by a crocodile only a few weeks earlier. Across the river we could just see a leopard stretched out on the branch of a tree.

Unlike Safari Parks I have visited in England and Germany, there were no tarmac roads, no fences, and no enclosures. Instead there was just a loose network of dirt and mud tracks. There was not even a map! We just had to drive slowly and carefully around. At one point we passed within about fifty yards of a small family of elephants: a large bull elephant flapped his enormous ears, raised his trunk, trumpeted loudly at us, and began to move towards us. We increased our speed and a few hundred yards on, found ourselves by the river with nowhere to go except back the way we had come!

The track was narrow and we turned around with some difficulty, grateful to be in a four-wheel drive vehicle! As we approached the elephants, the bull made it obvious that he was even less pleased to see us than before, and we sped past as fast as we could! Incidentally, it wasn't necessary to visit game reserves to view wild life, as there was plenty to be seen as we moved around the training areas. One memorable sight was of giraffes running alongside the road and without slowing down; lowering their long necks to pass under the branches of trees.

A few miles from Nanyuki on the lower slopes of Mount Kenya was a wooden lodge overlooking a waterhole. Powerful spotlights had been mounted outside the lodge illuminating the water hole, and a number of platforms erected on which meat was placed at certain times. Over the course of time, the animals had got used to the spotlights and mounted the platforms to eat. I spent a night in the lodge and was awakened by a member of the staff in the middle of the night. I crept very quietly from my room and out on to the veranda where I saw, not more than four yards away, a leopard on the platform tucking in to an early breakfast! The next hour saw a number of animals visiting the waterhole: elephants, various types of gazelles and monkeys. I remember thinking how fortunate I was. Tourists paid lots of money to visit these places, and I was getting paid for being there!

One day I had a visit from a Chaplain serving with the Kenyan Army, and based at a Barracks not far from Nanyuki. He invited me to visit his Church the following Sunday and preach the sermon. He said, "You can preach in English of course, but you must pause after every sentence so that I can translate what you have said into Swahili for the congregation". I agreed and it was a most enjoyable Service, although I did find it difficult to preach in such a staccato manner!

There were several mountaineers in the Battalion who wanted to see how far they could climb up the mountain, which was snow covered. There was insufficient time available for them to make a serious attempt to reach the summit, but they managed to climb to a considerable height. I joined a less ambitious party who just wanted to climb for the day! We set off after an early breakfast and after a few hours, came to a ravine, which we crossed using a wooden bridge, which had been erected a few years earlier by a Squadron of Royal Engineers. At the end of the bridge there was a wooden notice board advertising this fact, and adding the words, 'ELEPHANTS ARE REQUESTED TO CROSS IN SINGLE FILE'. Shortly after crossing the bridge, we had to climb up through an area known as 'The Vertical Bog'! As the title suggests, we had to squelch our way up, moving slowly and with some difficulty between what looked like giant cabbages several feet high and ringing wet! Emerging from the 'Bog' we walked onwards and upwards for about another hour until exhaustion forced us to take a break. The views were magnificent, making all our efforts worth while. We made our way down again, descending through the 'Bog', which was if anything, more difficult than climbing up!

The Kenyan Army had a Parachute Company, and it had been agreed that some of the Battalion would make a parachute jump with them. The aircraft they used was a small Caribou, which only took about sixteen paratroops at a time. Jumping from the Caribou meant leaving the aircraft by jumping off the back (tailgating) instead of through a door. Those of us selected to jump had to undergo the usual two hours 'synthetic' training beforehand. It was decided that we should alternate with the Kenyans. The first to jump would be a Kenyan, then a British man and so on. The Dropping Zone was right on the Equator and on the day it was pouring with rain! That wasn't a problem in itself: the problem was rolling up a soaking wet parachute, stuffing it back into its bag, and securing it with pieces of thread to carry it off the Dropping Zone!

That evening we were entertained by the Kenyans at a social evening, and presented with a tie to commemorate the event. The tie is a lovely shade of green, with parachutes and a shield and spear on it. It has always been one of my favourites and still hangs on my tie rack today.

The training was deemed to be a great success and the Commanding Officer decided to hold a Cocktail Party to thank those who had made it possible. I didn't know if he was giving me the opportunity to redeem myself for the debt I'd run up for the Mess in Cyprus, or if he just thought I was one of the few with time to spare: anyway, he gave me the task of organising it! The acting Mess Sergeant was a man who was experienced, resourceful, and reliable. He winked at me, gave me a broad smile, and said, "Don't worry Padre, we'll soon sort this one out"! He soon discovered the nearest 'Cash & Carry', arranged for a vehicle, and we went shopping. The Adjutant had told us roughly the numbers invited and arranged for extra waiters to be available on the night. It was a very successful evening and was completed within budget!

One of the guests was an RAF Wing Commander from the British Embassy in Nairobi. As I was chatting to him, he mentioned that in addition to British Troops visiting Kenya for training purposes, the RAF occasionally flew to Australia and New Zealand. This was done in order to exercise their right to 'fly the routes', and sometimes they were able to take 'indulgence' passengers. This gave me something to think about, not for myself, but for an Australian Corporal who worked in the Battalion Medical Centre. He was separated from his wife, who lived in New Zealand, and wished to marry a girl from Aldershot with whom he had been living for some time. His wife had agreed to a divorce, but had failed to respond to any communication from either the Corporal or his solicitor. He had said to me some time before that if he could only get to New Zealand, he would be able to find his wife and get her to sign the necessary papers. I discussed this later with the Commanding Officer, and he agreed that when we returned to England, he would grant the Corporal thirty days leave, so that he could use the next available indulgence flight and sort out his domestic affairs. This duly happened although it took slightly longer than thirty days, as the Corporal was forced to give up his seat in Singapore to a more important passenger (which is a risk faced by all indulgence passengers!). After waiting for almost a week, he managed to get a flight. It was a happy day when I officiated at his marriage a few months later.

My Roman Catholic colleague followed his own routine and had an enjoyable time. We had shared two Services together. Now there were just a couple of days left before we returned home, and we decided to spend them together visiting Nairobi. We arranged to stay with the Royal Engineers Squadron just outside the City at Kahawa. They were kept busy doing jobs for the Kenyan Government, like building roads, bridges, and even a school. These were good Community Relations projects, and I think helped in part to pay for the training facilities used by the British Army. Saturday was spent looking around the City, particularly the markets, looking for souvenirs. My colleague, spent hours looking for a pair of elephants, which he insisted, had to be at least a foot tall. Eventually he found a pair. The next morning, being Sunday, he declared, "I think I'll go to Mass at the Cathedral". I decided to go with him. The Cathedral was already quite crowded and noisy when we arrived, and when it was time for Mass, it was packed! The congregation seemed to be as multi-coloured as their costumes, and the atmosphere was electric. A bell rang, signifying the commencement of the Mass, and the congregation were silent. A priest emerged from the Sacristy, stood in front of the congregation, and in a broad Irish brogue said, "Good mornin everyone, 'Tis luvly to see yer here". It was quite an experience: the music and the singing were memorable. The following day we boarded a VC 10 and flew back to England.

Back in Aldershot, the Commanding Officer began his battle to take Bayley to Berlin with the Battalion! The initial request was refused on the grounds that there was already a Church of Scotland Chaplain, and an elderly Methodist Minister, who was Warden Of Wesley House in Spandau. There were three Church of England Chaplains (including the Deputy Assistant Chaplain General) DACG. Eventually after prolonged negotiations, authority was obtained for me to go to Berlin with I PARA. Before that day arrived, there was much to be done.

The Parachute Regiment Free Fall Team, 'The Red Devils', organised basic courses for aspiring free fall parachutists. Their aircraft was a small red Islander, and the drop zone an area of sports fields a few hundred yards from my home. I decided to do the course! It was a very different experience to what I would call, the Military business of paratrooping! The parachutes were different, giving greater control, and even the training height of 2,000 feet was twice what I had been used to, giving more time to have a good look around! I had almost completed the course when we received some tragic news.

We got up one Sunday morning to find a note had been pushed through our letterbox, informing us that my friend from the 50s and Munster; the Adjutant of 23rd Parachute Field Ambulance, had been killed in a parachuting accident the day before. He had collided with another parachutist, been rendered unconscious, and therefore unable to open his parachutes. To add to the tragedy, his wife and two of their four children had seen it happen. He had been a very experienced free fall parachutist, and it was a real shock that he should die in this way. In the days that followed my wife and I spent many hours with his family.

The Commanding Officer of the Field Ambulance Unit and his wife were also very supportive, as were many of their friends. He was given a Military Funeral, which I conducted, and buried in Aldershot Military Cemetery. Afterwards, my wife said to me, "What you have to do as Padre with I PARA, you have to do. What you don't have to do is free fall parachuting." There was no answer to that, so I didn't complete the course and did only what I had to do.

Before returning to the Army as a Chaplain, I had enjoyed excellent working relationships with the local Church of England Clergy. I was most surprised and saddened to discover that in the Army, things were very different and developments years behind what was happening in the civilian Churches. Considering the role of the Army, I expected the reverse to be true. Talking with other Methodist and Free Church Chaplains confirmed that I was certainly not alone in this assessment. We were definitely treated as second class citizens! Roman Catholic Chaplains didn't have these problems as they had their own 'chain of command', and were not part of the so-called 'United Department'. Their responsibilities were clear; they were responsible for looking after all Roman Catholics in a Garrison, and were not attached to or responsible for any particular Regiment or Battalion. I came across a little verse somewhere, which adequately summed up the situation. It was entitled, 'The Anglican Song of Unity

"Jesus bids us shine with a pure clear light,

like a little candle burning in the night,

in this world of darkness so we must shine;

you in your small corner, **and I in the middle of the room!"**

One day a Corporal from I PARA came to see me to arrange a Baptism. I explained to him that as a Methodist, I would be happy to baptise his baby in one of the two Garrison Methodist Churches. He told me that his other two children had been baptised in the Royal Garrison Church, and would very much like his new baby to be baptised there too. I told him I would be happy to perform the ceremony there, but would need to obtain permission. I made my request, and the four Anglican Chaplains on the staff of the Royal Garrison Church had a meeting about it. I was informed that they would be happy for me to share in the service, but that one of them would have to do the actual Baptism! I declined the offer and informed the Corporal, who said he would come to the Methodist Church. This reminded me of the problems I had encountered in Northern Ireland!

A Chaplains Exercise, similar to the one in Germany was held in the Aldershot area for all Chaplains in South East District. This was called 'Pardon's Penance' and gave us an opportunity to practice and be tested on our military skills. At the end of the Exercise, a Service of Holy Communion was held for all the participants in one of the Anglican Garrison Churches.

Both the Chaplains who officiated at this Service were Anglicans, and I just couldn't believe it when a small group of Anglican Chaplains refused to take Communion because of the presence of a number of Free Church Chaplains! During the years that followed there were a number of distressing incidents, but I'm happy to say that things gradually improved.

As a Minister, I have conducted hundreds of funerals over the years. They were always very sad occasions and the vast majority were of elderly people. Funerals in the Army community were always particularly sad, and sometimes extremely difficult because it is a young community. The deceased were young soldiers, or a soldier's wife, and all too often, children. As the Army is a close-knit community, in many ways just like a large family; many people were deeply affected by these tragedies.

One day I was attending a meeting of the Methodist District Synod, which was being held in the Methodist Garrison Church in Aldershot; when a Police Officer came into the Church and informed me that I was to return to I PARA immediately. I went straightaway to see the Commanding Officer, who was manifestly most distressed. The two young sons of one of our Sergeants were dead. They had dug a den for themselves in the side of a hill just below the Military Hospital. Then they had made a fire, and been suffocated by the smoke and fumes. It was an absolutely devastating blow for the Sergeant, his wife, and their young daughter who was just a few years older than her brothers. I visited their home to discover that a Doctor had already been and prescribed medication for the boy's mother, who was in a state of shock and now partially sedated: a number of friends were with her. The Sergeant mad been taken out by some of his friends, and got drunk as he cried and raged in his grief. His wife was, very sadly, not allowed to grieve properly by her well meaning, but misguided friends, who insisted on giving her more tablets every time she was on the verge of having a good cry!

The funeral for those two small boys at Aldershot Crematorium, was one of the most difficult services I ever had to take. Their poor mother went through the entire proceedings in a complete daze. It was some weeks later in Berlin, before the real tragedy of her loss overwhelmed her and she was enabled to express her grief. At the Inquest, the Coroner was most sympathetic, but just offered the old adage that 'boys will be boys'. Thereafter, whenever tragedy struck someone in my community, I always tried to visit the next of kin as soon as possible. In this way I was able to advise, and hopefully convince relatives and friends to allow people to grieve.

Only a few weeks later, a Sergeant helicopter pilot from the Parachute Brigade's Army Air Corps Squadron, died in Northern Ireland after his rotor blades struck some wires, which weren't marked on his map! He was a married man, but had no children. After a Service in Aldershot, I travelled with his family to his home in the Midlands for his burial. His wife had been allowed to grieve, and of course would continue to grieve, but she had been aware of all that was happening, and told me she was grateful for the memories of the Funeral and the support of the Squadron.

Parachute training continued, culminating in an Exercise on Salisbury Plain in which the whole Battalion and its equipment were dropped. It was the biggest 'drop' I had taken part in since a NATO Exercise in Norway back in 1959. The RAF were unable on this occasion to provide all the Hercules aircraft needed for this Exercise, and we had to 'borrow' four from the Canadians. I was amongst the first troops on the ground, and it was a most impressive sight to see all the others come in. Within minutes of all the troops landing, aircraft were overhead dropping all our heavy equipment and vehicles on platforms; each one supported by 6 x 60 foot parachutes! Immediately these platforms hit the ground, teams of 'de-riggers' were all over them to release the equipment, and we were on our way. We knew that opportunities for para-chuting would be severely limited during our forthcoming tour in Berlin, so there was much satisfaction in the Battalion that we had managed to complete such an Exercise before leaving England. At the same time, we were preparing for a much more significant event.

On 15th July 1974, Her Majesty Queen Elizabeth II, would be visiting Aldershot to present new Colours to the three Regular Battalions of the Parachute Regiment, and to one Territorial Army Battalion. This was to take place in Rushmoor Arena, and lots of rehearsals would be needed! The new Colours were to be consecrated by the Chaplain General before being presented to the Battalions; and the four Battalion Chaplains would also need to be involved in the rehearsals. A couple living in a little cottage on the edge of the arena kindly offered to let the Chaplains use their living room to change into their robes before the ceremony. The dress rehearsal went off well, except for the weather! It poured with rain and everyone on Parade, wearing their best uniforms, were absolutely soaked. We consoled ourselves with the thought that it couldn't possibly be as bad on the day: but sadly it was!

In addition to the soldiers on Parade, many hundreds of veterans were expected to attend. At the end of the official proceedings they were expected to form up, and march past the Queen; who would be in a glass covered saluting base. It would take an estimated twenty minutes to gather the veterans together, and someone came up with the suggestion that the Chaplains should join the Queen in the saluting base, and chat with her while this was being organised!

On the day, accurately predicting the volume of traffic converging on the arena, all the Chaplains arrived early at the cottage: except the Chaplain General! As the minutes ticked by, and knowing that the Queen would arrive exactly on time, we grew more and more anxious. Eventually I left the cottage to look for him, being careful not to venture too far away from the cottage myself! I saw him in the act of climbing over the perimeter fence struggling with a suitcase containing his robes. I hurried to help him and guide him to the cottage, where he changed into his robes with only minutes to spare. His Staff Car had become completely blocked in by the traffic, so he had abandoned it and made his way across country! We were escorted to our places just in time to see the Queen arrive.

The four Battalions formed up in the arena; and the old Colours were paraded through the ranks. They were then slowly marched off the Parade Ground for the last time, as the massed bands of The Parachute Regiment played, 'For The Sake Of Auld Lang Syne'. As this was taking place, the odd tear was shed by some of the 'old' soldiers who had served under those Colours for many years. One in particular, still a serving soldier, had been an Escort to those Colours, when they had been presented to the Regiment by King George VI some twenty five years earlier. The Queen, accompanied by

the Chaplains, then moved to the dais on which the new Colours were laid across the Regiment's drums. The new Colours, after being consecrated there then handed to the Queen, who presented them to the Colour Parties of each Battalion. The Queen then returned to the glass covered saluting base, and the Chaplains returned to their places. All four Battalions, new Colours held proudly aloft, marched past and saluted the Queen, while the bands played the Regimental March of the Parachute Regiment, 'The Ride of the Valkyries'. The Chaplains then entered the glass covered saluting base and, after paying their respects, chatted informally with the Queen (Her Majesty of course, taking the initiative in this matter) for about twenty minutes while the Veterans were mustered. I was surprised to see how small she was, and how quickly she made us all feel at ease as we talked.

The hundreds of Veterans marched proudly past, some using sticks; others being pushed in wheelchairs by comrades. The Officers of each Battalion had a photograph taken with the Queen (my copy is on the study wall in front of me even as I type). Several large marquees had been erected, and the Officers and their wives had lunch with the Queen. In spite of the weather, the day evoked feelings of pride in belonging, and gratitude for the privilege of being able to play a small part in the proceedings.

Having been without a car for just over a year, and discovering the awful inadequacies of public transport, I was really looking forward to buying a tax free car before going to Berlin. The NAAFI, in consultation with the Battalion, organised a day when many car dealers exhibited their models on the Regimental Square. I spent a couple of hours looking around and getting in and out of various cars before deciding on a particular model. NAAFI Staff were available to help in organising help with finance. I ordered a car and paid a deposit. I was given a delivery date which came and went with no sign of the car! After numerous telephone calls it became apparent that the car wasn't going to arrive before our departure date, so I cancelled the order and the NAAFI encouraged the firm to return my deposit! I toured the local car showrooms seeking a small estate car, which was readily available for immediate collection. All I could find was a Simca and as I had run out of options, I bought it!

One member of my family was most unhappy about the move to Berlin. Our eldest daughter Vivien was now almost fifteen years of age, and had made some good friends in Aldershot. She dreaded the prospect of losing them and became very depressed. The situation wasn't helped by the information we had received that there was no Secondary Education in Berlin. There were insufficient children in that age group to warrant a School. Those children not already at Boarding School, and there were several in I PARA, would have to go to a Boarding School at Hamm, which was three hundred miles from Berlin! It was a BFES (British Forces Education Service) school, and was attended by Servicemen's children from many parts of Germany. About twenty of the children in the Battalion would have to go to school there.

Most of the families would be flown out to Berlin. I, like most husbands, would drive there with the car packed to capacity with possessions we didn't want to entrust to the tender care of the MFO (Married Families Organisation), who would be moving our packing cases to Berlin. I chose the long sea crossing and the shorter drive, booking a passage on the ferry from Harwich to Hamburg.

1ST BATTALION, THE PARACHUTE REGIMENT

BERLIN – AUGUST 1974 – JULY 1976

Leaving Hamburg I travelled south to join the Autobahn heading east to West Berlin, which was just over one hundred miles inside what was then East Germany. Travelling by road, there was only one route to Berlin, and that was by using what was known as 'the Corridor', which was controlled by the East Germans, but had a Russian checkpoint at either end. I was about to experience the first of many tedious journeys in and out of Berlin! The western end of the Corridor began at Helmstedt, near Bruswick, where there was a Royal Military Police base and NAAFI facilities for toilets and refreshments. In order to travel in and out of Berlin, a Berlin Travel Document (BTD) was necessary, together with Identity Card and Passport. The BTD had to be completed in the most meticulous way, even to the correct placing of full stops and commas! If the Russian Border Guards found the slightest mistake or discrepancy in the documentation, the traveller would be turned back. The Military Police checked the documents and gave each driver a very thorough briefing before allowing them to proceed.

There were very specific rules to be adhered to. The speed limit, which was strictly enforced, was 100 kilometres an hour (approximately 62 mph). Considering the awful state of the road surface, it was more then enough! The driver was not allowed to stop except in an emergency or vehicle breakdown. Not allowed to leave the Autobahn, and must take no longer than two hours to book in at the Royal Military Police post at the other end of the Corridor. The drivers time of departure and vehicle registration were telephoned through to the other end, and if a vehicle failed to turn up, a Police Patrol would be sent to find it! There were frequent Royal Military Police and East German Police patrols up an down the Corridor. A few miles from Berlin the driver would encounter the Autobahn Ring around the City, and there were three junctions with signs that had to be memorised. Taking the wrong one would take the driver into either East Berlin, or East Germany!

I signed a form signifying that I had been properly briefed and was given a piece of paper to hand to the East German Border Guard. Several barriers overlooked by watch towers were raised, and I made my way to the Russian Checkpoint. A young Russian soldier signalled me to halt and get out of the car. He saluted me and I returned his salute. This was necessary even if a driver was in civilian clothes and not wearing a hat. Any passengers remained in the car. My documents were checked, and he motioned for me to go into a prefabricated office building at the side of the road. Inside was a table on which a couple of Russian newspapers had been placed, a couple of chairs, and a slit in one wall, through which I passed my passport and travel documents. On the wall were a couple of pictures of Russian Presidents. As I sat and waited for my documents to be returned, the young sentry outside was examining my car. Eventually my documents were pushed back to me through the slit in the wall, and I was to discover that this procedure could take anything from a few minutes to half an hour.

No explanation was given and no human being was seen, unless some fault had been discovered; when an official would come and point it out to you, before sending you back to Helmstedt! I returned to the car and presented my documents to the soldier, who went through the motions of checking them again! We exchanged salutes and I got back into the car. After passing through several more barriers I was at last on the bumpy Corridor to Berlin. After two hours and having followed the correct signs at the Autobahn junctions, I arrived at the Russian Checkpoint on the border of West Berlin. There I went through the same tedious process as before, and was then allowed to proceed to the East German Border Guard; and finally on to the British Military Police Border post. Here my documents were given a final check and I confirmed that nothing untoward had happened on my way up the Corridor. Then it was a quick and much needed visit to the toilet, followed by a cup of tea, and finally back to the car and on into the City: Phew!!

I PARA was stationed in Montgomery Barracks, Kladow, which, as the crow flies, was no distance at all from the Corridor. However, there was a huge lake called the Havel, which prevented a direct route and I had to drive through the American Sector into the City and all around the lake to get there; a journey of about twenty miles! If you could imagine a map of West Berlin, Kladow would be in the bottom left hand corner. Making my way through the southern end of the City, I turned west, joining a dual carriageway called the Heerstrasse, where for the first time I encountered synchronised traffic lights! Overhead lights advised drivers to keep to the recommended speed; which, if followed, enabled the traveller to arrive at all subsequent traffic lights when they were on green. Exceed the advised speed limit and the lights would be on red! After a few miles I came to a major road junction. Straight ahead led to the Autobahn to Hamburg. How much easier it would have been had we been allowed to use that road! A right turn led to Spandau, the French Sector, and Tegel Airport. I turned left for the final six miles to Kladow. Passing RAF Gatow on my right, I finally arrived at Montgomery Barracks. The six miles from the Heerstrasse became a very regular and boring road, as it was the only road from Kladow to Berlin!

Montgomery Barracks was half surrounded by the Berlin Wall, which in fact was only a 'wall' as it passed through the City. The rest of the encirclement (it came as something of a surprise to discover that West Berlin wasn't divided by the Wall, but completely encircled) was by a high wire fence, through which could be seen a wide raked strip of land which was mined and regularly patrolled. There were also watch towers at regular intervals: one of which overlooked the Barracks, and was only a few hundred yards from my Church!

I went first of all to see the Officer Commanding the Advance Party, who was also our new Unit Families Officer. He was an ex-Regimental Sergeant Major with a distinguished record of service, particularly in Northern Ireland. To put it mildly, he was a most reluctant Families Officer who turned out to be an absolute gem, and we worked extremely well together.

My office was next door to his department! I had been allocated a lovely corner house about two hundred yards from the Havel, and five minutes walk from the Barracks. I officially took over the house and arranged for my packing cases to be delivered. It would be a few more days before the family arrived, so I had all the cases put into one of the many cellars so they could easily be unpacked without getting in the way! We also had a new Quartermaster, and I arranged with his staff to 'take over' and sign for my Church. Being a corner house meant that we had a large garden to care for; but as my wife was an enthusiastic gardener, my role was usually to just to cut the grass! There was only one disadvantage: being so close to the lake meant that at certain times of the year, we were plagued with mosquitoes. This problem was officially recognised, in that the Quartermaster issued a number of large cans of anti-mosquito spray to all families living anywhere near the water! Every evening, all the bedrooms had to be sprayed. One evening the front door was unintentionally left open when the hall light was on. There was such a cloud of mosquitoes it took a couple of cans to quell the invasion, and we literally hovered them up off the carpets!

As in Munster, I had to take another 'tick test' in order to obtain a British Forces, Germany driving licence, BFG number plates for my car, and an allocation of petrol coupons. There were three other things, all peculiar to Berlin. Firstly, there were BAFs (British Armed Forces paper money) to get used to. This was a bit like Monopoly money, and had to be used for shopping in the NAAFI shops in the Barracks and in Berlin. This currency, which was happily phased out during our tour, was obtained from the Battalion Pay Office which acted as our Bank. By presenting a cheque, I could draw so much in BAFs and so much in Deutchmarks.

Secondly there was FRIS (Forces Ration Issue Supplement). By filling in a special order form, we could buy most of the family groceries very cheaply, and have them delivered to the door in large metal trays twice a week! Many items especially meat were plentiful and cheap; and the NAAFI did a roaring trade selling chest freezers! Payment for these was deducted from my monthly pay cheque. We were informed that this was to rotate food stocks, which were now stockpiled in the City, as a direct result of the Russian blockade of the City in 1948, which resulted in the Berlin Air Lift when everything the City needed had to be brought in by air. Outside Templehof Airport is a Memorial to the aircrews who lost their lives during that critical period.

Thirdly, to provide employment and subsidised by the Berlin Budget, was the Hausfrau scheme. A cleaning lady was supplied at minimal cost to us. We were fortunate in being allocated a most efficient lady who was half German/ half Swiss, who would come to the house for two hours, five days a week, and help with the cleaning and ironing etc. This was a luxury never to be repeated anywhere else I served!

In addition to I PARA, I had pastoral responsibility for a an Army Air Corps Flight of helicopters based at RAF Gatow, an Armoured Squadron (Tanks), and a Squadron of Royal Engineers, both based in Spandau. Close by was the prison with its solitary inmate, the infamous Rudolf Hess, who was guarded in turn by troops from the four Occupying Powers of Britain, America, France, and Russia. In Spandau were also two more Infantry Battalions, each with its own Chaplain. A couple of miles towards the City; were the Headquarters of the Berlin Infantry Brigade, (where the Senior Chaplain had his office) next to the building housing the British Military Government. Nearby could be seen the Stadium, used when Germany hosted the 1936 Olympic Games, and which was now used by the Army for events like the Queen's Birthday Parade. The British Military Hospital (BMH) and the Roman Catholic Church were also in this area, so it was necessary for me to spend some time away from Montgomery Barracks.

The time came for the Secondary School children to go to the Boarding School at Hamm, and transport arrangements were made to take them there. We fervently hoped that Vivien would make new friends and settle down. When she came home for half term it was obvious that she hadn't settled and was very unhappy. I adopted the stern but supportive father approach, and told her that she really hadn't given herself a chance, and that it would soon be Christmas. A few weeks later there was an 'Open Day' at the School and we drove down for the day. As it was a six hundred mile round trip, we didn't have much time at the School. My daughter did tell us that she was being bullied, and had been branded as a lesbian by some of the other girls. We spoke to members of the Staff about this, and they promised to do all they could to help, and I'm sure they did. When Christmas came, nothing had changed and so we decided there was no way we could allow our daughter to return to Hamm. We spoke to my in-laws about this, and they agreed that she could live with them in Rotherham, and attend a local School just around the corner from where they lived. After Christmas we travelled to Rotherham and left Vivien with her Grandparents. She quickly settled there, and we flew her to Berlin to spend her holidays with us between terms.

The Methodist Church had a building, called Wesley House in Spandau. This came under the auspices of the Forces Board of the Methodist Church, whose offices were in Westminster Central Hall. A Methodist Minister was the Warden, ably assisted by his wife, who managed the commercial side of the work. They had been working there for eight years and were widely known and respected for the contribution they made to the Military Community. Wesley House had a gift shop, a canteen, a quiet room, and a Chapel where services were held on Sunday evenings. The Warden also conducted a Service on Sunday mornings at the Church of Scotland and Free Church Chapel at RAF Gatow. A significant part of their work was the provision of refreshments around the small military training areas and barracks in the Garrison. To do this they had four mobile canteens, with locally employed drivers. Work in Wesley House began at 6.00am in making sandwiches and stocking up the mobile canteens. Some local people and a few servicemen's wives were employed in the House.

One elderly German lady had been there for many years. I was informed that when the Russians invaded Berlin, both she and her daughter had been raped, and her teenage son taken away, never to be seen again.

Shortly after our arrival we were shown a film that was not, as far as I am aware, ever publicly released. The title was, 'A Day In July'. In July 1945, shortly after the end of the War, an aircraft fitted with cameras, flew back and forth across the whole area of the City. There was not a single building that hadn't been seriously damaged in the Battle for Berlin. Not a roof or a window was to be seen anywhere. The City had suffered bombing day and night by the British and the Americans. The Russians had launched the final battle for the City with two hundred Divisions, about two million soldiers. They had suffered approximately one hundred thousand casualties, who are buried in a Memorial Cemetery at Treptow Park, in East Berlin. The Berliners who survived, did so by living in the cellars under their homes, and were desperately short of food, water, and medical supplies. As soon as the War was over, they emerged and immediately began to clear away the rubble and repair their homes. The rubble they cleared was enough to build a small mountain, which I had seen as I entered the City. On the top are now radio/radar transmitters, and during the winter months, it is a popular venue for skiers! It is called Teufels Berg, (The Devil's Mountain).

There were many sites of historical interest in West Berlin, from the Brandenberg Gate to the Reichstag and the bullet scarred walls, still to be seen in many parts of the City. One of the most memorable places I visited was in an old prison at Plotzenzee, in the Northern part of the City, in the French Sector. It is a Memorial to the German victims of Fascism. Just outside the entrance is a large stone urn containing soil from the Concentration Camps. Inside were two small rooms where almost two thousand Germans had been executed, many suspected of being involved in the bomb plot to kill Hitler. The women had been guillotined, and the men hung using piano wire. When the executions first began, they were filmed: but the cameramen became so sickened, the filming stopped. Literature is available in many languages telling the awful story of what happened there. I remember taking a group of hardened Paratroopers to visit the place: and they were very, very quiet afterwards. I was informed that all youth groups visiting the City from West Germany were obliged to visit Plotzensee and the Memorial. They had been taught so much about the terrible atrocities committed by their Nation during the War: the visit to the Memorial helped a little to redress the balance and remind them that there had also been Germans who paid the supreme penalty for opposing Hitler.

In Munster, the code name for the deployment of troops in an emergency had been 'Quick Train': in Berlin it was ' Rocking Horse'. As before, this Exercise could be used to test procedures from Battalion level upwards, and troops would never know the level or the time scale involved. I was a Chaplain, not a political analyst or military strategist, and could only surmise that our prime role would be one of internal security. Surrounded as we were by dozens of Russian Army Divisions, we, and our French and American allies were certainly in no position to defend the City! However, 'The Threat' was perceived to be real and we took our training very seriously.

Allied forces in Berlin were allowed to use each others shopping facilities, and we made frequent visits to the American PX (Post Exchange), who would accept only dollars, and occasional visits to the French Economat, who would accept only francs! Many of the items on sale were considerably cheaper and people took advantage of that and stocked up! The main bargains purchased from the PX were spirits, beer, bedding, towels, and some items of clothing, notably jeans. Spirits like gin, were so cheap that in winter, people used it to fill the windscreen washer reservoirs of their cars, because it was cheaper than anti-freeze! People visiting the Economat were usually those who loved French wines, bread, and their wide variety of cheeses.

Public transport was cheap and reliable, and included an excellent bus service to and around the City. In the City there was a choice of the 'U' Bahn (underground railway), and the 'S' Bahn, (overhead railway). There were also Water Buses plying around the lakes. There were so many ways of getting around and seeing the sights, which were multitudinous: and I was really surprised and saddened that many people, particularly young soldiers who were happy to jump out of aeroplanes, never ventured far from the Barracks!

I PARA decided to mark their arrival in Berlin by arranging a huge Cocktail Party! A host of people were invited. The General Officer Commanding the British sector of the City, and members of the Military Government. The

Brigadier Commanding the Berlin Infantry Brigade and members of his Staff: Notables from the American and French sectors, both Military and civilians; and German representatives of the City. The weather was hot, the Battalion Band played, and the atmosphere was most convivial. There was only one slight problem. The Officers and Sergeants Messes were unable to provide enough waiters to cope with the crowds of people, so a number of soldiers had been issued with white shirts etc., and co-opted as waiters for the evening. They were inexperienced and had received minimal instruction. Large bowls of Pimms had been prepared beforehand, which were soon emptied by our many thirsty guests. Before long they were waving their empty glasses at passing waiters requesting more! Many were unfortunate (or fortunate depending on your point of view!) in securing the services of an untrained waiter; who went to the outdoor bar, looked for a bottle of Pimms, and filled the guest's glass. They had not been informed that Pimms needed to be diluted, and served it up neat! Before too long there were a number of very happy, glassy eyed and unstable guests, who left for home proclaiming that it had been a most excellent party!

One day I was visiting the main NAAFI building in Berlin, and found myself having a cup of coffee at the same table as an American Army Chaplain. We talked for a while and then I excused myself, saying that I had to visit people in our Military Hospital. "Do you have many in your drugs ward"? He asked, and was quite amazed when I informed him that we didn't have a drugs ward in the Hospital.

When he pushed me for a reason as to why we didn't have a drugs ward, he was most surprised when I told him that drugs were not a problem with our soldiers. Not that we were complacent, because our soldiers received regular presentations on the dangers associated with all kinds of drugs, including alcohol. I PARA were affiliated with an American Regiment in Berlin and on occasions, trained and socialised with them. I knew that my Commanding Officer was most anxious lest any of his soldiers came into contact with drugs because of this affiliation. By the end of our two years tour in the City and regular contacts with American Servicemen; not a single case of a soldier in the Battalion being involved with drugs in any way had been reported. When I asked a group of soldiers why they thought this was so, they replied, "Well, we don't need them, do we"

Going through 'Check Point Charlie' was the only way we were allowed to visit East Berlin, which all members of the Allied Forces and their families were entitled to do. It was necessary to inform Brigade Headquarters and carry a Passport and Identity card. A military car belonging to our Intelligence Section made regular visits, and there was usually a spare seat: so I decided my first visit would be as a passenger. It gave me the opportunity to check the route and also to have a guided tour. There were the usual thorough checks by the East Germans manning the check-point, not only of our documents, but also of the car. The checks were even more exhaustive on our return trip, with the car boot and engine space being examined, and a mirror being wheeled underneath. A visit to the 'Escape Museum', by 'Check Point Charlie', showed many of the ingenious methods people had used to escape to the West, and is a place visited by tourists as a priority. At many places around the Wall were black Crosses, marking the site where someone had been killed whilst trying to escape. For people not wishing to pass through the checkpoint, there were a number of viewing platforms, so that a person could at least look at a small part of East Berlin. The first thing that struck me was the number of war-damaged buildings that hadn't been demolished or repaired in any way. Then there was the lack of colour. This was something noticeable throughout East Germany, not just East Berlin.

Every time our car passed through an intersection, or went by a Policeman, we could see that our location was being reported, for all were equipped with portable radios. Big Brother was indeed watching us! I was shown the way to places I would visit several times later, like the famous Pergamon Museum, and the Russian War Cemetery at Treptow Park. After driving around for a couple of hours, we stopped at a café for some refreshments. We had acquired some East German Deutchmarks before leaving, so things were very inexpensive. In 1974 the exchange rate was four East German Marks for one West German Mark. It was important to estimate roughly how much money to change, because it was not possible to change it back again! It was the first of several very interesting visits I made to East Berlin, and I always felt a sense of relief when I returned to the West. Talking to others, I found that this was a common experience!

Church Services were held every Sunday Morning at the Church in Montgomery Barracks. The congregation was small but faithful, and we managed to run a small Sunday School. Occasionally I would 'exchange pulpits' with other Chaplains in the Garrison, and with the Warden of Wesley House. Most Sunday evenings we would attend the Service at Wesley House, and I would sometimes give the Warden a break by taking the Service for him! Afterwards we would stay for refreshments with the rest of the small congregation. One of the 'regulars' had been a Senior Police Officer in a City in the Midlands, and was now working as the Police Liaison Officer with the British Military Government. He was also the Choirmaster of the British Choir, which I joined.

A major event in the calendar was the Allied Christmas Carol Service, which was held in what was known as 'The Blue Church' in the centre of Berlin. At the end of the Kurfurstendam, one of the main roads leading to the City centre; was the Kaiser Wilhelm Memorial Church. A war-damaged tower had been preserved, and alongside; a large round Church had been built, which had amazing blue windows. Even though it stood in the centre of a very busy City, it was always remarkably quiet inside! The annual Allied Carol Service was high on the social calendar and it was a 'ticket only' affair! One of the pieces offered by the British Choir was always, 'The Hallelujah Chorus'. The American and French choirs made their contributions: and one year a Russian choir took part and sang magnificently, without any musical accompaniment whatsoever.

We hadn't been in Berlin very long before we suffered our first tragedy. Just a few miles up the road towards the City was the British Yacht Club, and several members of I PARA had taken the opportunity to learn to sail. It was also a good place for social gatherings. One day I received an urgent request to go to the Club because the six years old son of one of our Sergeant Majors was missing. I arrived just in time to see the boy's body being lifted out of the water: he had slipped unnoticed off the jetty and was not able to swim. Sadly, he had been in the water for too long, and all efforts to revive him failed. The family, and indeed all those present at the Club, were deeply shocked and every effort was made to comfort and support them. Later, I conducted a Service for the little boy, who was then buried in Berlin Military Cemetery in a plot reserved especially for children.

As I hadn't been to the Military Cemetery before, I made a visit so that I would know exactly the lay out and procedure. I should point out that in Germany, the Army didn't use civilian undertakers. Preliminary preparations were carried out by the Hospital staff who then placed the deceased in an appropriate coffin. It was the responsibility of the Battalion to collect the coffin and supply the bearers. In the case of a child, it was usually the Chaplain who would collect the little white coffin from the Hospital Mortuary and transport it to the cemetery. During the ten years I served as a Chaplain in Germany, I usually carried the little coffin from the Chapel and laid it in the grave.

The person in charge of the Military Cemetery would be responsible for digging the grave and ensuring the Chapel was properly prepared. Anyone who has visited Military Cemeteries anywhere in the world will know how beautifully they are maintained.

As I walked around the Cemetery, I was surprised to find about a dozen headstones with the badge of the Parachute Regiment engraved on them. The Commanding Officer was also surprised when I told him of my discovery. I visited the Cemetery again and made a careful note of all the details on the headstones, which I sent to the Airborne Forces Depot in Aldershot for their information: and also to ask if they had any idea how members of the Regiment came to be buried in Berlin. Eventually I received a reply. Some of the soldiers had been captured in Normandy in June 1944: others had been captured at Arnhem in September 1944, and one had been captured in Italy.

Apparently, all had been in Prisoner-of-War camps East of Berlin. Some had died in the camps, others as they were moved West ahead of the advancing Russians. After the War, their bodies had been exhumed and reburied in Berlin.

Because of the limited training facilities in West Berlin, soldiers needed to travel down to West Germany, usually referred to as 'The Zone' to practice some of their military skills. It was during one such training period that another tragedy occurred when a mortar bomb exploded on the firing position. Two soldiers were killed out-right; no one else was even injured. I understand that sometimes, such bizarre things happen after explosions. One of the fatalities was sent back to England for a family funeral. The other was to receive a full Military Funeral and be buried in Berlin. Preparations were made for the funeral service to be held in the Church in Montgomery Barracks. The bearers rehearsed their duties using a vehicle inspection pit with a coffin borrowed from the Hospital. The Commanding Officer obtained a gun carriage on which the coffin would be transported, under police escort, the eight miles to the Military Cemetery. The use of a gun carriage was frowned upon from 'on high', as custom dictated they should not be used for ordinary soldiers, but only for those of senior rank. The Commanding Officer was determined, and shrugged off the disapproval of others!

The real problems began when the coffin arrived at the Barracks a few hours before the Funeral, having been brought up from West Germany by military transport. Following the accident, the casualties had been taken to the nearest Hospital, which was a German civilian Hospital: and they had carried out the necessary procedures and placed the soldier in a typical German coffin, which was much deeper, wider, and higher than the standard English type! The Church was packed: the Military contingent being headed by the Brigade Commander. The first problem was that the coffin was just a little too wide to pass through the door of the Church, and had to be forced through, leaving ridges in the door-posts! After the Service the coffin was laid on the gun carriage, but the straps weren't quite long enough to go over and secure it!

There was a period of almost half on hour before suitable ropes could be found and the coffin securely bound to the gun carriage. The journey to the Cemetery was uneventful, but we encountered a major problem when we arrived at the graveside. The soil in Berlin is very sandy, and the grave had been shored up with timber. Like us, the Cemetery staff had not been expecting a German style coffin: and the grave was too narrow for the coffin to be lowered! I'm sure you can imagine the looks of horror and consternation on the faces of the crowd around the graveside: so I made the decision. The coffin was placed on the ground and I completed the Service, except for the actual committal, and suggested that everyone except the bearer party leave, and return to Montgomery Barracks. The soldier's family were most understanding, but the Brigadier as he left, was heard muttering something about, 'attention to detail'! When all had departed, the Cemetery Staff were summoned, the timber removed, the coffin was lowered, and the Service completed. Considering the completely unforeseen circumstances, and the distress felt by all, I think everyone coped very well. It was a sequence of events I ensured were never repeated, at least not in any funeral Service I had any part in!

The daughter of one of our Warrant Officers was admitted to the British Military Hospital as she was having problems with one of her legs. She was a lovely, lively girl who would soon be a teenager. She remained in Hospital for almost six weeks before being sent back to Cambridge Military Hospital in Aldershot for further investigation and treatment. The physicians there discovered that she was suffering from a form of cancer and began immediate treatment. They were hopeful that the treatment would be successful, and her parents, who I knew well as they were regular members of my congregation, were somewhat reassured. Shortly afterwards I had to attend a Conference at Bagshot Park, and went to visit her. I had heard that she was a fan of 'The Bay City Rollers' and managed to obtain a cassette to take with me as a little present. She was pleased to see me, and even more pleased with the cassette! The Doctor informed me that they were waiting for the results of more tests, which would show the full extent of the disease. "The best we can hope for", he said, "Is that she will lose a leg: if the cancer is also elsewhere, there will be no point in doing that." I returned to Berlin, hoping against hope that she would respond to the continuing treatment. She was such a brave and positive little girl.

The Commanding Officer, who invariably tried to help and support me in my work, suggested I might benefit from having my own driver. I wasn't too sure about it, but he insisted, and a broad Glaswegian became my driver. He had to spend a lot of time waiting around while I did other things, but he didn't deem to mind: and all the other drivers thought he had landed a 'cushy' number! I was happy to have him though, for one particular occasion. A senior Russian Orthodox priest, with the high ecclesiastical rank of Metropolitan, was due to make an official visit to East Berlin. All Allied Forces Chaplains were invited to attend a formal reception.

All the other British Chaplains had prior engagements, so I was the only one able to attend. I dressed in my best uniform and ordered my driver to do the same. We set off from home in good time, having in mind that we had the vagaries of 'Check point Charlie' to contend with! We found the venue, parked the car, and went into the building. I found a suitable place inside for my driver to wait, and went into the main hall which was already quite crowded. I looked in vain for any American or French Army Chaplains, but none were there: nor did any arrive later. I was the sole representative Chaplain from the Allied Forces in West Berlin!

The reception began with a word of welcome from an East German official, which was translated into Russian and English. Then followed interminable speeches in Russian and German, each of which had to be translated. There was a very large table in the hall, weighed down with food and drink, which was distributed when all the speeches had been completed. As the only Military Chaplain present, I was regarded with some curiosity and soon surrounded by people who had many questions for me! When they discovered I had a driver outside, they insisted he join us and a very uncomfortable Glaswegian came and stood by my side. Several people from the Russian Embassy questioned me about my role as an Army Chaplain. I knew from intelligence briefings that the Russians considered Chaplains and Education Officers to be responsible for propaganda, and the 'brainwashing' of British Serviceman and women. We were left under no illusions that if the Russians ever did invade the West: we would be the first to be shot, as we were regarded as 'Commissars'! I don't suppose I did much to counter this misapprehension when I was asked by one, "You are a man of peace"? I agreed. "But do you shoot people"? "No", I replied, nodding in the direction of my driver and suppressing a grin, "He shoots them for me"! My driver went a funny colour and choked on his beer! I was offered a glass of Brandy, which I sipped appreciatively. "You like"? I was asked. "Very much", I replied, "It's very good". "It should be", my host replied, "We used to supply your Winston Churchill with crates of it"! "You Russians make excellent Brandy": I complimented him. "It's not Russian", he almost snarled at me. "It's Ukrainian"!

A most attractive young woman then approached us, accompanied by a short, ugly little man, puffing on a cigarette and badly in need of a shave. She spoke excellent English and worked at the Russian Embassy. We had a lively conversation and then I thought it was my turn to ask a few questions. "You are atheists with no belief in God", I said. She agreed, "So, why are you here this evening at this function in honour of a prominent Churchman", I asked. "Ah well you see", she smiled disarmingly, "It's my husband," she nodded in the direction of the ugly little man who hadn't uttered a word: " he's in charge of Church Affairs"! It was my turn to almost choke on my Brandy!

I was glad of the opportunity to meet the Russian Orthodox priest I had met only briefly at the Allied Carol Service. He informed me that he had a small Church and congregation in West Berlin, and was allowed through Check-Point Charlie to conduct a weekly Service. He was not however, permitted to take his wife and children with him on these visits!

An official then came and informed me that the Metropolitan wished to meet me. He was a very big man with a great, bushy beard, and wearing his tall hat he seemed positively enormous! Through an interpreter he said he was very pleased I had been able to attend the reception, and wished me Peace in my work. I replied in similar vein. He then requested we pose together for photographs, and several were taken. I still have a copy somewhere showing me receiving a great bear hug as the picture was taken! It was a most interesting evening, and very late when we returned home. I really appreciated having a driver! What a pity it was that no other Allied Military Chaplain was able to attend!

Padre Brian Dougall, who had been my Padre in 1958, and Deputy Warden at Bagshot Park when I joined the Royal Army Chaplains Department, was now the Deputy Chaplain General. He had remained a friend of my Commanding Officer since they had served together in 2 PARA in the late 1950s, and he and his wife were due to visit Berlin for a few days. Knowing that Brian's wife was a very good singer and a lover of opera, I suggested we all go to the famous Berlin Opera during their visit. This suggestion was enthusiastically welcomed, and I managed to obtain tickets for a performance of 'Madam Butterfly', which we all thoroughly enjoyed!

Padre Douggie Dennis, who had been such a great help to me when I was considering offering for the Methodist Ministry, was now Deputy Assistant Chaplain General at 4th Armoured Division, at Herford in West Germany. I suggested to the Commanding Officer that we invite him to visit the Battalion the following September, and preach at our Service to commemorate the Battle of Arnhem, which would be held in the Regimental Gymnasium. After being assured by me that Douggie was an excellent preacher, he was duly invited; and he and his wife came to stay with us for a few days. How the years had flown and circumstances changed. It didn't seem so long since I used to baby-sit for them when I was a young soldier! It was quite a coincidence to have two of my 'old' Padres visit us in Berlin in the same year. Douggie's sermon at the Arnhem Service was much appreciated by the Battalion, and before returning to Herford, he insisted on taking us out for a meal. He had obviously done his homework, and had decided exactly where to take us for a sumptuous meal. The people of Berlin boasted that a person could 'eat out' every night for about fifteen years, without visiting the same place twice!

A couple of months later, the Battalion went to Schleswig Holstein, north east of Hamburg for two weeks military training. We took with us a 'hand picked' Platoon, about thirty soldiers, from our affiliated American Regiment. They were lovely people and very easy to get along with, but within a few days it became apparent that even though they had trained hard, their standards of physical fitness and military skills were well below those of the Parachute Regiment. Two examples will suffice. One morning the Battalion set off on foot on an 'advance to contact' exercise. This meant that the troops would move across country until they made contact with 'the enemy', and would then react according to their assessment of the situation.

After less than two hours marching the exercise had to be halted, and a helicopter called in to evacuate two American soldiers who were suffering from heat exhaustion: and this was in the Autumn! The problem was that they were wearing far too much clothing and equipment. On a similar Exercise, I was travelling in a Land Rover with a Sergeant from the Reconnaissance Platoon, who had seen service with the SAS. We were driving on the fringes of the Exercise area to meet up with the Battalion. I asked the Sergeant how he knew exactly where the Battalion were to be found. He smiled, pulled off the track and switched off the engine. "Listen", he said, "and you will hear the Americans coming three fields away"! They were seriously lacking in basic field craft techniques. We had just come to the end of our training when we heard that the little girl in Hospital in Aldershot had died.

I drove straight back to Berlin and immediately contacted her parents, who asked me if I would go to Cornwall to conduct the funeral. A flight was arranged for me and I flew back to England and caught a train to Cornwall. She had been an only child with great potential, and it was a very sad occasion. A posting was arranged for the Warrant Officer, and he and his wife remained in England.

When I returned to Berlin, I set about organising a Parade Service in Church for the Cubs and Brownies in Montgomery Barracks, and had chosen to prepare an address on 'The Whole Armour of God'. A few days before the Service I was visiting the Tank Squadron in Spandau. After walking around the tank park talking to the soldiers, I was having a cup of coffee with the Squadron Leader. During our conversation I asked in a jocular fashion, "Any chance of borrowing a tank for the weekend? It would be a marvellous visual aid for my talk to the children". I almost dropped my cup when he replied quite seriously, "Certainly Padre, "How many do you want"? He said, "It will be a marvellous opportunity to get my tanks out of barracks. Except for the odd deployment exercise, all we do is move them out of the garages, clean and service them, and put them back again. As we are not allowed to have them on the roads at weekends, we'll have to bring it on Friday and leave it with you until Monday. Leave it with me and I'll make all the necessary arrangements." Late on the Friday afternoon, the local residents were amazed and a little puzzled to see four Chieftain tanks, (the Squadron Leader had taken the opportunity to take a whole Troop for a drive out!) with a German Police escort with flashing lights at the front and rear. The convoy entered Montgomery Barracks, rove through the camp, and parked outside my Church.

I would have loved to know what sort of reaction this provoked inside the East German Watch Tower overlooking the scene! Tanks had never been seen in Montgomery Barracks before, and I bet the telephones were very busy for a while. Three of the tanks then returned to Spandau with their Police escort, leaving one parked outside the Church for the weekend. I had asked the tank crew to be present during the Service so that I could ask them questions about, the mobility of the tank, the strength of the armour, and the fire- power of the weapons.

This they were happy to do without divulging any military secrets, and I was able to relate this to the Scripture passage in Ephesians Chapter 6. After the Service, the children enjoyed themselves climbing all over and inside the tank! On Monday morning the rest of the Troop returned with their escort to collect the tank. We had enjoyed a good Service, and the tank crews had enjoyed their trip out, so everyone was happy!

The Battalions next trip to West Germany for training was to Vogelsang, in the beautiful Eifel region, south of Cologne. We stayed at a camp not far from the Belgian border, and administered by the Belgian Army. The camp had originally been built to train young German Officers, and I remember standing on the spot in the outdoor arena from which Adolf Hitler used to address them. The area afforded good training facilities including firing ranges for rifles and machine guns. It also had a special 'walk through 'range which required great concentration to react to the 'pop up' targets which presented themselves as the soldier walked through. It was during one such 'walk through', that a thirty two year old Corporal suffered a massive heart attack. I travelled with him in the ambulance to the nearest Hospital, while one of our medical assistants, a Sergeant, gave him mouth to mouth resuscitation all the way there and right into the Emergency Ward. The Commanding Officer was there when we arrived, and we waited together, saying our prayers, while the 'crash team' tried to restart his heart: sadly without any success.

The Corporal was married but had no children. The Commanding Officer told me to return to Berlin immediately and break the news to his wife, and to try to get there before she heard via the 'bush telegraph'. His Staff Car took me to Bonn airport, where I caught the first available flight to Berlin. The Families Officer had arranged for a car to meet me at the airport, and I was soon back in Montgomery Barracks. I drove to the Corporals house, only to find that his wife wasn't there! Neighbours gave me the addresses of some of her friends, and eventually I found her and told her the awful news. She was devastated. He had been a young, fit, and healthy man, as would be expected of a Corporal in the Parachute Regiment: and there had been no previous symptoms of any kind. His wife contacted her in-laws in South Wales, and between them they decided they wanted his Funeral Service to be held there, and that he be buried in the local cemetery in the Valley he came from. In order for the Corporal to be buried according to Military and Regimental tradition, the Commanding Officer again 'bent the rules' to give his soldier the Funeral he deserved, and which his friends in the Battalion expected.

The rules stated, and they were quite clear, that if a Serviceman died outside Britain, he could have a full Military Funeral where he was stationed. If however, the family decided on a Funeral in Britain, the coffin would be flown back at public expense, but from the moment the aircraft landed, it would become the sole responsibility of the family, and further Military involvement or any public expense expressly forbidden.

It was decided that I, and the bearer party would be flown to England with the costs being met from Battalion Funds. A Mini Bus would be hired from the Airborne Forces Depot in Aldershot to take us to South Wales, and any soldier serving in the Depot who knew the Corporal, and there were several, would be informed of the arrangements. They made their own way to the Service, as did others who were on training courses at Brecon. On the day, there was a sizeable contingent of soldiers wearing Red Berets, one of whom had brought a bugle and the Corporal was given a proper Regimental Funeral, much to the satisfaction of his family and the Commanding Officer.

Periods of Leave were usually spent visiting relatives in England. We would usually try to divide the time equally between Bradwell and Rotherham. Berlin was 600 miles from Calais, so I booked a passage on an early morning Hovercraft and decided to drive overnight. I had driven about half way down the Corridor, when a warning light appeared on the dashboard informing me that the dynamo wasn't charging the battery! Fortunately it went off again and we arrived at Helmstedt. After taking a short break we carried on, but the light kept coming on intermittently and by the time we reached a Motel/Service station near Hannover, I decided to call out the ADAC, which had a reciprocal arrangement with the AA. The mechanic shook his head sadly, and told me I needed a new dynamo: however it was now 3.a.m. and the nearest Simca garage was about twenty miles away and wouldn't be open until 8.a.m. I booked a couple of rooms in the Motel, and the mechanic told me he would return at 7.30a.m. and guide me to the garage. When he arrived, I left the family in the Motel and followed the ADAC man to the garage. They examined the car, and informed me that they didn't have a replacement dynamo in stock for my car, but could probably obtain one in about two hours. I had no choice but to wait until a new dynamo was obtained and fitted. I managed to telephone the Motel and get a message to the family. By the time we eventually left Hannover it was mid afternoon: so much for catching an early morning Hovercraft!

By the time we reached Calais it was late evening: all Hovercaft sailings had been cancelled due to appalling weather conditions, but I managed to book a passage on a ferry due to leave at 11.00p.m. It was a very rough crossing and it was a great relief when we finally arrived in Dover. There was still a long drive ahead of us to South Yorkshire, and I was beginning to feel very tired. I drove from Dover to and through London to reach the MI motorway. On the way North I had stop at every service station for a break, drink strong coffee, and walk around for a while to keep myself awake! When we arrived in Rotherham, I slept for a long time! My wife was feeling very guilty because she had been unable to share the driving, and expressed a determination to learn as soon as we returned to Berlin. She had tried a couple of times before to learn to drive, and had convinced herself that it was something she could never do. The awful journey from Berlin had given her a strong motive to try again. On our return I taught her to drive in wintry conditions, and she passed her test first time! I'd had several problems with the Simca, and the latest experience was enough to persuade me to change it for something better. I visited the NAAFI car salesman in Berlin and ordered a new Renault 12 Estate.

I had the choice of collecting it from either London or Paris, so I chose London and collected it from a depot near Heathrow Airport, returning to Berlin via Hamburg

Arrangements had been made, at long last, for us to do some parachuting. After the usual time of 'synthetic' training, I boarded a Hercules at RAF Gatow with two main parachutes. We flew to a dropping zone in West Germany and parachuted down. We were then loaded on to trucks and taken to a German Airfield, where our Hercules was waiting to take us up for a second jump. It was a hectic day but all went well, and that was the last time I parachuted.

We all felt the need for a bit of light relief and I discussed with the Commanding Officer the possibility of putting on a Battalion Concert. A meeting was arranged, and enough enthusiastic people turned up to encourage me to go ahead with the organisation. Others who where slightly less enthusiastic joined in after a little gentle persuading! It was decided the Concert would in fact be a Pantomime – 'Cinderella'. The Battalion Adjutant was soon to leave, not only the Battalion: but the Army. He wanted to study medicine and become a Doctor. Instead of finding someone whose dainty foot would fit into a glass slipper, the plot was to find a bottom that would fit into the Adjutant's chair! After a limited number of rehearsals, the Pantomime was performed in front of a packed 'House'. The performance began with a drum roll, which usually precedes the playing of the National Anthem. The audience stood up to attention; and the Band played . . . . "When The Saints Go Marching In"! The audience sat down again laughing, which certainly enabled the Pantomime to get off to a good start! Eventually of course, a perfectly shaped bottom was found. I will forever remember the sight of the Provost Sergeant (the Regimental Policeman in charge of a very tough Guard Room), appropriately dressed, singing 'I Feel Pretty' from 'West Side Story'. The Adjutant completed his medical training, and is now a GP somewhere in the Midlands.

It was in Berlin that I had my first experience of broadcasting! The British Forces Broadcasting Service (BFBS) were based in Cologne, but had a studio in Berlin. At 0750 hrs, Monday to Friday, there was a Program entitled, 'Just a Minute', which was a 'thought for the day' given by one of the Chaplains. I hadn't been in Munster long enough for them to catch me, but now they had: or rather, Chaplain's Branch at HQ BAOR had! I was required to prepare five talks, each one lasting approximately four minutes. The manuscripts had to be sent to HQ BAOR in advance to receive the approval of the Assistant Chaplain General, because the talks were broadcast live! It was something I dreaded, but did, and it was well received. During my several tours of duty in Germany, there were other occasions when I had to 'go on the air', including more 'Just a Minute ' sessions, organising an 'Any Questions' program, and a 'studio' Church Service. Unlike some others I never developed a love or a talent for broadcasting. There is a world of difference between preaching, speaking at meetings, and broadcasting: and I always preferred the former two. I like to see people's faces, and I never felt comfortable talking to a microphone!

The Chaplains' Department informed me that when I PARA completed it's tour of duty in August 1976, I was to be posted to 11th Armoured Brigade in Minden, and become Chaplain to The Duke Of Wellington's Regiment, the only Regiment in the British Army to be named after a Commoner. Before that day arrived, there was another major event in Berlin: The Berlin Military Tattoo, which was to be held in The Deutschland Halle, the Berlin equivalent of Earls Court. The Battalion, especially the Second-in-Command, was to play a significant role in organising, as well as participating in this. The theme tune for the Tattoo was 'Ode to Joy' which we had come to associate with the European Common Market, which many of us had voted to join the previous year. The scenery for the Tattoo was so magnificent that the General arranged for it to be transported to Scotland. He was shortly to take up the post of General Officer Commanding Scotland, and his intention was to use it in the Edinburgh Military Tattoo! I suppose there's little point in being a General if you can't organise things like that!

I drove down to Minden to meet the Senior Chaplain and talk about important things, such as the availability of married quarters! I was assured there would be no problem: in fact it turned out to be quite a problem! The Advance Party of the Duke of Wellington's Regiment had arrived (the remainder being still in Aldershot) and so I went to introduce myself to them. They informed me that most of their soldiers came from Yorkshire, and that they were the Army Rugby Champions! As an incoming Battalion, they had far more married soldiers than the Battalion they were replacing, and one of the main tasks of the Advance Party, was to acquire private accommodation for about 45 families until married quarters gradually became available for them. More about the problems this was to cause later! I was informed that I would also be Chaplain to 11th Armoured Workshops, Royal Electrical and Mechanical Engineers, and to the School for Army Children next door to Clifton Barracks, soon to be occupied by The Duke's.

The Schools in Berlin were located in the grounds of RAF Gatow, and I had visited them regularly to conduct morning Assemblies. I also discovered that I would be sharing the Garrison Church with a Church of England Chaplain, who was in fact my predecessor as Chaplain with I PARA, so we had already met. He was an extremely charming man, but I didn't particularly relish the prospect of having to share a Church with him, especially as he would be my Senior Chaplin and our convictions about the form and content of Services very different; but I knew I would have to make the best of the situation.

At the beginning of July 1976, having served for six years and received the required recommendations, I was promoted to Chaplain to the Forces 3rd Class (Major). Back in Berlin I reported on my visit to Minden, and was informed that the Advance Party of the Green Howards had arrived, and that when their Battalion moved in, my house would be allocated to their Second-in-Command. There were a number of 'farewell' functions to attend, and I was formally 'dined out' of the Officer's Mess. I concluded my 'grace' with these words:-

'And now this Padre passes on,

Mid joyful cries, 'Thank God he's gone.

So speed him on to distant places,

And subject others to his Graces!'

I had served with the Battalion for four years, and was presented with a bronze model of an Airborne Soldier wearing parachutes, which is one of my most treasured possessions. With my previous service as a Regular Soldier, I had served a total of eight years with Airborne Forces, and felt proud to have done so. I was also grateful for the way the Parachute Brigade, and those I had served with, helped shape my life and my character.

1ST BATTALION, THE DUKE OF WELLINGTON'S REGIMENT MINDEN, GERMANY;

AUGUST 1976 – SEPTEMBER 1978

The packing crates were filled again, and I left for Minden, hoping to return and collect the family within a few days. It turned out to be more than a few days! When I visited the Station Staff Officer and the Families Officer, I was informed that it might be a little while before a house became available for me. I was less then pleased with the outgoing Senior Chaplain, who had already departed, for the inaccurate assurances he had given to me! While I was waiting I lived in the Mess, and began to find my way around the Garrison. It was a very hot summer and my little Army Mini felt just like a greenhouse! There are very few roundabouts in Germany, but there are many sets of traffic lights! My initial impression of Minden was of a town where I seemed to spend an incredible amount of time being baked alive while I waited at traffic lights!

Minden is a delightful City, located on the River Weser a few miles north of the Autobahn leading to Hannover and Berlin, and about thirty miles north of Hamlin, where the legend of the Pied Piper is re-enacted at weekends during the summer months. To the west of the City is a lovely range of hills, broken by the Weser as it passes through the Minden Gap before turning South towards Hamlin. The Minden Gap has been the scene of many battles down the centuries because of its strategic position. The Battle Honour, 'Minden', appears on the Colours of many British Regiments. The Gap is overlooked on the north side by a large and impressive statue of the Kaiser, which attracts many visitors to the area: as does the range of hills, which is favoured by lots of walkers: a favourite German pastime! Also in Minden is the largest lock in Europe, which raises and lowers huge barges from the Weser to the Mittleland Canal. Another **must** for visitors to the area.

The Church was at the north end of the Garrison, in barracks occupied by The Cheshire Regiment, and very near to Brigade Headquarters: the Brigadier being a regular member of the congregation. I was given a very warm welcome and soon made to feel at home. The Army is understandably composed of itinerants, so there is always sympathy and understanding for the problems faced by all new arrivals! I made regular visits and telephone calls to the Station Staff Officer and the Unit Families Officer about my need for accommodation. They were also under considerable pressure from Berlin. The Second-in-Command of the Green Howards had arrived and desperately wanted to move his family into my house! As a direct result of this, we were offered temporary accommodation in a ground floor flat not far from Clifton Barracks. It was a lovely flat and I accepted it on the understanding that I would move to a four bed roomed house as soon as one became available. I informed Berlin and made arrangements to return and collect my family.

There were still elements of I PARA Rear Party there, and they arranged a working party and a vehicle to transport my packing cases to Minden. They arrived on schedule and unloaded the cases into my cellar, from where, as in Munster, we unpacked only those things we really needed. I continued to be a 'thorn in the side' of the Housing authority until we were allocated a house two months later. The Dukes had spent two years in Aldershot, but hadn't seen very much of the place. From there they had served on tours in Cyprus and Northern Ireland, and been involved in NATO Exercises. Returning to Germany, they moved from being an 'Air Portable', to a 'Mechanised Infantry' Battalion: and this required spending a lot of time re-training. Most of the young soldiers, especially those who had joined the Battalion during the past two years, had never even seen an APC (Armoured Personnel Carrier): now they had about 90 to drive, clean, maintain, and prepare to use in a battle situation.

I spent a lot of time initially visiting the families: and as I went around I received many requests for babies and young children to be baptised. It was often a case of, "Padre, while you are doing the baby, can we have the others done as well"! The Battalion had been committed in so many ways for so long: now they looked like being settled for a while, it was time to catch up on things like baptisms! I looked carefully at the Battalion's commitments for the next few months, and found only one weekend when everyone would be together in Barracks. On the Sunday afternoon of that weekend I arranged two Services: and baptised twenty three children. Never again! It was absolute chaos, and I was quite exhausted by the end of the afternoon. Many families had no transport of their own, so I arranged for an Army Coach to collect them, and take them home again after each Service.

As I mentioned earlier, on my first visit the Advance Party were looking for private accommodation for more than forty families. They had been successful, but we now had young families in private accommodation scattered within a five miles radius of the Barracks. Most had insufficient service and therefore few points; which placed them at or near the bottom of the waiting list for a married quarter. Most of the young wives, some with babies, had never been away from home before. Now they were in a foreign land, unable to speak the language, without transport; and with husbands away much of the time. The accommodation was fine, and sometimes there was a little German shop within walking distance: but when they needed to visit the Medical Centre, or shop at the NAAFI, or visit the Families Office; a car had to be sent to collect them. It was a far from ideal situation, and I seriously questioned the wisdom of allowing them to leave England before proper quarters were available, and they could be within a supportive community and close to all the necessary facilities. So many were very young wives who really missed not having Mum anywhere near them, and were often desperately unhappy.

Two other places came within the Garrison orbit. Buckerberg, a small town about eight miles from Minden, where a Field Ambulance unit was stationed, and which had a number of married quarters and an Army School, which I occasionally visited to conduct Morning Assemblies. It also had in the town a Helicopter Museum, which housed exhibits and information tracing the development of the machine. It was a popular tourist attraction. Nienberg was another small town about twenty-five miles north of Minden, and was the base for a Regiment of Royal Engineers. At that time they had no Chaplain of their own, but there was a Church in the camp so the Minden Chaplains took turns in taking Services for them. There were now four Chaplains in the Garrison, including the Roman Catholic Chaplain. His Church was near the town centre by the building housing the Station Staff Office. The Cheshire Regiment had just welcomed a new Chaplain: the old one having left the Army.

The Chaplains Centre in Germany was known as Church House, British Army of the Rhein, and was in Wuppertal, just north of Cologne. It was to Church House that soldiers were sent on Christian Information Courses, and Chaplains used for Conferences and Retreats. The old system of 'Padres Hours' had been discontinued in the 1960s, and replaced with an annual 'Character Training Program', which now came under the Director of Army Training. This meant that Commanders and Chaplains had an obligation to implement it, and Theme Notes were compiled and sent out annually by the Staff at Bagshot Park. Ideally this meant that Chaplains should meet soldiers of all ranks, every two months to work through the program. In practice, and due to ever increasing Military commitments, particularly in Northern Ireland, it was usually a case of 'as and when' possible. Many informal sessions took place with small groups sitting in the back of APCs during the interminable periods of 'waiting', which have always been a feature of Army life!

Just before leaving Berlin I attended a meeting, which was addressed by a senior General from the Ministry of Defence. We were informed that new physical fitness tests were soon to be incorporated into routine military training. They would be known as (BFTs) 'Battle Fitness Tests' and would apply to all serving soldiers. Extra time would be allowed for older soldiers up to the age of 55 years to complete them! When the Turkish Army invaded and divided Cyprus in 1974, the British Garrison were mobilised and deployed. During this unexpected deployment, as it says in the Bible; 'some fell by the wayside'!

Our soldiers had proved that they were not as physically fit as they should have been. I'm sure the 'laid back' way of life in Cyprus was responsible for this, but now the rest of the Army had to consistently work to maintain a higher standard. The test consisted of jogging as a squad for one and a half miles: and then running back to the starting point individually as fast as possible! Strict time limits were imposed, and those failing to complete the test within the required time, were given extra training until they succeeded! The Dukes decided to do this by Platoons, and I just 'tagged on' to whichever Platoon was taking the test when I was available. Having run regularly for some years, I had no trouble in meeting the required standard for my age!

I paid regular visits to the REME Workshops and we became good friends with the Adjutant and his wife. It was this unit, which suffered the first tragic event of my Minden tour. The eight years old son of a Sergeant and his wife fell into a nearby canal and drowned. The couple were absolutely devastated and wished to take their son to their home near Derby for the funeral. As it was not possible for this to be done at public expense, the Workshops raised enough money to make this possible for them. I needed to see them many times when they returned, as they were not only grieving; but their grief was causing great problems with their own relationship. In England, it would be normal for a family network to provided help and support for relatives coping with bereavement and loss. For servicemen and their families overseas, the supporting network is provided by a whole team consisting in the first place, of their Military unit, supported by the Chaplain, Doctor, Families Officer, and SSAFA (Soldiers, Sailors, & Air mans Families Association) Social Worker.

It was about this time that the practice of Hospitals disposing of stillborn babies was radically changed: and this was brought about by pressure from a number of Chaplains. Stillborn babies were now given a proper funeral and buried in the Military Cemetery. Furthermore, the mothers were encouraged to hold their babies, and even have them photographed. This acknowledged the reality of their loss and helped parents through the grieving process.

Having heard of the Duke's prowess on the playing field, I strolled along the touchline at their next rugby match. As I mingled with the supporters, an Officer said to me in a rather gruff, but bantering manner, "This is the only religion you'll find here Padre"! Unusually, the Duke's lost the match, and I was able to retort, "Well, it seems your Church is in a worse state than mine"! Later on in the season, the Dukes reached the final of the Army cup again, and I went with them to Sennelager to watch the match, which was played against their traditional rivals, the Royal Regiment of Wales. It was a most exciting and nailbiting game, which the Dukes won by 13 points to 12!

There were two major events in 1977. The celebrations marking the Queen's Silver Jubilee; and a four months tour of duty in Northern Ireland. A Parade was planned for the former, at which Her Majesty was to be present. Instead of the traditional March Past; a Drive Past was planned with all Armoured Vehicles from 4th Armoured Division taking part. This was to take place at Sennelager, not far from the City of Paderborn. It is a large training area containing extensive ranges; which soldiers from all over Germany visit, in order to fire their personal weapons and demonstrate an acceptable level of proficiency. This is known as 'annual classification', and failure to reach the required standard would jeopardise a soldier's pay and promotion prospects. We were informed that Sennelager was the place where Hitler trained his Penal Battalions, who had a reputation for fighting fearlessly and ferociously, because failure was not an option!

A limited number of special Medals were struck to mark the Queen's Silver Jubilee, but it was never made clear who should receive them! This was the subject of much discussion. Ideally, all those serving at the time should have received one, but that was out of the question. Some felt very strongly that all those who had served for the twentyfive years of the Queen's Reign should receive a Medal. I don't know what happened in the higher formations, but it was decided that at the lower level, each Regiment and Battalion would receive six Medals, and the Commanding Officer was given the unenviable task of deciding who should receive one. To my utter astonishment and I'm sure the chagrin of many, I was presented with a Silver Jubilee Medal. I don't think the Commanding Officer had any trouble deciding who should receive the first five, and chose to give the sixth to the Chaplain; probably thinking that wouldn't be controversial. He was wrong! There were several in the Battalion who considered themselves to be more worthy; and I was left in no doubt about the jealousy felt by some.

Unlike the day three years earlier when the Parachute Regiment received their new Colours in the pouring rain, the weather for the Silver Jubilee Parade was fine and sunny, and the thousands attending the Celebration had a most enjoyable day.

The Battalion had already begun preparing for their tour in Northern Ireland, and the training of soldiers for that role had been vastly improved since my first tour of duty in 1971/2. The training was now organised and supervised by the Northern Ireland Training & Advisory Team (NITAT). Many hard lessons had been learned, and much 'Intelligence' gathered since the Army had first been deployed there in 1969. Now the soldiers and their Commanders would receive the most up-to-date information and tactical training. A special training facility had been built in Sennelager, so that intensive training could be given in combating urban terrorism; and staying alive in the process! Let no one underestimate the dangers faced by the men and women who served in the Province; many of them very young and serving their first tour of duty. The climax of the training took place in 'Fort Night', so called because it lasted for two weeks! Half the Company taking part acted as the civilian population (Civpop), and lived for a week in makeshift houses knocked up out of breeze- blocks. It was their role to make life unpleasant for the other half, by rioting and setting up ambushes etc. The NITAT would set up a number of scenarios for the patrolling soldiers to deal with, and all this was captured on CCTV, which would be watched by the soldiers afterwards. It was an excellent training technique! After a week roles would be exchanged.

Soldier's wives and their families in England, were naturally very concerned when a Battalion was going to Northern Ireland. To put things in perspective, I pointed out to them that more soldiers were killed on the roads of Germany than were killed by terrorists: and that's a fact! The tour of duty would last for four months: and a comprehensive support system was organised by the Unit Families Officer and his Staff. An interesting program of events and activities was prepared, and free flights were available for those who wished to visit their home in England.

Soldiers were also given a long weekend back in Germany about half way through the tour. Chaplains would usually return for two liaison visits during the tour, depending on the needs of the Rear Party and the Battalion.

The Battalion was based in Londonderry, with Rifle Companies stationed in various locations around the City. I was based in a place known as Fort George, about half a mile from Battalion HQ. Fort George was the home of the Quartermaster's department, together with the REME (Light Aid Detachment) LAD, and other supporting staff. It was five years since I had been in Londonderry and it hadn't changed much! The old City, so dear to the hearts of the Protestant community, was situated on the west side of the River Foyle, whereas most of the Protestants living outside the old City walls, lived on the east side, known as the Waterside. There had been a significant Protestant community north of Fort George, but the Church of Ireland Clergyman, whom I had met on my previous visit, told me that sadly, most of his congregation had moved to the other side of the river, where they felt less vulnerable. The most significant difference I noticed in the Military composition was the enormous size of the Intelligence Section in each location. The operational emphasis had definitely changed.

I had a civilian car so I could get around the City and visit Hospitals and other Chaplains. The area was compact enough for me to walk to most places, which I usually did, day and night; wearing civilian clothes and my clerical collar. There were two Chaplains based in the City, at Ebrington Barracks in the Waterside district. Brigade HQ was also located there. The Church of England Chaplain was a very worried man. He told me that he, and the Roman Catholic Chaplain were to take part in a Television Program in the BBC 'Everyman' series, on the role of, 'The Army Chaplains in Northern Ireland'. He said, "The people responsible for making this program have been to see us. They know nothing about the Army, nothing about Northern Ireland, and nothing about the Church: is it any wonder that I'm worried?" I certainly shared his concern and did my best to reassure him, though I feared the possible outcome.

I was reminded of the occasion a few years earlier when I gave a lift to two English students who were walking along the road between Ballykelly and Londonderry. I asked them why they were going to Londonderry. One of them informed me that they were doing a project on 'the way the people of the Bogside and Creggan are being treated by the British Army'. I pulled into a lay bye and introduced myself! I told them that I was on my way to the Hospital to visit some of my soldiers who had been badly injured in the City. I readily answered many of their questions; and informed them of the realities of the situation. It was obvious they had many preconceived ideas picked up from television programs and tabloid newspapers. As they had not planned to talk to anyone in the Army, I was pleased to have been able to make my contribution to their 'Project'!

The television crew duly arrived and the program was made: soon afterwards it was shown on BBC TV. It was a disaster, just as the Chaplains had feared. There were a number of contrived situations, and of course the production team had complete editorial control. The Chaplains were made to look silly and the status of the Ministry of the Church in the Army diminished. However, what was more upsetting for the Chaplains was the complete lack of response from the hierarchy of the Chaplain's Department! The Church of England Chaplain said, "If only someone from the Ministry of Defence (Chaplains' Branch), would get on the 'phone and say something like, ' Well, you made a right mess of that, but thanks for trying ', but there hasn't been a word". I really felt the Chaplains involved had been badly let down. There was to be another chapter to this incident later.

One Rifle Company was based in the middle of the old City at a place known as 'The Masonic Car Park'. Space was very limited and soldiers were sleeping in three tier bunk beds. A young Officer arrived to join the Regiment fresh from Sandhurst and full of enthusiasm. He was shown around and saw the cramped conditions. "Sir", said one of the Sergeants, "You can see how things are here: until we can get something sorted out for you, you'll have to sleep out here". He was shown to a large kennel where one of the 'sniffer' dogs was normally kept. Completely taken in, the young Officer did just that, but for only one night! It was fairly quiet at the time with little to do except routine tasks. The young Officer grew impatient and demanded to know where the 'aggro' (aggression) was. That same evening, there was a small riotous situation to be quelled and a Platoon was deployed to deal with it. The young Officer ran out into the fray and was hit in the face by a brick. Fortunately he wasn't badly hurt and the company Medical Orderly dressed his wound. One of his Corporals remarked dryly, "Well Sir I see you found your 'aggro'!" The Dukes had a habit, almost a tradition, of 'taking the Micky' out of Officers who they thought deserved it. It was done in good humour, but not always appreciated. I had already seen an example of this in Minden. In the Army; The

Royal Military Academy, Sandhurst, is sometimes referred to as 'The Rupert Factory'. At Christmas, the Officers were invited to the Sergeants Mess for drinks. During he preceding year, any Officer who was unfortunate enough to make a mistake, and was seen to make it: that could be anything from being improperly dressed to misplacing the base plate of a mortar; would have the incident reported to the Regimental Quartermaster Sergeant (RQMS). During the Christmas drinks, the nominations would be read out, and the 'Rupert of the Year ' award presented amidst cries of great hilarity; and relief from those who had escaped! The little doll like, properly dressed 'Rupert Bear' would, before the end of the festivities, be given back to the RQMS who would take good care of it until the next Christmas.

The Battalion Band had planned to visit us for a week, and in addition to their few public engagements, I suggested an evening's entertainment in each Company location. I consulted the Bandmaster and each Company Sergeant Major, and made them an offer they couldn't refuse!

Each Company was asked to provide at least an hours entertainment: the Band and I would provide another hour. I had more than enough songs, monologues, and jokes to make my contribution, and also to act as Master of Ceremonies. The Companies responded with enthusiasm to the challenge, and three excellent Concerts were performed. In fact they produced so much unexpected talent, each Concert lasted about three hours! In the light of this discovery, we decided that when we returned to Minden, we would put on a Concert so that all the families could enjoy it. A few possible dates were agreed, and during one of my visits back to Minden I found a German Gasthouse, not very far from the Barracks with a large enough hall to accommodate us, and made a provisional booking.

Back in 1956 when I finished at Cliff College, I was 'killing time' waiting to be called up to do my National Service. I lived for several months with a family in Sheffield, who had four sons, the youngest still in nappies. We became great friends and have kept in touch through the years. When I became a Methodist Minister, it was their expressed wish that I should officiate at the marriages of their sons. Sadly, due to Military commitments I was not available for the marriages of the first three boys. Now I was invited to assist at the marriage of their youngest son, who was to marry an Austrian girl the following Easter Monday, in a little village in southern Austria near the Yugoslavian border. Normally this would have been out of the question. Whoever heard of a Chaplain taking leave at Easter? However, as there were now four Chaplains in Minden I considered three would be more than enough to meet the Easter commitments: so I applied for leave, and it was granted! I informed my friends in Sheffield, and they promised to send me more details and a route map nearer the time.

In Londonderry, several soldiers had suffered minor injuries in the performance of their duties in quelling civil disorder. One day, and quite unexpectedly, someone walked up to a young soldier on duty at one of the gates leading into the City from the Bogside, pulled out a pistol and shot him through the forehead. A medical orderly who just happened to be working nearby; gave the soldier mouth to mouth resuscitation until an ambulance arrived and took him to Hospital. He was immediately taken by helicopter to the Royal Victoria Hospital in Belfast. The bullet had not passed through his skull, but was lodged in his brain. His parents in Yorkshire were informed and flown out to Belfast. I met them at the airport and took them to the Hospital. Their son had a seven hours operation to remove the bullet, which had destroyed part of his brain. He survived the operation and was placed on a life support machine in the intensive care unit. His parents were informed that it was most unlikely that he would survive. After consultations with the family, the Battalion contacted their Depot in Yorkshire, and preparations began for a Military Funeral to be held there. After a few days, the decision was made to turn off the life support machine, and to everyone's amazement, the young soldier kept breathing! After several weeks in Hospital, he was sent back to England for rehabilitation. He had lost part of his brain, but was certainly not a 'cabbage'!

He was a great rugby fan, and the following year the Battalion flew him out to Minden to see an important game. He was in a wheelchair and would obviously never recover completely: he could talk and enjoyed a pint of beer as he watched the game! Looking back now over my several tours in the Province, and remembering the awful injuries some soldiers received: I cannot commend highly enough the skill and care of the surgeons and nursing staff working in the Hospitals there. They performed miracles.

On our return to Minden, and after the Battalion had taken some well-deserved leave, I confirmed the arrangements provisionally made with the Gasthouse and began to organise the promised Concert. After only minimal rehearsals, the Concert was held and the hall was packed to capacity. The soldiers performed even better than they had in Londonderry. Having more confidence, most expanded their contribution, and the Concert lasted for four hours!

Before going to Northern Ireland, plans had been made to convert a building next to the Station Staff Office into a Garrison Church, which would then be near the town centre, and not out on the edge of the Garrison like the present Church. A considerable amount of work was needed to turn this building into an acceptable place of worship, but that work was now well advanced. The Brigade had a new Commander, who was a most dynamic character and certainly got things done! The lights in Brigade Headquarters were frequently burning long after others had gone home, and the Brigade Staff were getting quite worn out! Of course the knock-on effect of this was that pressure was increased on all Brigade Units to improve their performance. I was being put under pressure in other ways.

11th Brigade was part of 4th Armoured Division, which had its HQ in Herford. One day, the Divisional Senior Chaplain sent for me and over a cup of coffee, told me about problems being experienced by the Garrison at Hamlin, where there were two Regiments of Royal Engineers, one of them Amphibious Engineers: there were also a couple of minor units, a Garrison Church, and a School. For various reasons, the last three Chaplains to serve there had left the Army. I hasten to add that it had been the Chaplain's own personal situations which had caused them to leave; not the duties or the Regiments in the Garrison! Minden was being well cared for, so I was asked to look after Hamlin Garrison for a few months until another Chaplain could be posted in. My Commanding Officer and the Brigade Commander had been informed of the situation, and so I was now to spend three days a week, and three Sundays out of four, working in Hamlin. It entailed a lot of driving, and of course a lot of time spent getting to know many more people.

The Church office, which also served as the Chaplain's office was in an awful mess; and so my first task was to go through and sort out the files in order to have some idea of what was happening in the Garrison. There was a good regular congregation who did all they could to help me. Because of the situation, there was a backlog of baptisms and impending marriages, as well as a number of families with particular problems.

For one soldier, his problems proved too difficult for him to cope with, and he took his own life. He was married with two children. I, and many others did our best to offer support and comfort, and the family were eventually found accommodation back in England not far from their relatives. In spite of the extra work, and missing out on many things happening in Minden, I enjoyed working with the Royal Engineers and gained insights into the way another part of the Army functioned.

It was the custom in Minden for the Annual Remembrance Day Service to be a Garrison Service. This required a sizeable venue, and relations with the German Churches being very good, we were invited to hold the Service in one of their two large town centre Churches: the Marienkirche (Roman Catholic), and the Martinikirche (Lutheran). The Garrison would alternate between the two. In 1977 it was the turn of the Marienkirche to host the Service, and my turn to preach the Sermon. The German Clergy were most helpful in cooperating with the Brigade Staff in organising the Service: and having recently returned from Northern Ireland, it was appropriate and meaningful for me to be the preacher. It says a lot for Anglo/German relations that we were able to hold our Remembrance Day Services in one of their Churches.

Every year all the Chaplains in Germany would meet for their annual

Conference, which was held at Church House in Wuppertal. It was always good to get together and meet old friends in a relaxed informal atmosphere, and catch up on all the gossip! There are guest speakers, free time, and a Dinner Night. The Chaplain General usually attended and brought all the Chaplains up to date with some of the latest developments taking place in the Army and the Department. This was a time when there were cuts in the Armed Services, and plans for more cuts: and this of course dictated the number of Chaplains required. Having said that, I can't remember a time when we weren't short of Chaplains!

On this occasion, the Chaplain General began his talk by attacking the BBC Program in the 'Everyman' series on the role of Chaplains in Northern Ireland, to which I referred earlier. One of his comments was that 'bad publicity is better than no publicity'! I strongly disagreed with this; and knew that he still hadn't contacted the Church of England Chaplain who had been involved in the making of the program! I had no idea what had happened regarding the Roman Catholic Chaplain, as he was answerable to the Principal RC Chaplain, not the Chaplain General. After Dinner and fortified by a couple of glasses of Port, I cornered the Chaplain General (who I knew pretty well), and told him how much I disagreed with his comments about 'bad publicity being better than no publicity'. "Programmes like that", I said, "We can do without! What's more, you still havn't contacted the Chaplain who was unfortunate enough to be lumbered with doing the program!" He said, "There's a letter on my desk now, ready to be sent off". "It's just a bit late isn't it", I retorted! Our conversation became more heated, and another Chaplain came and shepherded me away. The CG's parting comment to me as I was led away was, "Well, you can do the next one Bayley".

About half a mile away from Clifton Barracks, was a German Army Amphibious Engineer Regiment, doing the same job as our Regiment in Hamlin. Both practised regularly on the River Weser. One day all the Duke's Officers were invited to the German Officers Mess for drinks at 5.00pm. It was a 'three line whip', so I went along. As we arrived and began to mix together, things were a little strained. The German officers' knowledge of the English language was better than our knowledge of German! Their Mess waiters were under the impression that all British Officers drank gin and tonic, but hadn't been informed of the ratio of gin to tonic. The mixture they served up was about 50/50%! Within a short time the language problem seemed to have disappeared and everyone was getting along famously! Amongst ourselves we were saying, "What an interesting bunch they are, we really must invite them to our Mess soon." Just when some of us were thinking of making a move, the German Commanding Officer called for everyone's attention. After saying how good it was to have us visiting them, he began to tell us something of the history of his Regiment. He spoke very good English and it was an interesting talk. As he concluded, several of us again began to make a move. We were halted in our tracks when he said in a loud voice, "And now, we shall go down to the Keller Bar and drink some beer!"

We went down some stairs to a large room with tables laden with food, and were met by waiters bearing Steins of beer! We all ate and drank well as the conversations continued. In the room was a Kegel Bahn (bowling alley). There was only one lane, but the challenges came thick and fast, and I think we acquitted ourselves well. When it came to the singing however, it was quite another matter! Germans love community singing, and the Army seem to have an inexhaustible repertoire of Marching Songs. Our contribution was by comparison insignificant; especially as Rugby songs were banned! Eventually the evening came to an end, and having expressed our heartfelt thanks for their tremendous hospitality and vowing to return it, we made our weary way homewards. Some teatime drinks session that was!

The new Garrison Church building had now been completely refurbished and a Service of Dedication was arranged. It was indeed a great improvement on the old wooden building which had served the Garrison for years, and it did result in an increased congregation. Another factor was that we now had four Chaplains who were all very different. The Senior Chaplain was a 'middle of the road' Anglican. I was a Methodist, and the other two Anglican Chaplains came from opposite wings of the Church; one being a low Church evangelical: the other continuing the Anglo Catholic tradition. This meant that all the people were happy with the Services some of the time!

Easter was drawing near and I received directions and information from my friends in Sheffield regarding the Marriage of their youngest son. The Wedding Ceremony was to take place in a beautiful Chapel in Schloss (castle) Seegau, which was in Leibnitz: a village some miles south of Graz. The Priest in charge had declared that he was happy to share the Service with me.

It was to be a long drive; and it had been arranged for us to stay over night with some wartime friends of the Groom's father; who owned a Gasthause in Bavaria, not far from the Austrian border. It took a whole day to drive down from Minden, and my children in the back were very well behaved! We were made most welcome at the Gasthause and extremely well fed. The following day I drove carefully over the Alps, which were still in places covered with snow, and arrived at our destination in the late afternoon on Easter Saturday. Schloss Seegau had ample accommodation and was administered by an Order of Nuns

Having made such a long journey, I had arranged for us to stay on for a couple of days after the Wedding. My instructions were to go first to the Bride's home, but when we arrived, only the Bride's mother and grandmother were there. The Bride's father had taken all the visitors from Yorkshire, about two dozen of them, on the Weinstrasse (the wine road) along the Austrian/ Yugoslavian border. The Bride's mother thought she might know where to find them and insisted on guiding us to join them on what was really a bit of a pub crawl! Eventually we caught up with them. It was good that they had their own coach, because most of them had never been on the Continent before, and were drinking wine as if it were the beer they were used to at home! By the time we set off back to the village, most were very merry to say the least! One of the Groom's brothers really had too much and was out cold by the time we arrived back at the Schloss. We got him up to bed, and I made sure he was in the semi-prone position before we left him!

There were many very sore heads the following morning, which was Easter Sunday. We went to Mass with the family in the beautiful Chapel, where the Marriage was to take place the following day. It was an area where 98% of the population were Roman Catholics; and it was unusual for them to see a Minister with a wife and children – we were quite a novelty! The Priest didn't show the slightest hesitation in offering us the Sacrament, and after the Service we had a Wedding rehearsal. It was agreed that the couple would make their vows in both languages, guided by their respective Clergyman.

Easter Monday dawned bright and quite warm. The outside of the Bride's house was completely covered with floral decorations, and all the neighbours came out to wish the couple well as the party left for the Civil Ceremony. Britain is the only country where a couple can be legally married in a Church Ceremony. On our way to the local Town Hall, the convoy was brought to a halt several times by children holding a small barrier made of flowers across the road. For the barrier to be removed, a few coins or sweets had to be given to the children. I was most impressed by the Civil Ceremony, which took much longer then a Register Office Marriage in England, and contained much more than the couple making the vows and affirmations required by law. After the Ceremony we returned to the Bride's home for a little while before going to the Chapel. The Bride's father was quite a character. He had only one arm and proudly showed me a wall in the kitchen, which was covered with certificates he had been awarded for safe driving.

Before we left, after the Wedding, he insisted on taking us for a drive in his large Opel saloon. He was indeed a very good driver: but being driven on normal roads at 100 mph by a man with only one arm was an unforgettable experience, and one I hope never to repeat!

The Chapel was full for the Marriage Ceremony, which was very moving, and for some, an emotional event. The Bride's family had understandably mixed feelings. They were very happy for their daughter on her Wedding Day, but saddened by the thought that she would soon be leaving them to live in England. At the end of the Service, several Nuns entered the Chapel carrying large trays, on which were glasses of wine: and for the next quarter of an hour everyone seemed to be toasting everyone else! Then it was off to the Reception. The Wedding cake was the most beautiful I have ever seen. It consisted of several tiers, which weren't just covered with icing, but were magnificently sculptured. Following the meal and the speeches the festivities really began! After a while someone announced that the Bride was nowhere to be found. She had in fact been 'kidnapped'! I was assured that this was nothing to worry about, as it was the custom for the Bride to be 'kidnapped' by thwarted suitors. I went off with most of the men in search of the Bride. It turned into a 'pub crawl' until we found her and all returned to the Reception. I think they knew where she was all the time: but custom had to be followed! The next couple of days were spent sight seeing and resting before making the long drive back to Minden.

Having spent so many holidays visiting relatives in England, we decided it was time to spend a holiday in the sun! We had heard so many people talking about the wonderful holidays they'd had; so I booked for us to spend a holiday in a caravan in the south of France. I was confident we could make the journey in two days and planned accordingly. In fact it took three days, and this is why! The first day was uneventful and we stayed at a small Gasthouse a couple of miles from the German/French border. We set off the following morning in high spirits after a good breakfast, and soon arrived at the main Autoroute to the south. What I didn't know, and what anyone who did know had failed to tell me, was that we had chosen to travel at the same time as millions of French people had their Annual Holidays! It seemed as though the entire population of Paris were on their way, with their caravans, to the south coast! We crept and crawled mile after mile as the temperature rose higher and higher. As evening approached I decided we would have to find somewhere to spend the night.

What a foolish man I was to imagine there would be a couple of empty rooms anywhere! I rejoined the crawl on the Autoroute until we came to a Service Station with a tourist sign on the entrance. I asked the receptionist if she could find us a couple of rooms, and after several phone calls informed me she had found a Hotel in Lyon, a large city about sixty miles south. She wrote the name and address of the Hotel on a card for me, which I appreciated as I do not speak French. I had no idea what a large City Lyon is, and after driving around for half an hour, I hailed a Taxi and showed the card to the driver.

I managed to make him understand that if he led me there, I would pay him. By this time it was 1.00am and we were all tired, hot, sweaty, and fractious! After a fast drive through half the City, trying desperately hard not to lose sight of the Taxi, we arrived at what was obviously an expensive Hotel, and my heart sank. I registered and we were shown to our rooms. The children thought it was a wonderful place, but they hadn't seen the tariff inside the wardrobe door! I gave them strict instructions not to have anything from the mini-bar in their room, and we all showered and collapsed into bed for a few hours.

In the morning we checked out and I paid the bill in cash (we didn't have Credit Cards then). It was £80, which was a lot of money in 1977, and a very large chunk of our holiday money! The cashier said, "But you have not had breakfast yet sir?" I muttered something about being late and getting something to eat on the way. A few miles down the road I stopped at a 'Take Away' and bought breakfast and a few cans of drinks.

The road was just as congested as the previous day, and so I looked at the map and decided on an alternative route. Sadly hundreds of people had done the same: every other vehicle was towing a caravan, and we weren't even on a dual carriageway! It was almost dark when we eventually arrived at the Campsite. The English rep was a very helpful young man who assisted us to get settled in and told us where all the facilities were located. None of the family had been to France before, and I had neglected to inform them that the toilet consisted of two pieces of wood to stand on, and a hole in the ground to aim for! They were appalled, but had no choice but to get used to it. It was a well-equipped caravan with a colourful awning so we could sit outside for our meals, but first we had to do some shopping for food and other necessities. Then it was time to find our way to the beach a few miles away. Having spent almost six months in Cyprus, I thought I was well qualified to warn he others of the danger of over exposure to the sun. The only one to get badly burned on that first day was ME! My legs below the knee, and my feet were very badly burned and I suffered for several days. When I got out of bed in the morning my skin was so tight I could hardly stand up. The nearest beach was frequented by nudists, which my 11 years old son found quite fascinating (of course I didn't!) for a couple of days until the novelty wore off! We explored the surrounding area and ate out a couple of times: then it was time to go home. On the way back, the roads in France were practically empty and we arrived at our Gasthaus in Germany in time for tea! As soon as we arrived home it was time to prepare to go to England.

By the time our son Simon, was 11 years of age, he had already attended five different schools. Remembering well the experiences of our eldest daughter, we had decided to send him to Boarding School. By doing this, his education would not be disrupted every time I was posted, and he would be able to retain his friendships. Having consulted several of my colleagues, we decided to send him to a Methodist School near Bury St Edmunds.

As a Methodist Minister, the fees would be slightly reduced, and the remainder almost covered by the grant from the Army. We had already visited the school and obtained the necessary items of uniform from the sole supplier in Bury St Edmunds. We were granted two free flights a year for him to come home for the holidays: the third we had to pay for. Not having any relatives in the south of England, we arranged for him to spend his half term holidays with his grandparents in Yorkshire. When Simon began his first term, we took him and saw him settled in. Thereafter, we took him to the airport, where there were many children on their way to Boarding Schools; and used an organisation called 'Country Cousins' to escort him across London to Liverpool Street Station. There he met up with other pupils on their way to Bury St Edmunds. At the railway station, a coach was waiting to take them to the School. At half term, the School Staff ensured he caught the right train to Yorkshire. When he came home for the Christmas vacation, he seemed to have settled in well and had made a number of friends.

The priority for the Battalion was now to prepare for their Battle Group training exercise in Canada. A Battle Group was made up of tanks, artillery, mechanised infantry, engineers, helicopters, and about twelve thousand troops. The Military units making up the Battle Group were stationed in various Garrisons in Germany, and it was necessary for them to spend time training together before going to Canada. Every year about six Battle Groups went to Canada from Germany, where the training was organised and supervised by the British Army Training Unit Suffield (BATUS), which was in a huge training area in the Province of Alberta, about one hundred and forty miles east of Calgary. The training area was much larger than any in Germany, and it was therefore possible for the armoured vehicles to move and fire their weaponry in ways not possible anywhere else. In such a situation, as we were to discover, SAFETY was a priority and we were rightly never allowed to forget that! BATUS held a stockpile of all the heavy equipment used by a Battle Group from tanks to land rovers, so it was not necessary to bring them from Germany.

The Duke of Wellington's Battle Group gathered together for preparatory training in one of the main training areas in north Germany in February. It was bitterly cold. During the night the temperature dropped to − 18 degrees, and the vehicle engines had to be started up several times during the night as the diesel was 'sludging' in the fuel tanks. As I would be the only Chaplain accompanying the Battle Group, it was a good opportunity for me to meet, and spend time with the other units. I was invited to drive one of the Chieftain tanks; only on the training area I hasten to add! The tank, which weighed about 60 tons, had five forward and five reverse gears: the method of changing gear was by using a foot, which was very much like the method used on my old motor bike! The direction of the tank was determined by means of the tillers, which controlled the tracks. It didn't take long to get used to it, and I had an enjoyable half an hour covering ground, which was only possible in a tracked vehicle.

I thanked the Troop Commander, a Lieutenant in the Blues And Royals, and was about to climb down off the tank, when he said, "Would you care for a glass of port before you go Padre?" I didn't really know if he was being serious or not, but replied, "That's very kind, I'd love one please". Out of the bowels of the tank appeared a small silver tray with two glasses of port on it! After enjoying the port, I placed my glass on the tray saying, "That was most enjoyable, I'll buy you a glass in Canada"!

Before leaving for Canada I received a Posting Order, informing me that I was to move at the beginning of September to Hohne (better known as Bergen/Hohne) which is only a couple of miles from the site of Belson Concentration Camp. My posting was to 1st The Queen's Dragoon Guards together with pastoral responsibility for 45 Regiment Royal Artillery; and a Royal Army Ordnance Corps Company. I would also have my own Church, which pleased me very much!

When the day came for us to depart for Canada, we left Minden very early in the morning for the RAF airfield from where we would be flown out to Calgary. We waited for several hours without any explanation. The RAF was living up to its ascribed motto "Hurry up and wait"! Eventually we took off, but had to land in England for the aircraft to top up its fuel tanks, before setting off across the Atlantic Ocean. We landed in Gander, Newfoundland for refuelling before setting off to Calgary. It took longer to fly from Gander to Calgary than it had to cross the Atlantic: which told us something about the size of Canada! We crossed several time zones, and it seemed that every time I managed to doze off, some one would wake me up for a meal! After landing at Calgary, we boarded coaches for the final leg of our journey to Suffield.

After looking at the boring landscape for several miles, some one asked the driver, "Is it like this for long"? The driver grinned and said, "only about three thousand miles!" Whenever we came to a level crossing the coach stopped, the driver opened the door, closed it again and drove across the railway line. It was possible to see for miles in both directions, but the law dictated that the driver always had to stop and open the coach door! If a train was coming, it was a long wait while it passed, because the trains were very, very long! There are very strict speed limits on the Trans Canadian Highway, but eventually the coach turned off north, and within a few miles we arrived at the BATUS camp. The accommodation was basic, but adequate and we soon sorted ourselves out and went to the cookhouse for a meal. The food was consistently very good and there was plenty of it. The first night in bed, I was so tired I went straight to sleep: but woke up in the middle of the night! It was my first experience of 'jet lag', and it took a couple of days to get back to normal.

Sitting in the sun outside our huts, it was quite fascinating to watch the gophers, which seemed to have their little holes everywhere. In the hut, which served as the Officers Mess, was a large television set which seemed to be permanently tuned to American channels. Trying to watch a film was difficult as there was no break for adverts: they just came on and went off without the slightest pause, so it was difficult at first to know whether you were watching a film or an advert!

The religious programmes were the cause of some amusement. I found most of them quite nauseating: a bit like having a cup of coffee with ten spoonfuls of sugar.

During the next few days, the crews checked and took over their vehicles and equipment. Officers went on reconnaissance trips around the training area, and we had lectures from the Safety Staff and the Military Police. We were warned to look out for rattlesnakes, which initially made everyone very wary! I saw only one, and at a safe distance! Some soldiers saw a couple one evening as they were preparing to bed down for the night, and decided to sleep on their tanks! The Police were particularly keen that every one should be aware of the Canadian laws regarding alcohol. In a bar, customers had to sit at a table and be served by a waiter. It was unlawful to stand at the bar! If a customer wanted to move to another table to talk to friends, he had to summon a waiter to carry his glass for him: it was unlawful to walk across the room carrying a glass! If a customer asked for a glass of beer, he was given two. Apparently, this was a hangover from the days when someone would come in from the prairie, hot and dusty, demanded a beer and drank it straight down before immediately demanding another one! Now the customer is given two beers as a matter of course! Fortunately Canadian beer is very weak! Outside a bar, beer can only be purchased from a bonded shop in sealed cardboard containers. These containers must not be opened until the customer gets home. It is illegal to drink on the street, or even at a picnic by the side of your car. As my own home town increasingly suffers from drunken yobs and loutish behaviour: instead of officials and the media continually agonising over the problems caused by alcohol; why don't we just adopt the Canadian system?

The landscape made distances very deceptive. There is a village called Ralston, which we could see from the Camp, where all the BATUS married men (British and Canadian) had their homes. It looked to be a few hundred yards away, but was in fact more than two miles! One morning I was walking from the Camp to BATUS HQ, when I saw two very weary looking soldiers coming towards me. I said to them, "You lads look a bit shattered, where have you been?" "Oh Padre", they answered wearily, "We went to Medicine Hat last night, and missed the transport to bring us back. We could see the lights of the Camp and decided to walk back". Medicine Hat is a town 35 miles from BATUS! There were a number of shops in Ralston, and a very well equipped Church, designed to serve all Christian Denominations. A Minister from the United Church of Canada and a Roman Catholic Priest made regular visits from Medicine Hat, but were happy to have Chaplains from visiting Battle

Groups relieve them whenever possible! There were more than 50 churches in Medicine Hat, which had a population of about 35,000. I mentioned this to the Minister asking, "Economically, how on earth can your town possibly support so many Churches"? He replied rather dryly, "It's the Americans just over the border; they think we're a Mission Area"! During my visit, I conducted a number of Services there and baptised several babies.

I only made two visits to Medicine Hat and on my second visit, went to the Cinema to see 'Grease'! That was before the film was shown in England!

The first part of the Exercise period was spent with the units composing the Battle Group; which now included a Mechanised Infantry Company from the Canadian Army, finding their way around the area and practicing for the big, live firing Exercises that were to come. Not having a vehicle of my own, I hitched rides with others like the Quartermasters Staff, and the Doctor, in order to have a look around the area and visit the troops. If I needed transport to visit Hospitals in Medicine Hat or Calgary, a self- drive car would be provided for me. Occasionally I would hitch a ride in a helicopter. When the live firing Exercises were taking place I would use a Land Rover, but would have to seek permission from the Control Centre as to where and when I could travel, and which routes I would have to take. The times of my arrivals and departures would be reported to the Control Centre. Anyone getting lost would be very unpopular, as the Exercise would have to be halted until they were found. Fortunately it never happened to me!

There were two events, which merited ensuring a 'grandstand' view. The first was the night firing exercise with a spectacular display of flares, rockets, and tracer rounds. The second was the firing by the Royal Engineers of the 'Giant Viper'. This was a device used for clearing a path through a minefield, wide enough for tanks to pass through. It consisted of a length of hose packed with explosives and wound around a huge drum. At the end of the hose was a rocket, which when fired, unwound the hose from the drum and propelled it over the minefield. As it landed on the ground, the whole length was detonated and exploded all the mines in the surrounding area. It was most impressive.

One day I drove to the Hospital in Calgary to visit some soldiers who had been injured, not seriously, in a traffic accident. The speed limit on the Trans Canadian Highway was 55mph, which was quite frustrating given the distance to be travelled and the fact there was so little traffic! When I arrived at the Hospital and took a lift to the floor where the soldiers were being treated, I was amazed to find myself sharing the lift with a dozen people, who were all speaking in German! I mentioned this to the Ward Sister, who informed me that there were more than 50,000 Germans living in Calgary. By reading the local Newspapers and Magazines, it was evident Calgary is a very cosmopolitan City!

At the end of the Exercises there was a considerable amount of clearing up to be done. All the vehicles and equipment had to be cleaned and serviced ready for the next Battle Group. When BATUS were satisfied, all personnel were allowed three or four days R & R (Rest and Recuperation). Some were anxious to go over the border and spend a few days in the United States Of America, others went on Adventure Training trips to the Rocky Mountains: while others hired cars and visited beauty spots in the Mountains.

A colleague and I planned to spend a few days based in Calgary at a good Hotel which offered us special rates; and look around the area from there. The Army Air Corps had a small Beaver light aircraft which made regular trips from Suffield to Calgary, and he had arranged a couple of seats for us. That saved us a few hours travelling time, though we would have to return by Grey Hound coach. As we flew to Calgary, I noticed how every farm and dwelling seemed to have its own scrap yard, made up of old rusty cars and machinery. I suppose being so far away from any large town left them with no alternative.

After landing at Calgary Airport, we took a taxi to the Hotel in the City. It was very comfortable and we were grateful to have received the recommendation. The following morning we took the lift to the top of a very high tower with a revolving restaurant on the top. We breakfasted on flapjacks with maple syrup and coffee: and as the restaurant revolved, had a magnificent view of the Rockies. We spent the day looking around the City, and were surprised how cheap the cars were: and that it was possible to buy one using a Credit Card! The shops were quite fascinating, but very expensive. Banff, a very popular tourist resort wasn't very far up into the mountains, so we booked a coach trip to go there the following day. That evening we decided to go for a meal and were overwhelmed by the choices available. Feeling hungry but not adventurous, we ended up in a German Restaurant and had an excellent meal at a very reasonable cost. Better the devil you know! On the way to Banff, the coach driver made a slight detour in order that we might see some Bison. Might was the operative word, because they decided not to come out that morning! At Banff we took a cable car to the top of a nearby mountain and enjoyed the views and the antics of some racoons. Once again we braved the shops and bought a few small presents and souvenirs. It was a most enjoyable day, and Banff was well worth the visit.

We returned to Suffield on a Greyhound coach, which dropped us off at the bottom of the road. My colleague 'phoned BATUS, and they sent a vehicle down to collect us. Then it was just a case of packing up and waiting for our flight back to Germany. The journey back was long and tedious, and again we needed a couple of days to get over 'jet lag'! While I had been away, my wife had cleaned the house ready for handover, except for the attic and cellars, which, because of the dust and spiders, were always my responsibility! Cleaning a married quarter before 'marching out', as it was called; was a long and tiring duty. The house and its continents had to be spotlessly clean and were inspected by the housing staff before we left. The inventory was checked against the condition of the contents, and compared with the 'marching in' documentation. Any damage, from scratch marks on furniture to stains on mattresses had to be paid for! On all our sixteen 'march' out documentation during my time in the Army, my wife always received a special commendation for the cleanliness of the property. When we had finished filling the packing cases and made final arrangements to move to Hohne: we said our 'goodbyes' to the Dukes and some good friends we had made in the Garrison. Because there wasn't time, I had to return several weeks later in order to be formerly 'dined out' in the Officers Mess.

As Hohne was only a couple of hours drive away, I had already visited the Garrison, met the Chaplain I was succeeding, who was also a Methodist, and ensured we had a married quarter to occupy as soon as we arrived! The Dukes provided a vehicle and working party to move my packing cases and we all travelled up to Hohne on the same day.

1ST THE QUEEN'S DRAGOON GUARDS & 45 REGIMENT, ROYAL ARTILLERY. SEPTERMBER 1978-OCTOBER 1980

Our Married Quarter was a lovely ground floor flat in a cul-de-sac in the village of Bergen, just two miles from the Garrison. A single-track railway line ran alongside our block, and just a few yards from our lounge window! On the other side of the track there was a wire fence, and over the fence the local cemetery, which, as is the norm in Germany, was beautifully maintained: and the many flowers made it pleasing to the eye and a pleasure to walk around. At Hohne were the ranges for Tanks and Artillery; and we had to get used to rattling windows and very loud bangs on most days! Some of the tanks and artillery were transported to the ranges by road. Others came by rail and past our lounge window. There was something a little sinister about it. It wasn't so many years earlier that prisoners on their way to Belsen had passed the same way. After the war the site of the concentration camp had been left derelict for some years, until the Jews cleared the site and turned it into an impressive Memorial.

There is a museum containing a model of the camp, and many photographs and newspaper articles. Around the site are a number of mass graves, a Memorial, and a Cenotaph. As visitors walk around the site, they pass through lightly wooded areas, and see a number of graves containing just one or two bodies. Belsen is visited by many thousands of people every year. In Hohne Camp, British Officers and Senior NCOs now occupy the houses once used by Senior Officers and Guards staffing the Camp. My father had a good friend, whom I met many times, who was one of the British Soldiers who discovered the Camp. His hair turned white, virtually overnight by the horrors he encountered. I remember reading a copy of an old local magazine in which there is an account of the local Burgermeister (Mayor), visiting the Camp to protest about the treatment of the prisoners. He was never seen again.

The nearest Military Hospital was more than an hours drive away in Hannover, and the Military Cemetery was also near Hannover, a few miles to the west of the City: so I was driving down from Hohne at least once a week, fortunately mostly to the Hospital.

When I arrived in Hohne, I took my family to the flat and then went to see the Adjutant of 1st The Queen's Dragoon Guards, to pay my respects and let him know that I had arrived. After exchanging greetings, he pushed into my hand a large Signal, (today it would be an 'E' Mail), saying. "I think you'd better read this"! I sat down and read the Signal with mounting apprehension. It was about an ATV (Now Central TV) series called 'JayWalking'. It was a series of programs presented by Susan Jay on Sunday evenings. The Chaplain General had been approached by the program makers, and had agreed to a programme being made showing the work of an Army Chaplain.

The Signal concluded with the words, "The Chaplain General has nominated the Revd Peter Bayley to do this programme"! He had made good his threat to me at the Chaplains' Conference the previous year, when we had been discussing the disastrous programme made by the BBC in the 'Everyman' series! Sue Jay and her producer came to see me a few weeks later to discuss the program. I insisted we agree on some 'ground rules'. I made it abundantly clear, that unless we could come to an agreement on certain things, I would refuse to participate in the making of the programme, no matter what the Chaplain General said! The priority was that there would be no contrived situations. I was more than happy to be interviewed on any aspect of my work, and that they could film me as I went about my various tasks in the Garrison. They planned to return in mid November, which would be right in the middle of a major Military Exercise, which would be an ideal setting. I was convinced that they were genuine in their stated objectives, and there was no hidden agenda. I realised of course, that neither I, nor the Chaplain General himself, would have any say at all in the way the programme was cut and edited. However, before then, there was a much more important event for 1QDG.

On 8th November 1978, Her Majesty, Queen Elizabeth The Queen Mother, would be presenting them with a new Standard, which would be consecrated by the Chaplain General. There were lots of rehearsals, and a slight problem regarding protocol. The Commanding Officer informed me that there would be a formal Lunch in the Officers Mess after the parade, and that the Dean of Windsor, who was in fact a Bishop, would be in attendance. The problem?

Who should the Commanding Officer invite to say Grace before the meal? The Bishop? The Chaplain General? Or the Regimental Chaplain? I didn't know the answer, but told the CO I would make enquiries. The answer was that I, as the Regimental Chaplain, should be the one to say Grace! It was a splendid occasion: the weather was kind, and it was a great pleasure to meet the Queen Mother.

After Lunch I took the opportunity to tell the Chaplain General of my meeting with Sue Jay and the producer of the proposed 'Jay Walking' programme. He gave me a wry grin and wished me well!

The NAAFI shop in the Garrison was in a large building known as 'The Roundhouse'. In addition to the shop and other facilities, there was a large hall: and it was here that the Remembrance Day Service was held. The hall held about 1,000 people, so wasn't large enough for the whole Garrison and their families, so a representative number from each Regiment attended. A collection was taken at the Service for the Earl Haig Fund. It added up to under 1,000 Deutchmarks, which I considered to be a miserly amount, especially given the extra Local Overseas Allowance paid to Servicemen in Germany: and the duty free items such as cigarettes, alcohol, cars, and cheap petrol!

The following year, it was my turn to preach and I pointedly drew attention to this. I reminded the gathering that we were assembled, not just to remember those who had died in two World Wars and many other conflicts, but also to 'keep faith' with those who still suffered and would continue to suffer. I said that if we, who wore the same uniform, didn't 'keep faith', then that would be a deplorable example to the community at large! I asked them, for example, to think about what they had spent on food and drink on the traditional 'Saturday night out'. The collection that year was more than double the previous year, but my comments weren't universally appreciated: especially by some Senior Officers, who were quick to comment that the soldiers had bought poppies! I think for the most part it was just sheer thoughtlessness. The old attitude, that when a collecting plate comes around, you just put a coin on it. I remember well when decimalisation was adopted in Britain, Church collections dropped because the half-a-crown had been discontinued!

1QDG were equipped with Scorpion and Scimitar light tanks and their role was primarily one of reconnaissance: to be the 'eyes and ears' of the Battle Groups and the Armoured Division. 45 Regiment was equipped with SP (self propelled) Abbot Guns, and an Air defence Battery equipped with hand held 'Blowpipe' anti aircraft missiles. In addition they had on attachment, a Royal Horse Artillery Battery, equipped with eight inch guns, capable of firing nuclear shells: and a small detachment of American Servicemen. The Senior Chaplain had pastoral responsibility for a Regiment equipped with 'Chieftain' main battle tanks, another Royal Artillery Regiment, and a Field Ambulance Unit; which he left to the care of a Church Army Captain.

There were two Primary Schools in Bergen, and one in Hohne Camp. In the Camp there was also a Secondary Modern School, which was attended by children from neighbouring Garrisons as well as our own. Conducting School assemblies was a regular commitment. There were three Churches, one a Roman Catholic, one Church of England; always known as 'The White Church', and my Church, which had a long tradition of serving Methodists, Presbyterians, and Baptists. To my great joy it was well equipped with Methodist Hymn Books!

All the Churches worked closely together, especially on what was known as 'The Hohne Churches Project'. There was a small committee, made up of representatives from the Churches. The Garrison Commander, a Brigadier, was also an enthusiastic supporter who attended the committee meetings. Every year, they would choose to support a particular charity, and raise a considerable amount of money together. One year, a Corporal from the Field Ambulance Unit, suggested we support the 'Across Trust', which enabled severely handicapped people to have a holiday overseas. We looked at literature and a video, as well as having a brief visit from the vehicle which made such holidays possible. It was called a 'Jumbulance', a large, long, 'Bendy'bus, capable of transporting people on stretchers: with each disabled person having a carer travelling with them.

The Across Trust is a Roman Catholic charity, but the disabled people didn't have to belong to any particular Church. The proposal was that we raise enough money to bring the 'Jumbulance' and it's passengers to Hohne, provide them with food and accommodation, and arrange for them to visit places of interest. The Medical Corps Corporal offered to be the liaison/coordinator for the visit. This suggestion was accepted unanimously by the committee, which had one slight reservation: would they be able to raise the amount of money required, which was far in excess of any amount previously raised? We decided to go ahead, and after a short publicity campaign, the Garrison responded magnificently, raising the required amount of several thousand pounds within a few months. People held coffee mornings, baked and sold cakes, made cash donations, and a Concert was held at the Senior School, at which my contribution was a couple of songs and monologues. The dates for the visit were planned when one of the Regiments would be away on 'block leave', which meant we could use some of their accommodation.

When the 'Jumbulance' arrived, I was pleasantly surprised by the number of soldiers who volunteered to help, not only by pushing wheelchairs, but also in helping to wash, dress, and feed our disabled visitors. They went on a number of trips to places of interest, and particularly enjoyed a visit to the Zoo in Hannover. The Garrison arranged an 'Open Day', when all the military vehicles and equipment were on display. Those in wheelchairs were hoisted by cranes onto trucks usually used for transporting ammunition, and said that it was more fun than visiting a fairground! On a more serious note: several of our visitors questioned the soldiers about their role in Germany, and one lady, realising how close we were to the East German Border, asked about the 'threat' from the vast numbers of Russians not very far away! A young Bombardier from one of the Artillery Regiments, unaware of my presence in a group behind them, replied reassuringly, "Don't you worry love, if ever they do come, we shall stop them. There may not be many of us left, but we shall stop them"! I felt quite proud and a little humbled by his response. When the 'Jumbulance' departed, all the visitors expressed their thanks for 'a wonderful holiday'. As I reflected on the events of the week and all the hard work beforehand, I thought that most of **us** had benefited more than our visitors from their time amongst us.

The 'Jaywalking' crew arrived just after the Autumn Military Exercise had started. The weather was cold, with some snow and hard frosts. We joined the Exercise, taking great care not to get in the way! The cameraman was able to get lots of shots of tanks, APCs, and helicopters: and I had my first interview standing by the aide of a tank. There were questions about how Christians could serve in the Military, where they might have to kill enemy soldiers, and how I, as a Christian Minister could be part of it. I maintained there was no area of life from which God was excluded, and that my role was to be the Man of God in the Military situation.

Several soldiers were interviewed as the armoured vehicles rolled by. Questions such as, "Do you go to Church? And, "What do you think of the Padre?" One soldier was asked, "Are you a Christian?" To which he replied, "No, I'm a Catholic!" I felt quite sure that would be 'edited out', but it wasn't! We moved on to where the Regimental Aid Post of 1QDG was temporarily located. More questions were asked of soldiers, and we moved inside the barn and sat down for a mug of coffee; in a pig sty! While the pigs made their own contribution, we continued our conversation. I was asked why I was in the Army as a Chaplain, and I explained that it had only been with the help and support of an Army Chaplain when I was a young soldier, that I was in the Church at all.

My 'Battle Station' was with the Regimental Aid Post, where battle casualties were brought to be examined, stabilised, and sent back to the Field Ambulance Unit; the next ink in the casualty evacuation chain. Casualties would obviously be in a state of shock and anxiety, and I would do my best to comfort and reassure them. More questions were asked about the reasons for the Church being involved in a fighting force. I pointed out that if the number of Soldiers, Sailors, and Airmen, were added up, plus their wives and families, and the many civilians who were part of the community, such as School Teachers, NAAFI staff, and many others: we were talking of more than half a million people, and that of course the Church must be available to minister to them.

We journeyed back to Hohne, to illustrate other parts of the Chaplain's role. I was filmed doing my Battle Fitness Test with a group of soldiers, which I completed ahead of many younger men. Still hot and sweaty, I was asked, "What do you feel like now?" To which I replied, "I feel like a pint". After a quick shower and change of clothes, we met up again in the Sergeant's Mess of the Royal Army Ordnance Corps Company. There, the members were asked questions about the Church and the role of the Padre, and I was asked about a Methodist Minister enjoying a pint! We then went to join a meeting of the Wives Club where more questions were asked about the role of the Chaplain. There was particular interest paid to the wives whose husbands were away serving in Northern Ireland.

The following morning I was due to take an Assembly at one of the Primary Schools, and that was filmed. I had a final interview in the vestry of my Church, where once again Sue Jay returned to the subject of 'how a Christian could be a soldier'. I was asked if I would kill to defend myself. "What with", I replied, "My bare hands?" Chaplains are none combatants, they do not carry weapons, and they do not train in the use of weapons. I confessed that it was not possible to state unequivocally what I would do if someone was trying to kill me! We talked more about war, and I made the point that armies do not wage war: Nations wage war, and it is not Generals who make the decision to

fight them, but politicians. I was asked about soldiers who might have problems about the morality of war: and emphasised the fact that British soldiers are professionals; we do not have a conscript Army where I could indeed envisage a few problems.

The production team visited the Chaplain's Depot at Bagshot Park and took some footage in the Museum, which set the role of the Army Chaplain in its historical context. It took almost four days filming to produce a programme, which lasted 25 minutes! My Senior Chaplain at 1st Armoured Division obtained an advance copy of the programme, and I went to Verden to see it. It was well received by a small, select audience, and I was satisfied with the final result. It was better than I had dared to hope!

It was due to be shown on ATV (now Central Television) one Sunday evening in the spring of 1979. Unfortunately it was postponed due to TV coverage of the Pope's visit! It was shown at a later date, and was very well received by the Army and the Methodist Church. The Army obtained a number of videos and 16mm films, which were used for many years in Training Establishments to illustrate and inform Officers and soldiers about the role of the Chaplain. The Home Mission Division of the Methodist Church (all Forces Chaplains come under that Division of the Church) did the same, and the programme was widely used in Methodist Churches around the country, usually at Home Mission Meetings. When I left the Army seven years later; the Church to which I was invited saw the film just before I arrived! I still have a copy of the video, which is now rather worn after nearly 25 years. The issues it deals with are still relevant, and it also serves to remind me how I used to be when I was 40!

Some friends we had met in Minden were now stationed in Fallingbostel and we met regularly. It took about half an hour to drive to their home if we took the road across the ranges. If that road was closed due to live firing, we would have to drive north towards Soltau and use the Hamburg – Hannover autobahn to get to Fallingbostel, which was almost twice the distance. They had asked to me officiate at the marriage of their daughter to a British serviceman. The day before the wedding there had been an exceptionally heavy fall of snow and we had difficulty getting to the church, as did many of the guests. The long path from the road to the church was covered by deep snow and several soldiers had laboured to clear the way to the church door, piling snow high on each side of the pathway. It was quite a sight to see the bride and her father making their way between walls of snow to the church door. I met them there and said to my friend, "I know you wanted a white wedding, but this is ridiculous!" After the ceremony it began to snow heavily again, and those of us who had come from outside the area thought it prudent to leave the reception early to ensure we were able to get back home before the roads were blocked. It proved to be a wise decision because though the authorities did their best to clear the roads, strong winds were blowing snow off the fields and blocking them again!

The large Cinema in the Garrison was advertising a showing of 'Grease'. I had already seen the film in Canada and thoroughly enjoyed it, but I booked tickets so that I could take the family. The Cinema was filled to capacity and everyone waited in eager anticipation: but there was a problem! The mechanism controlling the huge curtains covering the screen had seized up. The Manager and his staff tried in vain to move the curtains, as the audience grew more and more restless and impatient. After almost half an hour, the Manager strode onto the stage, and with a great effort, ripped the curtains down and the film commenced to loud cheers. I think he was afraid of being lynched unless he did something drastic!

Our first winter in Hohne was the worst I had ever known. We had been invited to a New Year's Eve Party at one of the homes in the Camp. During the evening it began to snow very heavily, and I wisely, as it turned out, decided to stay at home. I phoned the party givers and gave our apologies. They informed me that others had already phoned for the same reason. It snowed heavily for days, and living in a cul-de-sac, we couldn't get out. Some people needed to get to the Medical Centre, and a tracked vehicle was sent to collect them! When the New Year break was over, people needed to get to work. It took quite some time to de-ice the cars and get down to the main road. Driving very, very carefully I managed to get into Camp. It continued to snow, and I was reminded of the words of the Christmas Carol, 'Snow had fallen, snow on snow'. People had to get around, and the road surfaces became deeply rutted as the snow became more and more compacted. It was six weeks before we saw the ground again. In the cul-de-sac; the residents were using hammers and chisels to break up the inches thick layers of ice that covered the road surface.

Not long after the snow had eventually disappeared, I went to Benbecula in the Hebrides with the Air Defence Battery for their annual 'live-firing' camp. I was very surprised to hear from the residents that they hadn't had any snow! They explained that they rarely had snow, because the strong winds usually blew it straight over the top of the island!

The target for the Gunners, with their hand held 'Blowpipe' missiles, was a drone towed a long way behind an aircraft towards the range, which was over the sea. It was very frustrating for them, as they didn't succeed in hitting the target once: and the bottle of Champagne, which was held in readiness, remained unopened. It was fortunate that before the Falklands War in 1982 these weapons had been replaced with Batteries of 'Rapier' anti-aircraft missiles, which were far superior to the 'Blowpipe'.

One evening I joined a group and went for an excellent meal at a restaurant down at the southern end of the island. I had the most beautiful salmon steak I have ever tasted! The venue actually appears in the 'Guiness Book of Records': not for its salmon steaks, but because it's bar boasted the greatest variety of whiskeys in the world! The week was also memorable because of the time many of us stayed up most of the night watching the results of the General Election; which the Conservative Party won, and Margaret Thatcher became the Prime Minister!

Within a few days of returning home, we received the news that my father-in-law had died. He had been suffering with heart trouble for a while, so the news did not come as a complete surprise. I immediately set the wheels in motion for my wife to travel home to Rotherham. The Movements Section handling Compassionate Cases were most efficient. My wife was granted Compassionate 'B' category and was given a flight to England the following day. Had my father-in-law been classed as VSI (Very Seriously Ill,) she would have been granted Category 'A' status and flown home immediately. I took her to Hannover Airport, and when the aircraft landed in England, she was met by a member of the Movements Staff with a car, taken to London and put on a train to Rotherham. She returned after the funeral, having made arrangements for her mother to come to Hohne for a month in June.

Soldiers wishing to get married in Germany were often faced with problems. If a soldier wished to marry a British girl: for example, the daughter of a serving soldier or a schoolteacher or a nurse: they could be married by a Chaplain under The Foreign Marriage Act. I would fill in forms provided by HQ British Army of the Rhine (BAOR), return them immediately after the marriage ceremony, and a Marriage Certificate would be issued. Having said that, the German lady clerk who worked in the office at HQ BAOR, was an absolute pedant, and returned the forms if there was the slightest error. That was fair enough, but I had a disagreement with her that went on for many weeks! A soldier had declared his place of birth to be Norwich, Norfolk. The clerk wanted to know which part or district of Norwich. The soldier was unable to produce his Birth Certificate, and it took weeks to persuade the lady that the soldier had been born simply in Norwich – no particular part or district – just Norwich. Other Chaplains had similar problems, and one told me he would open a bottle of Champagne if he could ever send Marriage Forms to HQ BAOR without them being returned for one reason or another. I don't believe he ever opened the bottle!

A soldier wishing to marry a German girl was required to give six months notice; and submit his request using special forms. If for any reason it was not possible to give six months notice: for example if the girl was heavily pregnant, or the soldier was being posted; the Commanding Officer would have to sign a Certificate waiving that requirement. The couple would then have to make arrangements with the German Civil Authority, and attend several times with an official translator, whom they had to pay: and who would sign a form declaring that he had accurately translated all that had been said. If the couple desired a marriage ceremony in Church: that would have to be held after the civil ceremony.

An Officer in 1QDG wished to marry a German girl, and have the religious ceremony in the 'White Church'. Unfortunately, his military commitments were such that he wasn't going to be around to make all the necessary visits to the German Civil Authority. There was great consternation as many plans had been made and people invited from England! I had a brainwave.

I suggested the Officer took a few days leave and went with his fiancée to England, where they could be married in three days by Special Licence: then come back to Germany for the Church Ceremony. They did just that, and I had great pleasure in conducting the ceremony in Church; omitting from the Service the legal declarations as they were already married. Also, I didn't have any paperwork to worry about!

In Hohne there was a Battalion of Dutch soldiers, and one of my soldiers wanted to marry a Dutch girl. Can you imagine the paperwork and time scale involved? British soldier marrying a Dutch girl, in Germany! I explained to the couple all that was involved, and advised them to allow plenty of time. They didn't heed my advice, and made plans for a date which I knew to be too optimistic. Had it been a marriage between two British people, I knew I could get on the telephone and attempt to hurry things along: but there is no way to hurry the German Civil Authority. At least two dozen guests flew from England for the Wedding: but the paperwork wasn't completed. Most stayed around for a week, and then returned home. A week later the authority came through, and the couple were married, but without many of their friends in attendance!

45 Regiment went to Northern Ireland for a four months tour of duty, and I went to spend some time with them. They had soldiers based at the Maze Prison, Porterdown, and small detachments manning border posts just south of Enniskillen. I based myself with the Battery at the Maze Prison. All around the perimeter were watchtowers manned by soldiers. The Army had no role inside the prison itself. I climbed up to visit those manning the watchtowers many times, but my main form of exercise was to run around the tarmac perimeter track, which was exactly two miles long. Most days I would do two laps, always making sure I informed the Control Room beforehand. They would notify the soldiers in the towers: "Padre running around the walls in an anti-clockwise direction"!

Just before our arrival in the Province, many members of the Parachute Regiment had been killed at Warrenpoint. A large bomb had been detonated and killed many: then when all the Emergency Services and others from the Regiment arrived on the scene, a second bomb was detonated, and most of them were also killed. I don't know for sure, but this was probably the greatest loss of life suffered by the Parachute Regiment since World War II. I visited some of the survivors in Hospital. They were deeply shocked at the loss of so many of their comrades.

One day as I was on my way to Porterdown, I passed the Methodist Church in Lurgan. As I drove past I glanced at the Church Notice Board, and was delighted to see that the Minister was the same man I had known in Limavady seven years earlier when I was based at Ballykelly with The Royal Green Jackets. I arranged to call on him and his wife, and after catching up on each other's news he said, "Are you going to come and preach for me one Sunday"? I agreed that would be possible and suggested a Sunday evening. He said, "Great: please come and have tea with us before the Service".

The Sunday I had offered was just before the Pope was due to visit the Republic of Ireland. Over tea, my friend said to me, "You're not going to mention the Pope's visit are you?" I replied that I intended mentioning it in my prayers of intercession. He said, "Please don't: this isn't Limavady. This area is what you might call 'hard Orange': and three members of my congregation have been murdered by the IRA". He went on to tell me that he had recently mentioned that he was thinking of changing his car, and buying a Volkswagen. He received a deputation from some Church officials, who said to him: "you can't drive around here in a Catholic car." He was very puzzled by this. Apparently, many of the local Priests and Nuns drove VWs, and many people were convinced the Catholic Church had shares in Volkswagen!

I followed the Pope's visit on TV, and was deeply moved by the Open Air Mass he conducted near Dublin, especially when he sank to his knees to pray for peace. Referring to the 'men of violence', he prayed for them to renounce their murderous campaign. "I **beg** you," he prayed: "on my knees, I **beg** you". But the 'men of violence', Republicans and Loyalists alike, were not listening.

The soldiers in Porterdown were operating out of pre-fabricated buildings. One day a group of visitors were being shown the workings of a Rocket Launcher. This weapon was sometimes used, by firing an inert round: (one without an explosive warhead) into a vehicle suspected of containing a bomb, in an attempt to explode it. Live, inert, and practice rounds had different coloured rings around them: the soldier demonstrating the Rocket Launcher believed he had loaded a practice round: but it was in fact an inert round. The next room was the Battery HQ, which was a hive of activity. A telephone was ringing and the person who should have answered it was busy, so the Battery Sergeant Major leaned over to pick up the receiver. As he did so, the soldier next door fired the Rocket Launcher. The round went through the wall, hit the BSM in the shoulder, demolished the Battery Office and the next two rooms; and ended up several hundred yards away.

The BSM was rushed to Craigavon Hospital and admitted to the Intensive Care Unit. He was classified as being Very Seriously Ill, and his wife was flown from Hohne to be with him. He remained in Intensive Care for many weeks before being transferred to Dundonald Hospital, south of Belfast, to be treated by some of the finest plastic surgeons in the world. They had treated so many people in the last twenty years suffering from terrible injuries. In the Hospital there is a Museum, depicting much of the work carried out by the surgeons. One part shows many, 'Before and After' photographs. The reconstruction, repair, and cosmetic work carried out, is truly one of the most remarkable exhibits I have ever seen.

Like most people, the BSM's wife had many preconceived ideas about Northern Ireland. She was totally unprepared, and therefore quite overwhelmed by the kindness and hospitality she received; and by the unstinting care given to her husband by the Hospital Staff at the two Hospitals mentioned. The BSM made a significant recovery, but the accident affected his promising career prospects. Had the accident happened elsewhere, it could well have cost him his life.

Back in germany again and time for an annual event in the Garrison: the Anglo/German/Dutch Advent Carol Service, which was held in the Lutheran Church in Bergen. I had already been involved in a number of Anglo/German Services, which were difficult enough to arrange: but to involve the Dutch as well made things even more complicated! I attended a number of planning meetings, and as usual one of the hardest things was finding hymns that all three nationalities knew. I rashly volunteered to preach the sermon in German! My command of the language was not nearly good enough to have done it without some assistance; but a German lady working in Garrison HQ, kindly offered to translate a simple sermon of mine from English into German: and tutored me in the correct pronunciation and emphasis. I produced a manuscript copy for the English and Dutch people in the congregation, and the Germans complimented me on my efforts! It went off well but was quite nerve-racking; and was something I never attempted again!

A young sergeant in 1QDG Band and his family were faithful members of my Church, and he felt the need to offer himself for full time work in the Church. He talked about going to a Bible College, knowing that it was quite easy to gain entrance to such colleges, but I reminded him that there was no guarantee of anything at the end of the course, and urged him to be realistic and practical; especially as he had a wife and children to consider. His wife was a Methodist and so I encouraged him to consider offering for the Methodist Ministry. There were difficulties, but because of my own experience of being in a similar position, I knew that such difficulties could be overcome.

The first thing he needed to do was to gain some experience and knowledge of Methodism, and become a Methodist Local Preacher. He really needed to go back to England and become involved with a local Methodist Church and Circuit, and see how things developed from there. I spoke to the Commanding Officer and explained the situation and the procedures involved. He promised to do what he could to help, and a few months later the Sergeant was posted as an Instructor to the Band of the Junior Leaders Regiment of the Royal Armoured Corps in Bovington, Dorset. He quickly became involved with the Poole Methodist Circuit, became a Local Preacher, and offered for the Ministry. He was accepted, and it was my great privilege and pleasure to attend his Ordination Service when the Methodist Conference met in Birmingham some years later.

Just before Christmas, we were invited to 45 Regiment Sergeants Mess Christmas Draw: a major social event! Towards the end of the evening I was aware of a row breaking out amongst people sitting at the other end of the room. The wife of one of the Sergeant Majors stormed out into the night. I noticed her because she and her husband regularly attended my Church. There was snow on the ground and it was bitterly cold. After a short while, her husband left the Mess to look for her: concluded that she had decided to walk home, and without thinking, jumped into his car to try and find her. He hadn't travelled many yards out of the Camp, when he was stopped by the Military Police and breathalysed. He was over the limit, which was an automatic Court Martial Offence. The sad thing was that transport was always laid on by the Regiments to take people home after social events, so there was never any need for those attending to drive themselves home. I made a point of attending his trial at the Divisional HQ as a Character witness and spoke on his behalf. However, Military Law is quite uncompromising on these matters, and rightly so. I can't remember what punishment he received, but it was enough to blight his career, and cost him his almost certain promotion to Regimental Sergeant Major.

Every year the President of the Methodist Conference would spend a few days visiting the Chaplains serving with the Armed Forces. This year it was the turn of the Army; and the President was Rev Bill Gowland, who, as Principal of Luton Industrial College had greatly influenced me during my final year in Theological College. He had inspired me to become involved in Industrial Chaplaincy, but was pleased to find me working as an Army Chaplain! His itinerary was very crowded and he had been programmed to spend only a short time with me in Hohne. I arranged a meeting for him to address, and I know that amongst others, the Brigadier was particularly impressed with what he had to say. The following morning I was scheduled to take the President to Hannover airport to catch a flight to Berlin. However, he expressed a strong desire to visit Belsen before he left, which meant a very early start. That wasn't a problem: the problem was getting the President to go to bed! He had a very strong constitution and spent half the night talking, while he smoked little cigars and drank countless cups of coffee. We arrived at Belsen Camp at 8.00am, only to find the gates were closed until 9.00am! As he had a flight to catch, we couldn't wait and he was unable to visit the Camp. Had I known before he arrived of his desire to visit the Camp, I would have suggested rear-ranging his programme.

45 Regiment had arranged to use the American Army Firing Ranges in Bavaria for a week, and I went with them. Having two major units, I was constantly juggling things to ensure I spent time with each of them, as well as making sure I had someone to take my Sunday morning Service if I was away for the weekend! The Ranges used by the American Army in Bavaria were much larger than Hohne, and were in use 364 days a year – Christmas Day being the only day there was silence. The American Army had lined up on the parking area, more Artillery guns than I had ever seen: our contingent was minute by comparison.

The training and live firing was very realistic, none more so than the firing of the eight inch guns with their nuclear capability. I had often heard the Battery Commander saying, "We shall be firing at 9.00pm," or whatever, and thought nothing of it. I discovered that when he said, 9.00pm, he meant it to the second! When targeting enemy armoured and troop concentrations, in front of your own troops with a battlefield nuclear weapon: it is vital they know exactly when to expect it! That evening we all synchronised our watches and set off into the forest. We stopped not far from one of the guns and waited. It was dark and I had no idea where the gun position was: until it fired! It was so close and so loud it almost scared the life out of me! Within 45 seconds the gun had been 'taken out of action', and was driven away to its next location. Later, I was talking to the Sergeant in charge of the gun (the No 1), and said to him, "I was taken completely by surprise because I didn't even hear you shout 'Fire'". He said, " I didn't shout: I whispered the command, because had it been a 'misfire', I could have given away my position". I was impressed by his professionalism, even if it was standard procedure!

At the end of a most successful exercise for the Regiment, precious time was saved when the Commanding Officer offered me a lift back to Hohne in his Staff Car. It gave us an opportunity to talk together. When I was serving with 2RGJ almost ten years earlier, I learned an important lesson. A Chaplain is the Chaplain to **everyone**, from the youngest soldier to the Commanding Officer, and later in his career, to the Brigadier and the General. Who else can these Officers, who carry so much responsibility talk to in confidence, or get something 'off their chest'? Who else, except the Doctor, who is not normally around at such times, is able to say to an obviously overtired Commander: "Sir, you really ought to get some sleep"!

My next Posting Order came through. I was go to the Royal Armoured Corps Centre in Bovington as Senior Chaplain: but not until the Autumn after a very big Military Exercise called 'Crusader 80' had been completed. This Exercise had been planned for a long time and involved troops from a number of countries, including America. It was so inclusive that a few people who weren't involved had special tee shirts made with the words, 'I Wasn't On Crusader 80' printed on them!

Before then, and before a summer holiday in Italy, I went with 1QDG to Vogelsang. It was a fairly routine training period, but one thing stands out in my memory. In the Camp there is a tower 150 feet high. It is possible to climb up inside the tower to an excellent viewing platform near the top. A Sergeant, who had been on the Army Everest Expedition a few years earlier, decided the tower would enable the soldiers to do a little 'Adventure Training': namely abseiling! He had brought all the necessary equipment; harnesses and ropes etc., and had chosen another area in the Camp to serve as 'nursery slopes'. These weren't very high and were for the benefit of those who hadn't done any abseiling before. That included me; but somehow I missed out on that important little bit of information! The first I knew about it was when people began descending from the tower. Then it was a case of, "Come on Padre, surely you can do this". I would most certainly have 'lost face' had I made excuses, so I climbed up to the platform and quietly informed the Sergeant that I had never done any abseiling before! For some reason he seemed quite pleased, and made a great show of instructing me in the correct procedures. When he and I were satisfied, I put on the harness, climbed on top of the wall surrounding the platform, and planted my feet firmly near the edge. Then I 'tested' the ropes to ensure they were secure, and leaned backwards away from the tower.

Looking down between my legs at the ground, I decided parachuting was a much easier way to the ground! I pushed off from the platform but was a little uncoordinated. I neglected to release the appropriate rope and found myself looking upwards at my feet. I wasn't in any danger, but felt very foolish! Eventually, and with a little advice from the now grinning Sergeant looking down at me, I managed to descend safely to the ground. At least I had provided a little light entertainment for the onlookers! The incident reminded me of the time in Berlin when I had watched two young Officers abseiling from the top of the Mercedes Building in the centre of the City. That building was many times higher than the tower in Vogelsang: and what's more, they had literally **run face downwards** to the ground!

It was now time to prepare myself, and my equipment for 'Crusader 80'. The Exercise would last approximately two weeks, and cover a wide area: I therefore needed a large map! There would be lots of movement and armoured vehicles would be everywhere. Villages and farm buildings would by occupied; as well as woodlands. Farmers would be paid for the use of their buildings, and for any damage caused.

Arrangements had already been made by Service Liaison Officers for the areas to be used: and damage assessment teams would follow the progress of the Exercise and agree compensation terms with farmers for any damage caused. I knew I would be driving many miles as I visited my soldiers in their various locations. Keeping track of them would be difficult, as they would not remain in any location for long. I knew from previous Exercises, that often by the time I had caught up with them, they would have moved: and I always hoped I would meet up with someone who could give me the grid reference of their new location. If all else failed, I would visit the main Exercise Control Centre, who would at least know where my Regimental HQs were!

Several days were always spent when everyone wore Nuclear, Biological, and Chemical (NBC) Warfare suits, so I made sure I had my two sets ready: and ensured that my gas mask was in good condition. I carefully packed my Bergen (a large back pack mounted on a frame) with everything I might need, including changes of clothing and spare boots. In my ammunition pouches and bum bags, which were worn on a belt with my water bottles, I would pack my Field Communion equipment. This consisted of a Chalice, a supply of Communion Wine and Wafers; a small portable Cross, and about 20 Army Prayer Books which contained Orders of Service and a number of well-known hymns. Other important items were a sleeping bag and fold up camp bed.

If the tailgate of the Land Rover was let down on its chain, an Army Camp Bed would just fit in the back of the vehicle. The rear canopy could be let down, and a waterproof ground sheet wrapped around the bottom, thereby ensuring I could sleep without getting frozen or soaked! I then prepared my Land Rover, checking the tyres, not forgetting the spare wheel: fuel, oil, and radiator levels: tool kit, pick & shovel, and camouflage net and poles which were secured on top of the vehicle by ropes and bungee elastics. In addition I carried spare fuel and water in jerrycans.

The Exercise commenced in pouring rain, which was not unusual: and I found a dry spot and spent some time marking up my map showing the initial locations of my Tank Squadrons, Gun Batteries, Tactical HQs, and Echelons where the Quartermasters would be! The latter were most important, because they would know where the rest were, otherwise they would be unable to feed and re-supply them! One evening I was with the Quartermaster of 1QDG and one of his Staff said to me, "Fancy coming out with us later tonight to do a rolling re-plen Padre?" I hadn't any idea what a rolling re-plen was, but I readily agreed to go if only to experience something new! We set off later in a Stalwart Truck, fully laden with jerrycans full of fuel and water, each containing four and a half gallons. The fuel and water were stowed in different parts of the truck and the cans were of a different colour. After driving for about an hour along tracks through the forest, the driver pulled the truck just off the track and switched off the engine. "They'll be here in exactly half an hour" said the Corporal. 'They', turned out to be tanks, and they arrived exactly on time. I was amazed how quietly they could move! It was very dark and they

With members of 45 Regt. R.A. Ex 'Crusade' 80

could just be heard coming slowly down the track towards us. They were not showing any lights at all.

I climbed on to the back of the truck, ready to help in handing the jerrycans to the tank crews as they passed. As each tank approached the front of the truck, a crewman would whisper quietly, how many jerrycans he needed. They were immediately passed over and empty jerrycans received in return. As they passed, the tanks slowed to a crawl, but didn't stop: hence the term 'rolling replenishment'(re-plen). By the time they had all disappeared again into the forest, my shoulders were aching from lugging the jerrycans over the side!

On another evening, I was with the Quartermaster of 45 Regiment. I found it was always worthwhile being with such people at that time of the day, because a good meal could always be guaranteed! The QM's Department had taken over some farm outhouses in a village, right next to the village Church. As we were clearing away after our meal, the Pastor from the Lutheran Church strolled over for a chat. He spoke very good English! He informed me about a Social event being held that evening in the Church Hall, and said that any who wished to attend would be made very welcome. I mentioned this to the QM, who said he wasn't expecting a move until sometime the following day: and that any of his Staff not on essential duties, could go along to the Social if they wished. About a dozen took up the offer, and even though they had to go in Combat Uniform: I ensured their boots were clean!

We were indeed made most welcome by the villagers, who insisted on involving us in a little German Folk Dancing. It was quite amusing to see the soldiers wearing their great boots attempting to get the steps right! Then the Pastor said to me, "Now you must teach us one of your English dances". The soldiers turned to me for suggestions, but I couldn't think of any! Then I had an idea. "What about the Hoky Coky"? I suggested: and as no one had a better idea, the Hoky Coky it was! It was quite hilarious and a good note on which to conclude the evening. Before we left the following day, the Pastor presented me with a small lead copy of the weathervane on the top of his Church. It was made up of four crosses representing the points of the compass, and still hangs on a wall in my house today.

The Exercise was judged a success and valuable lessons were learned. I was impressed by the enthusiasm and sheer professionalism of our soldiers. Some had served for a number of years but were still keen to improve their skills. The American soldiers, friendly and good natured as they were, rarely seemed to take things very seriously. While we were running around in NBC kit and camouflaging our vehicles and guns every time we stopped, they were sitting alongside their tanks in deck chairs. I overheard one British Officer mutter, "If there is another war in Europe, thank God the Germans will be on our side"! The German Army had regained its professionalism and their performance on the Exercise was impressive. I was given to understand that the active participation of Germany in NATO had brought about a significant change in NATO planning.

When I first began serving in Germany, the plan was, that if the Russians invaded: the task of the Allies was to hold a line by the River Weser until reinforcements arrived from Britain and the United States. At that time there was a lot of media speculation that the Russians could over run Germany within a couple of days. I remember the German Defence Minister saying, that the only way that would be possible, was if the German Army acted as traffic policemen! The Germans were determined to defend their border and not permit the Russians to have a free run across half of Germany before attempting to stop them! Thereafter, our Military Exercises concentrated on defending the Inner German Border: that was the border between East and West Germany.

On returning to Hohne, there was the usual sorting out and handing in equipment: then it was time to fill the packing cases yet again and prepare to move to Bovington. As we were only one hours drive away from Hamburg, I booked a passage from there to Harwich. So ended six years in Germany, and we were looking forward to spending some time back in England. My successor was another Methodist Chaplain who had just joined the Department. 24 years later he was to become the first Methodist Chaplain General. By that time it would have taken 208 years for the Royal Army Chaplains' Department to become a true meritocracy!

THE ROYAL ARMOURED CORPS CENTRE, BOVINGTON, DORSET.

OCTOBER 1980 – JULY 1982

We moved into a married quarter right away and spent a few days getting unpacked and sorted out. We were getting quite used to the routine by now and it didn't take too long! My next door neighbour was a most enthusiastic young Chaplain, serving with the RAC Junior Leaders Regiment: and next door to him lived my predecessor, a Church of England Clergyman, who had just retired from the Army; but was still looking for a Parish. While he was waiting, he was advised to 'sign on the dole'; which he did! The very idea of a Parson 'on the dole' gave my father much amusement! The Garrison had a few shops, a Bank, and a Junior School, which was in an awful state of disrepair, thanks to Government Policy at that time. Our youngest daughter attended that school for the first year, before moving to a school in Wareham.

At the southern end of the Garrison was the village of Wool, which had a Railway Station with regular trains to London, Waterloo: and was by the main road between Wareham and Weymouth. The Garrison itself had been beautifully landscaped, and most of the buildings were comparatively new. One notable exception being the Garrison Church, which was an old wooden building which had a running track on one side, and faced the Tank Museum a couple of hundred yards away. The Church property was the responsibility of the Quartermaster of the Junior Leaders Regiment. There was a small hall attached to the Church, which my colleague, the JLR Chaplain used for 'Padres Hours' with the boys.

I was a great believer in encouraging the Congregation to remain for a while after the Service on Sunday mornings, for coffee, tea, and biscuits: so that they could meet each other socially. The hall was the obvious place, but contained only a supply of chairs and a couple of tables. It took several weeks before I managed, by various means, to have a sink installed, a cupboard to store the crockery, and an urn to boil the water! Drawing up a list of volunteers to make the refreshments and do the washing up was easy by comparison!

The Garrison Commander was a Brigadier from the Life Guards, a most charming man, to whom I was answerable. There were a number of units in the RAC Centre. The Gunnery School was down at Lulworth Cove, the Driving and Maintenance Wing (D&M) was close by my office, the Junior Leaders

Regiment was across the road from the Tank Museum; and the Armoured Trials Development Unit very close to where I lived! At the time of my arrival, trials were being carried out on the Challenger Tank, which would eventually replace the Chieftain as the Army's Main Battle Tank. For our first few weeks, the Challenger engine was being extensively tested and was being run for hours at a time. It made for a very noisy environment and sometimes, sleepless nights!

The Centre Regiment, which was responsible for providing the manpower for the day to day running of the Garrison, was 16/5th The Queen's Royal Lancers, my own County Armoured Regiment. It had been a Squadron of 16/5th I had met when I was serving with the United Nations Force in Cyprus in 1973. They were quite happy with their posting to Bovington after all the pressures of Germany. There was plenty to do, but working hours were fairly predictable and they were able to spend more time with their families. The younger Officers were more than happy, as it was so easy for them to get to London!

I made contact with the Superintendent Minister of the Poole Methodist Circuit, and he invited me to attend the Circuit Staff Meetings. Because I only had a Morning Service in the Garrison, which I shared with my younger colleague, I was able to offer a number of dates each quarter when I would be available to take Services in the Circuit. After six years in Germany when my only contact with Methodism was through the Church Newspaper, I wanted to get back in touch with 'grass roots' Methodism, and was delighted and reassured to find that things hadn't changed as much as I'd been led to believe! After a while I commented on the large number of elderly people living in he area. The Superintendent smiled and said; "Ah yes; people come down to the south coast to die: and then they forget why they've come!"

During the past six years I had been under pressure from the younger members of the family for us to have a dog. My standard reply was to say, "Not while we're in Germany"! Now I had no excuse and we scanned the local newspapers, visited kennels and breeders: and eventually chose a gorgeous Corgi puppy. We were all singularly lacking in imagination and named him Sandy! He had a very good pedigree, and according to the information with it, one of his ancestors had sired a litter for the Queen. With my participation in past Royal Occasions, this seemed quite appropriate!! He turned out to be a real character: only ever bit one person, and that was one of my nephews who tormented him! He was to be part of the family for the next thirteen years.

My colleague was having trouble with his Army car, which he needed for visiting families and Hospitals. I checked on this and discovered that the Garrison Transport Workshops were waiting for a new handbrake cable, which had been on order for weeks. I was astonished that this was the only reason the vehicle was not considered roadworthy! This was one of those times, and there were several during my service, when the Military were being forced into adopting cost cutting measures. I remember for example, when I was in Aldershot prior to going to Berlin, being forbidden to use my Army car to go home for lunch!

I said to the Warrant Officer in charge of the Workshops, "Go and buy a hand brake cable from the local Garage, and I'll pay for it out of Church Funds". He said, "Oh you can't do that Padre, or the Supply Depot will expect us to find the money to buy the other spare parts we need"!

The Commanding Officer of the Junior Leaders Regiment offered his Chaplain the use of his Staff Car, but after being knocked up for the keys late one night, that offer was withdrawn; but it resulted in more pressure being put on the re-supply system, and a hand brake cable was soon available!

On Remembrance Sunday, the Service was held in the Church. The Junior Leaders had their own Service, but the Garrison Church was full, and there was no 'three line whip'. In addition to serving soldiers, there were a number of Ex-Servicemen who lived in the neighbourhood, including some members of the local branch of the Royal British Legion. Shortly afterwards I received a request from the County Officials of the RBL. They were making plans to celebrate the Diamond Jubilee of the RBL and asked if I would conduct a Service for them in Bovington, at which all the branches in Dorset would be represented. Of course I agreed and the Service was duly held. It was a most impressive occasion to see every Branch in the County on Parade with their Colours. I enjoyed the Service, but it was far more difficult to arrange than any Garrison Service. Trying to contact the correct officials and get them to make decisions was most frustrating! I have tremendous respect for the RBL and the work they do; but working **with** them, as I did on a number of occasions was always a little difficult! I think this was probably because being out of the Army; their officials operated in a consultative rather then an authoritative manner!

Sometimes, Regiments serving overseas experienced problems with individuals and families, which were too serious to be solved by the Medical or Welfare facilities available to them: and they were often posted back to their Regimental or Corps Depots in England. A nurse serving in one of our Military Hospitals in Germany once said to me, "The worst thing about being over here, is that when we have a patient with a serious or unusual medical condition, they always send them back to England: which means we don't get comprehensive nursing experience".

One day I happened to overhear two lady cleaners talking about a soldier's wife who had been sent back to Bovington from Germany because she was suffering from cancer. I asked them if they would mind telling me about her, as no one else had mentioned the matter to me! They told me that she was a local girl from Lulworth who had married a soldier in the Royal Armoured

Corps, had four children, the youngest being a babe-in-arms; and while serving in Germany, had been diagnosed with terminal cancer. She was now in the Douglas Macmillan Hospice in Christchurch. I made enquiries and tracked down the soldier, who was with his wife's family. In addition to making frequent visits to the Hospice, her family were helping to look after the children.

I was most annoyed to find out about this tragic situation by accident! I visited the soldier's wife who was only twentyeight years of age several times a week until she died: and did my best to hep her husband and family to cope with their loss and their grief. This was the first time I had experienced the unstinting care given to the terminally ill and their families by the Hospice Movement: and I couldn't have been more impressed.

The medical and supporting staff were absolutely marvellous, before and after the woman's death.

The young soldiers in the Junior Leaders Regiment always had their own Church Service, conducted by their Chaplain and 'tailored ' to suit them. They also had a morning Assembly once a week, again conducted by their own Chaplain. I was a little concerned that they weren't having any experience of what a Church Service was really like. Roman Catholic young men went to Mass: joined other members of the Garrison, and nothing 'special' was arranged for their benefit. They experienced worship in the Church as it is. I believed that Protestant young men should be afforded the same opportunity, particularly during their basic training and introduction to life in the Army. If they didn't like it, at least they would have an opportunity of finding out what it was they were rejecting!

I discussed this at length with my colleague, and he was quite enthusiastic about the idea. My suggestion was that one Company at a time should attend the Garrison Church Service, help with minor duties such as giving out books and taking the offertory, share the Service with the regular congregation; and join them for refreshments afterwards. The Garrison Commander and the Director of the Royal Armoured Corps, (DRAC) a Major General, who was incidentally a member of the Prayer Book Society (1662 and all that), frequently worshipped in the Garrison Church. I made it clear that my colleague and I, who would share the Services, would, in our planning and conduct of the Service; make it clear that we were aware of the presence of the young men, without arranging the Service specifically for **them**! The Commanding Officer of the JLR wasn't initially impressed by the idea, and had some reservations. I think he thought I was invading his 'space', or interfering with his Command! My only motive was that the young men should have, in that formative part of their Military Training, a more 'rounded' idea of what the Church was really about.

Aware that we were breaking new ground, we gave a lot of time and thought to the first Service. It had been agreed that the JLR Company should attend the Service in 'casual' dress to avoid any idea that it was a Parade. The Service went well and was enjoyed by everyone. I was gratified to notice during refreshments, many of the usual congregation, including a number of Senior Officers chatting informally with the Junior Leaders. One memorable, amusing, if slightly embarrassing incident took place during the Service, when one of the young men walking down the aisle taking the Offertory to be dedicated; was seen to have the words, **SOD OFF** printed on the back his jeans! The new format worked well, and achieved something I should have thought about but hadn't. It enabled some young men who wished to attend Church, to do so without making it obvious to the others!

Every year, two Forces Chaplains nominated by the Forces Board of the Methodist Church, attended the annual meeting of the Methodist Conference, the Church's Governing Body. In 1981 I was nominated to attend, with a Chaplain from the Royal Air Force. That year the Conference was being held in Norwich. I hadn't attended Conference since my Ordination in 1968 so was more than happy to go, especially as there were issues bothering me, which I hoped to be able to air. Some senior members and officials of the Methodist Church were pacifists, active members of CND, or just anti anything Military. They were of course perfectly entitled to hold and advertise their convictions. I think they were given media coverage disproportionate to the numbers they claimed to speak for. Senior Ministers usually failed to make it clear that they were speaking for themselves and not on behalf of the Methodist Church. It is only the Methodist Conference which can speak for the Methodist Church!

I had to explain this to the DRAC. One morning the General sent for me, sat me down with a up of coffee and said, "Padre, what the hell are you Methodists playing at"? As he asked the question he stabbed his finger at a newspaper on his desk in which was printed an article by the President of the Conference: a passionate pacifist who frequently made newsworthy comments about issues like for example, the amount of money the Nation spent on Defence. At a time when the Army was faced with more cuts, and some tanks for example not being able to move through lack of spare parts: the General was understandably a little sensitive!

Posters greeting the traveller entering Norwich advertise it as being 'A Fine City', and I certainly found it to be so. My only regret was that I had to spend so much time in the Conference Hall there was very little time to explore the City. Accommodation had been arranged me for me with a lovely family who lived about twenty miles south of the City. On a good day the journey would take about half an hour. Conference hours were such that I saw very little of the family, but did take them out for a good meal before I left, as a 'thank you' for their kindness.

One of the highlights of Conference is the acceptance by the Church of those who had completed their theological training and Probationary period. Now they attended the Conference, lined up on the platform, and were formerly accepted as Ministers. The family and friends of the Ordinands would attend this ceremony. That same evening, Ordination Services were held in a number of Churches in towns in the district. I obtained a ticket and attended an Ordination Service being held in Lowestoft. Following the Ordination of the Ministers was a Service of Holy Communion: and what had been a very moving occasion, was now marred by using the traditional Methodist practice of giving communion to small groups of people kneeling at the Communion Rail. After receiving Communion, the group would wait to be dismissed with a short prayer offered by one of the officiating Ministers. This took an interminable time and became very tedious. Some Methodist Churches with large congregations now use the 'continuous flow' method of dispensing the Sacrament.

Roman Catholic and Anglican Churches have always used this method, which in no way detracts from the solemnity of the occasion, and enables large numbers of people to receive the Sacrament in a comparatively short time.

The Conference Agenda was huge and much of the business routine. I, and my RAF colleague stoically sat through every session, but probably had more than our share of coffee breaks! It was good to meet some old friends and acquaintances, particularly those I hadn't seen since leaving Theological College in 1965.

There was a short, impassioned debate about the problems in our Cities, proposed by one of our regular 'firebrands'. The media had obviously been 'tipped off' and were in attendance. The motion was overwhelmingly passed, as would a motion against sin, and the media and the initiator left the Conference! For several years afterwards, 'Mission Alongside the Poor' was on the agenda of Church Councils and Circuit Meetings. Shortly afterwards I bumped into Revd Bill Gowland, an ex President who had stayed with us n Hohne. He growled at me as we passed in a corridor, "Typical Conference, very good at passing resolutions, and then finding out the facts"!

One hot and sticky afternoon, a Representative from Northern Ireland addressed the Conference on the situation there. As he was speaking I made my way to stand by the podium and when he had finished speaking, seized the opportunity to speak in support of what he had said; adding a few comments drawing on my own experience in the Province. Later, during a discussion on the arms trade and military expenditure, I was again able to mount the podium and began to speak about some of the issues bothering me. I had only been speaking for about two minutes when I was asked to draw my comments to a close. I protested to the President, saying that as a serving Army Chaplain,

I was unable to take part in the usual forms of this ongoing debate as others could; by writing to the Press etc: and as a Representative from the Forces Board to the Conference, I should be given the opportunity to speak. There were murmurs of agreement from the Conference, and I was permitted to continue. I told them about the soldiers who had asked me, "Padre, why is the Church against us?" and went on to speak for another ten minutes and then, conscious of the restlessness on the platform beside me, drew to a close, wishing I had another half an hour! In the days that followed, many people approached me and thanked me for what I had said, usually adding, "It was something that needed saying".

My son was due to come home for the summer vacation, and I drove down to Wool station to collect him. The train duly arrived and people got off, but there was no sign of Simon. I concluded that he had missed the train and would arrive on the next one. I was just leaving the station when I heard a plaintive cry of "Dad!" I turned around and saw a young 'skinhead' approaching me! With a few of his friends, he had all his hair cut off 'for a dare'; and I couldn't even recognise my own son. It was something he never repeated!

Earlier in the year, I had interviewed a soldier wishing to arrange a date for his marriage. When he gave me the date I said, "I'm terribly sorry, but I can't marry you on that date." He said, "But you have to, we've arranged the Reception"! I said, "I can't marry you on that date as I shall be on holiday in Majorca: you really ought to have cleared the date with me before making any other arrangements!" Only a few weeks earlier, I had been in the office at the Gunnery School in Lulworth, when a young WRAC (Women's Royal Army Corps) girl, almost hugging herself with excitement, said to me, "I'm getting married in a few weeks Padre". "I'm very pleased for you," I said. "Where are you getting married?" She mentioned a Parish Church a few miles away. "Have you arranged to have your Banns Called?" I enquired. "What are Banns?" She asked. I explained the legal requirements involved and suggested she and her fiancée arrange to visit the Vicar as soon as possible.

One day, a friend of mine was once the Senior Chaplain in Munster, Germany. One Saturday, he was doing a bit of tidying up in the little garden by the Garrison Church, when to his horror, he saw two smart cars approaching bringing a Wedding Party! He hurriedly consulted his diary – nothing! He dashed into the vestry to look at the Church Diary, as two other Chaplains used the same Church – nothing! He then went and introduced himself to the happy party, who looked at him in a funny way because of the way he was dressed. "Have you made arrangements with one of the Chaplains to be married here today"? He asked. The Groom replied, "Well, no, but you're open aren't you"? My friend told them that there was a little more to it than that: explained to them what they had to do, and married them a few weeks later. It was incidents such as these, which lead to the Chaplain's Department organising 'Marriage Preparation' Courses, which were held regularly at Bagshot Park, and in Germany. Soldiers and their fiancées were encouraged to attend these courses, which dealt with marriage in general, and marriage in the Army in particular.

After our holiday in Majorca, it was time to prepare for the annual Chaplain's Exercise, 'Parsons' Penance', which in 1981 was held in the Kielder Forest in Northumberland. The base for the Exercise was Otterburn Camp, which I had last visited in 1958. It was a long drive from Bovington to Otterburn, so another Chaplain who had a house in Preston, suggested we spend the night there, before driving up to Northumberland. It was a welcome offer! We were informed that Land Rovers would not be required on this occasion, so my colleague and I travelled up in my Ford Escort Estate.

The Exercise had been organised by an Infantry Brigade which was training in the same area; and was without any doubt, the most physically demanding Chaplain's Exercise I had taken part in! I think those who set the tasks had neglected to take account of the age of some of the Chaplains; and I felt particularly for some of the Territorial Army Chaplains who had a real struggle.

The following year Argentina invaded the Falkland Islands and the plans of many had to be changed as the Task Force was assembled. Bovinton was largely unaffected; only a small number of soldiers with special skills were taken, and all thankfully returned safely. I had already been informed that my next posting was to be in July, when I was to take up the post of Senior Chaplain 12th Armoured Brigade and Osnabruck Garrison in Germany. However, with so many soldiers, including of course, Chaplains, preparing to leave for the Falklands, there was a shortage of Chaplains in Northern Ireland: so I was sent there for a few weeks to help out. I flew from Heathrow Airport, and for the first time experienced the new, cheap, 'do it yourself' system of boarding the aircraft. After checking in and going through the usual security checks, I had to carry my luggage, which consisted of two large heavy suitcases and a bag over my shoulder, to the Departure Gate at the very end of the Terminal. By the time I completed the trek my arms had almost been pulled out of their sockets and I was completely exhausted! It didn't take long to fly to Aldergrove Airport, just outside Belfast, and I was relieved to be met by the Senior Chaplain, a Methodist colleague, who helped to load my luggage into a car.

He informed me that I was to be based with 2nd Battalion, The Light Infantry (2LI), whose Headquarters were in an old factory at Bessbrook in South Armagh. As well as the soldiers in the factory, there were Companies in Crossmaglen, Forkhill, and a number of smaller locations. For some time this notorious area had been known as 'bandit country', and even though I had been provided with a car, travel was usually by helicopter, the car being used mainly to visit people in Hospital near Belfast, or the HQ in Lisburn.

Near the helicopter site were two corrugated iron huts. One was the control centre, known as 'Buzzard Operations (Ops)'; and the other, a waiting room. People needing to visit the Military units in the area, and that included workmen as well as Military personnel; would 'book in' at Buzzard Ops, inform them of their destination, and then go to the waiting room. It was a very busy place, and as each helicopter came in, its destination would be announced over the intercom and passengers would prepare to board. Helicopters were vulnerable to attack and the crews were obviously anxious to spend the minimum amount of time loading and off loading. Consequently, when it landed the engine was not switched off, and the passengers ran to board, keeping low to avoid the main rotor blades, and approaching at an angle to keep well away from the tail rotor blade. As soon as everyone was on board, it took off for its destination. Some of the locations visited were very small, and I marvelled at the skill of the pilots in getting in at all! Several types of helicopter were in use: the smaller ones flown by pilots from the Army Air Corps, and the larger ones by Royal Air Force crews and occasionally there was a Sea King helicopter with a Royal Navy crew.

I had my own little bedroom and a small portable television set. In the room serving as the Officers Mess there was another TV, and because of the unfolding situation as the Task Force sailed to the Falklands, all those not on essential duties would crowd in for every news bulletin.

Almost everyone knew someone who was in the Force. 2 and 3 PARA were part of the Task Force and I knew that with inter-battalion postings, some of those I had served with in 1 PARA were with them. 1 PARA was in Northern Ireland and bitterly disappointed that they had been left behind. I heard that the Commanding Officer begged the Ministry of Defence to include his Battalion, but his request was denied!

The Minister of the Church in Bessbrook kindly invited me for a meal one evening. He and his wife told me how the village was still traumatised following the atrocity inflicted on them a few years earlier. A minibus full of men from the village who were on their way to work; had been stopped by the IRA; and every man had been shot dead. It will take much more than a ceasefire or a peace process to heal such wounds.

I made regular visits to Crossmaglen and Forkhill. Sometimes when I had arranged to conduct a Service, I would arrive only to discover the soldiers had been deployed to deal with some emergency. Intelligence reports would sometimes send them off by helicopter to mount a quick Vehicle Check Point (VCP) on a country road. Because of recent mortar attacks on the bases, the tops of all the buildings were in the process of being fitted with what were known as 'sacrificial roofs': which ensured that mortar bombs would be detonated before they hit living and working accommodation. The living accommodation was very small and cramped with three tier bunks and no privacy at all. In spite of this and being always ready for immediate deployment, morale was very high and I never heard anyone complain. By comparison the Factory at Bessbrook was spacious and luxurious!

An additional benefit was that the top floor of the Factory in the roof space; had a stone floor: and previous occupants had marked out a running track of about 60 yards around the pillars. I seem to remember it was about 30 laps to the mile! On most days I would climb up to the top and run for three miles. As well as being good exercise, it was good therapy and helped to dispel stress and anxiety! When running outdoors, I always found it possible, either to let my mind relax, or use the time to make plans and sort out problems. Running in the factory required concentration to avoid colliding with a pillar!

The Task Force arrived in the Falklands and whenever possible, everyone was following the events taking place 8,000 miles away. The first troops landed successfully, but the Argentinian Air Force was inflicting serious damage on the Royal Navy. I don't think anyone who was following those events will ever forget the sepulchral tone and manner of the BBC announcer as he reported what had happened! Mercifully the conflict was not prolonged, but I grieved for those who had been lost, on both sides.

When I returned to Bovington it was time to fill the packing cases again and prepare to move back to Germany. Having done less than two years in Bovington I was surprised and a little disappointed to be moving back to Germany so soon, especially as we now had a dog! The family would fly out to Germany a few days after I had gone by sea with the dog. I booked an overnight passage from Sheerness to Flushing in Holland, having first received assurances that I would be able to keep the Corgi, Sandy, in the cabin with me. I took him for a good walk before the ferry sailed, and he was very well behaved on the boat!

OSNABRUCK GARRISON GERMANY
JULY 1982 – OCTOBER 1864

On arrival in Osnabruck I stayed for a few days in the Officers Mess of 1st Battalion, The Kings Regiment until my predecessor had vacated the house we were to occupy. A 'Mission' directed at Officers had recently been held in the Garrison. I was a little puzzled by this, because if there is one group who are not noticeably absent from Church Services, it is the Officers! The 'Mission' had little effect on the Officers, but a number of Officer's wives had been strongly influenced and met regularly together. On my first evening I was invited to supper at a house where many of them were present. They had made an assumption that, because I was a Methodist, I would be very evangelical and fit in with the group. They couldn't have been more wrong. Theologically, we weren't even on the same planet! The lady running the group greeted me with the words, "I suppose you've heard about our great Revival in Osnabruck?" I replied rather dryly, "Yes, they've sent me here to stop it"! She laughed gaily, failing to realise that I was quite serious!

There were two Brigade HQs in Osnabruck; 12th Armoured Brigade, and 24th Infantry Brigade, which had some units in the Garrison, and others based in England. I had already picked up from the Staff in both Brigades, ripples of concern about the effects of 'The Mission'. These good ladies were 'on a high', which was inevitably followed by 'a low'. "Oh", said one, I think I need another 'experience'! I pointed out that having faith didn't always mean feeling good and happy. While 'mountain top' experiences could be real and valuable, most of life was lived 'in the valleys', and that the Christian faith was not an insurance policy against things going wrong in life. I had to make this point as many of the group attributed the things going wrong in their lives to a lack of faith! Like many (not all) evangelicals, they were unable to accept pain, loss, and failure, without blaming themselves. The Church, all denominations, has a lot to answer for because of the way it has for centuries, concentrated on making people feel GUILTY!

Shortly after my arrival, we were invited to the Garrison Commanders home for dinner. When we arrived at the Brigadiers home, we found that among the other guests, there was another Brigadier (24 Infantry Brigade Commander) and three Colonels and their wives. I enjoyed the evening and welcomed the opportunity of meeting socially some of the Senior Officers of the Garrison. My wife hated it. The past twelve years in the Army had done little to change her appetite for such gatherings.

My married quarter was a large detached house with an even larger garden; which my predecessor informed me was in a ' lovely natural state', which actually meant he hadn't bothered to do anything with it! Furthermore, it was situated next to a large open space where another house should have been. I was informed that it was my responsibility to keep that piece of land tidy as well as my own garden. I therefore had to buy a heavy-duty grass cutter! It took several months of hard work to bring the wilderness under control. We even discovered a lovely sunken garden!

The first major problem we had was to make the garden Corgi proof, and what a job that was! Every time we thought we'd succeeded, the resourceful little monster would discover some way out only to be eventually dragged home by a sympathetic local resident. As we lived quite near a busy main road, it was a wonder he survived! Whenever we took him for a walk the local German residents made quite a fuss of him: most had never seen a Corgi before but were aware that the Queen had several. I swear one or two German ladies we met only just stopped themselves from curtsying! Some others thought we had a fox on a lead! Finally we made the garden secure and were able to let Sandy out without feeling a sense of impending disaster! We also had a major problem with moles. There were numerous little piles of earth in both areas. Once I actually succeeded in trapping one and put it in a bucket while I considered what to do with it. It looked so small and pathetic and after wrestling with my conscience for several hours, I had to let it go! I just couldn't bring myself to kill the little animal.

The garden of every married quarter we occupied during my sixteen years as a Chaplain needed lots of work to make it presentable. In a way this was understandable as people stayed such a short time and husbands spent long periods away from home on Military duties. Gardens take a lot of time and effort. Fortunately my wife was a keen gardener and I just provided the muscle while she made it pretty! I can honestly say that as we moved around, we left every garden in a much better state than we found it.

In 1982 Osnabruck was the largest Garrison in Germany with eight major units (a Lieutenant Colonel's Command) and many minor units. There were 2 Mechanised Infantry Battalions, 1 Air Portable Infantry Battalion (part of 24 Bde), 1 Tank Regiment, 1 Royal Artillery Regiment, 2 Regiments of Royal Engineers (one being part of 24 Bde), and the Divisional Field Ambulance Unit. In addition there was a Royal Corps of Transport Regiment based at Bunde, a small Garrison about thirty miles to the south east. Adding together the soldiers, their families, and the civilians, for example School Teachers; there was a British Military community of about seventeen thousand

To cater for the spiritual needs of the Garrison there were six Chaplains, each with his own Church. As Senior Chaplain, I was responsible for each Brigade Headquarters and their Royal Signals Squadrons, The King's Regiment, which had been formed years before by an amalgamation of the Liverpool and Manchester Regiments; and a Royal Army Ordnance Corps Company which occupied an old German Army Barracks which had in fact been used in the making of the TV Series, 'Colditz'.

My Church was located in the lines of The King's Regiment, and much of my time was spent with them. Their soldiers were recruited mainly from Liverpool and Manchester, and while they weren't always the least trouble-some soldiers in the Garrison; they were just the kind of soldiers I would want to go to war with! They were very professional and in the Regiment there were many unforgettable 'characters'.

At times I thought there was an unofficial competition between them and The King's Own Scottish Borderers as to whose Guardroom had the great-est number of prisoners! The Regimental Sergeant Major of The King's Regi-ment was a small, stocky Liverpudlian with a great sense of humour; referred to by his soldiers quite affectionately, as ' Hagar the Horrible'! The Regiment held the title of Army Boxing Champions. A few weeks after I joined them, I discovered that they were to box against 1 PARA 'at home'. On the day of the match I bumped into the RSM. "RSM", I said, "I've only been with you a few weeks; I spent four years with 1 PARA. Can I wear my Red Beret at the match tonight?" He fixed me with a hard stare and said, "Padre, much as we love yer, you turn up in a Red Beret tonight, and we shall hang yer from the nearest f****** lamp post!" I hadn't been at all serious in my request, but thought I'd be a bit provocative! The King's beat 1 PARA, but only just!

Another great character was the Quartermaster. He had been with the Regiment since he was a recruit, and although like many Quartermasters I met, he came cross as gruff and fearsome; he cared deeply about the well being of the soldiers and ensured they always had the best food, equipment, and accommodation available. During Military Training periods in Germany or Canada; whatever the conditions, which were sometimes severe; he would always be on hand during the night, chivvying his cooks to make sure there was plenty of hot food and drink available for the soldiers on their return.

As he was responsible for the fabric and maintenance of my Church I had to visit his office regularly. We would usually spend the first few minutes exchanging insults: then I would say, "Come on you miserable old sod, let's get down to business"! He would laugh like a drain, order two mugs of coffee, and then I'd get what I had come for. It came to be quite a ritual and we actually became good friends.

One morning I was pottering about in the Church when two civilians came in. They were both wearing blazers with embroidered military badges. They informed me that there were about four hundred British ex-patriots living in the area. Most had retired from the Army, and having married Ger-man girls, remained in Osnabruck. Some were still working for the Army, while others were working for German firms. Their reason for coming to see me was to inform me that they were in the process of forming a new branch of the Royal British Legion. I knew there were Branches of the RBL in Berlin and Hamburg and I readily understood why they wanted to form one in Osnabruck.

The Garrison Commander had arranged for premises to be made available for them to hold their meetings, and they had two questions for me. Would I be their Chaplain, and would it be possible for them to display their Colours in my Church? Of course I agreed to both requests. In an attempt to inform and hopefully recruit members, they had recently arranged for a Notice to be inserted in the local German newspapers. This Notice appeared at the time the British Task Force was on its way to the Falklands. To their great amusement, they received lots of telephone calls from Germans volunteering to join the Legion in order to fight the Argentinians; and had to explain that the RBL wasn't being formed for that purpose!

The Branch was duly formed and their Colours displayed in my Church. Within a year they had over a hundred members and I used to enjoy my visits to their Club. As a newly formed Branch, they were invited to send their Standard Bearer with their Colours to the next Festival Of Remembrance in the Albert Hall. They were absolutely delighted, but on the day the Standard Bearer was so nervous he was out of step as he marched into the arena: and this was witnessed by the millions watching the Ceremony on TV, and that included most of Osnabruck Garrison! It cost the poor man a few pints when he returned!

One day a member of the Legion came to see me with an unusual request. He told me he was due to travel to England in the near future for a major heart operation. "Padre", he said; "if I die will you do my funeral Service"? In Germany the population pay a Church Tax, which accounts for the excellent condition of all the Churches, and the decent standard of living enjoyed by the Clergy! However, it is possible to opt out of paying this tax; but those who do are not then entitled to any of the services provided by the Church, such as Baptisms, Wedding, or Funerals. The man's wife was German and they were both very worried about what would happen if he didn't come through the operation successfully! I assured him that if the worst came to the worst, I would personally ensure he had a good and proper funeral. Thankfully the operation was successful and he returned literally with a new lease of life!

As well as a heavy workload, I found it very difficult to work with two of my colleagues. They were from the Conservative Evangelical wing of the Church of England, and we weren't on the same wavelength at all. During my Ministry I had always worked well with Clergy of all denominations, so this was a new and at times distressing experience. I knew exactly where they were coming from as they represented something I had rejected and moved on from twenty years earlier. Fortunately, I got on very well with and received great support from the Garrison Roman Catholic Chaplain, and the Chaplain to the King's Own Scottish Borderers, who was an Irish Presbyterian.

Having said that, one of the Church of England Chaplains, who had only just joined the Army, did a tremendous job following a most tragic event. Two soldiers had too much to drink one night. They took an armoured personnel carrier, a tracked vehicle weighing about 16 tons, and were hit by an express train on a level crossing. Both soldiers were killed. Fortunately there were no German casualties. By the time the British and German investigations had been completed, the British Services Liaison Officer (SLO) had a file inches thick on the matter. He was a retired Officer who had served in the Royal Army Education Corps and the Parachute Brigade; and we became good friends. This was one of several incidents involving 'joy riding' in armoured vehicles: the others mercifully without causing accidents. However, the word went around, whether there was any truth in it or not I couldn't say; that the German Police planned to shoot the drivers of any other armoured vehicles endangering the public. This was a perfectly understandable reaction from the German authorities.

After all, what other way is there of stopping an armoured vehicle? There were no further incidents, at least not in the next two years!

Even though I had a large team of Chaplains, there were rarely more than two in station at any one time. Regiments were away in Canada or on tours in Northern Ireland, and Chaplains were on leave or retreats and courses. This meant the remaining Chaplains being involved with all units. It was basically a case of whoever was left looking after whoever was left! To add to the 'overstretch', we were without a Chaplain in Bunde for several months. As their Sunday morning Service was at 9.00am, it was just possible, especially using the Autobahn, for a Chaplain to conduct the Service there, and be back in Osnabruck just in time to conduct the Service in his own Church.

My first Garrison Service on Remembrance Sunday was held in the open air on one of the Parade Grounds. About five thousand soldiers and many of their wives and children attended the Service. The weather was bitterly cold; but anyone who complained about having to stand in the cold and drizzle for over an hour; was quickly reminded by others of the awful conditions suffered by those we were commemorating! The main problem as far as I was concerned was the inadequate and unreliable public address system; which meant that many people were unable to hear what was being said. The following year, with a new Garrison Commander, the Service was held in a huge hanger used for garaging armoured vehicles. Far better that they were outside getting soaked than thousands of people! An efficient public address system was hired for the occasion, and that was to become the pattern in future years.

The HQ Staff of 12 Armoured Brigade used to go for a run at 7.00am every Monday morning. This was a '3 line whip'; and therefore included myself, and my Roman Catholic colleague, who was rather large and quite unfit. RC Chaplains were quite illusive characters. They had a wide area of responsibility and people were always appreciative when they **did** put in an appearance. The first time my colleague joined us for a run, we ran together. After less then half a mile I thought he was going to die, he was in such a state! Our new Brigade Commander was a Roman Catholic, and he was determined that 'his' priest was going to achieve a level of physical fitness to enable him to pass his Battle Fitness test. He therefore assigned a Physical Training Instructor to take his priest out for training every morning. It was a long hard slog and I really felt for him, but within a year the objective had been achieved!

There are not many Methodists in Germany and I was delighted to discover that there was a small Methodist Church in Osnabruck. I made contact with the Minister and we arranged to meet. Fortunately he spoke very good English so we were able to discuss many things. He informed me that as Osnabruck was 'twinned' with Derby, he and his congregation had formed an attachment with a Methodist Church there, and were in the habit of visiting each other. One year a party from Derby would visit Osnabruck, and the following year a party from Osnabruck would visit Derby.

They had been doing this for several years and firm friendships had been established. The following year I was able to meet the party from Derby. The Minister also informed me that he had never been invited to any of the meetings held periodically between the German clergy and the Army Chaplains. I promised to rectify that, and the first opportunity was only a few weeks away.

Every year there was an Anglo/German Advent Carol Service in the City, held alternately in the Roman Catholic and Lutheran Churches. This entailed holding a number of planning meetings with the German clergy and I ensured the Methodist Minister was invited to attend, and offered a part in the conduct of the Service. I was very grateful on these occasions for the help of the Service Liaison Officer. One of the biggest problems we had as usual; was finding appropriate hymns that were known by both communities. The Germans made much more of the season of Advent than the British and consequently had more hymns; very few of which were known by the British! They found it difficult to understand our practice of singing Christmas Carols before Christmas Eve! These Services were very popular with both communities and the Church was always filled to capacity.

When I was not away on Military Training Exercises, a considerable amount of time would be spent visiting families. Sometimes because they had serious problems, and I emphasise again, that I would usually be just **one** of several people involved. Occasionally it would be necessary to seek the help of a SSAFA (Soldiers, Sailors, & Airmen's Families Association) Social Worker. These highly trained professionals were often a bit 'thin on the ground' and usually covered more than one Garrison. The SSAFA network in Britain was also used when there were problems 'at home'. A Marriage Guidance Counselling Service had recently been set up in Germany, and this was a welcome addition to the resources available to us. Considering the Military way of life, and it is a way of life, not merely a job of work; it was surprising how well the vast majority of families coped. A Battalion would have about three hundred and fifty families, and the number of 'problem families', as opposed to families experiencing a problem, could usually be counted on one hand.

Chaplains would organise regular Marriage Preparation Courses at Church House in Germany; and soldiers and their fiancées where possible would be encouraged to attend. I persuaded one young soldier from The King's Regiment to attend one of these courses with his fiancée. I saw him a few weeks later and asked him if they had enjoyed the Course. "Oh man", he said; "It's given us so much to think about, we've postponed the wedding for six months"! Baptisms were another reason for visiting a family. On one visit some friends of the family were present. As most lived in blocks of flats, this was not unusual!. The lady asked me if I was the Padre who conducted Assemblies at the local School. I didn't as that particular School was the responsibility of one of my colleagues. She related the following incident. Her daughter, who was six years of age, was sitting on the toilet one day, with the toilet seat cover pulled down across her back. "Why are you sitting like that", her mother asked.

The little girl answered, "The Padre who comes to my School, says that God is everywhere, and sees everything; and I don't want him to see my bottom"!

In order to keep fit and also because I enjoyed it, I would go for a run of three or four miles on most days. Sometimes I would run on tarmac and at others I would run through woods and around a lake not far from home. It became quite addictive and if I was unable to run for a few days due to other commitments, I would suffer withdrawal symptoms! When I was asked to take part in a Brigade cross-country run through the woods near Bunde, I readily agreed. I completed the course in good time, in spite of spraining an ankle about three quarters of the way around the course. To my surprise I was awarded a 'Veteran's' Medal: this was because I was over forty years of age. It came as a sobering thought that I was now, as a youngster (that's really how I **felt**) of 45 years of age; actually older than the Brigadier!

Because I enjoy singing I was delighted to join a newly formed Garrison Choir. They met for Choir Practice once a week so I was able to attend most meetings. In preparation for Easter, the Choirmaster decided the Choir should perform Stainer's 'Crucifixion', and I was prevailed upon to be the Bass soloist. My range is fairly wide and I can sing Tenor or Bass, usually filing in where there is a shortage. I was quite apprehensive about this part, as I don't read music very well and had previously only sung much 'lighter' parts! Someone who understood my dilemma; suggested I obtain a cassette of 'The Crucifixion' and learn my part 'by ear', which is exactly what I did. On the day of the public performance, I managed to sing my part to the Choirmaster's satisfaction!

The King's Regiment were now preparing to go to Canada for a months Battle Group training, and as I was going with them, several weeks were spent on preliminary training Exercises with the rest of the Battle Group. We left for Canada at the beginning of May 1983 and unlike my previous visit in 1978, were flown out, not by the RAF, but by huge aircraft chartered from Caledonian Airways. There was no necessity to stop on the way to refuel the aircraft, and we flew directly to Calgary Airport; which had been closed the previous day because of snow! Such is the unpredictability of the weather in that part of Canada! The temperature quickly rose, and as it did so, the clouds of mosquitoes appeared! We were issued with special sprays and cream to protect us from being driven mad by these pests, which many years before had been responsible for the migration of vast herds of animals.

The British Army Training Unit in Suffield (BATUS) had changed little since my last visit in 1978. The Training Program was the same as before. With so much live ammunition being used, safety was still paramount, and everyone was again briefed by the Military Police about how to enjoy them selves without upsetting the Canadian authorities! I visited the Church again in Ralston village and arranged to conduct Services there on the Sundays I was in station.

The routine was very much the same as 1978 so I will not repeat it. There were however two incidents which stand out, as they **were** different. The first was a flight in a Lynx helicopter. I had previously flown in five different types of helicopter, but the Lynx was by far the fastest. I was treated to a demonstration of 'tactical flying'. The Lynx flew very fast and low, following the contours of the ground. It really was a 'white knuckle ride'! Its primary role was to be an anti-tank weapon. It was equipped with air to ground missiles. It would hug the ground until directed to a target, then rise briefly to fire its missiles and then drop down again out of sight. It was a strange experience to hear these aircraft around you on the prairie and not be able to see them!

The second involved answering the call of nature! There were of course no toilets on the prairie. The soldiers called it, 'going on shovel patrol'. One day I went on shovel patrol and eventually found a small hollow, out of sight, and dug my hole. I had just dropped my trousers and squatted down when a troop of tanks appeared from nowhere and passed within fifty yards of my toilet! The Troop Commander in the leading tank, recognised me instantly, grinned broadly, threw up a smart salute and shouted loudly, "Good morning Padre". I returned his greeting but not his salute as my right hand was otherwise engaged; and in any case had I tried, I would probably have fallen over!

At the end of the Training Exercise, the Quartermaster and I decided to spend a few days relaxing in the town of Medicine Hat about 35 miles away. We soon discovered several others had the same idea. One evening we visited a typical 'Country & Western' Bar. I like 'Country & Western' music so I really enjoyed the experience. At one point in the evening a competition was held to discover which table could make the best effort at singing the song. 'Oh Lord, It's Hard To Be Humble, When You're Perfect In Every Way'. Our table won; and were given a bottle of wine as a prize!

The flight back to Germany was memorable for two reasons. The aircraft flew over the North Pole and the scenery was spectacular: but there was more than one silent prayer offered that we wouldn't have to make an emergency landing in that vast, inhospitable wasteland! As we descended over northern Europe, the aircraft entered a thick cloudbank, which seemed to go on and on as we looked anxiously for sight of the ground. When we eventually broke through directly over RAF Gutersloh, the visibility was appalling and the aircraft was obviously not able to land as it was too high and more than half way along the runway! The engines roared and we gained height quickly, back into the thick cloud. For what seemed an eternity, the aircraft flew on, turning and banking; the sound of the engines changing every few minutes. We listened in vain for information about what was happening. None of the passengers uttered a sound! Were we just flying around waiting for a break in the weather? Were we being diverted to another airfield? At last we broke through the cloud just short of the runway at RAF Gutersloh and landed safely. As we taxied along the runway the passengers all clapped and cheered with obvious relief.

I have flown many, many times; but never experienced anything quite like that before or since!

The Summer holidays were approaching and I decided that the only way Chaplains were gong to get any leave was if we closed each of the Churches for a couple of weeks during the summer months. This was not a popular decision, and was vigorously opposed by some of the Commanding Officers. One of them, in an attitude of sheer disbelief said; " Padre, you can't close **my** Church"! I insisted that I could because there wouldn't be a Chaplain available to conduct the Service; and pointed out that everyone had a car, or at least access to one, and it would be no hardship for them to drive three or four miles to one of the other Garrison Churches. As it was, the remaining Chaplains would be dashing about looking after the other four Churches!

In October 1983 we were celebrating our Silver Wedding Anniversary. We had a lovely meal with a few good friends who had travelled from various parts of Germany to be with us; then spent a few days exploring the delights and the wines of the Mosel valley! It didn't take very long to drive down from

Osnabruck and we spent our first night in Cochem. As it was a special occasion, I ordered one of the more expensive bottles of wine; and to my surprise it was delivered to our table and served at room temperature! I queried this with the waiter, and was assured that their white wine was always served at room temperature. I thought to myself, 'well; this is where they grow the grapes and make the wine; they aught to know!' Even so, I still prefer to drink white wine, chilled! We took a trip by boat down the river to Trier. It was a most enjoyable trip as the river wound its way between hills covered with vines; and the sun was so hot, I was sunburned! We then drove to Trier and came back along the south side of the river, spending the night at Bernkastel. It was most interesting to stop at little villages on the way whose names we'd only previously seen on wine labels!

12th Armoured Brigade planned an Exercise, as part of the build up to the biggest Exercise ever to be held in Germany in the autumn: codenamed 'LION HEART'. I went to join the Brigade Exercise and arrived just as the Brigadier really upset a Tank Regiment my informing them that all their tanks had been destroyed; and that for the next phase of the Exercise, they were to act as Infantry! To say the least, they were not at all pleased at this development. Many didn't even have proper boots: after all, who knows what tank crews wear when they are inside their tanks? They were given two hours to prepare for a Night March; and then mount a dawn attack on an Infantry Battalion well 'dug in' and waiting for them! I joined the March with one of the Staff Officers from Brigade Headquarters. The Cavalrymen entered into the spirit of things and acquitted themselves extremely well. As we were recovering from the night's exertions, two Chinook helicopters touched down, and all Staff and Commanders were ordered aboard. "What now?" we asked ourselves. Imagine our surprise when we touched down in the grounds of a German Hotel, and were treated to a Champagne Breakfast!

The Divisional Senior Chaplain had planned a mini 'Parson's Pleasure Exercise for all the Chaplains in 1st Armoured Division. We were put in teams of four and spent four days being tested on our military skills. For the first two days we were required to carry with us at all times, a heavy metal box! This certainly tested our patience and resourcefulness. The First Aid test was most interesting. We came across an APC, which had been 'hit' and damaged by shellfire. Inside were four badly injured soldiers, twisted and sprawled in seemingly inaccessible places! Our task was to treat and remove the casualties from the APC. Under normal circumstances, we would have made them as comfortable as possible, ensuring that their airways were clear and that they weren't bleeding to death. Then we would have waited for professional medical assistance, as moving them could have led to more serious injuries. However, we were told that the position was going to come under mortar attack in ten minutes. There was no alternative but to drag the casualties out anyway we could and get them away from the position. We reasoned that the possibility of being more seriously injured was preferable to being dead! That, we were told later, had been the correct decision.

The final day involved going over an Assault Course. This would not normally have been a problem; but it was wet and my boots were very muddy. Walking on a tree trunk to cross a ditch, my boots slipped and I fell to the bottom of the ditch, hitting my thigh on the trunk on the way down. I was hurt and badly shaken and needed help to get out of the ditch. I had great difficulty in walking at all! The next day I returned to Osnabruck and went to the Medical Centre. My right leg was very bruised where it had hit the trunk: in fact the thigh muscle was black. It was treated with ice packs to reduce the swelling, and I had to have physiotherapy for several weeks. It was a few months before I could run again, but eventually it was possible.

Our youngest daughter, Karena, was now approaching the age when she would be going to boarding school. Before deciding on a school, I felt it important to discover where I was to be posted next, so that initially we wouldn't be too far away while she settled in. I shared this concern with the Chaplains' Branch at the Ministry of Defence, and after a few weeks was informed that I would be posted to a job in Cambridgeshire in the autumn. I was pleased about that as it meant we could apply to the same Methodist Boarding School my son had attended near Bury St. Edmunds. We made a quick trip to England, visited the school, and bought all the necessary items of school uniform. My daughter seemed quite happy at the prospect, especially as we wouldn't be too far away and she would be able to come home for exeat weekends: something my son had been unable to do.

My mother, whose health had been deteriorating over recent years suffered a mild heart attack and was admitted to hospital. I took a few days leave and went home by train and ferry to visit her. My father, who had always been so dependant on her, was extremely concerned. She seemed to recover well and was allowed home. I returned to Germany knowing that my sister, who lived very near, would do her best to look after both of them; and keep me informed of any developments.

For our summer holidays that year we went to Italy again. In spite of the long drive, (it was a round trip of over one thousand six hundred miles) it was well worth it. When we returned home I looked through the pile of letters that had accumulated during our absence. I just couldn't believe it when I read a letter giving a long list of Chaplain's postings. My posting had been changed, and the letter was dated well before our departure on holiday. I was to be posted as Senior Chaplain, Arborfield Garrison, a few miles south of Reading. It could hardly have been worse. I was absolutely furious: it was much too late to find another school for my daughter. I telephoned the Ministry of Defence, but the Senior Chaplain responsible for postings was away on leave. I telephoned the Senior Chaplain in Germany, knowing full that he wouldn't be able to do anything about it; but I had to vent my spleen on someone in authority! What upset me most of all was that the Ministry of Defence hadn't taken the trouble to telephone me and tell me that my posting had to be changed. I had been in the Army long enough to accept the exigencies of Service life, but this was an example of man management that left much to be desired! I was due to move to Arborfield as soon as possible after the end of Exercise 'LIONHEART', but first we had to make another quick trip to England to take my daughter to Boarding School. She wasn't very happy when we left her, but we hoped she would soon settle down and make friends.

When I returned, the Brigade had already deployed for 'LIONHEART'. They were not very far away and I planned to join them after I had conducted my Sunday Morning Service. Having been given a grid reference, I found the Headquarters in a couple of old barns. One served as the Operational Headquarters, and the other accommodated the Staff. It was very crowded and I only just managed to find a space for my sleeping bag, leaving the rest of my equipment in my Ford Escort Estate car tucked away under cover. The Brigadier asked me where his priest was, and I said that I was sure he would be turning up before the evening was out. He didn't put in an appearance until the following morning. "What happened to you"? He was asked, "You should have been here last night". "I was", he replied. "I came to the stable and discovered that there was no room, so I went to an Inn". Brilliant!

Exercise 'LIONHEART' had taken a couple of years to plan and there were troops from half a dozen Nations taking part. It would be covering a very wide area, so my first task was to visit the main Exercise Control point, which would be static, so that I knew where to go if I lost touch with any of my units; including the Territorial Army Units and their Chaplains from England who were taking part. It was a very testing time, especially for Commanders. Colonels would be tested and their performance assessed by Brigadiers. Brigadiers would be tested and assessed by Generals: and they in their turn would be tested and assessed by more Senior Generals controlling the Exercise. We all soon learned to expect the unexpected, because that's what happens in warfare.

Having trained hard and prepared for a particular operation, and being deprived of sleep for a couple of days; the orders would sometimes be changed and the Regiments, the Brigades, and sometimes the Divisions, would be sent off to do something quite different.

There were troops absolutely everywhere. There were also many 'Enemy' troops, and they could be identified by the different coloured markings on their vehicles. Umpires were also around and they had white crosses on their vehicles, which meant they were sometime mistaken for Chaplains! It was impossible to find a village or a hamlet, or even an isolated farm building that wasn't the temporary home for a unit of soldiers and their equipment. There were camouflaged armoured vehicles everywhere: and as one unit moved out, another moved in to take its place. The local people were quite used to this and showed great patience with us; they allowed us to use their outhouses and toilet facilities, and were compensated for any inconvenience or damage caused.

I drove many hundreds of miles visiting my units and Chaplains. The Exercise was very realistic, and even Chaplains became 'casualties' and had to be evacuated or 'buried'. This enabled those held in reserve to be brought forward to replace them. The second weekend involved most of the soldiers digging defensive positions. In places even the tanks were being dug in, It rained heavily, and on the Sunday, as there being no possibility of holding even a small Open Air Service; I put on all my waterproofs over my Combat Uniform and wandered around the trenches to talk to the soldiers. I came to one trench being dug by a couple of soldiers from The Kings Regiment. "Allo Padre", said one, "What you doin 'ere"? "I've come to see you", I replied. He looked up at me, the rain streaming down his face. "Yeah, but you done **ave** to be 'ere do yer"? "No," I replied, " I don't **have** to be here, but I've just come to see you". He wiped the rain from his face and said, "Well then, yer must be f****** stupid". I hoped that later, when he was dry and warm, he might revise his opinion!

My Brigadier, always the realist, believed that in the event of war; there was no way that we would be hiding in forests, but would simply take over and use civilian accommodation. He therefore always ensured that his Head-quarters was located in a German Gasthous and its outbuildings. Always of course with the agreement of the Landlord, who was invariably delighted to have our custom! The Mess Sergeant parked his 4 ton vehicle, containing the Mess rations etc. as close to the building as possible; and we fed well: though some decided to eat in the Gasthous, and even pay for a bed for the night!

As the Exercise drew to a close, the Brigadier planned a Dinner Night for his Commanders and Staff, before we returned to Osnabruck. It was still my custom to offer what I hoped to be an appropriate 'Grace' before formal meals. The Brigadier said to me, "Padre, I expect something about 'LIONHEART' in the 'Grace' tomorrow"! When the time came I offered the following:-

> 'Thank God for food, and friends who come
>
> By APC and Rover:
>
> All gathered here to celebrate,
>
> That 'LIONHEART' is over'!

When I returned to Osnabruk there was much to do before departing to

Arborfield. We were saddened to discover that my daughter had not settled down happily at Boarding School. She had been frequently telephoning my other daughter, who had married a soldier in the Royal Electrical and Mechanical Engineers (REME), and was now living in Bordon, Hampshire. Now she began to 'phone us. I assured her that we would soon be back in England and would review the situation. It was now a priority to arrange for Sandy to go into Quarantine Kennels for six months. I received several recommendations from colleagues and chose one not very far from Dover. It was not our intention to visit him in kennels. A Removal Service was now in operation so it was no longer necessary to pack everything in crates and packing cases.

This time we travelled together as a family for a change, taking Sandy with us. We planned to arrive in Arborfield on the same day as the Removal Van. I was sad at leaving Osnabruck and Germany, as I had thoroughly enjoyed my service there and found it professionally to be very satisfying. I knew from my Confidential Reports that I had done a very good job as Senior Chaplain in such a large Garrison, and had been recommended for promotion; but I was also acutely aware of my failure in relating to and supporting some of the Chaplains in my team.

When we arrived at the harbour in Calais, I explained that we had a dog going into quarantine in Dover, and was instructed to park well away from other vehicles waiting to board the ferry. When everyone else had boarded, we were directed down into the bowels of the ferry. Not very far from the engines was a cage. Understandably, none of the crew would go anywhere near Sandy. I had to put him in the cage and lock it. It was hot, smelly, and noisy by the engines, and he looked at us so pitifully as we left him to go upstairs. On arriving in Dover, my car and family were driven off the ferry by a member of the crew. I had to wait until all vehicles had left and then a van from the Quarantine Kennels came on board. The driver wouldn't touch Sandy, and I had to take him out of the cage and carry him to another cage in the back of the van. We didn't see him again for six months, by which time I had paid out over £600 in fees!

SENIOR CHAPLAIN ARBORFIELD GARRISON

OCT 1984 – AUG 1986

When we arrived in Arborfield, we were in for another disappointment. The lovely house we had been allocated was in the process of being rewired, and fitted with a new kitchen! The work would not be completed for at least six – eight weeks. The Station Staff Officer suggested we move temporarily into another, smaller house until the work was completed. Having done just that three times before; I had had enough and refused. I telephoned my daughter in Bordon, about ten miles away and suggested we stay with her for a few weeks. She readily agreed. I arranged with the Removal Firm to store everything for us at their Depot in Camberley, and also arranged to have a room in the Officers Mess in case I needed to stay overnight. It was not a very auspicious beginning to my time in Arborfield, which was the Depot and Training Regiment for the REME. Also in the Garrison were the School of Electronic Engineering (SEE), the REME Officers School, and the REME Army Apprentice College with more than six hundred boys aged between $15^1/_2$ and $17^1/_2$. The College had it's own Chaplain, a lovely Welshman with whom it was a pleasure to work.

The following day I met with the Garrison Commander, a Brigadier, and amongst other things we discussed I explained my decision to commute from Bordon for a few weeks! He was very supportive and I felt we would work well together, which proved to be the case. My office was in Garrison HQ and I spent most of my first day looking through files and listening to the many messages on my answer phone. Most were from Platoon Commanders at the Training Regiment trying to fix dates for Padres Hours for the recruits.

Recruits had ten weeks basic training and during that time each Platoon had three sessions with me, and attended one Service at the Garrison Church. 1400 recruits a year passed through the Training Regiment, with 'Pass Out' Parades and new intakes every two weeks. The REME was now the largest Corps in the Army; an indication of the mechanical and technological expertise needed by the Army. It was now mid October, and organising the Remembrance Day Sunday Garrison Service was a priority. However, the immediate task was to organise my first Service in the Church. In some ways the Garrison reminded me of Bovington. There were lots of new buildings; the grounds were beautifully laid out and well maintained: and the Garrison Church was a grotty old wooden building! This policy had to be an indication of the importance placed by the Ministry of Defence on the spiritual needs of the Military Community!

My Church had previously been the Dental Centre and was a long, narrow building. My predecessor and the College Chaplain had arranged the interior so that the Lectern (there was no pulpit) was in the centre by one of the long walls of the rectangular building, with the chairs arranged in an arc around it. That didn't suit me at all. When conducting a Service, I like to see the faces of my congregation. Preaching in this building was more like being an Umpire at Wimbledon: I had to turn my head from side to side every few seconds! So I changed it around.

There was an old barn at Bagshot Park filled with items of furniture salvaged from Army Churches, which had closed over the years. Chaplains were encouraged to search through the barn and remove anything useful to them. Having a good rummage through the barn, I found an old large Eagle Lectern made of brass, which had been dismantled into about six parts: and a small pulpit! I arranged to have these collected and taken to Arborfield. The pulpit was quickly cleaned up and installed in the Church. It took a little longer for the Lectern to be assembled, lacquered, and because of its weight, securely bolted on to a substantial base. It was an impressive sight and was called by some irreverent soldiers, 'The Celestial Budgie'!

The Roman Catholic Church was also a converted old building in need of repair and refurbishment. The Garrison shared a Priest with the Royal Military Academy at Sandhurst, where of course they had beautiful, purpose built Churches! I was delighted to discover that the Roman Catholic Chaplain was my old colleague from Osnabruck.

I inherited a system of 'Sponsored Services', whereby the different units in the Garrison, including students attending Courses at SEE, took responsibility for Stewarding, Reading Lessons, Collecting the Offertory, and providing tea and coffee for the congregation after the Service. They also did the washing up! A small number of people from Arborfield village were regular members of the congregation. Some had been attending the Garrison Church for many years, including the Organist. One lady in her 90s was an unforgettable character. She lived alone in a small council bungalow. Her daughter had tried to find a place for he in a residential home. After only two weeks she returned home, saying, "I can't possibly stay in that place, it's full of geriatrics"! The Apprentices had their own Service as well as a mid week Assembly, which I occasionally conducted.

During the night of Saturday 21/22 October I received a telephone call from my sister, informing me that my mother had suffered another heart attack and died. I told my sister we would come home on Sunday afternoon, straight after my first Service, which, under the circumstances, was a most difficult Service for me. I informed my Senior Chaplain at HQ South East District, the Brigadier and my colleague at the Apprentice College that I would be away for two weeks. Karena was on half term from school and came home with us.

The journey to Bury St Edmunds had been long and tedious as the M25 had not yet been completed and there were many road works to contend with. Some years earlier my parents had moved from their three bedroom house in Bradwell, to a small, one bedroom flat in Newcastle-under-Lyme. For the last few years, my mother had chosen to sleep on the sofa in the lounge. Whenever we had visited them, we had slept on airbeds on the floor. For many reasons, my sister and I had never been close to our mother, but **were** very close to our father. He was most distressed and this concerned us greatly because we wondered how he was going to manage without her. In spite of her many periods of illness, my mother had always been the one who made all the decisions and controlled the family affairs. My mother was 71 when she died and my father was then 67.

The Bayley family had used the same undertaker for many years, and my father suggested we went to see my mother in the Chapel of Rest. Karena wanted to come as well and I was quite willing that she should. I had been about the same age when my Granddad Thornhill had died. However, the term 'Chapel of Rest' was a misnomer. My mother was laid in her coffin in what was the undertaker's garage cum workshop. What was far worse was that they had tried to put her false teeth back in and hadn't been able to do the job properly; so that my mother looked quite grotesque. Karena took one look, cried out and fled! I made very sure eleven years later when my father died that we employed the services of another undertaker!

Mother's spiritual roots were in the Salvation Army and her Funeral Service was held in the local Citadel, followed by cremation at Bradwell Crematorium; which my father had helped to build. His sense of humour was such, that when he was building the chimney in 1965 he sat on he top and said, "Well Harry lad, I wonder how long it'le be before you're comin up 'ere?"

There were many at the Service: relatives, friends, neighbours, and old colleagues from mother's working days. We had to practically carry my father through the day. In the days that followed he regained his composure, as we sorted out mother's affairs and possessions. Most of her clothing was bagged up and taken to the Salvation Army. Once we were sorted out in Arborfield, my father came and stayed with us for a while. In the meantime he leaned very heavily on my sister; who was a great help and comfort to him.

I had left instructions and an Order of Service for the Remembrance Day Service before I left, and I was pleased that everything had been arranged by the time I returned to duty. The Service went well, in spite of the usual complaints about the length of the Service in freezing temperatures. Most Senior Officers in the Army belong to the Church of England, and had a fixed idea that sermons should last for seven minutes and no more. Now to ask a Methodist to preach for only seven minutes is to inflict a peculiar kind of torture and is against all his training and tradition; and I refused to compromise!

My elder daughter, who by now had two children, coped well with having us living with them in Bordon: in fact I think she was quite glad of a little help from Grandma! My son-in-law was now a Sergeant, and was about half way through his two year Artificers course. Some good friends of ours from my tour in Minden were also stationed there, and it was good to be able to spend some time with them again.

Life in Arborfield was busy and fulfilling, but it was routine and usually predictable. Only rarely did I have to work unsocial hours, which was a pleasant change from the hyperactive lifestyle demanded of the Army in Germany. I had never worked with recruits before and it was an interesting experience. I soon discovered that I was the first Clergyman most of them had ever met, and very few knew anything at all about the Church. My first session with them was spent telling them a bit about myself as a real human being; and then explaining the role of Chaplains in the Army, giving some historical background. I emphasised the fact that all soldiers have the right of direct access to the Chaplain, without going through the usual 'chain of command'. I felt it was important to warn them that they would be 'pushed' harder than they ever had been before, and that they would learn an awful lot about themselves. Later, many of them told me how accurate my comments had been!

Two short films had recently been made for the Army. One was called "Life and Soul of the Party", and graphically portrayed some of the dire consequences of drinking too much alcohol and the effects this had, particularly on the lives of others. The other film was entitled, " For Better, For Worse", and dealt with the subject of marriage. I used these films as an introduction to the subjects with all Recruits. Others lectured them on the issue of drugs. I took each Platoon to the Chaplains Depot at Bagshot Park for half a day where, in addition to having a conducted tour of the House and a meal; they heard about the Courses available to them. These included basic Christian Information and Marriage Preparation Courses.

Work progressed slowly on our house and I pestered the Station Staff Office to put some pressure on the contractors. The firm storing all our worldly goods had informed me that unless I could give them a date very soon, they could not guarantee delivery before Christmas. After pulling all the strings I could, we moved in just over a week before Christmas! There were going to be nine of us at home for Christmas, so it was a race against the clock to get things unpacked and the house sorted out!

Every other Friday there was a Pass Out Parade for two Platoons who had successfully completed their ten weeks basic training. Sadly, some had been unable to complete their training and had returned to civilian life. I spoke to many of them and the reason for their failure was that they had been unable to achieve the standard of physical fitness required. The usual comment was, "I expected the discipline to be tough and was prepared for it, but I didn't expect it to be so physically demanding".

Wives, parents, and girl friends, were invited to attend and many did. The REME Staff Band played and a dignitary, usually a Senior Officer was invited to inspect the Recruits and take the Salute. Concord, which had just taken off from Heathrow Airport, usually flew over the camp at this point. It seemed quite fitting! Before the 'March Past', I, in my formal robes, stepped forward and offered a short prayer, which was the REME Collect; a special prayer for the Corps. Everyone then went to the Gymnasium where the Recruits put on an impressive display. Refreshments followed and there was an opportunity to mix with the guests. So many parents were genuinely amazed at the transformation of their sons from boys into men in ten weeks, and expressed their heartfelt appreciation to the Staff. The Officers then adjourned to the Mess for a formal lunch with the Inspecting Officer, before which I was expected to offer an appropriate Grace, usually including at some point a reference to the Inspecting Officer!

After some well deserved leave, the recruits would move on to do their Trade Training. Those selected to train as Electronic Engineers, would remain in Arborfield as students at the School of Electronic Engineering. Aspiring vehicle mechanics, and that meant the repair and maintenance of everything from Land Rovers to Chieftain Tanks (they were referred to in the Corps as 'the black hand gang'), went to Bordon: as did those training as Armourers; whose training ranged from the understanding and maintenance of pistols, rifles, and machine guns, to tanks and heavy artillery.

One evening, while I was running around Borden, I began to experience a strange sensation in my right leg, which seemed to be disobeying the signals from my brain to run. I was forced to stop before I fell over! This puzzled me because nothing like this had ever happed to me before. I rested for a few minutes and then carried on without any further problem. In Arborfield I had worked out a three and four mile circuit for my regular runs, and as I now regularly had minor problems with my leg, decided to see the Doctor and told him what I was experiencing. He was not a military man, but a local Doctor from the village who worked in the Medical Centre. He asked me how old I was, and when I told him I was 46, said, "Well, if I were you, I would stop running"! I know now that I was experiencing the first symptoms of Multiple Sclerosis, which would not be diagnosed for a further four years! I can't help but wonder now what path my life might have taken, had that Doctor referred me, or if I had insisted on further investigation! A few years earlier, another Chaplain had been diagnosed with MS and continued to serve until he was 55 years of age: even completing a tour as Senior Chaplain in Northern Ireland.

Arborfield was situated in the Reading and Silchester Methodist Circuit; the nearest Methodist Church being in Wokingham, about four miles away. I met with the Superintendent Minister and the Staff, and offered to take Services in the evenings. I enjoyed preaching in the Circuit Churches and speaking occasionally at mid week meetings. I also attended meetings of the Southampton Methodist District Synod. All Forces Chaplains are officially members of the London South West District, but it was customary to attend the Synod of the District where you were stationed.

We continued to make the awful journey to and from Bury St Edmunds every few weeks. My daughter had a friend who lived in Abingdon, and we made arrangements with her parents to share the chore! Sometimes we would drop Karena off at Abingdon to be taken the rest of the way by her friend's parents; and at other times we would collect her friend from School and drop her off at Abingdon. It was a slight improvement! Sandy had served his time in quarantine, and we drove down to the kennels near Folkstone to collect him. As we drove down we were wondering how much he might have been affected by his enforced imprisonment! We needn't have worried; he came racing out, ears flapping and stump wagging as though he'd been there for 24 hours instead of six months!

An Instructor, a Major, working in the REME Officers School was a Licensed Church of England Lay Reader, who was later to be Ordained. We became good friends and he was able to take Services for me occasionally. Being a very practical man, he helped me to convert a small part of the Church into a REME Memorial Chapel. He and his wife became very fond of Sandy and were more then happy to look after him any time we were away. They had a lovely Golden Retriever and a cat: she soon taught Sandy to have a healthy respect for cats! For the first time in fourteen years, I had a regular Church Council Meeting! The Brigadier attended without fail, and this certainly enabled us to get things done to improve the Church, which otherwise would have taken ages!

Even working in this comfortable and predictable environment didn't prevent me from having to deal with the occasional tragedy. A young member of the Corps was killed in a road accident in Germany. As his home was not far from Arborfield, his mother requested a Military Funeral be held in the Garrison, followed by burial in a local Cemetery. I visited the Cemetery Superintendent to discuss the arrangements. The grave was less than 100 yards from the perimeter fence of a Primary School; and the Headmistress, backed up by the Cemetery Superintendent, objected strongly to the firing of the final salute over the grave, on the grounds that because of periodic 'terrorist' warnings; the children would be scared. I made the point that providing the children were informed beforehand about what was happening; they wouldn't be scared at all! During a Military Funeral; once the coffin has been lowered into the grave, three shots are fired (using blank ammunition of course) as a final tribute and salute. The Bearer Party, under the command of a Sergeant Major and some of the soldier's friends, were coming from Germany for the funeral.

I shared this problem with the Brigadier, who discussed the matter with the Mayor; and the objections were overruled. The Sergeant Major informed me before he left, that whatever the consequences, he would order the firing of the salute! His soldier was entitled to a proper Military Funeral; and that was exactly what he was going to have!

It was shortly after this I was called upon to conduct another funeral at which I was to be one of the mourners. My old friend, the Quartermaster of The King's Regiment, had died suddenly. His widow and the Battalion wanted me to take his Funeral Service. The Battalion was now stationed in Chester and had no Chaplain of their own; a Chaplain from Preston visited them occasionally. The Funeral Service was to be held in the Regimental Chapel in Manchester Cathedral. I drove to Chester the day before the Service to discuss the arrangements with the Commanding Officer and the QMs widow. I travelled to the Cathedral in a Staff Car, and conducted the funeral of a 'rough diamond' of a man; who had served so well the Regiment he had joined as a teenager. After the Service, the cortege made its way to a Cemetery at the southern end of the City, with a Police Motor Cycle escort. I spent the night with the Battalion and drove back to Arborfield the following day.

On a much happier note, the young Sergeant from the Queen's Dragoon Guards who had been accepted into the Methodist Ministry; having completed his theological training and Probationary period; was due to be Ordained at the Methodist Conference which was to meet in Birmingham. He requested my attendance as an Assisting Minister at his Ordination Service: each Ordinand being permitted to invite one Minister to assist at his/her Ordination. I considered it a privilege to be invited and we travelled to Birmingham for this joyous event. It was a most enjoyable Service and so good to see him and his family again.

A Bandsman from the Staff Band had joined the Choir at Arborfield Parish Church. He informed me that they planned to sing Stainer's 'Crucifixion'; and that he was singing the solo part I had sung in Osnabruck. A few days before the performance he caught the 'flu; and before he took to his bed, informed the Choirmaster that I was familiar with the part! The Choirmaster came to see me, and after one rehearsal with the Choir, I sang the part on the following Sunday.

A letter from the Ministry of Defence informed me that I had been selected for promotion. I was now a Chaplain to the Forces Second Class (Lieutenant Colonel). It took a few weeks to train everyone to still refer to me as 'Padre', and **not** 'Colonel'! I have often been asked about Chaplains holding a Military Rank. The Royal Navy is usually quoted as an example of Chaplains not holding any rank. A Methodist Naval Chaplain once told me that their practice is good in theory, as the Chaplain is expected to assume the rank of the person he is dealing with. "But," he said, " That's all very well, but you try it with an Admiral"! Any Chaplain, whatever his 'rank', will have no trouble putting Servicemen and Women at their ease.

A Chaplain's rank is also an indication of his length of Service and experience, and most Commanders will be assured by it, and therefore have realistic expectations of their Chaplain. I always found rank was useful in helping soldiers, and especially in dealing with Officers, who would invariably look at the badges on my shoulders before noticing the crosses in my lapels or the clerical collar around my neck! The Chaplain General would now sometimes invite me to accompany him on his visits to the Staff College, and other Officer Training Establishments; where we would talk to the Senior Officers of the future about the role of the Chaplain.

There was a bizarre problem concerning a soldier getting married. One Friday afternoon I received a visit from a very agitated soldier from SEE. "Padre", he gasped, "I'm supposed to be getting married tomorrow at the Register Office in Reading, but the Registrar has just informed me that he can't do it"! The Reception was arranged, and a coach load of relatives and friends were on their way from the North East of England. I sat the soldier down and telephoned the Registrar; who explained what had happened. Some months earlier the soldier had telephoned the Registrar and asked if he could be married there on the date now at hand. The Registrar consulted his diary and confirmed the date and time was available. "Thank you very much", said the soldier, and put the phone down before the Registrar had chance to explain the procedure to him! I was glad the soldier concerned had passed through the Training Regiment before my arrival! I felt very sorry for the young man and thought of a compromise solution. I offered to conduct a Service of Blessing for them in the Church, emphasising that it would not be a Marriage Ceremony, as all the legal declarations would be omitted. They would then be able to have the reception, and organise with the Registrar for the legal ceremony to be held by Special Licence in a few days time. I began the Service by explaining to the congregation that what was about to take place was not a legal Marriage Ceremony!

Chaplains serving in Depots, and with Training Establishments, still had an Active Service Unit to report to in the event of Mobilisation. I was one of three Chaplains whose role was to serve with 2 Field Hospital. Their small Headquarters with its Administrative Company was based in Aldershot. I remembered that it was the same Field Hospital, which took over and used my Church premises in Ballykelly back in 1972 during Operation Motorman, which cleared all the barricades in Londonderry! They would practice their Mobilisation procedures at least once a year, and deploy the Hospital, which was all under canvas; sometimes in England, sometimes overseas.

The Consultants, Doctors, Nurses, and Medical Assistants; were drawn from all over the country: many already serving with the Territorial Army. The one Exercise I was involved in took place in England. The Hospital was of a considerable size and like any other Hospital, consisted of a Reception Area where patients were initially assessed: and a number of Wards and Operating Theatres.

As the Hospital had to be prepared to treat casualties from an attack by Nuclear, Biological, and Chemical agents, there were decontamination areas, airlocks in the corridors, and sterile Operating Theatres. Everyone entering these areas had to wear appropriate clothing. What really amazed me was the speed with which the staff could dismantle, pack up, move the entire Hospital to a different location; and erect it again.

The Roman Catholic Church in the Garrison was faced with closure for a few months while it underwent some long overdue repairs and refurbishment. Their Sunday Morning Mass was early, so I suggested they use my Church while the work was being done. They gladly agreed and asked if they could install a Crucifix, the Stations of the Cross; and a receptacle for the Reserved Sacrament. On the first Sunday of this arrangement I went to the Church early to ensure our visitors had found everything they needed: and was informed, rather bluntly by a crusty old Major. "We have a Priest, that's all we need"!

One afternoon in the early summer of 1985, I was sitting in the garden thinking about the future, and the kind of jobs likely to be open to me. They would doubtless be responsible positions, but of an administrative nature with responsibility for other Chaplains, and little to do with soldiers. There would still be regular moves with all the stress that involved; periods of separation, and a social life with more Senior Officers if I continued to climb the career ladder: prospects which greatly concerned my wife. My youngest daughter had come to terms with life at Boarding School, but wasn't very happy. My son was serving in the Army and wouldn't be affected by any decision I made. By 1986 I would have completed sixteen years Service and be eligible for a Pension. From the viewpoint of Methodist Circuits seeking Ministers, I would still be young enough to be a ' marketable commodity'! I thought and prayed about it for a while and made my decision. I would leave the Army in 1986 and return to Circuit Ministry. This was my own decision; and was not made due to anyone pressurising me in any way.

In 1985 the Methodist Church planned the movement of its Ministers at least eighteen months ahead, so I knew that most posts for September 1986 would already have been filled. I telephoned the Chairman of the London South West District, informed him of my decision; and asked for his help in finding a suitable position. As I'd expected, he informed me that most posts had already been filled, but that he would make enquiries of other Chairmen and get back to me. Of course I informed the Chaplain General, but my formal letter of resignation would not be required until much later. Within a couple of weeks I heard that an unexpected vacancy had come up and I was invited to travel to London to meet with the Chairman of the London North East District, who thought he might have something suitable for me.

We met in Westminster, and over lunch he told me about the vacancy. When I told him I would consider the position he had in mind, he left it to the Senior Circuit Steward to make contact with me.

A few days later I received a telephone call asking me to consider the post of Superintendent Minister of the Wanstead and Woodford Circuit, with particular responsibility for a new Church to be built in Loughton, near Epping Forest. He was most surprised when I told him that I'd never heard of Loughton, and had to get a map out to see exactly where it was! My wife and I visited Loughton and met the Senior Church Steward, Eddie Hayes at the Church, which he informed me, was shortly to be demolished due to extensive problems with dry rot; and a new Church costing half a million pounds built on the same site. It was a prime site on the main road and the Church Leaders had wisely resisted the temptation to build the new Church elsewhere in the town. I immediately warmed to the man and listened intently to all he had to tell me. We talked for a while and then went to see the Manse where we would be living, and to meet the present Minister. He was Revd Leslie Griffiths, who many will now have heard due to his frequent contributions on the radio. He was most helpful and encouraging, and though it was certainly never my intention to seek a Superintendent Minister's post, I was attracted by the challenge presented by Loughton; and informed the Circuit I would consider the appointment if I were to be formerly invited.

They contacted the Reading Circuit to enquire when and where I was due to conduct Services; and one Sunday evening a number of the Loughton Stewards together with Circuit Representatives, turned up in the congregation. After the Service the Church made a room available, and I was interviewed for half an hour. They reported back to the Circuit Meeting, and I received a letter from the Secretary informing me that the Meeting had unanimously voted to invite me to the Circuit as Superintendent Minister.

There was still almost a year to go before I was due to leave the Army, so I got on with the job in Arborfield. On the weekends when we weren't going to and from Bury St Edmunds, we toured the area looking at furniture! In the

Army, all the main items of furniture are provided. We were now faced with the prospect and the expense of furnishing a house with four bedrooms: the Circuit providing only carpets, curtains, and a cooker! My wife was quite delighted at the prospect of having all her own furniture instead of that not only chosen by other people, but also having the same as all the neighbours: she therefore really enjoyed these expeditions!

My son-in-law successfully completed his Artificers Course at Bordon and was now a Staff Sergeant. He was posted to Germany to serve with one of the Royal Engineer Regiments in Hamlin: and my daughter suggested we have a holiday with them, and take my father along as well. We took up the invitation and had an enjoyable holiday.

Many German Gasthouses have their own little bowling alley, called a Kegelbahn. One evening we visited one, had a couple of pints of good German beer and a hilarious game of bowls. On the way out I caught my foot on a small kerbstone, and much to the amusement of the family, lost my balance and did a simulated parachute roll into the roadway! I wasn't hurt at all, but puzzled over why I should have fallen so easily.

Later I realised it was another small symptom of what was to come; as were the muscle spasms in my legs which were causing me to have disturbed nights. It was suggested to me that raising the foot of the bed might alleviate this, but it didn't.

Every year the President of the Methodist Conference spent a couple of days with all the Forces Chaplains. We usually met at Bagshot Park, the arrangements being made by the Secretary of the Forces Board. It so happened that two others were also leaving in 1986; one from the RAF, and the other from the Royal Navy. At one of our gatherings, the Secretary asked all three of us to speak, and reflect on our time in the Services. We did not confer, but what we said was remarkably similar. All of us had enjoyed our time in the Services and were grateful that the Methodist Church had given us the opportunity to serve in this way. However, we all agreed that it was our wives and children who had paid the price; which we all thought was considerable. The frequent moves, the loss of friends, the periods of separation; and the distances from parents and relations when we were out of the country: all these while we were generally enjoying ourselves and doing our 'own thing'! The atmosphere in the meeting became quite sombre and at times emotional. It reminded some of an old fashioned Methodist 'Class Meeting'! It was also unusual because all three of us were returning to Circuit Ministry. There had been many years when Chaplains leaving the Services went on to do other things, and there had been a degree of reluctance to send men into the Forces; because very few ever came back into Circuit Ministry!

As I was coming to the end of my service, I was entitled to a Resettlement

Course. I obviously didn't need one to prepare for future employment, so I opted for a course on Household Maintenance. Never having been a practical person I had much to learn! The course was held in Aldershot and lasted for four weeks. During that time I learned something about plumbing, electrics, bricklaying, decorating, and tiling. It was interesting and valuable, especially as I left with a thick folder covering all we had been taught, and more!

It was about this time I heard that the next Chaplain General was to be a Church of Scotland Chaplain. Since its formation in 1796, every Chaplain General had been a Priest of the Church of England; so this appointment was very significant and most welcome by every other Protestant Church!

The Methodist Church provided a special Course for those about to become Superintendent Ministers. It was held at Luton Industrial College and was divided into two parts: one week prior to taking up the appointment, and another week a few months later when the Minister had been doing the job for a while and discovering some of the difficulties! The 'instructors' were mainly from Westminster Central Hall, the HQ of Methodism, and the Property Division in Manchester. There was also an important session on insurance matters, because whether he liked it or not, a Superintendent Minister is the Agent in the Circuit for the Methodist Insurance Company! For this he is paid a small commission, based on a Church's annual premium, which is taxable and not worth the amount of work involved!

A highlight of the course was the showing of a short film starring John Cleese entitled, "Meetings, Bloody Meetings". This was most appropriate as I was soon to discover. The restructuring of the Methodist Church, which had taken place during my time in the Army had created more meetings, not less! The membership was considerably less, and the paperwork considerably more! I left the Course with piles of paper and a sense of foreboding that after so many years away from Circuit work, during which time there had been so many changes, it would prove to be too much for me to handle. I had been assured that if (it should have been when) I made any mistakes, there would always be someone at the end of a telephone to 'put me straight'!

My wife and I continued to shop around and order furniture. It was fortunate we were able to do this well in advance, as we discovered it would take months for some of the major items we ordered to be delivered. At our time of life, I considered it prudent to invest in good quality furniture that would last the rest of our lives; and that by commuting part of my pension I would have enough money to pay for it!

I was determined that we should have a good holiday before leaving Arborfield and going to Loughton. After looking at the options I booked a holiday on the Island of Rhodes. It wasn't the best time of year to go due to the temperature, but we had little choice; and I did choose a hotel with air conditioning! The hotel was very good and had an Olympic size swimming pool. During our stay there I swam a mile every day. Most days we stayed by the pool and had our lunch there; only going out in the evenings when it was much cooler. We travelled by public transport to the City of Rhodes, and soon discovered that there was no such thing as a full bus! No matter how many people were at the bus stops, everybody always got on the bus!

One day we decided to go on a short boat trip to the Island of Symi, which was renowned for its sponges. On the way we passed within a hundred yards of the Turkish mainland. The Greek woman, who was our guide, insisted on referring to it as Asia Minor! On arriving on Symi early in the morning, we found the temperature was already over 100 degrees and getting hotter. After looking around the picturesque village; we found a discreet little doorway, stripped off, and went for a swim in the harbour! As it does on holidays, the time soon passed and it was time to leave. We'd had a good rest and felt ready to tackle the rest of the packing and the move to Loughton.

Before leaving, there was the usual round of 'farewell' meetings to attend; but this time they were far more poignant as I was not just leaving Arborfield: I was leaving the Army and a way of life I had really enjoyed. At last the packing was finished, the Removal Van arrived on time, the car was loaded up; and with mixed feelings I drove out of Arborfield and headed for Loughton.

SOME REFLECTIONS

After serving as a Regular Soldier and later spending sixteen years as an Army Chaplain, I have tremendous admiration for the British Soldier and his professionalism. Of course there are exceptions and there will always be the odd individual who will act irresponsibly, and bring his Regiment and the Army into disrepute. In Northern Ireland in particular I saw soldiers on many occasions 'keeping their cool', and maintaining discipline under the utmost provocation. Warrant Officers and Senior Non Commissioned Officers remain the 'backbone' of the Army; and the lives of soldiers and the careers of Officers would be seriously affected without their experience, their loyalty, and their dedication. Officers are highly trained, and to attain Senior rank must demonstrate exceptional ability not only in understanding and implementing military strategy and tactics; but also in diplomacy and the care of soldiers and their families. I have the utmost respect for those I have served under; having seen something of the demands placed upon them; and the relentless pressure due to 'overstretch'; and often the lack of resources in manpower and equipment.

I was privileged to be with people during some of the happiest moments of their lives; such as Marriage and the birth or Baptism of a child: and also to be alongside them during times of illness and bereavement. These times were particularly difficult, not just for me, but for the community, due to the young ages of the men, women and children who suffered and died. It was also a privilege to share with my Regiments as they commemorated significant events in their history, or when they received new Colours and a Standard from members of the Royal Family.

Someone once said that 'to live is to change': and my time as a Chaplain definitely changed me. I was not the same man, or the same Minister as I had been in 1970. The experiences I had undergone and the people I met; changed the way I looked at things. I was more open minded, more tolerant, and less 'cock sure' about things in general, and my faith in particular. I had learned to appreciate what others deemed important, and that there was always another side or another way. My Faith was stronger, but different; and I was, and still am, increasingly concerned about the growth of fundamentalism and biblical literalism in the Churches.

As an Army Chaplain, I was often asked about the differences between my role and that of a civilian Minister. The main difference is that a civilian Minister spends the majority of his time working with and for a Church congregation. A Chaplain spends most of his time working with and for people who are not Church people, and who never will be. He is the Man of God in the Military situation. Because of frequent postings, Military Training, conferences, continuation training, and involvement in welfare matters, I found it difficult to actually 'build', anything. Every posting meant learning to work in a different environment, and no matter how much I might have achieved in a previous situation; every move meant starting again from 'square one'!

I know that over the years I influenced some people, helped many through times of great distress, and challenged others to think differently. Most important was the fact that I SHARED a whole way of life with those I lived and worked with and for. Postings; separation; problems with married quarters; and anxiety over the effects of Army life on wives and children; I SHARED them all. I wasn't a visitor who popped in from time to time, like for example, a part time Industrial Chaplain: I was an integral part of the Military community, with all its joys and sorrows, and was therefore able to identify with people in a way not possible in civilian life. If I were to take a sheet of paper and write down lists of the pluses and minuses of Service life, there would be more pluses.

Above: Peter with his father Harry and Valerie with her mother Joan

Below left: Peter in 1977 with an Arab
Below right: relaxing in Israel 1977

Ministers past and present at the 200th anniversary celebrations of
Newcastle Methodist Church

PART III – HEAVY LANDINGS

LOUGHTON METHODIST CHURCH
AUGUST 1986 – JULY 1995

We arrived at the Manse in Loughton to find a small group of people, not simply there to give us an extremely warm welcome, but to provide much needed practical help. The Manse was a lovely house, but not nearly as well equipped as the Army Married Quarters we'd been used to; and I couldn't resist saying so! The entire contents of the kitchen consisted of a sink, an old cooker, one small cupboard on the wall; and a very old and dilapidated French dresser. There was not a single working surface. The Circuit Stewards promised to get some new kitchen units, which they quickly did, and a very practical member of the Church spent a couple of months in his spare time, fitting them, together with an adequate number of working surfaces.

There was a garden at the front of the house and a large garden at the rear. The wooden panel fence was in need of renewal, but it would take several years before it was all replaced. It was a case of doing a little each year as money became available. There were a number of other things in need of replacement; but we felt we couldn't keep on asking for more. Having 'put up' with so many things over the years, we were anxious for our new home to be as we wanted, and within the first few weeks spent over £1,000 of our own money.

The removal van arrived just before all the new furniture we had ordered, so there was much to do. Fortunately there was a large useable attic, in which we put many of the packing cases while we found enough room for the contents! Army quarters always had attics, and I was used to lugging heavy cases and crates up and down loft ladders. However, on this occasion, I found it particularly difficult and tiring, and couldn't understand why.

The old Church had been raised to the ground, and the new building was about a third of the way up! The Sunday morning Services were being held in the Roman Catholic Church Hall just across the road, on condition that they finished by 12 o' clock when the bar was due to open! Evening Services were held in Wesley Hall, the Methodist hall behind the Church, which had not been demolished. A considerable amount of money had already been raised to pay for this most ambitious project, much of it by the members themselves. Various grants had been obtained from Methodist sources, including the Joseph Rank Benevolent Fund.

A letter requesting assistance had even been sent to the Roman Catholic Church, who had already given us the use of their hall, and another room in which some of our young people met.

It was a Jesuit Parish with three Priests, and the Priest in charge sent a letter back saying, "I regret that we cannot possibly give you a donation towards the building of a new Methodist Church, but I enclose a donation of £1,000 towards the demolition of the old one"!

There were two Welcome Services. The Circuit Welcome Meeting and Induction Service was held at Hermon Hill Methodist Church in Wanstead, and conducted by the Chairman of the District. It was a memorable Service for me, and I was surprised and pleased that quite a number of my colleagues from the Chaplains Department; including the Chaplain General Designate, had made the journey to share in it.

All the Churches in Loughton had recently entered into a formal Covenant, and the second Welcome Service was held on a Sunday Evening at Loughton Union Church, and organised by the local Council of Churches. All this was before my first Service with my own people, which was on the following Sunday morning. There were about two hundred and fifty church members and the Catholic Church Hall was filled to capacity. Having listened for so long to the feeble attempts at singing by Garrison Church congregations, the first thing I wanted was to hear my congregation sing: I told them so, and was not disappointed!

The Catholic Sacristy became our Vestry, and the atmosphere was heavy with incense. It hit the back if my throat, made my eyes water; but cleared my sinuses! After the Service the congregation filed out, shook my hand, introduced themselves, and welcomed me to the Church. How on earth was I ever going to remember the names of such a multitude? Eventually of course I did, and more, because there was still many on the Church Community Roll and the rest of the Circuit I still had to meet.

Debden, my other Church, was on a large post war Council Estate two miles away. The Church and hall had been built in the 1950s; and were very similar to those on the Bradwell and Blurton Estates. I felt very much at home, and wasn't at all surprised when I discovered the history and current problems were very much the same. In its early years it had been the centre for work amongst children and the youth of the Estate. They had grown up and left the area leaving less than a dozen members, mostly elderly ladies. I arranged to conduct the Sunday Service there once a month. A scheme had been organised by the Loughton Church to transport some of the more elderly members to and from Church on a Sunday. Its survival was due entirely to the fact that a retired psychiatric nurse and her husband had established a Day Care Centre for about twenty elderly people, some of whom were a little confused. They met in the Church hall every Tuesday and Thursday. An old ambulance had been converted and was used to transport people to the Centre. Volunteers cooked an excellent meal for them and provided a little entertainment before they returned home. On Thursday afternoons there was a short act of Worship, which I conducted once a month. A daughter Church of the Parish Church of St. Johns, called St. Gabriels was also struggling to survive on the Estate, with a Curate in Charge.

The other two Churches in the Circuit were at Wanstead and Woodford. They had a full time Minister and the assistance of an Active Supernumerary Minister who also helped out at Debden and Loughton. With three Ministers and only four Churches, making the Circuit Quarterly Preaching Plan was quick and easy; enabling many of our Local Preachers to help out in neighbouring Circuits.

In Loughton there were two Church of England Parishes, one 'High' Church, and the other 'Low' Church. The Union Church was composed of people from Congregational/Presbyterian/Baptist traditions; but the Minister was always a Baptist. Along with the Roman Catholic and Methodists Churches, all these had signed a formal Covenant to work and worship more closely together, and not to do separately, what could and should be done jointly. Loughton was an Ecumenical Flagship and the Dioceses of Chelmsford (Church of England), Brentwood (Roman Catholic), and the London North East District of the Methodist Church; all played an active part in working for its success.

Every Monday morning, all the Clergy would meet for Prayers at 8.00 a.m.; each taking his turn to act as host and lead the prayers. The Council of Churches (soon to be renamed 'Churches Together'), met regularly, and together with the Minister's Fraternal, which met monthly, planned joint Study Courses, made arrangements for the Week of Prayer for Christian Unity; the March of Witness on Good Friday, and many other events. I was an enthusiastic supporter of the Covenant, but it did add more meetings and another layer of administration on to an already overcrowded schedule. Eventually I felt guilty about constantly urging my congregation to support our own Church events, Circuit Events, and Ecumenical Events. My own Church had lots of different Committees, each with their own agendas demanding support. One of the first things I encouraged my people to do, was to appreciate that there was such a thing as 'A Life after Church'! Many were commuters, working in London, and would often come directly to meetings without having been home for a meal! I thought this might change after they had achieved their goal and the new Church was open and paid for; but it didn't. If anything it became worse.

Running was still important to me, and I worked out a couple of circuits, trying to find time at least three times a week to run; which helped me to think and get rid of my frustrations! My runs became less pleasurable as they became more of an effort, so I decided to talk to my Doctor. He listened carefully, said it probably wasn't anything, but that he would refer me for some tests; muttering something about, 'a cloud no bigger than a man's hand'. For those who don't know the Biblical story, that small cloud developed into quite a storm!

The new Church building was coming along well, and I regularly attended meetings of the Development Committee. As a 'latecomer' I said little but listened carefully. There were a number of professional people on the committee who knew exactly what they were doing and I was happy for them to get on with things! I did get involved with the sub committee, which was set up to purchase the interior furnishings. We obtained the services of an Israeli carpenter who designed and made the communion table, the communion rails, the pulpit, and the lectern. We spent a lot of money on hundreds of comfortable chairs, which could be linked together when necessary. The design of the Church was unique, and created a lot of interest in architectural circles.

There was a large 'Welcome Area', which opened directly onto the High Road and had its own small kitchen. As well as being a place where the congregation could gather before and after Services, it was to be open to the community five and a half days a week as a Coffee Bar. The Church and the integral Hall were designed as multi-purpose areas, and could be divided several ways by means of huge partitions which, when not in use, folded easily away in their own storage room. Upstairs there was a large meeting place, which was named the Joseph Rank Room, and a smaller room underneath the spire, known as the Tower Room, which could comfortably accommodate a dozen people.

When the spire was ready, a helicopter was brought in to lower it into position, which certainly caught the attention of the local people! On top of the spire was a Cross. The architect had a problem: and that was how to illuminate the Cross at night. Any kind of bulb was out of the question, as we certainly couldn't bring in a helicopter every time a bulb needed changing! He got the answer from a friend who was a surgeon. The Cross was illuminated using a bulb set in the Tower Room, and the light transferred to and through the Cross by fibre optic tubes. This system had never been used before, and it worked!

It was anticipated that the Church would be ready by Easter 1987 and that Revd. Dr. Leslie Griffiths (now Lord Leslie Griffiths) at my suggestion, be invited to preach at the Service of Dedication on Easter Saturday. A very small minority didn't agree, but I know that without his drive and inspiration, the new Church would never have been built; and the Minister who can please everyone hasn't been born yet! I insisted on planning the Service of Dedication myself. There was no way I was going hand that task over to another

Committee! The Order of Service was professionally designed and printed. It cost a lot, but then again, so did every part of the Church!

When I was in Arborfield I had conducted the Marriage Service for the daughter of the Director of Music for the REME Staff Band. He was now the Director of Music for one of the Guards Regiments in London. I contacted him and asked if we could hire two Trumpeters. Six hundred people where expected to attend the Service, and I thought a Fanfare would be an appropriate and fitting way to get every ones attention and commence the Service! It was a most inspiring and joyful Service, with all the Circuit Staff taking part; and the Church Members were justifiably proud of what they had achieved. The local Clergy were in attendance, as was the Chairman of the Epping Forest District Council; whose name I unfortunately couldn't remember when I welcomed everyone! The Chairman of the District, Revd Brian Galliers, who had not been able to join us for the Dedication Service, conducted the Service on Easter Day, bringing to a conclusion an unforgettable weekend of celebrations.

The Welcome Area ' opened for business' the following week, with many of the Church Members volunteering to work in the Coffee Bar. It didn't take long before it was being used regularly by a considerable number of people; and it was apparent that many of them were quite lonely people who came for the company rather than the coffee! One of the Church Members quickly became aware of this and suggested a 'Friendship Club' be formed. Leaflets were left on the coffee tables to assess the demand for such a club, and we were delighted when the offer was enthusiastically accepted; and within a few months there was a waiting list of people wishing to join the club! There were a number of rooms available for hire, and it didn't take long before we were accepting many regular bookings. There was a need for someone to coordinate the letting of rooms and the Property Committee drew up a list of costs and terms; and also recommended the employment of a part time caretaker, who would also act as 'lettings steward' and be responsible for the security of the property. LMC (Loughton Methodist Church) became such a popular venue every room was soon fully booked! This provided a valuable source of income and soon enabled the Church to employ a full time Administrator. The post was advertised and there were a number of applicants. A small sub-committee was formed to interview the applicants: one member of the sub-committee being the local Undertaker who said he would be happy to serve as he was used to firing people! One of our own Church Members was eventually appointed and did an excellent job in putting LMC 'on the map'.

As the Wanstead & Woodford Circuit was very small by Methodist standards, the job of being Superintendent Minister was not an onerous one. There were the usual number of meetings, but I was blessed with having a competent Staff and Circuit Officials, which was a great help! It was not destined to remain like that for long, as there was a policy of creating larger Circuits, and following a visit from the Boundaries Commission, we would soon be obliged to consider amalgamating with one or more neighbouring Circuits.

Looking through the Church Newspaper, The Methodist Recorder one week; I saw a notice from 'Holy Land Christian Tours' offering a cheap 'familiarisation visit' to The Holy Land for Ministers considering taking a party on a pilgrimage to Israel. Anyone interested was invited to attend a meeting to be held at a Hotel near to Heathrow Airport in order to receive more details. I had wanted to return to Israel since 1958 and this seemed to be an ideal opportunity. I passed the word around the Church and Circuit, and was gratified that there was enough interest to warrant me attending the meeting. The Hotel was further from the nearest Underground Station than I had anticipated, and my legs felt very weak by the time I arrived! I received much information and literature, and agreed to go on the familiarisation visit planned for January 1988.

There were about a dozen in the group and the week we spent in Jerusalem and Galilee was very hectic. We toured the main Holy sites, visited many Hotels, met with and were escorted by several official guides, both Arab and Israeli: and attended many meetings setting out in detail the way to organise and lead a party on its Pilgrimage.

There was a lot of work involved, but Holy Land Christian Tours (HLCT) provided excellent support and backing at every stage. I agreed to lead a Party in May 1989; drafted out my own itinerary; and chose the Hotels and Guide I wanted. No Party is allowed to tour Israel without an official Guide. HLCT printed lots of attractive brochures outlining the thirteen day itinerary to circulate around the Circuit.

When I returned home, my wife informed me that she had attended a Modern Sequence Dancing Club. This was something she had wanted to do for many years, but because of the Army way of life, this had not been possible. I agreed to learn and went to the Club with her whenever I could. Unfortunately my legs weren't really up to mastering the intricacies of Modern Sequence Dances, especially as new dances were being introduced almost every week! However I did my best, but soon discovered that for most members, it wasn't just a hobby, it was a way of life; and many went to several different clubs every week. I remember one couple saying to me, "This is something that breaks up many marriages you know"! It was said in a rather jocular manner, and I passed it off. After all, I had been very happily married for thirty years!

Every ten years Methodist Ministers are expected to go away for two weeks, meet with others who had served for the same length of time; and under the guidance of senior Ministers discuss and evaluate their respective ministries. It is a time of reflection, sharing, learning, and growth. Being in the Army I had missed the first; and with all that was going on in Loughton, asked for the 20 year course be postponed. So it was 1988 before I presented myself to Hengrave Hall, near Bury St. Edmunds together with a couple of dozen Ministers. I was really looking forward to the course, especially as I knew I would be meeting friends I hadn't seen for many years; and it would be a good opportunity for me to stand back and assess my Ministry since leaving the Army. It really was good to meet up again with old friends and colleagues; and to learn about all they and their families had been doing. I appreciated the input and advice of the Directing Staff; and gained much from the small group sessions we held: but at the end came away feeling quite depressed at the amount of pain being experienced by most of the Ministers.

They told of difficulties caused by inadequate Stipends and allowances, unrealistic expectations of their congregations, problems with relationships, particularly with some Church Officials; and the heartaches caused by having to move so often and the effect this had on their wives and children. My time in the Army had cushioned me from some of these, but I was soon to discover pain in other situations.

At long last I received an appointment to see a Specialist at the Royal London Hospital in Whitechapel about the problems I was having with my legs. He questioned me, examined me, and sent me to another Hospital for a Magnetic Resonance Scan. The results were inconclusive, and I was referred to a Consultant Neurologist. In the spring of 1988 I spent two weeks in the Royal London Hospital undergoing tests on my eyes; had a brain scan; and a lumbar puncture.

The diagnosis was Multiple Sclerosis. The Consultant said, "It's very mild; it might not get any worse: there's nothing we can do for you, so go away, do the best you can and come back and see me in a years time"! Later, many people with MS told me they had also been dismissed in the same perfunctory manner after being diagnosed.

There was a sense in which I was relieved: at least I knew now that there was indeed something wrong: but I didn't know what to do; or what not to do. What would help, or what might exacerbate the condition. I determined to find out what I could. I discovered that the MS Society had its head office in London, so I got on the Underground and presented myself at the Head office of the Society in Fulham. The two ladies in the office were a little taken aback when I went in and said, "I've just been diagnosed with MS; do you have any advice for me, or any literature to help me understand something about this disease?" They rummaged through draws and filing cabinets and gave me a few leaflets and photocopies of articles about MS, from which I learned that MS is a degenerative disease of the central nervous system. There are two main types of MS: relapsing/remitting; which is when people have 'attacks', followed by periods of remission: and chronic progressive, when the condition of the patient slowly and inexorably deteriorates. It soon became apparent that I was suffering from the latter. Having said that; no two people have exactly the same symptoms. One symptom however is common to all, and that is fatigue. Now I knew why I was getting tired so easily! It was probably a delayed reaction to the diagnosis, but I began to suffer periods of depression when I would just sit and break into uncontrollable bouts of sobbing. My wife also had difficulty in coming to terms with the diagnosis and in a sense went into denial. I was both bewildered and upset when she said: "well you've had 50 good years, and it isn't life threatening"! There have been a number of occasions since then when I really wished it **was** life threatening. I am not afraid of dying; but I am afraid of ending up as a bed bound, helpless cripple! My GP prescribed something to help, and after a few weeks the dark cloud of depression lifted. I was definitely going to have to learn to pace myself and seriously considered moving from Loughton to a less demanding job. I discussed this with one of the senior Circuit Stewards who was a Member at Loughton, and he said, "We would rather have you firing on four cylinders than anyone else firing on six!"

Two significant things then happened to help me even more. Another Church Member who was a Douglas Macmillan Nurse came to see me. She had some knowledge of MS and told me that I couldn't make the condition any worse by pushing myself; and that I should do my best to avoid stress, which would only exacerbate the condition. The first was music to my ears! It reminded me of my Parachute Selection Course when I had been told, "You can lie down in the gutter and die: but you don't give up; you don't stop"! She also reminded me of the old maxim, 'If you don't use it, you'll lose it'. So I began to take more exercise and walk regularly. Avoiding stress was much more difficult, and that was to become a major problem. Another lady who had recently left Loughton sent me a copy of a book she had bought from a second hand bookstall. Its title was, 'MS & How To Manage It'.

The book had been written by a woman who was herself suffering with MS. She was a journalist who had employed her journalistic skills in researching the disease. The book contained lots of useful information about the disease itself, ways of combating and controlling the symptoms; and hopefully slowing down its progression. Evening Primrose oil was strongly recommended, and I have been taking that and many other supplements for the past fifteen years. A low fat diet was also strongly recommended.

Several other people encouraged me to get in touch with an organisation called ARMS (Action for Research into MS), and try Hyperbaric Oxygen Treatment. (HBO) This meant going into a chamber, like the ones used by Divers suffering from 'the bends'. The chamber, which would seat six people, would then be pressurised to the equivalent of 8, 16, or 33 feet: and a mask worn in order that a person could breath pure oxygen under pressure for one hour. The chamber is then depressurised and the occupants released. Some found it helpful, others didn't. I decided to give it a try, to see if I could get any benefit from it; but first I needed a certificate from my GP, in case I had other problems which might make such treatment inadvisable. I went to see my GP who said, "Well it can't do you any harm, so try it".

The nearest ARMS Centre (there were more than 60 in the country) was located on an Industrial Estate in Walthamstow, just off the North Circular Road, about five miles from Loughton. In order to obtain maximum benefit from the treatment, it is strongly recommended that a person has twenty 'dives' in the first month to get lots of oxygen into the blood stream, and then regular 'top ups' every week or two. ARMS is a Charity and receives no public funding. The centre had a paid Administrator, and there were lots of volunteers. The rent paid to the owners of the Unit was £17,000 a year; so there were lots of fund raising efforts. Each 'dive' cost the member £6, which I soon discovered was for me, a worthwhile investment. It certainly helped to combat fatigue. Previously, I had been like a night storage radiator: good in the morning after a night's sleep; but then gradually being used up until there was nothing left. I still got tired; but now I found that if I had a short rest, I could 'bounce back' again and carry on. A physiotherapist was also available at the Centre, and after an assessment, gave me a list of exercises to carry out daily when possible. So there it was: I had a new regime to follow, I felt better, and more confident about the future. I continued to work hard, but disciplined myself to take a break whenever necessary. My Church Members were very understanding and supportive; and lightened my workload whenever possible. I remember talking about this to my predecessor, Revd Leslie Griffiths, who was still in London; and he said to me, "You couldn't be in a better place; the Loughton people will be a great help to you".

The couple responsible for running the Day Care Centre at Debden decided to leave the area, but others, appreciating the value of the Centre to the community, stepped in to ensure its survival.

Lady Heather Murray and the Senior Steward at Debden took over the kitchen and cooking responsibilities; and I remember well seeing Lord Murray, sleeves rolled up, peeling carrots in the sink! Much of the equipment in the kitchen was very old; and in order to comply with new Health & Safety regulations, the Church resolved to have a new kitchen installed. Several of the people attending the Centre were in wheelchairs; and so a small lift was installed to enable them to reach the main building, where one of the toilets had been extended to accommodate them. All this proved expensive, and we applied for and received a number of grants: the remainder being raised by the people.

Transport proved to be one of the biggest problems, and I undertook the responsibility for organising it. Epping Forest District Council had recently acquired two new Mini-Bus Ambulances, and they agreed to give us the use of one of them every Tuesday and Thursday; but we had to provide the drivers, who had to pass a County Driving Test first! I managed to get a small group of volunteers from Loughton and St. John's Parish Church, and I put myself on the list. It took about an hour and a half, and three trips around the area to bring everyone in: and the same length of time to take them all home again in the late afternoon. The lady who was the Senior Steward at Debden acted as escort and guide for those drivers who didn't know their way around the Estate; and also assisted those who needed help getting on and off the transport. For some of those elderly people it was a real lifeline, as it was the only time they ever got out of the house: and it gave the carers of those with disabilities a welcome break. It became one of my priorities to ensure those people were always collected. If for any reason it was not possible for a driver to fulfil the commitment; I would try to find another driver; and if that proved impossible, I would rearrange my own commitments and drive myself.

There was another, smaller Day Care Centre on the edge of the Estate which had been set up by St. John's Parish and the Methodist Church in Loughton. It was staffed by people from both Churches, and met once a week in a small building owned by the local Council. This Day Care Centre was organised and run by a small committee and they asked me to be the Chairman! Transport and cooking arrangements were well established so there wasn't a great deal of work involved as far as I was concerned. I Chaired the Annual General Meeting; and conducted a Service for them at Christmas and Easter, as well as providing a little light entertainment!

A lot of thought was being put into the matter of amalgamating Circuits referred to earlier; and now the Boundaries Commission was expecting a response from us. The predominant reaction from people was still one of sadness: they didn't want to see the Wanstead and Woodford Circuit disappear. The stark choice was that we either came to some agreement with neighbouring Circuits, or a scheme would be imposed on us. Extensive consultations were held to discover people's feelings and preferences. The consensus was that few were in favour of linking up with Harlow to the north of us; especially as they were already seeking closer links with the United Reform Churches in the area: and most were against linking up with Ilford (Redbridge) to the south east.

Many people, having moved up from the south and the south west of the Circuit suggested we explore possibilities in those areas.

Eventually it was proposed that we join with the Walthamstow and Chingford Circuit, and half of the Leytonstone and Forest Gate Circuit; the other half of that Circuit going elsewhere. This would create a Circuit of seventeen Churches following the line of the Lea Valley. There would be eight Ministers. I personally agreed that this was a good proposal, but emphasised that I would not wish to be the Superintendent Minister! It was agreed that the new Circuit, to be known as the London (Forest) Circuit, would come into being in September 1989: and that the Superintendent would be the present Superintendent of the Walthamstow and Chingford Circuit, for one year: a new Superintendent from outside the area would be sought for September 1990.

Both Churches on the Debden Estate were struggling to survive. The Anglican Curate and I worked well together, and felt that for the work of the Church to be meaningful; our Churches should work more closely together, and even explore the possibility of uniting. The Methodist Church had the best set of premises by far and was the obvious place for the work of the Church to be based. Just off the Estate was another very small old church, which also belonged to the Parish; and was looked after by a non Stipendiary Priest. We consulted our respective superiors, and with their agreement and encouragement, began to work towards having the area designated as a Local Ecumenical Project: (an LEP). A lot of work was involved to bring this about, and my Anglican Colleague did most of it, mainly because it was acknowledged that I had more and wider responsibilities. The main proposals were: that the three Churches should not only work together; but also worship together, have one Church Council; and one Bank Account! As was to be expected, there were a few 'personality clashes' as those who had been big fishes in little ponds, jockeyed for positions in a much bigger pool! It was decided that the Church be renamed 'Trinity'; and because the majority of the congregation would be Anglicans, three out of four Services each month would be conducted by one of the Anglican Priests, and the fourth my me or one of my Methodist colleagues. There were a few 'teething troubles' to begin with; but I was surprised and delighted by the way it all worked out so well, and the new Church prospered and grew in membership and influence in the community.

A Church Member at Loughton was a Senior Officer in the Metropolitan Police. One of his contributions in raising money for the new Church had been to arrange for the Metropolitan Police Band to give a couple of Concerts, which were a sell out! They expressed a desire to give another Concert in the new Church; this was a most welcome offer, which was gratefully accepted. It was an excellent Concert and the Church was packed to capacity. One of the 'highlights' of the evening was a duet sung by me, and the now ex-Senior Steward, Eddie Hayes; who was also a retired Police Officer.

We sang 'The Bold Gendarmes' wearing little Police Helmets, waving truncheons, and dancing a jig between the verses. It was the most memorable contribution to a very successful evening!

My wife was now more involved in the dancing world and I was rarely able to go with her. I really understood her love of dancing and that she was making up for lost time. The problem was that she was spreading her wings at the same time as I was having mine clipped! I felt that we were growing apart and had nightmares about losing her. We talked about it, and I was accused of being paranoid. I sought the help of a counsellor. It was good to share my fears and anxieties, but obviously did nothing to change the situation.

Our Pilgrimage to the Holy Land was drawing near and I was busy finalising the arrangements. There were thirty people in the group and we had two meetings to prepare ourselves; and for me to pass on important information. A coach had been hired to take us to Heathrow Airport. As we were flying with El Al, the Israeli National Airline, we were required to check in at least two hours before take off and submit ourselves to extensive security checks and interviews. The flight to Tel Aviv took about four hours, and the Israeli Guide I had booked was there to meet us. We boarded the waiting coach and drove up to Jerusalem, arriving at our Hotel where a warm welcome and a snack awaited us before it was time for bed.

I had arranged for us to spend seven nights in Jerusalem, which included two half days and one full day free. This was to enable people to go shopping and to re-visit any of the sites we had seen together. For most people, it was a once in a lifetime visit; and I felt it was important to give them time to themselves. The problem with the shorter; for example the eight day tours, is that with having so many places that just have to be visited, there's no time for anything else! One day was spent down in the Jordan Valley where it was very hot! We visited the traditional site of Christ's Baptism, Qumran where the Dead Sea Scrolls had been discovered: and the mountain fortress at Masada, where Jewish zealots had held out against the might of Rome following the destruction of Jerusalem in AD 70. The enormous ramp the Romans had to construct in order to conquer the fortress still occupies a prominent position. Most of the group took the opportunity to have a swim in the Dead Sea, which is so salty it is impossible for a person to sink! Swimming properly is also impossible, and watching people try was the source of much amusement.

Another place we visited which moved everyone very deeply was the Holocaust Memorial at Yad Vashem; particularly the Children's Memorial. This building is dark inside, with mirrors and candles. Visitors hold a rail to guide them through: and as they proceed, the names and ages of the children who were killed are continually read out. In total, one and a half million children perished; and when we emerged from the Memorial, several members of the group were in tears. There was insufficient time to see and read all that was on display; and some members of the group returned on one of their free days.

On the first Sunday morning most joined the congregation for worship at the Garden Tomb, others decided to go to St. John's Cathedral. After a fascinating week in Jerusalem, we journeyed north to a Hotel by the Sea of Galilee for five days; which again included free time. From there we visited Nazareth, and crossed the lake to Capernaum. The wearing of shorts by men and women is forbidden in Capernaum. We were given ample notice of this and all the women took a skirt to slip on, and the men took a pair of trousers: one young man either forgot or chose to ignore this advice and was not allowed off the boat! The same was expected of visitors to the Dome of the Rock in Jerusalem; which is a Holy Site for Muslims and Jews, as well as Christians: as it is built on top of Mount Moriah where Abraham was prepared to sacrifice his son Isaac. The Muslim 'Guardians' of the site even remonstrated with a couple of our ladies who sat down!

On the Sunday morning I conducted a Service of Holy Communion for the group on the Mount of The Beatitudes overlooking Galilee. There are a number of special sites set apart for such Services; the wine and wafers being provided for us by the nuns who cared for the beautiful Church on the Mount. It was a fitting climax to what had been an inspiring Pilgrimage.

The advantage in having an Israeli Guide instead of a Christian; is that without detracting in any way from the Christian Pilgrimage, we were also given a Jewish perspective; and I came to see how much of our Jewish heritage the Christian Church has neglected or chosen to ignore! The group had enjoyed themselves so much; we planned a reunion when everyone brought their photographs! They urged me to organise another Church Holiday the following year: not another pilgrimage, but a holiday. I realised that there were many people who had no one to go on holiday with; and to be part of a Church group fulfilled a real need. The success of this trip led to me to organise a Church Holiday every year for the next five years.

The time came when all my anxieties, fears, and nightmares became reality when I discovered, most definitely, that my wife was having an affair. I was absolutely devastated. I felt as though my insides had been ripped out and replaced with a ball of iron. Even so, as with the diagnosis of MS, I felt a sense of relief; as I believed that the discovery would end the matter and we could rebuild our relationship. I was certainly very determined that we should. My wife was most contrite and begged my forgiveness, swearing that the affair was now finished. I was still very much in love with her and could not, after so many years together, even imagine life without her; so I readily forgave her. Now it had been admitted, I really believed we could make a fresh start. My first instinct was to arrange to leave Loughton and I investigated that option with the Chairman of the District, who was most helpful and promised to support me in any decision I made. I seriously considered returning to the Army, and spoke to the Deputy Chaplain General using the Chairman's telephone. The DCG consulted the Army Medical Services, and informed me that as my MS was still in its early stages, they would be able to find a job for me.

My major concern was for my youngest daughter, who, having spent all her life moving around because of my job, had settled down well in Loughton and made some good friends. My other two children were old enough not to be affected by my movements. I agonised over the situation, and as it isn't really in my nature to run away from things, I decided to stay and try to work things out. With the Chairman's encouragement, and at the Districts expense, my wife and I agreed to go for Counselling: each of us seeing a Counsellor specialising in helping clergymen and their wives through marital difficulties. We went to several sessions, but before we reached the stage when all four of us would have to meet together, my wife withdrew. I insisted she cease dancing, which made her very unhappy. I continued to work as best I could: people attributing my 'off days' to MS, which became a convenient cloak to hide behind! I was not convinced that the affair was over, even though my wife maintained that they were now just 'good friends'.

Six months later, and additional tensions had emerged: my wife was very unhappy because she wished to continue her dancing; and as a result I became equally distressed. I was embroiled in the very thing I had been strongly advised to avoid: lots of stress. I reluctantly agreed that she could resume dancing; and because I could no longer even attempt to dance, she encouraged me to join a choir. Eddie Hayes, who had an excellent bass voice, and his wife Valerie had recently joined the New Essex Choral Society, which met for rehearsals in a school hall in Barkingside (London Borough of Redbridge). I asked if I might join them, and was made very welcome by the Choir, especially as they were short of tenors!

The Passion Play at Oberammergau in Bavaria was due to be held in 1990, and I was encouraged by some of those who had been on the Holy Land Pilgrimage to organise a holiday; which would include seeing the Passion Play. I approached a coach company which claimed to have tickets for the play; and who also offered to arrange accommodation for a fortnights holiday. The first week being spent in an Austrian village not far from Oberammergau; and the second week in a village in northern Italy, very close to the Brenner Pass. The holiday price included overnight Hotel accommodation in Holland on the outward and return journeys: as well as a number of day trips, which I could arrange in consultation with the drivers.

I circulated the information around the Church and Circuit, and 44 people signed up for the trip. Not long before we were due to leave, the news broke that many thousands of tickets for the Passion Play had been misappropriated. The Company we had booked with were one of the many victims; and even tough there was great disappointment at not being able to see the Play, we resolved to continue with our holiday arrangements. The fraudster had made a lot of money and was eventually traced to somewhere in South America. I don't know what happened to him, but I do know that the German Authorities assumed greater control over the distribution of tickets before the next Passion Play in the year 2000!

Our Hotel in Austria was an old wooden building with lots of character. Most of us were initially a little disappointed as we had expected something more modern! However it was a family concern, and the staff were excellent. The food was very good and there was plenty of it. As the leader of the party, I had to check that everyone was happy with their rooms, and that there weren't any problems with electrics or plumbing etc. There were always too few single rooms, and it was always a little difficult to 'pair' people to share a room. Most were very happy and sorted things out between themselves. On this occasion however, one lady was complaining bitterly because the person she was sharing with snored so loudly she was unable to sleep! I spoke to the owner of the Hotel, and he managed to sort things out. By the end of the week we had all grown so attached to the place, we were sorry to be leaving. Even though we were unable to see the Play, we did visit Oberammergau, wandered around the famous Open Air theatre, and saw the costumes worn by the players. Having visited Austria several times, it is for me, the most beautiful Country in Europe: and after a number of coach trips to local beauty spots, I think most in the party would agree with me!

It didn't take long to drive from our village in Austria to the village in Northern Italy. The Hotel was more modern, but extremely noisy! This was due to a very fast flowing mountain stream, which passed within a few yards of our bedrooms. It was just like an express train, the only difference being, there was no end to it! There was a town not far away, which was renowned for its shopping facilities and 'bargain' buys, so we really had to visit it; the ladies insisted! The undoubted highlight of the week was a day spent in the Dolomites. The morning began dull and misty; and the drivers told us not to get our hopes up. We were fortunate as the cloud lifted and the mist disappeared by mid morning, and we had a gloriously sunny day. The Dolomites are incredible rock formations of various heights and shapes, each one standing alone. As the coach drove around, we were confronted by one breathtaking vista after another. They were truly unforgettable sights. A few weeks after returning home we held a reunion, and the main question was, 'Where are we going next year?' I had already anticipated this and given it some thought. I suggested a holiday in Germany; spending one week in Hannover; which would be a good base from which to visit other places of interest: then moving up to Berlin for the second week. The group were more than happy with this, so dates were fixed and I made preliminary bookings.

On the day after the Harvest Festival in October 1990, Eddie Hayes suffered a massive heart attack and died. His wife Valerie was absolutely devastated and inconsolable. Revd. Dr. Leslie Griffiths and I conducted Eddie's Funeral service. The Church had lost a strong and dependable leader; and I had lost a stalwart friend and supporter.

It was several weeks before Valerie felt able to return to Church, but I encouraged her to continue attending Choir rehearsals. She loved singing and found it to be quite therapeutic in coming to terms with her loss. I collected her and we travelled together to Barkingside; eventually taking turns to do the driving.

I enjoyed belonging to the Choir; and even though I found it difficult to cope with singing a part rather than a solo, soon managed to learn enough to sing my part to the Choirmasters satisfaction; but I always made sure I was standing next to a tenor who was able to read the music!

The new London (Forest) Circuit, under the guiding hand of its new Superintendent; an experienced and resourceful Minister, was now in being and working hard to establish its own identity. With eight Ministers on the staff, the Churches benefited from the availability of a wide range of talents and abilities. All Ministers have a Circuit responsibility of some description, and I volunteered to carry on doing the Circuit Quarterly Preaching Plan, which I had been doing for the past year during the change over. With seventeen Churches it was a considerable and a time consuming task. I enjoyed getting to know the new Churches in the Circuit; especially those with a large proportion of black Members; whose families had originally come from the West Indies and West Africa.

In Redbridge (Ilford) there was a very active branch of the Council of Christians and Jews, (CCJ) and my colleague, the Supernumerary Minister and his wife regularly attended their meetings. As a direct result of my experiences in Israel in 1989, I wanted to find out more about the organisation and decided to accompany them. This was to be the beginning of a significant change in my faith pilgrimage, and soon led to an increased interest and involvement in inter-faith matters. Valerie, who had been brought up in an environment where there were people of other Faiths; and as a school teacher taught in schools where there were children from different ethnic backgrounds, knew more than I did. She had also been on the 1989 pilgrimage to Israel, and had decided to explore what CCJ had to offer, making her own significant and well-informed contributions to the discussions!

Loughton Methodist Church was a hive of activity. With such a large Church and Community membership, it was able to sustain a wide variety of Fellowship groups and clubs. There was something on every evening of the week, in addition to what was taking place during the day. There were the usual number of Church Committees; but I only had to 'Chair' two of them:

the Church Council, and the Pastoral Committee. Fortunately, there were enough talented lay people to 'Chair' the other Committees: which I attended when possible, and was kept up to date by receiving the 'Minutes' of the meetings.

Again, as might be expected; there was a wide range of theological emphasis manifested in the groups of the Church; each with their own agendas. As I was very definitely on the 'liberal' wing of the Church, I wasn't the sort of Minister the evangelicals would have chosen; and this sometimes led to friction between us. As in the Army, I appreciated that I was the Minister to the whole Church community; and did my best to accommodate all shades of opinion and conviction. In a way it was like driving a coach and four horses, with each one trying to go its own way! My task was to occasionally give them their head; while at the same time striving to keep them together and travelling in the same direction!

Another thing I was acutely aware of, particularly in my preaching, was the danger of sharing my conclusions with so many people who had not shared my faith pilgrimage. The life I had led, and the events I had experienced had challenged me to continually rethink my beliefs and revise my priorities. Some members of my congregation were fairly new Members of the Church; others were mature Christians whose faith had also changed over the years: then there were those who had long ago accepted a system of beliefs, dug deep defensive positions, and spent their time rationalising and justifying what they had accepted many years ago.

During my nine years at Loughton, I confirmed more than fifty new Members. At the first meeting of the Membership preparation course, I would say to them, "the Methodist Church is what might be called 'a broad Church'. We do not expect you to accept a 'package' of beliefs. You will be embarking on a journey, a pilgrimage: and as on all journeys, as you travel along, the scenery around you will change, and you will be affected by those changes. It is perfectly acceptable that you should have many questions and doubts; hurtful things will surely happen in your life; and you will need to wrestle and sometimes even agonise to discover what is acceptable truth for you. Truth is not something that can be imposed on you by others. When I encourage you to become Members of the Church, I don't expect you to leave either your brains or your critical faculties at the door!"

Many years ago, when I was a student I had been helped, as had many others, by the Commentaries on the books of the New Testament written by William Barclay. One of his comments puzzled me at the time when he wrote; "We must beware of elevating Jesus into an idol who hides God from us". Over the past thirty years I have become increasingly aware of those parts of the Church, which have done just that! There has been a growth of what a friend of mine once termed; 'the doctrine of Jesuology'. I have been at pains over the years to emphasise; from the pulpit and in discussion groups, that Jesus came to **reveal** the Father, not to **replace** Him! It has been my aim to encourage and lead people into a relationship with God; **not** to have a love affair with Jesus!

Some people will use the doctrine of The Trinity, which one of my College lecturers used to describe as 'a profound mystery'; and certain Biblical texts to justify this 'elevation' of Jesus. To embark upon this path is to attempt to cross a quagmire wearing Wellington boots: one is more likely to be swallowed up before reaching solid ground. That is of course always assuming that there is solid ground at the other end of the swamp! From my reading, study, and interpretation of the New Testament; Jesus, who was first and foremost a good Jew, would I am sure, be puzzled and dismayed by the way in which his coming amongst us has been interpreted and used.

The new Church building had now been paid for, and attention was now concentrated on the refurbishment of Wesley Hall.

In a conscious effort to give something back to the wider Church and community; both at home and overseas: events were organised to raise money, which was all given away!

Most mornings I would try to pop into the Welcome Area and have a coffee and a chat. It was a good way of getting to know a lot of people! Baptisms and Funerals required home visits, and the Church was proving to be very popular for Weddings. There were always people to be visited in the many Hospitals in the area. Most were in the 'local' Hospitals in Epping, Harlow, and Walthamstow: but others requiring more specialised treatment would be in one of the many London Hospitals. Because of the distances, a considerable amount of time was spent in travelling; either by road or by the Underground.

In 1983, one of the local Anglican Clergymen had founded an organisation known as Loughton Community Care; (soon to be renamed 'The Loughton Voluntary Care Association'). When the Clergyman moved to another Parish, I was asked to be the Chairman. The Association had more than 100 volunteers on its books, the majority from the local Churches; but a significant minority having no Church connections. The Association had an Administrator, and a small Executive Committee, which met monthly. There was a small group of dedicated 'Duty Officers' who manned the telephones and contacted volunteers until someone was found to fulfil the request. The majority of requests were for people to be transported to and from Hospital appointments. There was no charge for this service, but the 'clients' were asked to make a contribution towards the cost of the driver's petrol. Some people asked, "Why don't these people use taxis"? The answer was simple. Most of the 'clients' were elderly, some infirmed, who needed help in getting out of their homes, into the car; and someone to remain with them at the Hospital. The volunteers did a commendable job and rendered a most valuable service to the community.

It was Holiday time again and we boarded our coach outside the Church. I had booked us on an early ferry from Dover to Calais so that we could arrive at our Hotel in Hannover the same evening. The terms were as before; which meant that the coach was ours for two weeks, and we could decide our own itinerary. It was to be a trip down memory lane for me and I was quite looking forward to it! We made good time, and I decided to make a short detour and visit the Mohne Dam (the scene of the famous 'Dam Busters' raid). When we had been living in Germany, it had been an interesting place to take any relatives and visitors who came to stay with us! There was a suitable place for refreshments, and a small museum in a building at one end of the Dam. It was possible to walk along the top of the Dam; and easy for those who were old enough to remember the event or who had seen the film; to imagine the Lancaster Bombers flying through anti-aircraft fire to drop their 'bouncing bombs' which breached the Dam. In the museum, people were shocked at the thousands who were drowned when the Dam burst: and amazed at how little time it took for the Germans to repair it!

We arrived at our Hotel in the centre of Hannover in time for a late evening meal. It was a comfortable Hotel just a couple of hundred yards from the main Railway Station. The following day was spent recovering from the journey, and people were free to explore the City centre. We spent a day visiting the picturesque town of Hamlin; and I resisted the temptation to 'pop in' to the Barracks still housing the Royal Engineer Regiments I had cared for back in 1977. All the personnel would have changed anyway! The day we visited the Harz Mountains was disappointing as the hills were covered by low cloud and we were not able to enjoy the lovely scenery. However, we had lunch in the ancient town of Goslar; and visited the largest all wooden Church on he Continent in the small town of Clausthal Zellerfeld. Souvenirs were bought from a small wood carvers shop I had bought items from on previous visits.

One day we spent the morning visiting the site of the old Belsen Concentration Camp. When we departed, the group were all in a sombre mood and were very quiet until we reached the town of Walsroda and visited its famous Bird Park. It is so large it would have been easy to spend the whole day there! There were birds from all over the world, including a whole section devoted to water birds. There was a huge covered area where exotic birds could be seen in free flight; and the sunny afternoon helped us to appreciate, not only the birds, but also the lovely gardens filled with gloriously coloured flowers and shrubs. I had deliberately planned to visit the Bird Park after, and not before our visit to Belsen. As a result, everyone was in a light hearted and relaxed mood when we arrived back at our Hotel.

The journey to Berlin bore no comparison to all my previous visits! The Berlin Wall had been demolished in 1989 and Germany was reunited. There were no checkpoints. The Watchtowers, the barriers, the Russians and the East German Border Guards had all gone; and we drove along a recently re-surfaced Autobahn to Berlin. Our Hotel was about a mile from the City centre and was only able to offer bed and breakfast facilities. The Travel Company had arranged for my party to have their evening meal at a good restaurant in the City centre. Because of parking restrictions we were unable to use the coach, so it was a matter of walking, or using the U Bahn (underground). After the evening meal, which was invariably of a high standard, most people stayed to explore the City's night-life. Others, who couldn't stand the pace, and that sometimes included me, made their way back to the Hotel!

Our coach driver had a few local contacts from previous visits, and found a guide for us to visit what used to be East Berlin. We visited the Escape Museum by the site of 'Checkpoint Charlie'; and then went on into the Eastern part of the City. I couldn't believe the transformation! Not only had the Wall gone, but also the old war damaged buildings had been demolished; and there were lots of new buildings rising from what had been a wasteland. We visited many of the sites I have described earlier; and it was good to be able to wander around without feeling that we were being watched and monitored at all times! There was one very noticeable difference in the City, and that was the presence of people begging.

Since the Wall had come down, so had most of the barriers on the frontiers: and many refugees were leaving countries in Eastern Europe and heading West through Berlin in the hope of finding a better life.

Being good Methodists, I had arranged for us to visit Wesley House in Spandau, which, under the leadership of a new Warden was continuing to do sterling work in the Garrison. On the Sunday morning we drove down to RAF Gatow, and joined the Free Church congregation for Morning Worship. Our coach load really swelled their numbers, and I was surprised and grateful that they had provided a buffet lunch for us all! After lunch I couldn't resist taking the coach the couple of miles down the road to Montgomery Barracks, and look at the house we used to live in. Then, because it was a very warm afternoon, I guided the driver around the lake and through the Grunewald (Green Forest) to a spot I knew had a sandy beach. I had advised the party of this possibility, and most had come prepared for a swim! Like 1 PARA seventeen years earlier, they were amazed at the number of lakes and woodland in Berlin.

As it was six hundred miles to Calais, I had arranged for an overnight stop in Holland, so we weren't too worn out when we arrived back in Loughton. Everyone agreed that we had enjoyed a most interesting holiday. The coach driver had served us well, and we had discussed the possibility of a holiday in 1992, visiting the Rheinland and Bavaria. We would discuss this further at our holiday reunion meeting, which now featured regularly on the calendar! Several people who had not been able to join the party in 1989, expressed an interest in a Pilgrimage to the Holy Land, so I arranged to go on another short familiarisation visit to bring myself up to date on the situation there.

I continued to go regularly to the ARMS Centre for my 'dives' and did my best with my diet and exercises. Provided I didn't 'over do it' I managed quite well in fulfilling my commitments. The amount of time my wife was out dancing was increasing; as there always seemed to be something 'special' arranged, usually on Saturday evenings. Things between us were not good; and I coped by 'burying' myself in my work. The Choir also held 'social' functions every couple of months, and I went to them with Valerie.

I'm sure most people will be familiar with the verse, or the picture called, 'Footprints'. On many occasions, and they were to become more frequent; I knew that I was being picked up and carried.

The Superintendent Minister now decided he would take responsibility for the quarterly Preaching Plan; so I took on the responsibility for Circuit Home and Overseas Missions. This meant raising the profile of the work of those Departments, arranging at least one major Circuit event each year to publicise and raise money: and of course, to 'Chair' the Circuit Missions Committee!

I went to Israel for a week to determine whether the security situation warranted me taking another party in 1992. Things had so obviously changed for the worst.

Relations between Jews and Palestinians had deteriorated, and the Hotel we had stayed in by the Sea of Galilee; was now occupied by Jewish refugees from Ethiopia. I received assurances, not only from the Travel Agents, but also from many local people, that Pilgrims were not only welcomed, but would be scrupulously cared for. I decided to make a booking, and to my delight, managed to book the services of the same Israeli guide who had served us so well in 1989. I publicised the details of the Pilgrimage planned for May 1992, and seventeen people took up the offer; none had been on the previous visit. I considered this to be a pleasurable 'duty' and continued plans for a holiday in August to the Rhein Land and Bavaria.

My initial invitation to the Circuit had been for five years, later to be extended to seven; which meant that unless that were to be extended, I would be leaving in 1993. I formerly requested a two years extension, which would take me to 1995; when I planned to seek early retirement on health grounds. The Circuit were in full agreement, but to my utter amazement; most of my Church Stewards at Loughton didn't agree. It soon transpired that the Stewards had failed in their basic duty in such matters; and had made little attempt to discover the mind of the Church. For example, none of the Chairmen of the Church Committees had been consulted. I knew I had my finger 'on the pulse' of the Church, and that the vast majority wanted me to stay. A small minority of the Stewards, who were strong characters, had convinced the others that it would be in my and the Churches best interests if I left in 1993. Three years earlier, when I had been seriously considering leaving Loughton at very short notice, I had in the strictest confidence, shared my problems with two Church officials, one from the Church, and the other from the Circuit. I had deemed this to be necessary just in case my domestic situation became unbearable and I wanted to leave at very short notice. Now I felt as if that confidence had been betrayed. I had spent many years working and living with men whom I knew, would if necessary die for me and I for them. Now, amongst the wonderful people of Loughton, I found there were a very tiny minority who would 'stab me in the back'!

An eastern mystic once said that, "The trouble with Christians is that they are usually prepared to sacrifice people for principles": which is a point worth pondering. The Church is not immune from people 'playing politics', and it was with sadness that I joined the game! A senior and much respected member of the Church told me he was convinced that there was a conspiracy; and that we should fight it! We did and we won. The Circuit Meeting voted overwhelmingly for my extension. As a result of this, things changed at Loughton. At the next Annual Church Meeting, a number of changes were made in the Members serving on the Church Council; and henceforth more proposals were put to the vote, instead of decisions being reached 'by consensus': which in the past had usually meant a few strong characters getting their own way!

The Holy Land Pilgrimage followed the same route as the previous group three years earlier, with a few notable differences. On my familiarisation visit a few months earlier, we had been taken to a site deep beneath the Church of the Holy Sepulchre: one of the Guardians having been generously 'rewarded' for unlocking the gates and allowing us to descend. It was a site not open to the mass of visitors. Only a few years earlier, a charcoal drawing of a Galilean fishing boat had been discovered on one of the walls. By the boat were written the words, (and I can't remember whether they were written in Greek or Aramaic) 'Lord, we have come'. The drawing and words had been carbon dated as being about AD 146, which seemed to indicate that from earliest times, the site had been a destination for pilgrims. I encouraged our guide to find and suitably reward one of the Guardians to allow my group to see the drawing. We descended and found that the drawing had now been framed to protect it, but we were able to view it through the glass.

When we took the boat trip across the Sea of Galilee, we were informed that the water level had dropped so much that we were unable to get into Capernaum, and had to land about half a mile away and walk to the village. Israel, Jordan, and Syria, were all taking so much water from the lake and

River Jordan that not only the waters of the Sea of Galilee were being diminished, but the Dead Sea was also shrinking alarmingly. This was due to evaporation and the reduction of water coming into it from the River Jordan. As there are substantial mineral deposits around the Dead Sea, we were told that Israel was seriously looking at the possibility of piping water from the Mediterranean to compensate for this reduction. This would be an enormous and costly undertaking.

As the water level of the Sea of Galilee dropped; an ancient Galilean fishing boat was revealed; which experts estimated to be about 2,000 years old! This really was considered to be a most significant discovery; and the same care and methods used in England to raise and restore the 'Mary Rose' were used to lift the boat from the mud. It is now housed in its own small museum, completely submerged in a special mixture of chemicals designed to preserve and restore it. The entire procedure was filmed; and visitors are able to look at a video in the museum showing the entire operation.

About ten years earlier, and only a few miles away at the northern end of the lake, a farmer uncovered a beautiful mosaic depicting a basket of bread and two fishes. This is now on display in a little Chapel, which many believe to be the site of 'The Feeding of the five thousand'.

A couple of months later, I set off with a coach load of holidaymakers for our trip to the Rheinland and Bavaria. We spent the first week at a Hotel on the east bank of the river, about an hours drive south of Koblenz, where the rivers Rhein and Mosel converge. Sleeping was rather difficult, as the Germans move much their freight by rail during the night; and the railway line was only a few yards from our Hotel! We spent a few days exploring the glories of the area with its many Castles, and were fortunate that our visit coincided with a spectacular event known as 'The Rhein in Flames'. We went north by coach and found a suitable viewing place just south of Koblenz.

As darkness fell we looked southwards and waited for the huge fleet of small ships, boats and barges. As they appeared we could see that each one was covered with lights; and as they passed there were firework displays from the many already floodlit Castles. More coloured floodlights, mounted on the riverside, were switched on as they passed; adding to the blaze of light and colour; which did indeed give the appearance of he river being in flames! It really was a magnificent sight and an unforgettable experience.

At the end of the week we journeyed south to Bad Tolz in Bavaria where excellent accommodation awaited us. The lovely little town was a health spa, and there was some hilarity in the party when one of the ladies decided to have a mud bath! There was an indoor swimming pool next door, and one day as we were getting changed into our swimming costumes; the voices of a man and a woman were heard coming from one of the cubicles. The voices and noises were such as to cause a few eyebrows to be raised as people wondered what was going on in the cubicle! We were surprised and a little ashamed when the cubicle door opened, and a woman emerged escorting a man who had only one leg. She had obviously been helping him to get changed; but our suspicious little minds had been going along another track!

The beauties of Bavaria are well known, and as we explored the area we understood the reasons why. There is so much impressive scenery around almost every bend in the road; and the floral decorations adorning every village added to our enjoyment and sense of wonder. We returned home with many happy memories and hundreds of photographs!

PART IV - LIFTED UP

It was about this time I accepted, that even after three stressful years and many hours of talking together, my wife and I had no future. I felt trapped in a situation I could do nothing about, so I ceased to care. It's difficult to contemplate a future with someone whom you know prefers to be with someone else. This painful realisation actually helped me, as in ceasing to care, it is hard to be hurt any more. I felt entirely alone as I felt I had lost not only the wife I had loved dearly for so many years, but also the person who I thought of as my best friend. There was also the feeling that everything I thought we had over the years had been devalued. The future seemed bleak indeed, and I lived one day at a time. The changes I was experiencing were noticed by Valerie during our weekly trips to the Choir, and over the several months that followed, I very gradually shared with her all that had happened over the past few years. This helped me and I was confident that what I had told her would go no further.

In November 1992 I went up to Newcastle-u-Lyme to spend a week with my father. Even though he had visited us in Loughton about twice a year, I had felt unable to leave home to spend time with him. In fact, the last time we had visited Newcastle was in October 1991 for my sisters Silver Wedding Anniversary. When I told Valerie I wouldn't be going to Choir that week, she asked for my father's address and while I was there I received a letter from her in which she wrote things she had been unable to tell me to my face. She felt she was falling in love with me. I had also been feeling a growing affection for her, but felt unable to say anything to her because I was still married; I was her Minister: and I was suffering from a degenerative disease. I read her letter many times; and that night after my father had gone to bed, I telephoned her. Being uncertain of my reaction to her letter, she was at first reluctant to speak to me. I said to her quite simply and directly: "Valerie, I think **I** am falling in love with **you**, and it scares the hell out of me"!

The implications were frightening, and the next time we met, we just hugged each other, and shed a few tears. The next couple of months were very busy and we only had opportunities to talk as we went to and from Choir rehearsals. At the end of February 1993 I had organised a special Service to mark the tenth anniversary of the founding of Loughton Voluntary Care Association, with the Guest Preacher being the Vicar who had founded it. An ad hoc Choir had been formed to sing at this Service, and Valerie and I were part of it. As we were milling around before the Service, my wife said to me, "Does Valerie know about our problems"? I answered simply, "Yes, she does". "Why"? My wife demanded. I said, "Well, when you get close to someone, you share things". "How close", my wife asked. "Close enough", I replied. "Are you having an affair"? She asked. "No", I replied, as whilst we were clearly in love, we certainly were **not** having an affair.

The day after that Service, I commenced a Three Months Sabbatical, which released me from all Church duties and responsibilities. My intention was to spend time exploring inter-faith matters, and I did manage to spend a lot of time doing just that. The first week however, was spent at The Chelmsford Diocesan Retreat House at Pleshy, for the Methodist District Ministers Annual Retreat. There was a certain amount of free time, and one night I telephoned Valerie, who was teaching in Bethnal Green at the time; and told her that I had the following afternoon free. She managed to reorganise her commitments, and we met in a car park in Ongar. We spent the entire afternoon sitting in a café, drinking endless cups of tea, and we talked, and talked, and talked. She and my wife had met and had talked together for a long time. Valerie had told her, and me, that if there was any possibility of us 'patching up' our marriage; she would drop out of the picture altogether, and move away from the area. She said to her; " All you have to do is tell me that you still love Peter, and I will go away". My wife responded saying that we had a long history, and that she was fond of me! She was determined to carry on as before, and I still couldn't at that time bring myself to initiate divorce proceedings. The implications of going along that road were too distressing to contemplate, so we carried on as we were; living under the same roof, but leading separate lives. When my wife went dancing, Valerie and I would drive out into the country, well away from Loughton for a meal; or if it was a Saturday, go to a Theatre or Concert outside the area.

I had promised my father that I would take him to Scarborough for a few days, so he could take a trip down 'memory lane': he had spent some time there at the beginning of the War before being sent overseas. Just before we left my brother in law was admitted to Hospital. He had been suffering pains in various parts of his body for some time; now he was admitted for investigation. On our second night in Scarborough, my sister Joyce 'phoned to say that her husband Eric, was in so much pain, he had been fitted with a morphine pump! We decided to return to Newcastle the next day. There was a slight problem in that Joyce, unbeknown to my father, had arranged for someone to redecorate his flat while we were away! This was to be a surprise, so my father and I booked into a local Hotel until the work was finished. After several more worrying days, Eric was moved to a neighbouring Hospital, and was diagnosed with Multiple Myeloma, which was gradually destroying his bones. He began to have regular chemotherapy and radiology

As part of my Sabbatical I had arranged to attend a Conference in Germany; which was being held in a village called Bendorf, not far from Koblenz. The Conference had been held annually for about twenty years, and was attended by Jews, Christians, and Muslims. I had first heard of the Conference at a CCJ meeting. The British contingent was organised by the Leo Beck Jewish Rabbinical Training College in North London and I arranged to travel to Germany with them. I met up with them at Heathrow Airport. As I went up the escalator, carrying my suitcase from the Underground platform to the Departure Lounge, I lost my balance and fell backwards as the escalator continued its ascent. Fortunately for me, there were a couple of men behind who caught me and helped me safely to the top. Apart from feeling a bit foolish, I was unhurt but rather shaken.

The experience knocked my confidence, and forced me to rethink some of the things I'd planned for my Sabbatical; such as making a trip on my own to Israel!

The theme of the Conference in 1993 was; "Are We Prisoners Of Our History"? There were three lectures on this subject; one from a representative of each of the Faiths attending the Conference. Many had attended previous Conferences and there were joyous reunions! The Principal of the Leo Beck College gave the opening address, and spoke to us about how the week would be organised. Problems experienced at previous Conferences had now been sorted out; one of the main issues being Jewish and Muslim dietary requirements. He smiled as he said, "It's good to have the Christians here, because they will eat anything"! There were about 150 people present; about half being German Theological students. During the week, we would pray together; morning devotions being taken in turn by members of all three Faiths; eat together, socialise, and study together. Friday was the Muslim Holy Day, and everyone attended prayers. An Imam from South Africa preached on the subject of 'Women's Liberation'!

There was also a most moving address from an Imam from Sarajevo, who told us that thousands of Muslims were being massacred and Mosques destroyed by the Serbs. He begged us to tell people about this when we returned home. Eventually of course, the United Nations sent forces into Bosnia, but they were largely ineffectual. Even now, in 2003, the perpetrators of the so-called, 'ethnic cleansing' are still being sought and brought to justice. Friday evening saw the start of the Jewish Sabbath, which was a joyful occasion. The end of the Sabbath on Saturday evening was followed by a most enjoyable social event with most people taking an active part as they made their own individual or group contributions to the evening's entertainment. The Christian Service on Sunday was quiet and subdued by comparison!

We were divided into groups of about a dozen, and met daily. There was no agenda and attendance was not compulsory! There were Hebrew and German speaking members in each group; so there were no problems regarding people's comments being translated. It was a little awkward at first, but as we gradually got to know each other, and appreciate each other's personal history, the group became more close and trusting: and attending the group meetings became a priority. Some, notably the Jewish members had tragic stories to tell. One middle aged Jewish man, now living in England, had lost most of his family in the Holocaust, and was visiting Germany for the first time. He was actually quite nervous about attending the Conference. He had travelled by car, and had his return journey carefully planned. It was good to see him gradually relax, and talk freely with the Germans in the group. An elderly Jewish man who had travelled from Israel; really gave us something to think about when we were discussing the Crucifixion of Jesus, and the Cross as the symbol of Christianity. He said, "I'll tell you what the Cross means to us: it is a sign which reminds us of all the pain and suffering inflicted on Jews by Christians over the past two thousand years"!

I later obtained a Video from CCJ entitled. 'Shadow on the Cross'; which had originally been a program shown on ITV Channel 4: and which was about the Christian roots of anti-Semitism. I later showed the video to many Christian groups, most of whom had been completely unaware of the part played by certain interpretations of Scripture: and the roles played by some prominent Church leaders; for example, Martin Luther.

One evening I stayed up very late in one of the village Gasthouses, in the company of a German Roman Catholic Priest, a young man training to be a Rabbi, and the author and ex Roman Catholic nun Karen Armstrong. We talked frankly about many things; and it was a memorable evening. There were a number of optional trips available, and I joined a party for an afternoon in Koblenz. We visited the site of the old Synagogue, which is now a museum/memorial. All the Jews in Koblenz had died in the Holocaust, and there were many pictures of what had been a thriving congregation. There was also a Reception Centre/Social Club for Muslims who came to live and work in Germany. That Centre provided invaluable support and guidance for many Muslims seeking a new life in Germany.

On the aircraft going back to England, I sat next to one of the Trainee Rabbis and thought deeply about what had been for me, what I can only describe as 'a mind blowing experience'! I was forced to concede that Jesus Christ was honoured and revered by the Jews and Muslims I had met, but most definitely not essential! They most certainly had a real love for and relationship with God; which was not dependant on Jesus. After fifty years in the Church, it took me a while to get my head around that. After clearing customs at Heathrow, my Jewish companion was met by his wife, who had driven from Newbury Park to collect him. They very kindly offered to make a detour and drop me off at home.

One of the corner stones of my conviction that inter-faith work is vital comes from the writings of Hans Kung, a Professor of Theology at Tubingen

University in Germany. He had been an advisor at the 2nd Vatican Council called by Pope John XXIII. He wrote:

'No peace among the nations, without peace among the religions.

No peace among the religions, without dialogue between the religions.

No dialogue between the religions, without investigation of the foundations of the religions.'

I visited the Mosque in Regents Park, and attended the Orthodox Synagogue in Loughton. I had to knock on the door to gain admission to the Synagogue: and was saddened that the Jews in my home community felt it necessary to take such precautions. I continued to make regular visits to see my father and help to support my sister. Eric was undergoing lots of treatment, and the future was very uncertain. I kept in touch with Valerie by telephone, and saw her whenever possible. Like me, she was tired of us having to sneak around like a pair of criminals, especially as neither of us had done anything wrong! She was very unsettled, and applied for a job at a boarding School in South Africa.

The Headmaster of the School came to London to interview the applicants, and Valerie was offered the job. She told me her feelings for me hadn't changed; and in any case she had two sons at University and an elderly mother living in Brentwood. She therefore planned to come home at the end of each term, but said she wouldn't accept the position without my agreement. With a heavy heart I felt I had no alternative but to encourage her to go. As the time for her departure drew near I became quite depressed and asked her not to go. She withdrew from the post, having not yet signed the contract, and we carried on as before.

The following year, 1994, part of the School in Bethnal Green was closing, and Valerie had to look for another job. She successfully applied for a post as IT Coordinator at a school in Petersfield, Hampshire. The post also required her to take on the role of Housemistress, which meant she was required to live in a flat at the School from Monday to Friday, and be on duty one weekend each month. She was happy with this arrangement, and planned to travel back to Loughton on Friday afternoons and go to Choir practice as usual.

The long period of uncertainty regarding our future together, had taken its toll. Just before she departed for Petersfield, she said to me, "I can't go on like this any more. I don't want you to write to me or telephone me". With a very heavy heart I agreed. This lasted for two weeks. The first weekend she came home, I went to her house to collect her for Choir practise; and we just fell into each other's arms in tears. The time had come when I had to 'grasp the nettle'; stop worrying about the Church and other people, and take decisive action: something I should have done years earlier.

My relationship with Valerie was very therapeutic. I was in many ways, a shattered man. Valerie and I spent many, many hours talking; and gradually I began to recover my sense of self worth and self esteem. She gave me renewed confidence in myself, built me up again, and encouraged me to think positively about the future. Some lines of a hymn by William Cowper, which we would later sing at our wedding, now come to mind.

"When comforts are declining,

He grants the soul again

A season of clear shining,

To cheer it after rain."

Hymns & Psalms No 571

My wife and I had a long talk about our futures, and we agreed to a divorce. I promised to find her somewhere to live, and give her financial support. I tried to contact Valerie but she was unavailable, so I left a message with her youngest son, who was still living at home, to tell her when she phoned him, that everything was going to be all right! On the following Saturday I drove down to Petersfield to see her; we now had a lot of things to sort out!

In early October 1994, I visited a Solicitor, who did work for the Methodist District. There was no property or young children to be considered, and as the divorce would not be contested, he told me I would be able to handle the matter myself. I went to the County Court in Romford and collected the necessary forms. The Staff there were most helpful. My wife signed the forms and I returned them to the Court.

The Chairman of the District had an office not far from Liverpool Street Station and we arranged to meet in a café there for lunch. I explained the situation fully to him and he promised me his full support. He pressed me to make a decision regarding my retirement, as time was running out to find appointments for September 1995. Now that the decision had been taken, I felt a great load had been lifted from my shoulders; and that I had been given a new lease of life! I believed I could take on one more appointment before I retired. My condition was slowly deteriorating, but was manageable, so I began looking through the list of available appointments. Valerie had settled down very well at Churchers College; and if possible, wished to stay there. I looked long and hard for an appointment within thirty miles of Petersfield, but was unable to find one. No one in the Church at Loughton had any idea what was happening, even though Valerie and I were now engaged. The Divorce papers had been submitted to the County Court, and I was informed that the Decree Nisi would be issued at the beginning of January, with the Decree Absolute following six weeks later. It was time for Valerie to meet my family in Newcastle: she had already met my children in Loughton and Southend. We came up for a weekend in November, Valerie coming directly from Petersfield. We chatted together with my father over tea, and then I excused myself to visit the toilet. While I was out of the room, my father's manner changed completely. He looked steadily into Valerie's eyes, and said in all seriousness: "I have only one question to ask you: do you love my son?" Valerie assured him that she truly did love me, and nothing more was said!

At the beginning of December I was still looking for an appointment. As I browsed through the 'Yellow Book' of vacancies, I noticed that there was a vacancy in my home-town Circuit of Newcastle-under-Lyme. I knew that the Superintendent Minister, someone I had met several times, was moving in 1995; but there was no mention of the Superintendent's job in the 'Yellow Book'. I telephoned him and asked about it. He said, "The Circuit has decided that the Superintendent will be based in another part of the Circuit from 1995". I said, "In that case, I'm interested in the job"! I had discussed this with Valerie; and even though she was disappointed that there was nothing available anywhere near Petersfield, she was happy about the prospect of moving to Newcastle if that could be arranged. Within a few days I received a call from the Senior Circuit Steward inviting me to attend for interviews the following week. I arranged to stay with my father, who was absolutely delighted at the possibility of me returning to Newcastle, as was my sister. I told my father that my wife and I were getting divorced; and he didn't seem at all surprised. When I asked him why he wasn't surprised, he smiled knowingly and said, "The wise old owl sat in the oak; the more heard the less he spoke; the less he spoke the more he heard: I try to be like that wise old bird".

It had been arranged that I should visit the three Churches that would be my pastoral responsibility, and meet the Church Stewards. Before that I arranged to see the Superintendent. I informed him that I was in the process of getting divorced and planned to remarry in July 1995. I explained the circumstances to him and suggested he check them with my District Chairman if he so wished. I said, "If the Circuit decide not to invite me, there will be no need for anything to be said; but if they do want to invite me, you must tell them about the situation". I had already sent my CV to the Circuit so they already knew about my history, and my MS.

I visited the three Churches and was interviewed by the Stewards. I had lunch with the Circuit Staff (four Ministers), which included the Minister who would be the Superintendent from the following September. In the afternoon I had tea with the Superintendent and all the Stewards; and answered more questions before leaving them to their deliberations. I returned to my father's flat, and within half an hour received a 'phone call offering me the post! That evening I phoned Valerie, my District Chairman, and the Office at Westminster where the 'Yellow Book' was compiled, informing them that the vacancy at Newcastle had been filled. My father and sister were overjoyed! There were now many things to be done, and not a lot of time to do them.

I arranged to meet the Chairman again at the café in Liverpool Street station, this time taking Valerie with me. The first thing he said when I had brought him up to date on the situation, was that he wanted to officiate at our Wedding! We looked at possible dates and decided on 12th July. We then discussed where we should get married. He said, "Why don't you get married at Wesley's Chapel in London; I'll fix it". We thought that would be ideal, and he arranged it with the resident Minister! One of the many things that worried me was that while the people in Newcastle knew what was happening; the people at Loughton didn't; and my wife certainly wasn't going to say anything. All they knew was that I'd accepted an appointment in Newcastle. The Chairman advised me not to worry about that for the time being. The Headmaster at Churchers College wasn't at all happy about losing Valerie so soon, as she had already made an impact: but when he had been informed about the situation he was quite supportive, advertised for a replacement and the post was soon filled. Valerie also had to find a new post in or around the Newcastle area. We looked through The Times Educational Supplement every week for the next six months without finding anything suitable. It was proving to be more difficult than we had imagined.

Valerie wanted to sell her house in Loughton and buy a suitable property in Newcastle. Even though we would initially live in the Manse, we had to consider where we would live when I retired. Valerie's brother was living in Bristol and frequently visited his mother, but it was decided that it would be better if she moved up to Newcastle with us. We visited Newcastle several times before we found what we were looking for. A new development consisting of only nineteen homes was being built in a cul-de-sac just a few minutes walk from a Supermarket, and ten minutes from Newcastle town centre.

There were several types of houses on the site; none of them yet competed. All had four bedrooms and a double garage. We were advised by the sales office to visit a site about ten miles away where the same design of homes had been completed. We did just that and decided on the type of house we wanted. There were only two of that design being built in Newcastle, and one of those had already been reserved. Valerie immediately paid a deposit to secure the other one! The Estate Agents handling the sales weren't very pleased when they discovered that Valerie had a house to sell in Essex, and tried to terminate the agreement. (We suspected that the house had already been unofficially 'promised' to someone else) However, Valerie had paid the deposit, had a receipt, threatened the Company with legal action, and against all the odds, managed to sell her house in within two weeks!

Revd Dr. Leslie Griffiths, was an old friend of Valerie's, and was that year, President of the Methodist Conference. Valerie wanted to see him and explain the situation. In the midst of a very crowded schedule, he made time to meet her for lunch in London. He and his wife were invited to the Wedding, and happily they were able to attend. His mother-in-law was, incidentally, a Member at the Newcastle Church, where his wife Margaret came from. Leslie also knew the history of my problems at Loughton.

The divorce Absolute Decree came through on 17th February 1995. It brought to an end the worst six years of my life; and medical research has now shown what I had long suspected. The stress of those years greatly exacerbated my condition, and accelerated my deterioration. In other words, I wouldn't be as disabled as I am if I had taken decisive action six years earlier! I liken the situation to that of a ship, which, after sailing the oceans for more than 30 years, and weathering the storms; hits and gets stuck on the rocks. All attempts to pull it off the rocks and re-float it fail. After being battered mercilessly by winds and waves over a long period of time; it finally breaks up and sinks.

My ex-wife and I continued to live in the Manse until alternative accommodation could be found for her. Simon, now 28, and Karena, now 24, were still living at home and now set about finding somewhere else to live.

I attended the District Minister's Retreat at Pleshy; and while I was there, drafted out a Statement to give to the Churches in Loughton and Debden, and the Circuit. I discussed it with the Chairman, and he advised me to say nothing at this stage about my relationship with Valerie and our forthcoming marriage. His advice was simply, 'one thing at a time'. The Statement contained little detail; just the fact that we had been growing apart for some time, and now wanted different things in life. We were parting on amicable terms and hoped to remain friends. The Divorce proceedings had been completed without the Church being involved in any way. A couple of weeks before Easter, I gave a copy of the Statement, which we had both signed, to all the Church Stewards, including those at Trinity, Debden; the Secretary of the Church Council, a few close friends, and the Church Administrator; asking them to make the contents widely known around the Church.

The vast majority of people, even though they were shocked and surprised; were very sympathetic and most supportive. There were some who were not at all surprised!

Many questions were being asked; and it wasn't long before rumours of my forthcoming marriage to Valerie began to circulate: with some people adding two and two together and making five! The Senior Steward asked me to put out another Statement, which I did immediately. This Statement made it clear that my marriage had been 'on the rocks' before Eddie Hayes had died;

and that Valerie was in no way involved in the break up of my marriage. It added that the Newcastle Circuit were fully aware of the situation, and waiting to welcome us. Even so, there were a few people, including some we thought we could count on, who were unable to accept the situation; and distanced themselves from us. I know it was only to be expected, but it was still very hurtful, especially as they didn't know all the facts. After all, given the time we had spent amongst them, was it so unreasonable to expect that we should be given the benefit of the doubt?

My eldest daughter Vivien, and her family were living in Southend-on-Sea; as was one of my ex-wife's dancing partners. Valerie, my ex-wife and I, looked around the area; and eventually found a two bedroom flat in Leigh-on-Sea giving her a few months to decorate and furnish it to her own liking before moving in.

The people who had bought Valerie's house in Loughton were in a hurry to take possession, and we had a week to move out! Fortunately it was half term and we were able to move that week. Unfortunately, the house we had bought in Newcastle wasn't completed, and everything had to go into store for a while. Another problem was finding a removal firm to move us at such short notice. Eventually I found a small firm in Newcastle, and they turned up at 7.a.m. one morning with a small van! Seeing the stricken look on my face the foreman assured me that there was another larger van on the way. It took until mid afternoon to load up the vans, leaving just enough room to collect items I was taking from the Manse. There wasn't a lot left as I had encouraged my ex-wife to take all she needed to furnish her flat. Simon and Karena had taken other items of furniture. The foreman knew what he was about, but the rest of the men he brought with him were obviously just casual labourers and had little idea about packing! A pile of post and instructions regarding for example the heating system in the house, were packed into a crate and had to be retrieved from the warehouse a couple of days later. When everything came out of storage a couple of months later, we found that raw onions had been packed in another crate!

Valerie still hadn't been able to find a job in the area for September; so she removed a couple of pages from the local telephone directory; and sent her CV with a covering latter to more than thirty schools in the area. She received about a dozen replies; two of them being definite possibilities. On a subsequent visit, Valerie was interviewed by the two Head Teachers; and offered part time employment. This meant she would be working two days a week at each school.

We had been informed that it was difficult for schoolteachers from outside the area to find employment in the County. The advice was to take anything to get 'your feet under the table', and then look around.

One Sunday morning in June, after the Morning Service at Loughton, there was a formal 'Farewell' lunch in Wesley Hall. The Senior Steward had arranged it so that she sat in the middle of a large table, with my ex-wife and I sitting at either end! The hall was packed; there were speeches, presentations, and a few tears. Valerie was on duty at Petersfield that weekend so was not present; nor was she even mentioned. We were both saddened by this, as she had been at Loughton much longer then I; and had worked with the Boys' Brigade, the Drama Group, been a regular member of the 'Tuesday Group' and Chaired the Property Committee. A similar 'Farewell', was held at Trinity Church, Debden. It was not possible for either my ex-wife or Valerie to be present, but Valerie was at least mentioned!

Valerie was now 'homeless', and spent the weekends she was able to come to Loughton in local Hotels. On the weekends she was on duty, I went to Petersfield. The flat in Leigh-on-Sea was now ready for occupation; and I arranged for my ex-wife's furniture etc. to be moved. The new house in New-castle was finished and we ordered new carpets from a local Company. As we would not be occupying the Manse until mid August, we arranged for a lim-ited amount to be brought out of storage. Valerie ordered new curtains from a shop in Petersfield. Now the Manse at Loughton was virtually empty, I had arranged to stay and sleep at the home of one of my Ministerial colleagues.

My last Sunday at the Church was on 2nd July. The past nine years had been eventful in so many ways; in my life and the life of the Church. It had mostly been as I had originally intended: a period of consolidation following the demolition of the old Church and the building of the new one. We had shared and accomplished many things together. I had nurtured new life in the Church, joined many couples together in matrimony; and conducted the funerals of many who had been not just members of the Church, but also good friends. Such is the lot and the privilege of being a Minister; to share in the joys and sorrows of his people. It was sad to be leaving so many people who had become my friends.

Simon and Karena had rented a flat together in Loughton until they could decide what they wanted to do. When my ex-wife and I were divorced, it wasn't just a partnership of thirty six years that was broken; the home we had spent all those years building up was gone, and the family were broken up and scattered. I was so looking forward to marrying Valerie in ten days time, and moving up to Newcastle to be with the rest of my family and take on the challenges of a new job. So, I was a bit mixed up inside!

Wednesday 5th July was my last night in Loughton. It was also Simon's birthday, so we went to one of the local pubs and had a couple of beers to-gether. I would be seeing him the following week, as he was to be the Best Man at our Wedding. The following morning I loaded into a hired Transit Van, the few things that remained in the Manse, handed in all my keys to the Church Office and set off for Petersfield. I knew my ex-wife would be coming back to the Manse, like a good Army wife to make sure everything was clean and tidy for the incoming Minister and his family. I left a simple card for her to find saying: 'Thank you for thirty good years, thank you for my children. Take care'.

When I arrived at Petersfield, we loaded the contents of Valerie's flat into the Transit. That evening there was a 'farewell' Dinner for Valerie and other members of Staff who were leaving. In response to the tributes she received for her contribution to the College, Valerie gave an excellent speech laced with humour. At 8.00a.m.the following morning, another van arrived with the curtains that Valerie had ordered for the new house. They just managed to fit on top of everything else in the van! I drove to Newcastle, and my sister and one of her neighbours helped me to unload the van. I spent the night with my father, and set off early the next morning to take the van back to Woodford. A friend with whom Valerie had left dozens of houseplants to be looked after, collected me and returned me to my car in Loughton. I drove back to Petersfield to collect Valerie and the rest of her belongings, before we both drove back to a Hotel near Loughton to spend Friday evening.

On the Saturday morning Valerie had an appointment with her hairdresser in preparation for the Wedding; and I had arranged to go to Wathamstow for my hyperbaric oxygen treatment. Unfortunately my car wouldn't start and I had to send for the AA! A new dynamo was needed so I had to wait while a new one was fetched and fitted. Valerie had her hair done, but I missed my appointment. We drove up to Newcastle and arranged to spend a couple of nights in a Hotel while we sorted a few things out in the house. We had arranged for some pine beds to be delivered, which had to be assembled, and for wooden battens to be fixed above all the windows so we could hang all the curtains. After our Wedding, we had arranged a fortnights Honeymoon in Austria, and Valerie's youngest son, William, who would be home from Glasgow University, would be living in the house while we were away. Valerie's eldest son, Matthew, was studying Medicine at Leeds University; and he would be working during the summer vacation.

Having done all we could in the time available, we set off on the Tuesday morning to drive to a Hotel near Gatwick, which had been recommended by a friend. On the way we had to call at Blythe Bridge High School (about ten miles away) for Valerie to sign some forms regarding her employment there in September. The Hotel near Gatwick was excellent; one of the bonus points being that we could leave our car there for the two weeks we would be away! To avoid the hassle of driving in and out of London, I booked a taxi to take us from Gatwick to Wesley's Chapel. All went well on the Wednesday morning until we crossed the Thames and ran into road works and traffic diversions!

The taxi driver didn't know his way around London as well as I'd antici-pated and got lost. Fortunately Valerie did know her way around London: and using the A to Z road map, directed the driver around the diversions. We arrived at Wesley's Chapel just twenty minutes before the Ceremony!

It had been our intention that just family members and a few close friends attend the Ceremony; but others had insisted on coming, so there was a goodly number in Church, and it was good to see them. Valerie's two sons, her mother, her brother and his partner, and an aunt were there; as were my three children and three grandchildren; together with my father and sister. My son Simon was Best Man. The Chairman of the District, and the Minister of Wesley's Chapel conducted the Ceremony; and the Organist was my Supernumerary colleague from Woodford. Valerie and I walked down the aisle together. I was determined not to use a walking stick, so we held hands instead! We had rehearsed the Legal Declarations and the Vows; so did not need to repeat them after the Minister. After a joyous and memorable Service, we went to an up-stairs room for a Buffet Reception. Photographs were taken by a professional photographer from the Church at Loughton: and we had a lovely Wedding Cake which had been made for us as a Wedding present by one of the ladies from Trinity Church, Debden.

The taxi took us back to the Hotel at Gatwick. As we had already eaten, we ordered a snack in our room, which turned out to be a huge Beefburger! This we washed down with an excellent bottle of Champagne, which had been bought for us by Matthew and William. Well: we were celebrating! We were still up the following morning in good time to catch our 7.00 am flight to Salzburg. We spent our Honeymoon at the White Horse Inn in St. Wolfgang. The Hotel is located on the edge of a beautiful lake; and the views across the lake to the surrounding mountains were stunning. The table at which we ate our meals was by the window, so in addition to the excellent food, we were able to enjoy the marvellous scenery. We swam in the lake, sunbathed on the terrace, and were served drinks and snacks from the lakeside bar. Our room was most comfortable but noisy! It was located above an alleyway, which led from the town centre; and late night revellers on their way back to their Hotels kept us awake until after midnight. Then we were woken up at 4.00am by the noise of workmen emptying bins, collecting bottles; and generally tidying up after the previous evening's festivities!

We visited Salzburg one evening for a Mozart Concert, performed mainly by students. One day we took a coach trip just over the border into Bavaria and visited the 'Eagle's Nest', which was Adolf Hitler's favourite retreat in the area. To reach the summit it was necessary to change coaches at the foot of the mountain, and use one fitted with especially low gears. Leaving the coach a little way below the summit, we walked through a short tunnel and entered a specially designed lift. The lift was able to accommodate a large number of people; and the walls were covered with mirrors, making it seem even bigger! It was still powered by a very quiet submarine engine, with another in reserve in case of a breakdown. Apparently, Hitler didn't like lifts and every effort had been made to help him feel secure. Valerie appreciated all that had been done, as she doesn't like lifts either!

Looking around the castle, which is now largely a museum, I couldn't help but be reminded of the film 'Where Eagles Dare', particularly the large fireplace. Instead of taking the lift down to the coach park, Valerie thought it would be good for me to walk down a steep and uneven path. Even with the aid of a walking stick, it was a bit precarious and I was relieved when we reached the bottom; but glad that I had been 'encouraged' to do it. Many people with MS sometimes need a little loving persuasion to do things!

We also took a coach trip to Austria's highest mountain, the Grossglockner. The dozens of hairpin bends on the way up were a real test of our driver's skill! The building of the road up the mountain had been achieved at some human cost; and we passed a Memorial Chapel built to commemorate the workmen who had lost their lives in the building of the road. Walking up the last two hundred yards from the coach park to the Hotel/Café at the top, we saw several marmots, which are large rodents of the squirrel family. They tend to be shy creatures and we were informed we were lucky to see them. After having a meal and looking at a glacier, we ended up like most visitors, in the souvenir shop. It didn't take Valerie long to decide what she wanted for a souvenir: and that was a lovely furry marmot. We named it Zigi, and he became coveted by holidaymakers all the way back to England!

During our second week and at my suggestion, we hired a car for a few days and drove into Germany to visit Bayreuth; famous for it's large Concert Hall dedicated to the performance of Wagnerian Operas. Valerie is a great lover of the music of Richard Wagner, and possesses considerable knowledge of his work. We visited his home/museum, but were only able to walk around the outside of the great Opera House as rehearsals were taking place inside in preparation for the annual Festival. Even so there were still many visitors, and a number of music stalls outside. Valerie was delighted to be able to purchase a CD of the opera 'Tristan and Isolde', performed by some of the most accomplished Wagnerian opera singers. The last few days of a wonderful Honeymoon passed all too quickly and we were back in Gatwick. We stayed the night at the Hotel where our car had been secured; then headed north to begin our new life together.

PART V - FULL CIRCLE

BACK TO NEWCASTLE-UNDER-LYME AUGUST 1995 - ?

There were still a few weeks before I was due to be inducted as the Minister at Newcastle; but there were lots of things to be sorted out in the new house; particularly the garden, which the builders had left looking like a tip! We planned to move into my official residence, the Manse: which was about a mile away in the middle of August. Before then we had to make another trip to Loughton to collect all Valerie's plants which had been looked after by a friend: and her dog, a long legged Beagle called Snoopy who had been left with another friend. Snoopy was actually William's dog; but since he had been at University, Snoopy had become Mum's responsibility! I got on well with Snoopy: he only ever bit me once; and that was my own fault!

The size and quantity of Valerie's plant collection was such as to necessitate the hiring of a high Transit van. Snoopy didn't take up much room! Valerie's brother David had arranged to sort out their mother's house in Brentwood, dispose of all she didn't want to keep; and bring her and her belongings up to Newcastle in September. She had her own little car, a three wheeled Reliant; known within the family as 'The Plastic Pig'. She had graduated to that from a motorbike! Her first name was Barbara; but she preferred to be known by her second name, which was Joan. This went back to when she was much younger, and there were others in the family with the same name. She was quite active, but a little hard of hearing.

The Sunday after we arrived back in Newcastle, Valerie and I decided to go to Church. As I hadn't yet been officially inducted, convention dictated I should not attend the Newcastle Churches, so I decided we should go to Bradwell. I knew many of the people there, and it was good to see them again. Some of them had played a significant part in my teenage development! I was particularly pleased to see Mrs Cumberbatch (Cumby), who had been a great help to me as I was growing up. We had kept in touch over the years, and she was now over 90 years of age. The Local Preacher appointed to conduct the Service was someone I had known for about forty years. As the Service proceeded, it was as though I was in a time warp. The Preacher was saying exactly the same things in exactly the same way as when we trained together in the 1950s! There was no evidence of any change, growth, or development in the Preacher's theology; and I found that quite disturbing. I was soon to discover that in the North Staffordshire area, this was by no means uncommon. It reminded me of the ultra conservatism of the Southern States of the USA; but thankfully not as extreme!

In the middle of August we moved into the Manse and had the rest of our furniture moved out of storage. The Manse was a large old property, which had previously been a Doctors house and Surgery. The Circuit had recently laid a number of new carpets, redecorated, and provided new curtains for several of the many rooms. It was a lovely house but constantly needed structural repairs. Within weeks of our arrival, major work had to be carried out in the downstairs toilet/cloakroom due to a collapsed drain.

Many of the widow frames had been painted over so many times we were unable to open them! Some of the frames needed replacing altogether as the wood had perished. To adequately repair all these things would take a lot of money; which the Circuit didn't have, and the problems with the windows were never sorted out. Parts of the roof were regularly in need of urgent attention, and that **had** to be a priority. I think I made a major contribution to the problem by persuading he Circuit to sell it four years later when we moved out, and buy a new Manse for my successor!

The Welcome/Induction Service; was conducted by the Chairman of the Chester & Stoke-on-Trent District. It was a Circuit occasion as one of the other three Ministers in the Circuit was taking over as Superintendent; so the Church was packed! My father and sister were present and my father was visibly moved by having his son; not only back in Newcastle after so many years, but also as the local Minister. Furthermore, not only the Minister at Newcastle, but of the Higherland Chapel where we had both been brought up; and I had been Baptised. I also had pastoral oversight of a smaller Church at Cross Heath, about a mile north of the town.

After the Service there were refreshments in the large hall upstairs when we were able to meet many people from my three Churches; and folk from the rest of the Circuit, which had twelve Churches. As we filed along the tables collecting our refreshments, a lady pouring cups of tea said to me: "Weren't you in 'Guys and Dolls'?" I said, "Good heavens, you've got a good memory; that was thirty years ago"! Soon we were exchanging information about people and events from that period. As usual on such occasions, we were a little bemused by the number of people we met; and knew it would take some time to remember not just their names, but the Churches to which they belonged. It was a real pleasure to meet those who had been kind and thoughtful enough to send us greetings on our Wedding day; and to offer us such a warm and sincere welcome to the Church. For the next few weeks I walked around the town with a fixed grin on my face, smiling at everyone who looked at me; just in case they expected me to recognise them!

We soon discovered some major disadvantages in living in the Manse. It was located on the corner of a road at the top of a hill leading out of Newcastle towards Burslem and Tunstall. The noise from the lorries, buses, and other heavy vehicles as they ground their way up the hill past the house was one thing: the pollution they belched out was another. Many trees surrounded the house and garden and when the leaves came off they were very oily; and it was impossible to keep the dirt out of the house. At weekends, we were kept awake by gangs of noisy swearing yobs; high on alcohol or drugs as they made their way past the house. They frequently used our garden and porch as a toilet and seemed incapable if walking past the house without kicking in a couple of fence panels. Things would probably have been even worse had it not been for Snoopy, who could sound like the Hound of the Baskervilles!

Tramps and beggars were regular visitors; some of them making a living by visiting regularly every Vicar and Minister in the area! We used to discuss them at the meetings of the local Minister's Fraternal. On the one occasion we offered one of them some work in the garden, he was unable to manage no more than fifteen minutes before he was exhausted! Sometimes they could appear quite intimidating; with one person being at the door, and another behind a bush. I told Valerie not to answer the door when I was out. Eventually the Circuit erected an iron gate in the porch, so that the person opening the door could see who was there.

Valerie began working two days a week at each of the two Schools where she had been offered part time employment. It was very difficult for her; as for a number of years she had been a Head of Department and Faculty teaching Information Technology and Computing to 'A' level standard. Now she was starting at the bottom again. The vast majority of the Staff came from the local area; and Valerie was very much 'the outsider'. She settled down well at Blythe Bridge High School and got on well with other members of the Department; who soon came to acknowledge and respect her experience and professionalism. Unfortunately things didn't work out well at the other school and she left after the first term.

The Headmistress at Blythe Bridge, and the Departmental Head had already appreciated what an asset they had in Valerie, and she was offered extra work there. The following September she applied for, and was offered a full time post. As she had to do a considerable amount of work at home we had to share an office! I found this difficult at first but we soon got used to it. I was out most evenings so she had the office to herself! In an attempt to make me 'computer literate', my typewriter mysteriously disappeared and I was forced to use the computer! I have yet to master 'E' Mail and the Internet; much preferring to leave that to Valerie, who is ten times faster than I am in any case; and stick to using the computer simply as a word processor!

Sadly the ARMS organisation had, for various reasons, been forced to close down; but was replaced by the Federation of MS Therapy Centres. These are independent, self-supporting Centres offering the same support services as ARMS. The nearest Centre to Newcastle is just outside Chester. There was no way I could forgo my hyperbaric oxygen treatment; so I drove to the Centre at Chester every week; a round trip of eighty miles. My right foot was beginning to twist over to the right, and the big toe was forcing itself upwards, which could be quite painful at times. I thought I might be in need of some physiotherapy and consulted by doctor. Instead of physiotherapy, the GP referred me to a Consultant in Rehabilitation Medicine; who insisted I had an MRI Scan before he would see me. After waiting for a year and being informed by the local Hospital that it was still not possible to give me any idea how much longer I had to wait, especially as I was an 'out patient'; I went back to my GP, who agreed I had waited long enough!

As it was a Fund Holding Practice my GP agreed to pay for the scan, picked up the telephone and called a local Private Clinic who asked what time I could attend for a scan the following day! I duly attended the Clinic and was informed by the radiographer that the scanner there was rarely used. I considered this to be absolutely scandalous when people were waiting well over a year for a scan at the local Hospital!

My appointment with the Consultant soon followed. When we met he gave me a quizzical look and said, "You're the wrong age and the wrong sex"! Apparently it is most unusual for anyone over fifty years of age to get MS: I had been fortynine when I was diagnosed, though I had experienced minor symptoms for several years. He noticed I was wearing one of my Army ties, and informed me that he had served as a Regimental Medical Officer for several years; and after a short discussion discovered we had a couple of mutual acquaintances! Then it was down to business. He gave me a thorough examination and discovered a degree of spasticity (stiffness) in my legs; something I had been completely unaware of. This stiffness actually masks the underlying weakness in the muscles. He prescribed baclofen tablets and suggested certain exercises. Addressing the problem of my twisted foot and big toe, he informed that he was conducting trials, which would involve injecting botulinus toxin into one of my calf muscles. This would in effect weaken the muscle and make the other calf muscle work harder to pull the foot around. He told me that one of the problems was that my legs were too muscular! He gave me time to consider this; then, when I agreed; invited me to attend a Seminar he was holding when he would be demonstrating this treatment to other physicians. I was to be his live 'visual aid'!

I was given several injections, which were monitored as they were being given using a small electronic device. The procedure didn't take long, and after a couple of weeks I noticed a distinct improvement in my foot. A few weeks later I attended another Seminar and received the same treatment; this time to correct the movement in my big toe. That worked as well! I was encouraged as this was the first time I had received any help from the Medical Profession. I experienced adverse side effects from the baclofen tablets; and as

I wasn't feeling particularly affected by the spasticity, I stopped taking them.

The Consultant also put me in touch with a local Home Care Team to ensure I was receiving all the care and support I needed. I was now using a walking stick and experiencing problems with balance. I was visited by a physiotherapist, who encouraged me to attend a weekly session for treatment at the Hospital in Newcastle. Here I joined a small group with similar problems. An Occupational Therapist who was part of the Team organised the installation of several grab/support rails in the toilets and shower: and a woman who understood the Benefits System helped me to fill in an enormous form applying for Disability Living Allowance. After being visited and assessed by a Doctor; I was awarded DLA for life. I had applied for DLA when I was in Loughton, encouraged by the staff at the ARMS centre in Walthamstow. They also helped me to fill in the lengthy application forms.

I was not seen or questioned by a Doctor and the application was turned down. Much later I was informed that I should have appealed against the ruling!

This Allowance is divided into two components; Mobility & Care. I was given the higher rate for mobility, which enabled me to acquire a car under the Motability Scheme: and the lower rate for care as I was still then able to do most things for myself. I was soon to discover that being disabled involves a lot of extra expenditure! Two years later I was advised to apply for the middle rate for care, as the list of things I was unable to safely do for myself was now longer. Lengthy forms were again filled in, and a few weeks later a Doctor telephoned. Valerie happened to be by the phone; and after answering a few questions was informed that the increased allowance would be granted.

The three Churches I was responsible for were all very different. Newcastle was a very traditional Methodist Church with just over a hundred members. It had been the main Church in the Circuit for many years and functioned in a typical Methodist way – 'by the book'. The office holders knew how things should be done; and performed their duties efficiently. There was a small very well organised Sunday school; but very few older children. A Women's Fellowship with a couple of dozen elderly ladies met weekly, and my mother-in-law soon became a regular member. The Church building was fairly modern; but there were additional premises, including a large hall and a number of smaller rooms which were quite old, and in need of regular maintenance. Most of these rooms were regularly hired by various outside organisations; and this provided a valuable source of income for the Church. A major programme of refurbishment had recently been completed, but there were still more than thirty items outstanding!

These jobs appeared on the agenda of every meeting of the Property Committee, and it seemed that no sooner had a couple of jobs been completed, than another couple were added to the list! I suggested to the Committee that we put all the jobs together; add the installation of a lift; as the main hall was up two flights of stairs, and put the whole scheme up to the Methodist Church Property Division as 'phase II' refurbishment. If they accepted the proposals; the Church would be entitled to apply for grants from a number of sources to meet the cost. The Church would have to commit itself to raising a proportion of the total cost.

Having recently paid off a considerable debt, some in the Church were understandably apprehensive about taking on a new project, especially as the total cost was expected to be around £100,000. However, we were given assurances that help would be available, and a specially convened Meeting of the whole Congregation agreed to commit themselves to raising the necessary finance. Another regular income came from the Coffee Morning held every Saturday morning. Many people popped in for coffee and cakes when they came into town to do their shopping.

The Higherland Church had about eighty members and was of the Primitive Methodist tradition. They were hard working, independent, and had well formed ideas regarding the role of the Minister! They had firm ideas about the way they wanted things done; and as they always succeeded in what they set out to do I was happy to let them get on with things! At my Welcome Meeting I had said that one of my policies was simple: 'if it 'aint broke, don't fix it'!

It was a strange feeling to be the Minister of the Church where I had been Baptised, and been a member of the Boys' Brigade. The youngest members of the Brigade were then known as 'Life Boys'; today they are called 'Anchor Boys'. I was delighted to discover that the young man, who had led the 'Life Boys' in 1946-8 when I had been a member, was still active in the Brigade and the Sunday school. He showed me the Register for 1946 where my name was recorded. I proudly showed him my father's Brigade Membership card for 1931-2; which had been issued and signed by **his** father! In addition to the Boys' Brigade Company, there was also an excellent Girls' Brigade Company! Every year there was an Awards Evening for the North Staffordshire Battalions, usually held in the Victoria Hall in Hanley. The Higherland Companies always carried off a significant number of Trophies; and I was proud to be there as their Chaplain. The most commendable thing about both Companies was that they weren't just attached to the Church and using the premises; as is often the case in many other Churches: but were fully integrated and played a full and active part in the total life of the Church. Indeed, I don't think it would be an overstatement to say that without the Companies, the Higherland Church would cease to exist.

The Christmas Pantomimes organised by them, but involving many others; was an event not to be missed! Some of the Officers, with the help of others, organised and cooked a Christmas meal for about 200 people. That was a special occasion. As a matter of routine; hot meals were prepared and served every Tuesday and Thursday lunchtimes at a very reasonable cost. There were regular diners as well as casual visitors. The same service was offered once a month on a Saturday. This not only raised money for the Church, it also provided a public service, which was much appreciated.

Through its work with children and young people over so many years, the Church was known, respected, and used by a large section of the community. There were lots of Baptisms; many Funerals, but not many Weddings. Whenever I visited people in their homes, I was amazed how many of them had connections with the Church; and also how many of them knew my father! I was even more surprised when I called at one house, and the little lady who opened the door said to me, "You know who I am don't you?" Glancing quickly at my notes I said, "Yes, you're Mrs So and So". "No", she said, "I'm the woman who delivered your sister"! In 1946 she had lived a few doors away and had indeed assisted at the birth of my sister!

Unlike Loughton, which had a very mobile and changing community; most of the people in Newcastle stay in the area. This is remarkable considering the demise of the Coal and Pottery industries, which had provided employment for many thousands of people.

One woman I visited told me she had eight children. I said, "I suppose they live all over the place now". "Oh no", she said: "seven of them live very nearby: only one son has moved away". "So where does he live?" I asked. "Oh, he's moved to Longton"; she said. Longton is about six miles away! One very good thing about this habit of staying near to home; is that it provides a very supportive family network. I noticed this particularly during times of serious illness and bereavement.

As an old and well established Church, it had, over the years, played a significant part in the founding of three other Churches in the Circuit; one of them being my other Church at Cross Heath. In recent years there has been much talk in the Methodist Church regarding what has been called, 'Church Planting'. In Newcastle they have been doing just that for about one hundred years!

The Church at Cross Heath is in an area, which is now designated as an area of serious deprivation; though the surrounding area is one of mixed development. The Church has a membership of about forty people who are well known in the Circuit for their dedication, hard work, and cheerfulness. A new Church Hall has recently been built and paid for well within the time expected. The Church has a long history of work amongst the children and young people of the area; and unlike many premises nearby, has very little trouble with vandalism. The community 'owns' the Church and appreciates the way it has served them over the years. Witness to this is the large number of people who travel considerable distances to attend the annual Sunday School Anniversary Services. Many of the visitors point to some of the most elderly in the congregation and say, "She used to be my Sunday School Teacher"! The Church was frequently packed for Baptisms: so much so that I was forced to limit to two, the number to be Baptised on a Sunday morning. Funerals also drew crowds of people making it necessary for many to wait outside the Church until the coffin had been taken inside: then the Undertakers had to wait while crowds went outside before it was possible to remove the coffin!

A few years ago, one much loved lady Local Preacher affectionately named them, 'The Cross Heathens'! They accepted this title in the spirit it was given; and still accept it with good grace.

Sometimes when I was preaching there, I felt like a Rabbi in a Synagogue; because it was quite usual to have a dialogue with members of the congregation! There were no Church Committees at Cross Heath. All the business was done at the Church Council; which was attended by most of the congregation! It was always a light hearted, if ill disciplined Meeting: with the Chairman frequently having to impose Order, as there were often two or three other 'meetings' going on in the room at the same time! Business was never done 'by the book', but eventually we got through the Agenda, and for Cross Heath Methodist Church with its deficiency in both method and discipline, the system seemed to work!

In the early hours of 15th December 1995 we were woken by a telephone call from my sister, asking us to go to her home as quickly as possible. My first thought was that her husband, who was very ill, had taken a turn for the worse, or even that he had died. Instead, the bad news was that my father had collapsed and died only a few yards from the door of his flat. When we arrived at my sister's home, the Police were already there, and after answering a lot of questions I went with them to the mortuary and formally identified my father's body. An active worker for the local Constituency Labour Party for more then forty years; (he had a framed Certificate of Service on his kitchen wall), he had just left the Christmas Party which had been held in their hall about one hundred and fifty yards away; carrying a bag containing a parting gift of a few cans of beer, when he collapsed. A neighbour saw him fall and called an ambulance; but it was too late to save him. It was exactly the way the way he would have chosen to die, and I was glad for him. I was genuinely surprised at how devastated I felt at his death, and how immensely saddened I was that he should die so soon after my return to Newcastle.

Later the same day, my brother-in-law **did** take a turn for the worse, and the Emergency Doctor had to be called. It took him several hours to arrive, as there had been a misunderstanding. He was under the impression that he had been called simply to give my sister a tranquilliser because she was upset by our father's death! The Doctor knew nothing of my brother-in-law's condition and precious time was wasted while the Consultant was contacted, and my brother-in-law was eventually admitted to hospital, where his condition was stabilised.

After my father's death, there was much to be done; but given the proximity of Christmas; the funeral could not be held until 27th December, the day before my father's 79th Birthday. I suffered a bad attack of influenza, which only served to increase my feelings of depression and led to bouts of uncontrollable tears. The Chairman of the District came to see me, and was visibly shocked and worried at my appearance and condition. I was relieved of all Ministerial duties, but was determined; in spite of all advice and offers of help, to conduct my father's funeral!

The Funeral Service was held at the Higherland Church, which was absolutely packed with people standing in every conceivable place. As I spoke about my father, my tiredness disappeared and I actually felt quite invigorated: it might have been the adrenalin, but I felt it was something more. I spoke of his tremendous sense of humour, his great love for my mother and his unstinting care during her long periods of illness. He had been a man who was constantly in awe of Creation, and exhibited a sense of wonder at the Universe, and Earth in particular. He loved to read books on all aspects of life on Earth; and carefully scrutinised TV listings for programmes on nature and wild life in particular. After the funeral a substantial donation was sent to the World Wild Life Fund. It took me a long time to come to terms with life without him; and I still miss him very much.

Over the years of my Ministry I have had many, many conversations with people as they strove to come to terms with the loss of someone very dear to them: but it was the first time I had lost someone who was so close to me. A few months after he died I had a very vivid dream about him, and awoke feeling quite elated. I can't recall ever having dreamt of him before or since that one occasion. Make of it what you will, but it gave me great comfort and reassurance.

As part of our contribution towards raising funds for the Newcastle Church redevelopment fund, Valerie offered to organise an Auction! In an attempt to acquire items to auction; dozens of letters were sent to businesses in the town, but with little response. Church members and friends managed to contribute enough items to enable the auction to take place. It was an event well supported by the Circuit and the local community. Valerie acted as the auctioneer as 'to the manner born', and we raised just over £1000!

We both missed our connection with the Council of Christians and Jews; the nearest branch now being in Manchester. It would have been impossible to drive into Manchester in time for an evening meeting; and even though it would have been possible to get there by train: it would have been impossible to get back as the last train back to Stoke left at 8.00pm! I was however, delighted to discover that there was a small group called 'Faiths in Friendship', which had been set up by the Archdeacon of Stoke-on-Trent, and covered the whole of North Staffordshire. As the meetings were always held at lunchtime, Valerie was only ever able to attend if there happened to be a meeting during school holidays. The President of the Hanley Synagogue, a senior Muslim from one of the Mosques, and a Hindu lady were stanch members: the rest of the group was made up of Anglican and Methodist clergymen. This was in stark contrast to the inter-faith activities we had enjoyed in North East London. I will never forget attending an event hosted by the Quaker Meeting House in Wanstead; when no fewer then twelve world Faiths were not only represented, but took an active part in the proceedings! The undoubted success of that evening gave us all a little more faith in the future!

In the autumn of 1997, we joined a Study Tour to Israel organised by CCJ. By now I was using a walking stick regularly, but knew there were places in Israel where it would be possible to use a wheelchair to save me getting too tired too quickly; so I arranged to borrow one for a couple of weeks! Using a wheelchair to travel by air couldn't have been easier: the Staff at Heathrow and Tel Aviv Airports; and the cabin crews were most helpful. The Study Tour was very well organised and didn't follow the usual Holy Land Pilgrim trails. CCJ had links with an organisation in Israel, which gave us access to some excellent scholars who really made things 'come alive' for us. In Jerusalem we stayed at the Mount Zion Hotel, from which we had a wonderful view of the Old City. Arrangements had been made for each individual or couple to share the Friday evening meal with a Jewish family, after attending the Synagogue with them. Taxis had been organised to take us to their homes and collect us at the end of the evening.

It was the man of the house who escorted us to the Synagogue, while his wife remained at home preparing the meal. It was a privilege to share with the community, and the rituals performed by the family entertaining us; and also to witness their unbridled joy at the commencement of the Sabbath.

On another evening, the whole group visited the Home of the Sisters of Zion for a meal. They are an Order dedicated to promoting greater understanding and cooperation between the Faiths in the Holy City and beyond. It is **not** their function to attempt to convert people of other faiths to Christianity: unlike some other Christian groups operating in Israel. How much healthier and commendable it would be if such groups concentrated on people with no faith at all; rather then trying to convert people from one Faith to another! Mother Theresa of Calcutta was once asked how many people she had converted to Christianity. She replied that her task was not to convert people to Christianity; but to encourage Hindus and Muslims to the **better** Hindus and Muslims!

We visited Bethlehem, but the coach was unable to get anywhere near Manger Square and had to park some distance away. This was because Bethlehem was preparing to celebrate the Millennium, and a lot of work was being carried out; much of it we were reliably informed, being paid for by Japan! Having visited the place several times, I decided to stay in the coach and let the others pick their way through all the construction sites to the Church of the Holy Nativity.

We had a meal in a local Café; but were then invited to the home of a leading Palestinian Christian for tea! He had a large house, and the entire group, including our Moroccan Jewish driver, packed into his living room. In addition to refreshments, our host gave us a long and passionate talk regarding the merits of the Palestinian cause. On the way back to Jerusalem we were sitting at the front of the coach; and the driver, who was a surprisingly erudite man, systematically answered all the arguments put forward by the Palestinian we had just been listening to! I don't really know why I should have been surprised. Under the 'Right of Return' policy of Israel, Jews were coming from all over the world; and bringing with them many skills. We were to learn more about this when we visited Haifa at the end of our tour.

Leaving Jerusalem we journeyed north to The Galilee, appending a few days at the Kibbutz Lavi (lion) Hotel. It was a superb Hotel run by people who lived on the Kibbutz. There were a number of visits organised to places of interest in the surrounding area, but I was beginning to feel the effects of so much activity, and we decided to have a day off and stay in the Kibbutz. There was a large indoor swimming pool with a gentle slope and handrails leading into the water at one end: so I was able to enjoy a swim. Swimming is such good exercise for people with mobility problems, it's a great pity better provision isn't made for them by local authorities. We have visited a number of pools claiming to provide facilities for the disabled, and found only one I could use: and that was only available for an hour a week, and then only during term time when all the children were at school!

Learning something about life on the Kibbutz was most interesting. We met people who had been there since the State of Israel was founded in 1948. A group had been allocated a bare hillside, and told to build a settlement! One elderly lady, who was still working for several hours a week in the Gift Shop, came from Golders Green in north London. No one 'retires' in the Kibbutz: even the elderly make whatever contribution they can. One evening we visited the Synagogue and met their Rabbi, who also worked as a full time Schoolteacher in a nearby town: all his salary going to the Kibbutz. All members of our group went to individual homes for a meal. Valerie and I went to the home of a young couple with children. By our standards the house was very small, and sparsely furnished. They explained that should they have another child; the governing Committee would arrange for another room to be built on to their existing dwelling. The father was studying to be a marine biologist, and spent a lot of time at the seaside resort of Eilat. This was paid for by the Kibbutz, which met any reasonable expenses. The cars we had seen around belonged to the Kibbutz, and residents could request the use of one. The request would go before the governing Committee for approval; thus ensuring everyone had an opportunity to use the available transport! It seemed a very happy community, but we were informed that the number of Israeli citizens choosing the Kibbutz lifestyle was shrinking.

We were based in Haifa for the last few days of our tour, which is Israel's main port and industrial centre. It is a cosmopolitan City, and has the reputation for being a place where people of different races and faiths live and work well together. Our Hotel was a very tall and imposing building, which sadly didn't live up to expectations. The cleanliness, the food, and the service were well below standard: so much so that many in the group decided to have most of their meals elsewhere!

The group visited two places in Haifa, which were of particular significance. The first was a Reception Centre where Jewish immigrants from all over the world received instruction regarding the rights and responsibilities of Israeli citizenship: and where those who didn't already speak Hebrew, were expected to learn the language before being granted work permits. It is a most difficult language, but the immigrants we met were very highly motivated. The class we 'sat in on' consisted of Jews from nine countries. When I was at Theological College, learning Hebrew was an option taken up by very few students; and I was not one of them! It would be most commendable if similar centres were to be set up in Great Britain to help refugees and asylum seekers to become more effectively integrated into the Country. Such a resettlement policy might well lead to a reduction in the establishment of ghettos with their associated problems; while still enabling people to retain their cultural identities.

The second was a visit to an Arab /Jewish cultural community youth and sports centre called Beit Hagefen. The Centre, operating at municipal, national and international level, was founded in 1963 in order to create a supportive atmosphere and a social and cultural meeting place for Jewish and Arab citizens of Haifa in particular; and the whole of Israel in general. While such places continue to operate, there is a glimmer of hope for the future of Israel and it's Jewish and Palestinian inhabitants.

We took a trip to the top of Mount Carmel, and saw the impressive statue of Elijah. There is also a small Carmelite Monastery and a large terrace with magnificent views of the surrounding area, where so many events in Israel's history took place: mainly battles. For those who believe in Armageddon where the final battle between Good and Evil will take place; that's the place to reserve your seat!

One member of our group was a Carmelite Nun. She informed us that the Mother House of her Order was in Haifa; and requested that we visit the Church for a short Service of Holy Communion. We were all agreeable, even the few Jewish members of our party; even though they would not take the Sacrament. An elderly South African priest, who was a convert from Judaism to Roman Catholicism, conducted the Service. His Sermon he was so unbelievably offensive to any who were not Roman Catholics that the two Roman Catholic priests in our party actually walked out of the Service! We wondered whether anyone had informed him about the composition of our group! We all felt very sorry for the Nun who had suggested the visit. She was so upset and apologetic; but we were all sad that what was to have been the highlight of her visit to Haifa had turned out so badly.

I was very sad when the time came for us to leave Israel and return home. It had been my sixth visit and I had gained something from every one. Now I knew it was most unlikely I would ever be able to make another visit.

After spending most of my life working in the Church and latterly discovering more about other Faiths, I have continually wrestled with theological issues. At this point in my life I am personally convinced of only two things. Firstly I believe absolutely that there is a God who loves me: and secondly that at the end of the day, I shall be amazed how much of it I have got wrong!

Back in Newcastle, good progress was being made with the refurbishment of the Church premises. The people had been encouraged by the assistance they were receiving from many different sources. Several members, especially the Organist, Senior Steward, the Treasurer, were putting in an awful lot of work. They were not only very practical people, but also adept at discovering more Charities able to make financial contributions! In this quest they had received help from people in another Church in the Circuit, who had recently completed a new building project. By the time our scheme was completed, the Church had amongst other things; two new kitchens, one upstairs and one down, which made the ladies of the Church very happy: a number of new floors, ceiling lights, and a lift enabling the elderly and infirm to attend functions held upstairs.

There was also already in place, an excellent toilet specifically designed for people with disabilities, including those in wheelchairs. I emphasise the latter because I now know from bitter experience, that so many so-called disabled toilets are so badly designed as to be virtually unusable by people in wheelchairs. For example, those with doors which open inwards making it impossible for wheelchair users to close the door or turn around: and those with insufficient or wrongly placed handrails!

Routine pastoral visitation was now a thing of the past. I visited people for a specific purpose. With an aging membership in the Churches, and many people in the local community cherishing their links with my Churches; it was not unusual for me to conduct two or three funerals in a week. I always visited people in their homes when there was a bereavement, to talk with them, particularly about their loved one who had died; and discuss funeral arrangements. There were too many for me to visit following a funeral unless there were particular problems. Other people in the Churches were very helpful in the way they supported those who had been bereaved, and some Churches in the Circuit, including the Higherland had a permanent Bereavement Support Group.

I always visited the families of those wishing to have children Baptised, and each Church had a Cradle Roll Secretary, who made regular visits after the Baptism. Couples wishing to get married in Church were invited to the Manse; and then I met them in the Church a few days before the Service for a rehearsal. There were always people to be visited because they were ill, or too frail to attend Church Services. Some would be in their own homes; others in one of the many Nursing/Care homes in the area. Sometimes I would share Holy Communion with them. Visiting those in the three local Hospitals was a priority; and my members were very good at informing me about those going into Hospital. The main one was an amalgamation of three Hospitals, and was therefore a huge complex.

The problem with visiting people in the main Hospital was one of parking! There were many parking lots, and even though I possessed badges which enabled me to use Disabled Parking facilities and park on double yellow lines; I was sometimes, even after driving around for twenty minutes, unable to find anywhere to park and gave up! It was most frustrating. My other problem was that I was now unable to walk very far. If I needed to visit several people in different parts of the Hospital, it usually meant moving my car and searching for another parking space! Climbing steps was not yet a problem, providing there was a handrail. Because I was now experiencing some difficulties with balance, there were a number of homes I was unable to visit if it meant climbing a few steps without a handrail.

In 1998 I was due for another Sabbatical and decided to continue with my inter-faith studies, and spend more time exercising and trying to keep fit. Travelling around visiting places was no longer an option, so I had to concentrate on reading and visiting the local Synagogue in Hanley.

At the end of my Sabbatical I was forced to accept that I would not be able to complete five years in the Circuit; and because the invitation system for Ministers had changed, I informed the Circuit Stewards and my Churches, that I would be applying for permission to retire in 1999. This would give them ample time to seek a replacement for me.

In the autumn we put into operation, plans we had made for when I retired when the house was bought. There was an integral double garage, and the one next to the house was converted into a lovely sitting room for my mother-in-law. We also had a conservatory built on to the back of the house. When members of our families came to stay with us we needed all the space we could get! One of the main reasons we had chosen the house was the large bedroom, which extended over the garage.

I carried on as best I could through the winter of 98/99, but was forced to stop work in April 1999. By this time I was relying on my colleagues to help me conduct funeral services. I could manage the Service in Church and at the Crematorium, but could no longer cope with the uneven ground in the Cemeteries My last Service was a Memorial Service at Cross Heath for the families of people whose Funerals had been held there during the past year. In consultation with the Chairman of the District, the Circuit agreed to accept a Probationer Minister in September 1999.

In order to help the Circuit, we moved out of the Manse at Easter into our own home; giving them time to hopefully sell the Manse and acquire a new one for my successor; who was married but without any children. It was only a mile from the Manse to our home, but we still needed to employ the services of a reputable Removal Company, who sadly did not live up to their reputation: in spite of examining the items to be moved and the house they were to be delivered to. I knew all about packing, and the firm used an extremely excessive amount of packaging. For example using a metre square piece of paper to wrap up an eggcup! They also laded the biggest, heaviest items first, which meant they were the last to be unloaded, when there was nowhere to put them, as the house was full of packing cases! My sister and a couple of people from the Church did what they could to help; especially Valerie's friend and hairdresser Sylvia who stayed very late. I just kept out of the way and cried with frustration because there was so much to do, and I could do nothing to help.

The stiffness and muscle spasms in my legs were now getting worse. I had discovered some time ago that the prescribed Baclofen tablets to ease this condition had unacceptable side effects. My Consultant recommended I seriously consider having an electronic pump fitted under the skin in my abdomen; to which would be attached a subcutaneous catheter connecting it to the spinal canal. By this method effective doses one thousand times smaller than via the oral route would be continuously given. The pump works by dripping minute quantities of the drug into the spine from a reservoir contained therein. To determine it's effectiveness for me meant going into Hospital for a few days.

I talked it over with Valerie, and decided I had nothing to lose, and possibly much to gain so I went into Hospital for tests. The trial meant having a small catheter inserted into my spine and an experimental quantity of the drug poured into my spinal canal. The procedure is exactly like having a lumbar puncture, and about as pleasant!

I had experienced a lumbar puncture before, but this time as he probed about, my Consultant touched the sciatic nerve. I had never experienced such pain; and my instantaneous reaction was to swear at him! He apologised to me, and I to him! My tolerance to the drug proved to be very low, and the experimental dose too high; and it took me off my legs altogether for a couple of days. There always seems to be a 'downside' to all medication: and while the Baclofen relieves the stiffness, it also unmasks the weakness of the muscles. It was obvious in my case that I would have to commence the treatment on a very low dosage; and then very gradually increase it until an acceptable balance was achieved. I went into Hospital using a walking stick. When I left, I needed to use two! About six weeks later I was determined to complete the trials; and went back into Hospital. This same procedure was used; but this time without touching the sciatic nerve: and a much, much lower dosage of the drug used. The next day a little more was added, and I was able to tolerate it. There followed a few days of exercises and physiotherapy, and we were satisfied that the trials had been successful.

Now we were informed of a major problem. The cost of the pump was £6,800 and the local NHS Trust would not provide the funding! Furthermore, a young man on the same Ward had similar problems due to a serious head injury. His parents informed us that they had managed to acquire a pump for their son; because his limbs were so spastic they had great difficulty moving him out of bed and into a wheelchair; and in and out of their car. They had been informed that their son would have to wait more than a year to have the pump fitted!

I was determined to go ahead with this; and with the aid of an explanatory letter from my Consultant, launched an appeal for £10,000 directed mainly at Army and Church Charitable bodies.

After six years of suffering and being cared for at home by my sister; my brother-in- law was admitted to the local Douglas Macmillan Hospice. He was to remain there until his death on 1st August. He was, and always had been, a self confessed atheist: and I conducted an appropriate Funeral Service for him in the Crematorium Chapel. For the sake of my sister and other mourners; I did include a popular hymn, and elements from the Christian ritual.

It is customary for a special Service to be held when a Minister leaves a Circuit; and this is usually organised by the Circuit Stewards. In my case I wasn't just leaving the Circuit; I was retiring after thirtyfour years in the Ministry.

We decided to organise the Service ourselves; though I have to confess that Valerie did most of the work, especially that involved with contacting former colleagues. The date was to be Saturday 17th July 1999, and I asked our excellent catering team from the Higherland Church to prepare a Buffet for 200 people. Many people I had worked with in the past were invited to attend, and some to participate in the Service; several being invited to say a few words about my Ministry as they had experienced it. Valerie opened the proceedings by welcoming everyone, and spoke about me using as headings the rules from the popular Radio 4 programme, 'Just a Minute'. She said that I had worked without Hesitation, Deviation, or Repetition. These comments were particularly well received by the couple of dozen people who had come up from Loughton! The Senior Circuit Steward spoke of my work in the Newcastle Circuit and presented me with a gift on behalf of all the Churches in the Circuit. The Superintendent Minister offered a short prayer and said a few words. A local Vicar, who had been the Anglican Curate I had worked with in Blurton during my first appointment then spoke about our work together.

The Senior Methodist Chaplain in the Army (who became the Chaplain General in May 04) spoke kindly about my Service as an Army Chaplain; as did the Colonel who had been my Commanding Officer in I PARA. The Secretary of the Royal Navy, Army, and Royal Air Force Board; who was an old friend from College days; led the Prayers. After the Service he presented me with a cheque for £1000 from the Aldershot Methodist Military Trust towards my Pump Appeal!

In response to the tributes I had received, I struggled up the pulpit steps to make my reply. I thanked everyone for their kindness and support; and especially mentioned our friends from Loughton, and colleagues from the Royal Army Chaplains' Department; who had all travelled considerable distances to be present. I also thanked the Methodist Church for enabling me to exercise my Ministry; and mentioned particularly the way I had been influenced in my youth by the people of Bradwell and the Higherland Churches. I quoted a sentence that had been in my mind for many years; having first seen it written on, of all places, the top of a Bingo ticket whilst enjoying an evening with my parents at Bradwell Workingmen's Club! The words were: 'Life is what happens to you while you are planning for the future'!

When I left the Army in 1986, I had all sorts of hopes and dreams for the future. These were soon shattered by the breakdown of my marriage and the onset of Multiple Sclerosis. I acknowledged with gratitude the love and support I received from Valerie in helping me to rebuild my life, and give me hope for the future.

At the end of the Service, Valerie was presented with a huge bouquet of flowers by one of the lady Stewards from Newcastle, and I was given a standing ovation as I was pushed out of Church in a wheelchair to the lift and taken upstairs to join the congregation for refreshments.

It was an opportunity to talk with old friends and colleagues, which rounded off an unforgettable evening. Just before leaving, I gave the Chairman of the District copies of the letters regarding my appeal for funds to obtain the Baclofen Pump. Just before we went on holiday to Jersey, I heard from the Royal Army Chaplains' Department Association promising to meet half the cost! I contacted my Consultant and informed him that we were well on the way to raising the funds required.

On our return from Jersey, we found a note from the Chairman of the District informing us that he had arranged for the entire amount to be provided from several Methodist Church Charitable organisations. I was quite overwhelmed by this; and most grateful to him for all the effort he had put in to arrange for such a large amount to be made available. I didn't feel it would be right for the money to come to me personally; so it was arranged with the District Treasurer that he should hold the money, and I would send him the bills to pay as and when I received them. The congregation at Loughton very kindly sent a cheque for £600. I thanked them very much, but informed them that our target had already been reached. They insisted I kept the money; and I put the amount towards the purchase of a new, lighter wheelchair.

I had attended the Wheelchair Assessment centre at one of the local Hospitals. After determining that none of the standard NHS wheelchairs met my particular needs; I was given a form specifying my personal requirements, and a voucher for more than £500: which I then took to a local dealer. The dealer had to arrange for a wheelchair to be made according to the exact specifications given by the Assessment centre; otherwise he would be unable to cash the voucher. The cost of the wheelchair was over £1200! I was soon to discover that any appliances needed by disabled people are always very expensive.

PART VI - RETIREMENT

I had assumed that once the money was available, arrangements could be made for me to have the pump fitted straight away. I was wrong! As this was a new form of treatment, assurances had to be obtained from the local Health Authority regarding any problems that could arise in the long term either with me, or the equipment. I know my Consultant was campaigning for funds to be made available in the coming year for a number of pumps to be provided. One of his reasons was that if the pump were to be made available to people with severe disabilities; the number of Carers could be reduced from three to two, and the cost of the pump recouped within a year! However, the reason in my case was to enable me to keep walking! First the pump had to be ordered from the manufacturer, and a mutually convenient date arranged for the team performing the operation. The people who were required to be present were: a Neurosurgeon, an Anaesthetist, my Consultant; and an employee from the Company manufacturing the pump; who would bring the pump on the day of the operation. It was just a case of waiting! In the meantime I had to meet with the neurosurgeon who was to perform the operation.

I assumed the role of Office Administrator: sorting out the filing system and paying all the bills! I was still able to get in and out of the house and car unaided, so I could get out and about; though two walking sticks did get in the way at times. My car was an automatic with hand controls so I was able to drive myself to the MS Therapy Centre in Chester. Every Wednesday morning I would drive there, leaving home at 8.00am. After having my hour and a half in the Oxygen Chamber, I would drive over forty miles to Blythe Bridge to meet Valerie for a pub lunch at the Duke of Wellington, which was just across the road from the School. It was the only day in the week she managed a lunch break; every other lunchtime being taken up working or supervising 'Computer Clubs' for the students. We only had half an hour for lunch, so I used to phone the order through beforehand; and the meal was on the table as Valerie walked through the door! In spite of road works, bad weather, tractors, and caravans; I was never late, nor was our dinner. One of my souvenirs was an ice bucket in the shape of a drum from the Duke of Wellington's Regiment. It was an item we never used, so I made the Landlady a present of it!

One evening while watching the School Pantomime, I became aware of blurred vision in my left eye. I went to an Optician, who advised me to see my Doctor; who referred me to a Specialist at the Hospital. After several visits and many tests, he informed me that I had nerve damage. I still had peripheral vision, but my central vision was permanently damaged. My right eye was still good, so I was still ale to read, watch TV, and drive. Sadly, my ability to drive ended in mid 2001 when it became impossible for me to get into the driving seat. My left leg is much weaker then my right; and with the hand controls and steering wheel it became impossible for me, even with help, to get into the drivers side of the car.

This was a real blow, because not only had I enjoyed driving for forty years; it cost me my independence, and meant that Valerie or my sister would now have to do all the driving. This was another major 're-drawing' of the boundaries. My world was inexorably shrinking.

I was unable to walk very far without my legs getting very tired and weak; and walking around the town and the shops was hazardous, to say the least! I soon became acutely aware of how many people never look where they are going; and many were the times I had to freeze and remain where I was until I judged it safe to move. On one occasion I was standing at the cash out in Boots waiting to pay, when a lady charged past me and knocked both my sticks away without even noticing what she had done! I automatically grabbed hold of the nearest thing to stop falling to the floor; which happened to be a lady standing in the queue next to me. She was most surprised, but fortunately quite understanding! Another major threat were people with push-chairs. I was almost glad when the time came when I had to use a wheelchair. I felt very secure and was more than a match for any of them!

Late one Saturday evening in November 1999 Valerie's mother, who had suffered periodic bouts of ill health for several years, had to be admitted to Hospital. She died peacefully a few days later. We were grateful that her son and two grandsons were able to visit her, and that she was well enough to appreciate their presence. I conducted her Funeral Service at Newcastle, which was well attended, particularly by people from the Church. She had been a quiet but popular member of the Church and the Women's Fellowship. After cremation at Bradwell we returned to Newcastle Church, where the ladies had prepared refreshments for us. Several months later, with Valerie's brother and his partner; we journeyed to Porlock on the north Devonshire coast, and after offering a short prayer; scattered her ashes in the heather overlooking the Bristol Channel. She had been very fond of that area, and had enjoyed many holidays there. It seemed fitting that it should be her final resting place.

At last the team was assembled for me to have the Baclofen pump fitted. I went into Hospital and had the operation on 13th December 1999. The procedure took much longer than we had anticipated; and Valerie was beginning to worry as I was in the Operating Theatre for so long! Inserting the pump into my abdomen was the easy part: the difficult and time consuming part, was threading the catheter from the pump around to my back and inserting it into my spine. I was blissfully unaware of this and began to recover consciousness on my way to the Recovery Room. The pump was electronically programmed to deliver 60 micrograms (mgms) per day; which, I was informed was a very low dosage. I remained in Hospital for a week; by which time it had gradually been increased to 75 mgms. The stitches were removed from my abdomen and spine and I was sent home. Over the next few months the dosage was gradually increased; and sometimes decreased according to its effectiveness and my tolerance.

A machine very similar to a lap top computer is used to increase or decrease the dosage. My details are entered and an instrument just like a computer mouse placed over the site of the pump. The new dosage is registered using the keyboard; the 'mouse' placed over the pump, which is then reprogrammed. The screen then shows the amount of the drug remaining in the reservoir; and the date it is due to be refilled. A low audible bleep sounds if the amount remaining in the reservoir becomes too low. This has only happened to me once! Usually the reservoir is refilled with ample time to spare. Obviously, he higher the dose, the more often the reservoir will need refilling. This is done by placing a template over the pump; indicating the position of the aperture. A needle is inserted and any remaining drug drawn out. A fresh quantity of the drug is then inserted; and the programme altered as required. It was later discovered that it is possible to programme the pump to deliver higher doses at certain times of the day, when the need is more obvious. At the time of writing; November 2003, I receive a higher dose between 4.00 am – 8.00 am; and from 6.00 pm – 10 pm. These extra dosages cover the times when I am getting ready for bed and getting up in the morning. This ensures my legs are supple enough for me to get undressed and into bed; and out of bed and dressed without assistance. On a 'bad' day however, I need help in getting in and out of bed, and also in getting dressed and undressed. The daily dosage is now, after almost four years, 300 mgms per day; and the reservoir needs refilling every three months.

I am absolutely convinced that had it not been for the pump; I wouldn't be able to walk at all, and would be confined to a wheelchair: or even bed bound. As it is I am able to use a walking frame to get around the house. I need help getting in and out of the house; but then I can use the frame to walk to and from the car.

One evening in June 2000 I found I was unable to climb up the stairs to go to bed; and had to spend the night in a chair. The next day I made enquiries about obtaining a stair lift. The house has a straight staircase, with no bends; so the installation could be carried out easily and quickly. A reconditioned stair lift cost almost £1700. I made enquiries to see if I could obtain any help from Social Services; and was informed that any help would be 'means tested'. The serious flaw is that it only takes into account, income; and takes no account at all of the families 'outgoings'. Quite simply this meant that as Valerie was working, and I was in receipt of a Pension from the Army; no help would be forthcoming. I was also informed that even if Social Services were able to help; I would have to wait about two years for the work to be carried out! Furthermore, it would soon be the policy not to install stair lifts at all; but only a through the floor wheelchair lift; which would seriously affect the usefulness of two rooms in the house! The District Treasurer was still holding about £1300 from the Pump Appeal; so I asked the Chairman if I could use that money towards the stair lift. He readily agreed, and the stair lift was installed within two days. Having said all that: the local Social Services have always been helpful and supportive within the limits of their budget. They have provided handrails and an additional step outside the front door; and fitted a number of grab rails and supports in the shower and toilets.

Early in 2002 it became increasingly difficult for me to use the shower. It was a small shower situated in the en suite off the main bedroom; and even with the grab rails and a small portable step I was unable to get in our out unaided. There was a growing possibility that I would have an accident and fall. If this happened, Valerie would be unable to support my weight and the consequences didn't bear thinking about! We explored the possibility of having a walk-in shower installed. The only possible place was in the bathroom, and it would mean having the bath removed. The estimate we received to have all this work carried out was about £4,000!

Three years earlier when I appealed for funds for the baclofen pump; I received offers of help from a number of Military charities. Owing to the generous help I received from the Methodist Church, it was not necessary for me to accept their kind offers. Now I decided to approach them again. I first of all contacted the Royal Army Chaplains' Department Association. They passed the request on to the Officers' Association, who would co-ordinate the appeal by seeking help from some of the Military Units I had served with. First of all, they arranged for me to be visited by two SSAFA (Soldiers, Sailors, & Airmen's Families Association) representatives. They brought with them a number of forms; which they filled in with the information I supplied. I gave them full details of my Military Service as a soldier, and as a Chaplain. They needed details of all income, including Valerie's salary and my Pensions and Disability Allowances: but most importantly they needed details of all expenditure! This included absolutely everything from household utilities and insurances; to the amount paid to hairdressers! My membership of the MS Therapy Centre and the cost of the treatment were also included: as was the cost of the weekly journey to Chester. The amount I spent on food supplements, like Evening Primrose Oil was also noted, as was the monthly allowance I paid to my ex-wife.

The representatives were very thorough, and I was encouraged by their understanding of the situation and grateful for their support. Within a few weeks the £4,000 had been obtained from several Military charities and the work of converting the bathroom began. It was satisfactorily completed within a week, and the invoices sent to the Officers' Association for payment. I wrote letters of thanks and appreciation to all the Charities who had contributed. I really am most grateful for all the help I have received; and wonder how others with serious disabilities cope while they wait for the painfully slow bureaucratic processes to cater for their needs!

I continue to go to the Hospital every week for two hours physiotherapy, and to Chester once a week for hyperbaric oxygen treatment. I am most fortunate in having a lovely sister who, during term time, willingly drives me anywhere I need to go. Every day I do exercises at home to strengthen particularly my leg and upper body muscles. One of the physiotherapists recently remarked that I had legs a professional footballer would be proud of! The problem is that the damage to my nerves means they don't work properly. Not long after I had been diagnosed, a person with MS said to me: "We have to work to keep as fit as possible, so that if a cure is ever found for this bloody disease, we shall be in a position to benefit from it!"

Extensive trials have recently been completed on the use of Cannabis to alleviate some of the symptoms of MS. The harmful elements were removed and a capsule or an under the tongue spray were used. The main hope of the trials, which were to relieve spasticity, was sadly not achieved. However, many taking part in the trials, and others using the drug as a matter of course; testify to its effectiveness in relieving muscle spasms, getting a good nights sleep, and generally feeling better! These are very positive benefits, and the sooner it becomes available on prescription for MS sufferers the better! In the early years following my diagnosis, I was unable to understand why people with MS were often referred to as 'sufferers'. Now I know! In the meantime I manage to stagger around the house using a walking frame, which is collapsible so I can take it upstairs on my stair lift. I am also helped by a splint which I wear on my left leg which helps to prevent 'foot drop'. All this is very tiring, but I am grateful to still enjoy a small measure of independence. For many people with MS, every day is like fighting a battle, knowing that however hard you fight; the war is one you cannot win. One day a cure will undoubtedly be found, but probably not in my lifetime! For myself I hope some other illness will carry me off before I become completely incapacitated.

I am now experiencing weakness in my left arm and hand and am usually unable to use a knife and fork properly. I also have problems with buttons. If any food needs cutting, Valerie has to cut it for me. I am doing exercises to strengthen the arm because the weakness means I have limited control over my wheelchair. I know it is possible to obtain a wheelchair that can be operated using only one arm. That may well be the next item on the shopping list! An alternative is an electrically operated chair; but the size and weight bring another set of problems, and I want to continue using my strong right arm for as long as possible.

As my health deteriorates, getting around becomes more and more difficult. In 2000 Valerie moved to a more responsible job as ICT Coordinator at a Catholic High School in Newcastle. There was much to do in setting up both 'O' and 'A' level courses and acquiring the necessary equipment for the number of students wishing to take the subject. I had become used to her working very long hours, but now she is required to do even more; and to do so without any help from me on the domestic front. This was a very stressful situation for her; and I began to feel guilty about having married her and brought her into this situation. When we married in 1995 I was still quite active and never thought I would become so dependant so quickly. Without the help of my sister we would have tremendous problems. It was suggested to me that I would probably benefit by talking to a Clinical Psychologist, as I obviously had a lot of things to get out of my system. I followed up this suggestion and for the past year have been having counselling sessions about every six weeks. This has been helpful.

What has been more helpful and definitely therapeutic has been the writing of this book.

Over recent years a number of people have suggested to me that I ought to write about my life; because it really has been an interesting one! I always passed off these suggestions: but a year ago Valerie extracted a promise from me that in January 2003, I would spend at least one hour a day on the computer and begin writing. This I did; and to my own astonishment really began to enjoy writing about my past history. So much so, that when Valerie comes home from School, I have to be 'ordered' off the computer so that she could do School work!

As I mentioned earlier, I have never kept a diary; but as my mind ranged over dates, places, and situations; memories came flooding back and by the middle of the year I had come to a natural break in the narrative. I had written about 60,000 words covering the years from 1938 to 1970. The title I chose was, "Pits, Parachutes, and Pulpits" (Reminiscences from a wheelchair). Several dozen copies of the manuscript, together with a synopsis, and a Foreword kindly written by Lord Murray of Epping Forest, have been sent to Publishers; so far without any success. I have however received letters of encouragement and helpful suggestions from some of them. There seems to be a growing trend towards 'self publishing' using the Internet; and 'Partnership' arrangements with certain publishers. Both require the author to make a financial contribution, and we are looking carefully at what is being offered. I am reluctant to use the former as it would mean a lot of work for Valerie, and she just doesn't have the time.

It had been my intention to write two books, but after thinking about it and seeking advice from publishers: I decided to revise, amend, and add to what was to have been Volume I, and press on aiming to produce just one book. This is now nearing completion and I am determined that one way or another, it will be published!

We do not attend Church Services very often now, as getting 'properly' dressed is a most exhausting business. I normally dress very casually because that is the easiest and least tiring. I have only worn a suit and tie once during the past two years, and given my history I'm sure the reader will understand that it goes very much 'against the grain' for me to go to Church or attend formal events improperly dressed! The other problem is that now I have to use a wheelchair or walking frame; to say nothing of the 'bump' created by the baclofen pump; my shape has changed! I have not gained a lot of weight, but my neck and shoulders are now considerably more muscular as I have to rely on my upper body strength to get around! I make a special effort to attend a Service during major Festivals such as Christmas and Easter; or when a Minister is leaving or being welcomed to the Circuit. Circuit colleagues visit me at home and we share Holy Communion. I also try to accompany Valerie when there are special events at School.

A few years ago we joined a small newly formed group, all of whom are from the more liberal part of the various Churches to which they belong. It is an inter-denominational meeting composed of Anglicans, Roman Catholics, Quakers, and Methodists.

The group came into being mainly as a reaction to the predominantly conservative evangelicalism of the area: its very existence advertising the fact that there is 'another way'! The group meets every two months, and initially met in each other's homes. Now I find it impossible to get into other people's homes, we always meet in our home. There is no formal agenda and we take it in turns to introduce a subject for discussion. This is usually topical and relevant to what is happening in the Church and in the world around us.

It is always a controversial and stimulating evening as we push out the boundaries of faith and practice. Some might say that we are heretical, but history has shown that what is considered heretical today often turns out to be the orthodoxy of tomorrow. One example is the Ordination of women. It was unthinkable when I became a Methodist Minister; now it is the norm in Methodism and is increasingly accepted in the Church of England. A few years ago, a local Church of England priest who sought a move to the Roman Catholic Church because of this issue was told, "Don't bother coming to us, because we are gradually moving in the same direction". One senior Roman Catholic was reported as saying, that at the next meeting of the Vatican Council; the Cardinals will bring their wives: and at the one after that, they will bring their husbands! It is regarded as a joke now; but as the saying goes, 'Watch this space'!

I have been asked many times if my faith has been affected by having MS; or whether I am angry with God because I have been so afflicted. Throughout my Ministry I have always emphasised that having faith in no way prevents awful things happening to people. I firmly believe that having a faith helps people to cope with what happens to them; and we really have no choice but to play the hand we have been dealt! I have already referred to my own experience of being convinced that I was being 'carried' through some very tough times. I have certainly never been angry about my condition and disability. Sometimes I have been depressed and frequently frustrated, but never angry. Many years ago I heard of a young man with a promising sporting career ahead of him, who permanently lost the use of his legs due to a terrible accident. Informed by the doctors that he would never walk again; he remained silent for quite a while as he thought about what he had been told. One of the doctors then said to him; " you do realise that this will colour your whole life don't you?" The young man thought for a little longer and then replied: "Yes, I understand that; but I'm going to choose the colour!" Well I have tried, not always successfully, to choose the colour. Mostly I can be bright and cheerful; but there are inevitably times when all seems dull and even dark; but I understand that is part of the disease and I have to work my way through it: hoping that eventually it will pass.

In recent years several of my Army colleagues have died; and speaking to others in the weeks leading up to Christmas 03, I discovered that others, or members of their family have serious health problems. Most of us are eventually afflicted with some illness or 'complaint', which will affect our way of life and our hopes and plans for the future. Mine happens to be MS, and we have to live with it as best we can. I say **we** because it affects not just me, but the whole family.

I remain grateful for all the good things that I have experienced over the years; bringing happiness and a sense of fulfilment. Faith and Love are not crutches; they are Lifelines.

During my first year in Theological College I heard much about a student who came from Stoke-on-Trent, and had to leave owing to ill health. He had a tumour on his spine and was not expected to live for very much longer. He had been a very popular student, and those who knew him were deeply moved when he died; especially as he had maintained a strong and radiant faith during his terminal illness. A Memorial Service was held, and what had been his favourite hymn was sung. It was the first time I had heard it, and parts of it have meant a lot to me ever since. The words are by Ray Palmer; who died over a hundred years ago. The last two verses will serve to end this autobiography.

"Though waves and storms go o'er my head,

Though health, and strength, and friends be gone,

Though joys be withered all and dead,

Though every comfort be withdrawn,

On this my steadfast soul relies –

Father, thy mercy never dies!

Fixed on this ground will I remain,

Though my heart fail and flesh decay;

This anchor shall my soul sustain,

When earth's foundations melt away;

Mercy's full power I then shall prove,

Loved with an everlasting love."

Hymns & Psalms No 684

Pits, Parachutes and Pulpits

Other Books published by THREE COUNTIES PUBLISHING (Books) LTD, which are all available by mail order from the publishers are: -

Roll of Honour	by C. W. Sheldon ISBN 0 9544080 - 3 - 9	*Price £ 15.95*
Policing The Potteries	by Alf Tunstall & Jeff Cowdell ISBN 0-9535239-9-3	*Price £ 17.95*
Hanley Wakes	by Derrick Woodward ISBN 0 9535239 - 8 - 5	*Price £ 7.95*
Where Have all the Years Gone	by Reg. Harvey ISBN 0 9544080 - 1 - 2	*Price £ 9.95*
A History of Longton	by Prof. J. H. Y. Briggs ISBN 0 9535239 - 1 - 8	*Price £14.95*
The Spirit of the Place	by M. J. W. Rogers ISBN 0 9535239 - 3 - 4	*Price £16.95*
In Name Only	by C. W. Sheldon ISBN 0 9535239 - 5 - 0	*Price £ 13.95*
Gently Thru' Life	by David Whitmore ISBN 0 9535239 - 4 - 2	*Price £ 12.95*
A Victorian Pottery	by Peter Beckett ISBN 0 9535239 - 6 - 9	*Price £ 8.95*
In Search of Fenton Castle	by Barbara Maddox ISBN 0 9535239 - 7 - 7	*Price £ 7.95*
Yasmins Curse	by Pamela Hurst ISBN 0 9544080 - 4 - 7	*Price £ 8.95*
Normacot and the Dukes of Sutherland	by Mary Wilkinson Freeman ISBN 0 9544080 - 5 - 5	*Price £ 16.95*

If you do not wish to order any books but would like to be sent our twice yearly newsletter on new publications please complete the address panel below and send it to us marked NEWSLETTER PLEASE

POSTAGE - PLEASE NOTE:

ORDER ONE BOOK	POSTAGE & PACKAGE ADD £ 2.50
ORDER TWO BOOKS	POSTAGE & PACKAGE ADD £ 4.50
ORDER ANY THREE BOOKS OR MORE	POSTAGE & PACKAGE **FREE**

TOTAL REMITTANCE Incl. POSTAGE   £   .   p

Your Name ....

Address ....

....

Post Code .... Tel. No. ....(for use only if difficulty with delivery)

Cheques should be made payable to **Three Counties Publishing (Books) Ltd**
and sent to **P.O. Box 435, Leek, Staffs, ST13 5TB**
Please allow up to 10 - 14 days for delivery of books in stock.
This Order Form may be photocopied if you require more or would like to pass one to a friend